THE PAPERS OF
BENJAMIN FRANKLIN

SPONSORED BY

The American Philosophical Society
and Yale University

Benjamin Franklin. Mezzotint by James McArdell after Wilson.

THE PAPERS OF

Benjamin Franklin

VOLUME 9 *January 1, 1760, through December 31, 1761*

LEONARD W. LABAREE, *Editor*

Helen C. Boatfield, Helene H. Fineman, and

James H. Hutson, Assistant Editors

New Haven and London YALE UNIVERSITY PRESS 1966

Designed by Alvin Eisenman and Walter Howe,
and printed in the United States of America
at The Lakeside Press,
R. R. Donnelley & Sons Company, Chicago, Illinois,
and Crawfordsville, Indiana.

Library of Congress catalogue number: 59–12697

Contents

1761

List of Illustrations

A year or so after Benjamin Wilson had painted his portrait of Franklin in 1759 (above, VIII, *frontispiece*) he completed an enlarged replica, undoubtedly in order that it might be reproduced in mezzotint. Franklin is now shown in three-quarter length with a book in his right hand; his left points to a town in the background being struck by lightning. A chair and table appear dimly in the lower right corner and a curtain above them. The mezzotint was the work of James McArdell (1728–1765), a leading London engraver in that medium; it was published in 1761. The print shows the stricken town far more clearly than does the oil painting, while overhead bright light shines symbolically through the clouds. In the lower right corner the table supports papers, two pens, and an electrostatic machine. The book in Franklin's hand is now labeled "Electric¹ Expts." The painting and, even more strikingly, the mezzotint are significant in the history of Franklin portraiture because for the first time they memorialize Franklin the electrical scientist as well as Franklin the man. Charles Coleman Sellers, *Benjamin Franklin in Portraiture* (New Haven and London, 1962), pp. 55–6, 412–13. Reproduced by courtesy of the Yale University Library.

Oil painting by David Martin (1737–1798). Son of the schoolmaster of Anstruther in Fife, Martin became a pupil of Allan Ramsay (see on the Dick portrait below) and also studied at the academy in St. Martin's Lane, London. Working both as a painter and as an engraver of distinction, he lived at various times in Scotland and in London. His famous "thumb portrait" of Franklin, painted in 1766 and now hanging in the White House, will be reproduced in a later volume of this edition. The portrait of Lord Kames, dressed in his robes as one of the lords of the Justiciary Court, is reproduced here with the courteous permission of its owner, the Scottish National Portrait Gallery.

This is the most important of Franklin's writings for the public during the years of his first mission to England. *The Interest of Great Britain Considered* was a major contribution to the discussion of whether Great Britain should retain the whole of Canada at the end of the Seven Years' War, or, as his opponents argued, return all or most of it to France and keep instead the sugar-producing island of Guadeloupe. Reproduced by permission of the Yale University Library. There were four other editions in 1760: one in Dublin, one by William Bradford in Philadelphia, and two by Benjamin Mecom in Boston. The original London publisher issued a "Second Edition" (actually a second printing) in 1761.

Franklin drew this sketch to show his young friend Polly Stevenson that the tide, traveling as a wave, raises and then lowers the level of water at successive points in an extended canal or river as the crest moves along its course, but does not significantly increase the total amount of water in it. This diagram, as drawn by Franklin, appears in the original letter and is reproduced here by courtesy of the Library of Congress. It was printed in somewhat conventionalized form in *Experiments and Observations on Electricity* (London, 1769), p. 450.

Oil painting by Allan Ramsay (1713–1784), son of Allan Ramsay, wigmaker and prominent Scottish poet. He studied painting as a youth at the academy in St. Martin's Lane, London, returning in 1735 to his native city of Edinburgh. The next year he and the subject of this painting (ten years his senior) were companions on a protracted tour of the Continent. Ramsay worked for three years in Rome and then settled in Edinburgh to practise his profession for several years before moving to London. He attained great popularity and in 1761 was appointed portrait painter to George III. The painting of his friend hangs in the Dick home, Prestonfield House, and is reproduced here by courtesy of Sir Alexander's descendant, Mrs. Janet Dick-Cunyngham.

Kinnersley devised this apparatus to determine the amount of heat created in the surrounding air by passing an electric current between two wires, F and G, mounted within an air-tight glass tube AB in such a way that their tips could be made to touch or be separated to such a distance as the experimenter desired. A long, thin glass tube K was passed down through the larger tube into a reservoir of colored water, and air was forced into tube AB until the water rose in K to approximately the point c. The large Leyden jar at the left represents the source of the electrical charge; contact with wire G was made through H at the bottom, and with wire F through the suspended bar at the top of the illustration and the hand-held hook N at the right. The heat of the discharge passing between F and G expanded the air in the tube AB, driving the colored water in K as high as point d. The hook I and weight M at the far left were used to suspend various substances in the tube AB in order to determine the effect of the discharge on them. The object at the lower right has nothing to do with this apparatus; it shows how the wire at the top of William West's lightning rod was melted down when it was struck during a thunder storm in the summer of 1760 (see below, p. 293). Kinnersley's original drawings are now lost; the illustration is reproduced here from the engraving in *Experiments and Observations on Electricity* (London, 1769), facing p. 389.

Contributors to Volume 9

The ownership of each manuscript, or the location of the particular copy used by the editors of each contemporary pamphlet or similar printed work, is indicated where the document appears in the text. The sponsors and editors are deeply grateful to the following institutions for permission to print in the present volume manuscripts or other materials which they own:

American Philosophical Society
Bibliothèque Nationale
Boston Public Library
Detroit Public Library
The Franklin Inn, Philadelphia
Glassboro (New Jersey) State
  Teachers College
Harvard College Library
Haverford College Library
Historical Society of Pennsylvania
Library Company of Philadelphia
Library of Congress
Massachusetts Historical Society
New Jersey Historical Society
New-York Historical Society
New York Public Library
Pennsylvania Historical and
  Museum Commission

Commissioner of Records,
  City of Philadelphia
Princeton University Library
Public Record Office, London
The Royal Society
Royal Society of Edinburgh
Edward Lawrence Doheny
  Memorial Library, St. John's
  Seminary, Camarillo,
  California
Feehan Memorial Library, St. Mary
  of the Lake Seminary, Mundelein,
  Illinois
Scottish Record Office
University of Chicago Library
University of Pennsylvania Library
University of Virginia Library
Western Reserve University Library
Yale University Library

Method of Textual Reproduction

An extended statement of the principles of selection, arrangement, form of presentation, and method of textual reproduction observed in this edition appears in the Introduction to the first volume, pp. xxxiv-xlvii. A condensation and revision of the portion relating to the method of reproducing the texts follows here.

Printed Material:

In general Franklin's writings printed under his direction should be regarded as his ultimate intention and should therefore be reproduced without change, except as modern typography requires. In fact, however, newspapers and pamphlets were often set by two or more journeymen with different notions of spelling, capitalization, and punctuation. Although the resulting inconsistencies and errors did not represent Franklin's intentions, they are not eliminated by the editors. Again, in cases where Franklin's writings were printed by another, they were sometimes carelessly or willfully revised without his consent. He once complained, for example, that an English printer had so corrected and excised one of his papers "that it can neither scratch nor bite. It seems only to paw and mumble."[1] What was thus printed was obviously not what Franklin wrote, but, in the absence of his manuscript, the editors have no alternative but to reprint it as it stands. Still other Franklin letters are known only in nineteenth-century printings, vigorously edited by William Temple Franklin, Duane, or Sparks. Here, too, the editors follow the texts as printed, only noting obvious misreadings.

In reproducing printed materials, the following general rules are observed:

1. The place and date of composition of letters are set at the top, regardless of their location in the original printing.

2. Proper nouns, including personal names, which were often printed in italics, are set in roman, except when the original was italicized for emphasis.

---

1. BF to William Franklin, Jan. 9, 1768.

3. Prefaces and other long passages, though italicized in the original, are set in roman. Long italicized quotations are set in roman within quotation marks.

4. Words in full capitals are set in small capitals, with initial letters in full capitals if required by Franklin's normal usage.

5. All signatures are set in capitals and small capitals.

6. Obvious typographical errors are silently corrected. An omitted parenthesis or quotation mark, for example, is inserted when the other of the pair was printed.

7. Every sentence is closed with a period or other appropriate mark of punctuation (usually a question mark).

8. Longhand insertions in the blanks of printed forms are set in italics, with space before and after.

Manuscript Material:

a. *Letters* are presented in the following form:

1. The place and date of composition are set at the top, regardless of their location in the original.

2. The complimentary close is set continuously with the text.

3. Addresses, endorsements, and docketing are so labeled and printed at the end of the letter.

b. *Spelling* of the original is retained. When, however, it is so abnormal as to obscure meaning, the correct form is supplied in brackets or footnote, as: "yf [wife]."

c. *Capitalization* has been retained as written, except that every sentence is made to begin with a capital. When there is doubt whether a letter is a capital, it is printed as like letters are in the same manuscript, or, that guide failing, as modern usage directs.

d. Words underlined once in the manuscript are printed in *italics;* words underlined twice or written in large letters or full capitals are printed in SMALL CAPITALS.

e. *Punctuation* has been retained as in the original, except:

1. Every sentence ends with a period or other appropriate mark (usually a question mark), unless it is not clear where the sentence ends, when the original punctuation (or lack of it) is preserved.

2. Dashes used in place of commas, semicolons, colons, or periods are replaced by the appropriate marks; and when a sentence ends with both a dash and a period, the dash is omitted.

3. Commas scattered meaninglessly through a manuscript are eliminated.

4. When a mark of punctuation is not clear or can be read as one of two marks, modern usage is followed.[2]

5. Some documents, especially those of a legal character, lack all punctuation. This is supplied with restraint, and the fact indicated in a footnote. In some other, inadequately punctuated documents, it is silently added when needed for clarity, as in a long series of names.

f. *Contractions and abbreviations* in general are expanded except in proper names. The ampersand is rendered as "and," except in the names of business firms, in the form "&c.," and in a few other cases. Letters represented by the thorn or tilde are printed. The tailed "p" is spelled out as per, pre, or pro. Symbols of weights, measures, and monetary values follow modern usage, as: £34. Superscript letters are lowered. Abbreviations in current use are retained, as: Col., Dr., N.Y., i.e.

g. *Omitted or illegible words or letters* are treated as follows:

1. If not more than four letters are missing, they are silently supplied when there is no doubt what they should be.

2. The omission of more than four letters or one or more words is supplied conjecturally within brackets. The addition of a question mark within the brackets indicates uncertainty as to the conjecture.

3. Other omissions are shown as follows: [*illegible*], [*torn*], [*remainder missing*], or the like.

4. Missing or illegible digits are indicated by suspension points in brackets, the number of points corresponding to the estimated number of missing figures.

5. Blank spaces are left as blanks.

2. The typescripts from which these papers are printed have been made from photocopies of the manuscripts, and marks of punctuation are sometimes blurred or lost in photography. It has often been impossible to consult the originals in these cases.

h. *Author's additions and corrections.*

1. Interlineations and brief marginal notes are brought into the text without comment. Longer notes are brought into the text with the notation [*in the margin*].

2. Author's footnotes are printed at the bottom of the appropriate pages between the text and any editorial footnotes.

3. Canceled words and phrases are in general omitted without notice; if significant, they are printed in footnotes. The canceled passages of important documents, such as drafts of treaties, are brought into the text enclosed in angle brackets *before* the words substituted.

4. When alternative words and phrases have been inserted in a manuscript but the original remains uncanceled, the alternatives are given in brackets, preceded by explanatory words in italics, as: "it is [*written above:* may be] true."

5. Variant readings of several versions are noted if important.

Abbreviations and Short Titles

Acts Privy Coun., *Col.*	W. L. Grant and James Munro, eds., *Acts of the Privy Council of England, Colonial Series, 1613–1783* (6 vols., London, 1908–12).
ADS	Autograph document signed.[1]
ALS	Autograph letter signed.
APS	American Philosophical Society.
Autobiog. (APS-Yale edit.)	Leonard W. Labaree, Ralph L. Ketcham, Helen C. Boatfield, Helene H. Fineman, eds., *The Autobiography of Benjamin Franklin* (New Haven, 1964).
BF	Benjamin Franklin
Bigelow, *Works*	John Bigelow, ed., *The Complete Works of Benjamin Franklin . . .* (10 vols., N.Y., 1887–88).
Board of Trade Journal	*Journal of the Commissioners for Trade and Plantations . . . April 1704 to . . . May 1782* (14 vols., London, 1920–38).
Cohen, *BF's Experiments*	I. Bernard Cohen, ed., *Benjamin Franklin's Experiments. A New Edition of Franklin's Experiments and Observations on Electricity* (Cambridge, Mass., 1941).
Colden Paps.	*The Letters and Papers of Cadwallader Colden.* New-York Historical Society *Collections* for 1917–23, 1934, 1935.
DAB	*Dictionary of American Biography.*
Dexter, *Biog. Sketches*	Franklin B. Dexter, *Biographical Sketches of the Graduates of Yale College . . .* (6 vols., N.Y. and New Haven, 1885–1912).
DF	Deborah Franklin
DNB	*Dictionary of National Biography.*
DS	Document signed.

1. For definitions of this and other kinds of manuscripts, see above, I, xliv-xlvii.

Duane, *Works*	William Duane, ed., *The Works of Dr. Benjamin Franklin*...(6 vols., Phila., 1808–18). Title varies in the several volumes.
Evans	Charles Evans, *American Bibliography* (14 vols., Chicago and Worcester, Mass., 1903–59). Surviving imprints are reproduced in full in microprint in Clifford K. Shipton, ed., *Early American Imprints, 1639–1800* (microprint, Worcester, Mass.).
Exper. and Obser.	*Experiments and Observations on Electricity, made at Philadelphia in America, by Mr. Benjamin Franklin,* . . . (London, 1751). Revised and enlarged editions were published in 1754, 1760, 1769, and 1774 with slightly varying titles. In each case the edition cited will be indicated, e.g., *Exper. and Obser.,* 1751 edit.
Gipson, British Empire	Lawrence H. Gipson, *The British Empire before the American Revolution* (10 vols., to date: Vols. 1–3, Caldwell, Idaho, 1936; Vols. 4–10, N.Y., 1939–61; Vols. 1–3, revised edit., N.Y., 1958–60).
Lib. Co. Phila.	Library Company of Philadelphia.
LS	Letter signed.
Montgomery, *Hist. Univ. Pa.*	Thomas H. Montgomery, *A History of the University of Pennsylvania from Its Foundation to A.D. 1770* (Phila., 1900).
MS, MSS	Manuscript, manuscripts.
Namier and Brooke, House of Commons	Sir Lewis Namier and John Brooke, *The History of Parliament. The House of Commons 1754–1790* (3 vols., London, N.Y., 1964).
N.J. Arch.	William A. Whitehead and others, eds., *Archives of the State of New Jersey* (2 series, Newark and elsewhere, 1880–). Editors, subtitles, and places of publication vary.

N.Y. Col. Docs.	E. B. O'Callaghan, ed., *Documents relative to the Colonial History of the State of New York* (15 vols., Albany, 1853–87).
Pa. Arch.	Samuel Hazard and others, eds., *Pennsylvania Archives* (9 series, Phila. and Harrisburg, 1852–1935).
Pa. Col. Recs.	*Minutes of the Provincial Council of Pennsylvania* . . . (16 vols., Phila., 1838–53). Title changes with Volume 11 to *Supreme Executive Council.*
Pa. Gaʒ.	*The Pennsylvania Gaʒette.*
Pa. Jour.	*The Pennsylvania Journal.*
Phil. Trans.	The Royal Society, *Philosophical Transactions.*
PMHB	*Pennsylvania Magaʒine of History and Biography.*
Sibley's Harvard Graduates	John L. Sibley, *Biographical Sketches of Graduates of Harvard University* (Cambridge, Mass., 1873–). Continued from Volume 4 by Clifford K. Shipton.
Smyth, *Writings*	Albert H. Smyth, ed., *The Writings of Benjamin Franklin* . . . (10 vols., N.Y., 1905–07).
Sparks, *Works*	Jared Sparks, ed., *The Works of Benjamin Franklin* . . . (10 vols., Boston, 1836–40).
Statutes at Large, Pa.	*The Statutes at Large of Pennsylvania from 1682 to 1801, Compiled under the Authority of the Act of May 19, 1887* . . . (Vols. 2–16, [Harrisburg], 1896–1911). Volume 1 was never published.
Van Doren, *Franklin*	Carl Van Doren, *Benjamin Franklin* (N.Y., 1938).
Van Doren, *Franklin-Mecom*	Carl Van Doren, ed., *The Letters of Benjamin Franklin & Jane Mecom* (Memoirs of the American Philosophical Society, XXVII, Princeton, 1950).
Van Doren and Boyd, *Indian Treaties*	Carl Van Doren and Julian P. Boyd, eds., *Indian Treaties Printed by Ben-*

	jamin Franklin 1736–1762 (Phila., 1938).
Votes	*Votes and Proceedings of the House of Representatives of the Province of Pennsylvania, Met at Philadelphia . . . 1750, and continued by Adjournments* (Phila., 1751–). Each annual collection of the journals of separate sittings is designated by the year for which that House was elected, e.g., *Votes, 1750–51.*
WF	William Franklin
WTF, *Memoirs*	William Temple Franklin, ed., *Memoirs of the Life and Writings of Benjamin Franklin, LL.D., F.R.S., &c. . . .* (3 vols., 4to, London, 1817–18).

Genealogical references. An editorial reference to one of Benjamin Franklin's relatives may be accompanied by a citation of the symbol assigned to that person in the genealogical tables and charts in volume I of this work, pp. xlix–lxxvii, as, for example: Thomas Franklin (A.5.2.1), Benjamin Mecom (C.17.3), or Benjamin Franklin Bache (D.3.1). These symbols begin with the letter A, B, C, or D. Similarly, a reference to one of Deborah Franklin's relatives may be accompanied by a symbol beginning with the letter E or F, as, for example, John Tiler (E.1.1.2), or Mary Leacock Hall (F.2.2.3). Such persons may be further identified by reference to the charts of the White and Cash families printed in the present volume, pp. 139–42.

Chronology

January 1, 1760, through December 31, 1761

1760

January 2: BF elected a member of the Associates of Dr. Bray; elected chairman, March 6; re-elected in the spring of 1761.

February 16: BF presents the Pennsylvania Agency Act (Sept. 29, 1759) to the Privy Council.

March 13: The Penns' agent presents to the Privy Council eighteen Pennsylvania acts of 1758–59; they oppose ten in addition to the Agency Act presented earlier.

April 15–17: BF's *The Interest of Great Britain Considered,* commonly called the "Canada Pamphlet," is published.

May 21–23, June 3: Hearings before the Board of Trade on the Pennsylvania acts.

June 24: The Board of Trade reports on the nineteen Pennsylvania acts, recommending the disallowance of seven, including the Supply Act of 1759, which taxes the proprietary estates.

July 4: BF and Robert Charles petition the King in Council for a hearing on the Board of Trade report.

August 27–28: Hearing before the Privy Council Committee; the Supply Act is severely criticized but allowed to stand after BF and Charles sign a pledge that amendments will be made and the Assembly will henceforth tax the Proprietors equitably; six other acts are recommended for disallowance.

September 2: Order in Council putting into effect the Council Committee's recommendations.

September 7: General Amherst receives surrender of French forces at Montreal, thereby completing the conquest of Canada.

September 17?–November 1?: BF and WF tour the west of England and part of Wales.

October 25: George II dies; is succeeded by George III.

November 4: BF receives from the Exchequer and deposits in the Bank

of England Pennsylvania's share of the parliamentary grant for colonial expenditures in the campaign of 1758.

December 3: BF elected co-chairman of the Society of Arts' Committee
of Colonies and Trade; re-elected the following December.

December 18: BF makes his first purchase of stock for the investment
of Pennsylvania's share of the parliamentary grant; other purchases
follow.

1761

June–September: Abortive peace negotiations conducted in London
and Paris.

August 14: BF makes the final payment on stock bought for Pennsylvania from its share of the parliamentary grant.

August 15?–September 20?: BF, WF, and Richard Jackson tour the
Austrian Netherlands and the Dutch Republic, arriving back in London in time for the coronation of George III, September 22.

October 5: William Pitt resigns as secretary of state.

November 26: BF begins sales of Pennsylvania stock, at substantial loss,
in order to pay bills of exchange drawn on him by the trustees of the
Loan Office.

THE PAPERS OF
BENJAMIN FRANKLIN

VOLUME 9

January 1, 1760, through December 31, 1761

To Sir Alexander Dick[1]

ALS: New York Public Library

Dear Sir,   London, Jan. 3, 1760

After we took leave of you, we spent some Weeks in Yorkshire and Lincolnshire, and at length arriv'd at our House here in good Health, having made a Tour of near 1500 Miles, in which we had enjoy'd a great deal of Pleasure, and receiv'd a great deal of useful Information.[2]

But no part of our Journey affords us, on Recollection, a more pleasing Remembrance, than that which relates to Scotland, particularly the time we so agreably spent with you, your Friends and Family. The many Civilities, Favours and Kindnesses heap'd upon us while we were among you, have made the most lasting Impression on our Minds, and have endeared that Country to us beyond Expression.

I hope Lady Dick continues well and chearful. Be pleased to present my most respectful Compliments and assure her I have great Faith in her parting-Prayers, that the Purse she honour'd me with will never be quite empty.[3]

I inclose you one of our Philadelphia Newspapers supposing it may give you and my good Lord Provost[4] some Pleasure, to see that we have imitated the Edinburgh Institution of an Infirmary in that remote Part of the World.[5] Thus they that do good, not only do good themselves, but by their Example are the Occasion of much Good being done by others. Pray present my best Respects to his Lordship, for whom if I had not a very great Esteem,

---

1. President of the College of Physicians of Edinburgh; see above, VIII, 440 n.

2. On BF and WF's travels in the north of England and in Scotland, August–October 1759, and their visit to Sir Alexander and Lady Dick at Prestonfield House, see above, VIII, 430–1, 440 n.

3. For the verses with which Lady Dick accompanied the gift of a purse, see above, VIII, 442–3.

4. On George Drummond, lord provost of Edinburgh, see above, VIII, 434 n.

5. Probably *Pa. Gaz.*, July 12, 1759, which contained "A General State of the Accounts of the Pennsylvania Hospital," dated May 5, 1759, and "An Abstract of Cases" there April 26, 1758, to April 28, 1759. The latter reported 154 patients treated during the year, of whom 36 remained under care at the end of the period.

I find I should be extreamly singular. You will see in the same Paper an Advertisement of the Acting of Douglas, one of your Scottish Tragedies, at our Theatre, which may show the regard we have for your Writers.[6] And as I remember to have heard some Complaints from Persons in Edinburgh, that their Letters to their Friends in America, did not get regularly to hand, I take the Liberty to send you another Paper, in which you will see the careful Method they take in those Countries, to advertise the Letters that remain in the Post Office; I think it is generally done every Quarter. By that List of Names, too, you may form some Judgment of the Proportion of North Britons in America, which I think you once enquir'd about.[7]

My Son joins in the sincerest Wishes of Happiness to you and all yours, and in the Compliments of the Season, with Dear Sir, Your most obliged, and most obedient humble Servant

B FRANKLIN

Please to acquaint honest Pythagoras[8] that I have not forgot what he desired of me, and that he shall hear from me soon.

Sir Alexander Dick.

6. *Pa. Gaẓ.*, July 12, 1759, advertised the performance "At the Theatre, on Society-Hill" of *Douglass*, "a new Tragedy, written by the Reverend Mr. Hume, Minister of the Kirk of Scotland." The author was John Home (1722–1808), minister at Athelstaneford. When the play was first produced in Edinburgh in 1756 it had a long and successful run, but the ruling party in the kirk, strongly opposed to theatrical performances in general, was outraged that the writer was himself a minister, and Home was cited to appear before his presbytery. Before action against him was completed he resigned his pastoral charge and soon afterwards became private secretary to Lord Bute and tutor to the Prince of Wales. *DNB*. The Philadelphia performance advertised in the *Gaẓette* was part of the repertory of the American Company, in which Lewis Hallam (*c.* 1740–1808) played the male leads. *DAB*. Presbyterian opposition to the theater in Philadelphia proved ineffectual.

7. *Pa. Gaẓ.*, Aug. 9, 1759, devoted the whole first page to a list of persons for whom letters were waiting in the Philadelphia post office. Additional names appeared in the issue of August 30, completing the alphabetical listing. On BF's procedure in this respect while himself postmaster at Philadelphia, see above, II, 181–2.

8. For Pythagoras, see above, VIII, 443, 445 n.

4

To Lord Kames[9]

ALS: Scottish Record Office

My dear Lord,   London, Jany. 3. 1760

I ought long before this time to have acknowledg'd the Receipt of your Favour of Nov. 2.[1] Your Lordship was pleas'd kindly to desire to have all my Publications. I had daily Expectations of procuring some of them from a Friend to whom I formerly sent them when I was in America, and postpon'd Writing till I should obtain them; but at length he tells me he cannot find them.[2] Very mortifying, this, to an Author, that his Works should so soon be lost! So I can now only send you my *Observations on the Peopling of Countries*, which happens to have been reprinted here;[3] The *Description of the Pennsylvanian Fireplace*, a Machine of my contriving;[4] and some little Sketches that have been printed in the Grand Magazine;

9. Henry Home, Lord Kames (1696–1782), Scottish judge, son of George Home, a country gentleman of Kames, Berwickshire, was indentured at the age of sixteen to an Edinburgh writer to the signet. He studied assiduously in his spare time and was admitted to the Scottish bar at twenty-eight. His published collection of legal decisions four years later brought him to professional attention; he prospered, and was appointed an ordinary lord of Session in 1752, whereupon he assumed the personal, non-hereditary title of Lord Kames. In 1763 he became one of the lords of the Justiciary Court, where he sat until a few days before his death. He had a wide variety of interests including the promotion of fisheries and manufacture and improvement in agriculture. He wrote voluminously on law, antiquities, ethics and natural religion, and criticism. His *Introduction to the Art of Thinking* (Edinburgh, 1761) and *Sketches of the History of Man* (1774) included versions of BF's "Parable against Persecution" (above, VI, 114–24). As a judge he was severe in criminal cases, but personally he was jovial and vivacious, with a ready, though coarse, humor. *DNB;* Alexander Fraser Tytler of Woodhouselee, *Memoirs of the Life and Writings of the Honourable Henry Home of Kames* (2d edit., 3 vols., Edinburgh, 1814).

1. Not found.

2. The friend to whom BF sent his publications may have been William Strahan, Peter Collinson, or possibly Richard Jackson.

3. For the text of BF's *Observations concerning the Increase of Mankind, Peopling of Countries, &c.* and for its first reprinting in London, see above, IV, 225–34.

4. For BF's *An Account Of the New Invented Pennsylvanian Fire-Places,* see above, II, 419–46. In 1768 Kames expressed a desire for a "Pennsylvania Grate" in his Edinburgh house, but BF would not recommend one of those made in England, because of their "fancied Improvements." Kames to BF, Feb. 18, 1768, APS; BF to Kames, Feb. 28, 1768, Scottish Record Office.

which I should hardly own, did not I flatter myself that your friendly Partiality would make them seem at least tolerable.[5]

How unfortunate I was, that I did not press you and Lady Kames more strongly, to favour us with your Company farther![6] How much more agreable would our Journey have been, if we could have enjoy'd you as far as York! Mr. Blake,[7] who we hop'd would have handed us along from Friend to Friend, was not at home, and so we knew nobody and convers'd with nobody on all that long Road, till we came thither. The being a Means of contributing in the least Degree to the restoring that good Lady's Health, would have contributed greatly to our Pleasures, and we could have beguil'd the Way by Discoursing 1000 Things that now we may never have an Opportunity of considering together; for Conversation warms the Mind, enlivens the Imagination, and is continually starting fresh Game that is immediately pursu'd and taken and which would never have occur'd in the duller Intercourse of Epistolary Correspondence. So that whenever I reflect on the great Pleasure and Advantage I receiv'd from the free Communication of Sentiments in the Conversation your Lordship honour'd me with at Kaims, and in the little agreable Rides to the Tweedside, I shall forever regret that unlucky premature Parting.

No one can rejoice more sincerely than I do on the Reduction of Canada; and this, not merely as I am a Colonist, but as I am a

5. Those of BF's "little Sketches" which have been identified in the *Grand Magazine of Universal Intelligence, and Monthly Chronicle of our Own Time* are: "How to Make a Striking Sundial" (above, VII, 75–6), "Father Abraham's Speech" (above, VII, 340–50), and "Humourous Reasons for Restoring Canada" (above, VIII, 449–52). These appeared in *Grand Mag.* in the issues of February and March 1758 and December 1759, respectively.

6. In October 1759 on their return trip from Scotland to London BF and WF spent a few days with Lord Kames and his wife, Mrs. Home, at his estate near the Tweed in Berwickshire; see above, VIII, 431, 443 n. BF always politely, but incorrectly, referred to Kames's wife as "Lady Kames," but until 1905 the wife of a Scottish law lord was not officially entitled to use herself the title he assumed upon attaining high judicial office. Technically, she remained plain "Mrs. Home" until 1766, when, on inheriting from her brother the family estate of Blair-Drummond, she resumed her maiden name and was thereafter called "Mrs. Drummond."

7. Probably Francis Blake (above, VIII, 360 n), who owned an estate in the county of Durham through which BF passed on his way to York.

Henry Home, Lord Kames.

Briton.[8] I have long been of Opinion, that the Foundations of the future Grandeur and Stability of the British Empire, lie in America; and tho', like other Foundations, they are low and little seen, they are nevertheless, broad and Strong enough to support the greatest Political Structure Human Wisdom ever yet erected. I am therefore by no means for restoring Canada. If we keep it, all the Country from St. Laurence to Missisipi, will in another Century be fill'd with British People; Britain itself will become vastly more populous by the immense Increase of its Commerce; the Atlantic Sea will be cover'd with your Trading Ships; and your naval Power thence continually increasing, will extend your Influence round the whole Globe, and awe the World! If the French remain in Canada, they will continually harass our Colonies by the Indians, impede if not prevent their Growth; your Progress to Greatness will at best be slow, and give room for many Accidents that may for ever prevent it. But I refrain, for I see you begin to think my Notions extravagant, and look upon them as the Ravings of a mad Prophet.

Your Lordship's kind Offer of Penn's Picture is extreamly obliging. But were it certainly his Picture, it would be too valuable a Curiosity for me to think of accepting it. I should only desire the Favour of Leave to take a Copy of it. I could wish to know the History of the Picture before it came into your Hands, and the Grounds for supposing it his. I have at present some Doubts about it;[9] first, because the primitive Quakers us'd to declare against Pictures as a vain Expence; a Man's suffering his Portrait to be taken was condemn'd as Pride; and I think to this day it is very

8. Gen. James Wolfe's victory over the French on the Plains of Abraham, Sept. 13, 1759, had raised hopes that Great Britain would soon become the master of Canada and had precipitated a debate in the British press about the advisability of retaining that province at a peace settlement. *A Letter Addressed to Two Great Men* and BF's "Humourous Reasons for Restoring Canada" (above, VIII, 449–52), both favoring the retention of Canada, had appeared in December 1759, and in April 1760 BF used some of the arguments advanced in this letter in his famous pro-Canada pamphlet *The Interest of Great Britain Considered*. See below, pp. 47–100.

9. BF had good reason to doubt the authenticity of Kames's alleged portrait of William Penn, the so-called "Whisker" portrait, because according to an expert on Penn portraiture it was "so obviously unauthentic that it fell entirely into oblivion." William I. Hull, *William Penn A Topical Biography* (N.Y., 1937), p. 300.

little practis'd among them. Then it is on a Board, and I imagine the Practice of painting Portraits on Boards did not come down so low as Penn's Time; but of this I am not certain. My other Reason is an Anecdote I have heard, viz. That when old Lord Cobham[1] was adorning his Gardens at Stowe with the Busts of famous Men, he made Enquiry of the Family for a Picture of Wm. Penn, in order to get a Bust form'd from it, but could find none. That Sylvanus Bevan, an old Quaker Apothecary,[2] remarkable for the Notice he takes of Countenances, and a Knack he has of cutting in Ivory strong Likenesses of Persons he has once seen, hearing of Lord Cobham's Desire, set himself to recollect Penn's Face, with which he had been well acquainted; and cut a little Bust of him in Ivory which he sent to Lord Cobham, without any Letter of Notice that it was Penn's. But my Lord who had personally known Penn, on seeing it, immediately cry'd out, Whence came this? It is William Penn himself! And from this little Bust, they say, the large one in the Gardens was formed.[3] I doubt, too, whether the Whisker was not quite out of Use at the time when Penn must have been of the Age appearing in the Face of that Picture. And yet notwithstanding these Reasons, I am not without some Hope that it may be his; because I know some eminent Quakers have had their Pictures privately drawn, and deposited with trusty Friends; and I know also that there is extant at Philadelphia a very good Picture of Mrs. Penn, his last Wife.[4] After

1. Sir Richard Temple, Viscount Cobham (1669?–1749), a distinguished soldier and Whig politician. Horace Walpole gives several lively accounts of visits to the gardens at Stowe in Buckinghamshire and it is possible that BF visited them on his "Ramble" through the English Midlands during the summer of 1758 (above, VIII, 133–46).

2. See above, VIII, 437 n.

3. For a photograph of Bevan's bust see Hull, *William Penn*, opp. p. 304. For the several portraits, statues, and medallions copied from it see *ibid.*, pp. 299–301 and Hull's *Eight First Biographies of William Penn* (Phila., 1936), pp. 119–20.

4. This portrait of Hannah Callowhill Penn (1664–1726) was probably the one which John Hesselius (1728–1778) copied about 1742. Although the original is "unlocated and possibly lost," the Hesselius copy has survived and now hangs in the Historical Society of Pennsylvania. It is described and reproduced in William Sawitzky, *Catalogue Descriptive and Critical of the Paintings and Miniatures in the Historical Society of Pennsylvania* (Phila., 1942), pp. 129, 218.

all, I own I have a strong Desire to be satisfy'd concerning this Picture; and as Bevan is yet living here, and some other old Quakers that remember William Penn, who died but in 1718, I could wish to have it sent me carefully pack'd in a Box by the Waggon (for I would not trust it by Sea) that I may obtain their Opinion, The Charges I shall very chearfully pay; and if it proves to be Penn's Picture, I shall be greatly oblig'd to your Lordship for Leave to take a Copy of it, and will carefully return the Original.[5]

My Son joins with me in the most respectful Compliments to you, to Lady Kaims, and your promising and amiable Son and Daughter.[6] He had the Pleasure of conversing more particularly with the latter than I did, and told me, when we were by our selves, that he was greatly surprized to find so much sensible Observation and solid Understanding in so young a Person; and suppos'd you must have us'd with your Children some uncommonly good Method of Education, to produce such Fruits so early.[7] Our Conversation till we came to York was chiefly a Recollection and Recapitulation of what we had seen and heard, the Pleasure we had enjoy'd and the Kindnesses we had receiv'd in Scotland, and how far that Country had exceeded our Expectations. On the whole, I must say, I think the Time we spent there, was Six Weeks of the *densest* Happiness I have met with in any Part of my Life. And the agreable and instructive Society we found there in such Plenty, has left so pleasing an Impression on my Memory, that did not strong Connections draw me elsewhere,

5. According to a biographer of Lord Kames, "Penn's Picture" was sent to BF, but never returned. Tytler, *Memoirs of . . . Henry Home of Kames,* I, 369 n.

6. As heir to his mother's estate at Blair-Drummond, the son George Home later changed his name to Drummond-Home. After his father's death he continued Kames's activities in developing and improving that estate. The daughter Jean married in 1762 Patrick Heron, a Scottish banker, who divorced her ten years later for adultery. William K. Wimsatt, Jr., and Frederick A. Pottle, eds., *Boswell for the Defense* (N.Y., [1959]), p. 77 n; Charles Ryskamp and Frederick A. Pottle, eds., *Boswell the Ominous Years* (N.Y., [1963]), p. 186 n.

7. For Kames's *Introduction to the Art of Thinking* (Edinburgh, 1761), see above, VI, 116–17, and below, p. 104. On his interest in education, see James Ramsay of Ochtertyre, *Scotland and Scotsmen in the Eighteenth Century* (Edinburgh and London, 1888), I, 205–7.

I believe Scotland would be the Country I should chuse to spend the Remainder of my Days in.

I have the Honour to be, with the sincerest Esteem and Affection, My Lord, Your Lordship's most obedient and most humble Servant   B FRANKLIN

PS. My Son puts me in mind that a Book published here last Winter, contains a number of Pieces wrote by me as a Member of the Assembly, in our late Controversies with the Proprietary Governors;[8] so I shall leave one of them at Millar's to be sent to you, it being too bulky to be sent per Post.

Ld. Kaims.

From Isaac Norris

Letterbook copy: Historical Society of Pennsylvania

Dear Friend B Franklin   Fairhill, Janry 4th. 1760

The Bearer Charles Monk[9] calling here in his way to N York from whence he is going to England. I send by him this short Letter for which I detain him on his Journey to inform you we have nothing very new or important in America since the reduction of Quebeck.[1] Our Forces are quiet and General Stanwix continues at Pitsburg (as I hear laid up with a Fit of the Gout).[2] Major Gates[3] left the Troops there very lately well and in good health. At our last sitting in December our House reduced our Forces to 150 Men intended to Garrison Fort

8. Richard Jackson, *An Historical Review of the Constitution and Government of Pennsylvania*, published in May 1759; see above, VIII, 360–2.

9. Not identified.

1. The French garrison at Quebec capitulated on Sept. 18, 1759, five days after Wolfe's decisive victory on the Plains of Abraham.

2. Gen. John Stanwix (above, VII, 45 n), Forbes's successor as commander of his Majesty's forces in Pa., was superintending the erection of a "respectable Fort" at Pittsburgh. On Dec. 24, 1759, he wrote Governor Hamilton that he had a "pretty severe fit of the Gout." *Pa. Col. Recs.*, VIII, 427; 1 *Pa. Arch.*, III, 697.

3. Horatio Gates (*c.*1728/9–1806), the American commander at Saratoga in 1777, was at this time military secretary to General Stanwix and acting major in the 45th Regiment. Samuel W. Patterson, *Horatio Gates* (N.Y., 1941), p. 19.

Augusta Littleton and Fort Allen with a Design to protect our Indian Trade.[4]

General Stanwix had kept the Province Forces, as the former Generals had done, at Pitsburg designing to have them there this Winter and bring the Regulars into Winter Quarters[5] if we had continued them, and if he had done so it would have been the Fourth Winter these poor Creatures had remained there from their Homes almost perishing for want of Necessaries whilst the Regulars were sent down (as they were last Year) to commit shocking Insults on the Inhabitants in their Quarters. The Highlanders who bear a most wretched Charracter here were particularly mischievious at Lancaster, last Winter, forced themselves into private Houses killed several in a most shameful Manner and committed every Disorder which could be expected or feard from such worthless miserable Creatures (set on as 'tis said by their Officers).[6] These and other Reasons as well as the Peaceable Prospect on our Frontiers and our Inability to support the Charge we have been at for several Years past, determined the House to ease the Province of the heavy Expence we were incurring every Year by the failure of our Taxes to discharge the Grants to the Crown.

4. This resolve passed the Assembly on Dec. 7, 1759. The next day Hamilton requested the House to reconsider its action and to "suspend the coming to any final Resolution" on the disbanding of the provincial forces until it considered Stanwix' letter to the former governor, William Denny, Oct. 18, 1759, in which the general suggested that he would need a substantial number of provincials for winter service. On the same day the Assembly decided to adhere to its resolve and adjourned until Feb. 11, 1760. *Pa. Col. Recs.*, VIII, 425–9.

5. Norris was misinformed about Stanwix' winter plans. The general meant to keep 150 Pa. troops, 150 Va. troops, and 400 Royal Americans at Pittsburgh, send the remainder of the "two old Battalions" of Pennsylvanians to posts guarding the line of communications between Pittsburgh and Fort Augusta, and disband the colony's "new Levies." Stanwix to Hamilton, Dec. 8, 24, 1759, 1 *Pa. Arch.*, III, 693–4, 696–7.

6. Pursuant to an order of the Pa. Assembly, March 13, 1759, to investigate the complaints of numerous inhabitants of Lancaster and Chester counties against Col. Archibald Montgomery's 77th Regiment, the Assembly's Committee of Grievances reported, April 6, 1759, that the "Oppression" practiced by Montgomery's Highlanders was "of so extraordinary a Nature, that it calls for immediate Redress." The Committee accused the Highlanders of assaults, seizure of property, and exaction of money, but not of murder. *Votes*, 1758–59, pp. 31–2, 56–9, 67, 71, 73.

We have not heard from you by the last Packet or Captain Nicholson who arrived just before the Winter set in,[7] so that it is a long Time since our last advices from you either to myself or the Committee. I am Your Assured Friend   I N

(Ensclosed in this Letter I sent)
  3d Bill Exchange for £200. Joshua Howell on Messrs. Wm and Richard Baker. No. 2001[8]

NB as I had not Four Bills I must get another drawn by Joshua Howell if those three already Sent should Miscarry–in order to which I took a Certified Copy of the above Third Bill examind by [Israel?] Morris before I sent it enclosed in the above Letter.

NB I have an Account from BF of the rect of the above Bill No. 2001 for £200 Ster

BF recd this ackd. Feb[9]

From John Waring   ALS: American Philosophical Society

Sir   Russel Street Jan. 4: 1760

  This is to inform You that the associates of the Late Dr. Bray unanimously chose You a Member of their Society.[1] The Prospect of Your kind Assistance induced them to accept of the proposal mentioned in their Advertisment,[2] and to resolve upon opening three Schools for Negroes with all convenient Speed: They adjourned to Thursday 17th. Instant with a View to ask Your Advice

7. The "last Packet," the *General Wall*, Capt. Walter Lutwidge, left Falmouth on Oct. 18, 1759, and arrived in New York, Dec. 10, 1759; the *William and Mary*, Capt. William Nicholson, arrived in Philadelphia, Dec. 18, 1759, after a ten-week voyage from London. *Pa. Gaz.*, Dec. 13, 20, 1759; *N.-Y. Mercury*, Dec. 17, 1759.

8. For this bill, see above, VIII, 437.

9. No letter from BF to Norris of Feb. 1760 survives.

1. BF was elected to membership in The Associates of Dr. Bray on Jan. 2, 1760. On March 6, 1760, he was appointed to the committee which audited the Society's accounts and on the same day he was elected chairman of the Society for the ensuing year. In the spring of 1761 he was re-elected chairman. Richard I. Shelling, "Benjamin Franklin and the Dr. Bray Associates," *PMHB*, LXIII (1939), 282–93. For BF's earlier relations with this society, see above, VII, 100–1, 252–3, 356, 377–9; VIII, 425.

2. The editors have not succeeded in locating a copy of this "Advertisement."

and Assistance in the establishment of these Schools, and hope to have the pleasure of meeting You on that Day at 10 oClock at Mr. Birds Bookseller in Ave Mary Lane near St. Pauls: to go upon Business at 11. precisely.[3] I am Sir Your most obedient humble Servant   JN. WARING

Addressed: To / Benj Franklin Esq,/in Craven Street/near/Charing Cross.

Endorsed: Mr Waring Jan 4. 60. recd Jan 5.

To John Hughes   Draft (incomplete): American Philosophical Society

Dear Sir,   London, Jan. 7. 1760

On my Return from our Northern Journey,[4] I found several of your obliging Favours; and have now before me those of June 20. July 4. 25, Aug. 9. 22, 23, Sept. 25. and two of Oct. 3. for which please to accept my hearty Thanks.[5]

I congratulate you on the glorious Successes of the [year p]ast. There has been for some time a Talk of [Peace], and probably we should have had one this Winter if the King of Prussia's late Misfortunes had not given the Enemy fresh Spirits,[6] and encourag'd them to try their Luck another Campaign and exert all their remaining Strength that if possible they may treat with Hanover in their Hands. If this should be the Case, possibly most of our Advantages may be given up again at the Treaty and some among our great Men begin already to prepare the Minds of People for this, by discoursing, that to keep Canada would draw on us the

3. For BF's recommendations at the meeting on Jan. 17, 1760, see below, pp. 20–1. John Bird (d. 1804) was a liveryman of the Company of Stationers. John Nichols, *Illustrations of the Literary History of the Eighteenth Century,* VIII (London, 1858), 472.

4. For BF's travels in the north of England and Scotland, Aug.–Oct., 1759, see above, VIII, 430–1.

5. None of these letters have been found.

6. On July 23, 1759, the Russians defeated the Prussian General Wedel near Frankfurt an der Oder; on Aug. 12, 1759, a combined Russian and Austrian force administered Frederick II the greatest defeat of his career at Kunersdorf; and in November the Prussian General Fink surrendered an army of 20,000 men to the Austrians and Imperialists near Maxen in Saxony. Gipson, *British Empire,* VIII, 36–8.

Envy of other Powers, and occasion a Confederacy against us; that the Country is too large for us to people, not worth possessing, and the like. These Notions I am every day and every where combating and I think not without some Success. The Event God only knows. The Argument that seems to have a principal Weight is, that in Case of another War, if we keep Possession of Canada the Nation will save two or three Million a Year now spent in Defending the American Colonies and be so much the stronger in Europe by the Addition of the Troops now employ'd on that Side of the Water: To this I add that the Colonies would thrive and increase in a much greater Degree, and a vast additional Demand arise for British Manufactures, to supply so great an Extent of Indian Country, &c. with many other Topics, which I urge occasionally, according to the Company I happen into or the Person I address.[7] And on the whole, I flatter myself that my being here at this time may be of some Service to the general Interest of America.

The Acts of the last Yea[r are] all come to hand, but not all in a Condition prop[er to] be laid before the King for his Approbation. [As] the Governor's propos'd Amendments are tack'd to 'em, and no Distinction which were agreed to, or whether any or none; so that in some of the most material Acts there is no Ascertaining what is intended to be Law and what not.[8] This Mistake was fallen into, I suppose, from the late Practice of sending home the Bills refus'd by the Governor, with his propos'd Amendments, certify'd by the Clerk of the House and under the Great Seal, that the true State of such refus'd Bills might be known here. But when Bills are pass'd into Laws, the Copies to be sent here should be taken from the Rolls Office after the Laws are deposited there, and certify'd by the Master of the Rolls to be true Copies; and then the Governor under the Great Seal certifys that the Master

7. In neither his "Humourous Reasons for Restoring Canada," *London Chron.*, Dec. 25–27, 1759 (above, VIII, 449–52), nor in his major presentation of the issue, *The Interest of Great Britain Considered* (below, pp. 47–100), did BF stress the argument on the saving of money and troops used in defending the colonies if Canada should be kept. In the latter pamphlet especially he emphasized the positive value of Canada to the British and the nonsense of fearing increased strength of the existing continental colonies.

8. WF complained similarly of these irregularities in a letter to Joseph Galloway, Dec. 28, 1759, Yale Univ. Lib.

of the Rolls is such Officer, and that Credit ought to be given to his Certificate; or otherwise, that those Copies are true Copies and agreable to the Laws pass'd by him as Governor. But the Certificates with these Laws only expresses, that such Bills were sent up to him for his Assent on such a Day, that he propos'd the Annex'd Amendments on such a Day and on such a Day he pass'd the Bills, without saying a Word whether the Amendments were agreed to or not. Indeed by that Part of the Minutes of March and April which came [*remainder missing*].

Mr. Hughes

To Joseph Galloway

Duplicate: Yale University Library

(Copy)[9]

Dear Sir   London, Jany. 9. 1760

The enclos'd are Copies of my last[1] to you per the Pacquet: Capt. House, who talk'd of sailing two Months ago is still here, but probably will now go in a Day or two, and by him I purpose to send this Letter.

Since Govr. Denny and the Assembly have at length come to so good an Agreement, I cannot but join with you in Wishes that he had been continued. But before that Agreement was known here, Mr. Hamilton's Appointment had taken Place.[2] I know not

9. This copy was prefixed to BF's letter to Galloway of Feb. 26, 1760 (below, p. 26). The original may never have reached Philadelphia, because the ship which carried it, the *Juliana*, Capt. House, was taken in West Indian waters by Capt. Sebière du Chateleau (above, VIII, 220–1 n) and carried into Cape François, Santo Domingo. On the other hand, Chateleau, after "diverting himself" with the letters carried on the *Juliana*, permitted some of them to be carried to Philadelphia and BF's may have been one of these. See below, pp. 221–2; see also *Pa. Gaz.*, May 22, 1760.

1. Probably not the letter of April 7, 1759 (above, VIII, 309–16), but a later one that has not been found.

2. The "Agreement" between Denny and the Assembly, procured by bribes of £3,000, produced the passage of several acts of an anti-proprietary character, the most important of them being the £100,000 Supply Act of April 17, 1759, which realized the Assembly's long-standing objective of taxing the proprietary estate. See above, VIII, 326–7 n, 419–20 n. WF had written Galloway, Dec. 28, 1759, that James Hamilton had been dissatisfied with his instructions and made difficulties with the Proprietors. Yale Univ. Lib., Hist. Soc. Pa.

15

on what Terms he accepted the Government; I wish they may be such as will allow him to make the People and himself easy: But I doubt, from some Tokens appearing here, that the Storm is still to continue longer.

The Acts pass'd are in themselves so just and reasonable, that I at first flatter'd myself the Proprietor would either not have the Face to oppose them, or that if he did oppose them it would be without Effect. I thought too, that the Death of Paris, to whose evil Influence most of his indiscreet Measures have been ascribed by his Friends, would have left him open to better Counsels.[3] But I this Day learn, that he is determin'd to oppose the Supply and Re-Emitting Acts and some of the others, but which of the others, I am not inform'd, except that he has already put in a Caveat at the Exchequer against paying me the Parliamentary Grant in Pursuance of your Act, till the King's Pleasure on that Act is known, which if possible he will get refus'd.[4] The Exchequer, as it does not at present abound in Money, are not displeas'd to see any Dispute, that gives a Colour for delaying Payment; and as it may be some time before this Matter is settled, I hope the Committee will not be over-hasty in Drawing for the Money.[5] What the Event of the other Bills may be, none can foresee: Only from some other Particulars I have of late observed, I have not all the Con-

3. The Penns' agent, Ferdinand John Paris (above, VII, 247–8 n), died on Dec. 16, 1759; upon the recommendation of James Hamilton and with the approval of Lord Mansfield and the attorney and solicitor general, they appointed Henry Wilmot (c.1710–1794) of Gray's Inn, secretary to the lord keeper of the great seal, and agent for the Leeward Islands, to succeed him. Thomas Penn to Richard Peters, Jan. 12, 1760, Penn Papers, Hist. Soc. Pa. WF had remarked to Galloway, Dec. 28, 1759, that "it may be some time before he [Thomas Penn] can find another Person infamous enough to do his Dirty work."

4. Beside the "Supply and Re-Emitting Acts" (above, VIII, 326–7 n, 419 n), and the act authorizing BF to receive Pa.'s share of the £200,000 voted by Parliament to compensate the colonies for their war expenditures (above, VIII, 333, 442 n), the proprietors opposed eight other acts passed by the Pa. Assembly in 1758–59. For the Board of Trade and Privy Council Committee hearings on these acts, see below, pp. 125–73, 196–211.

5. The act appointing BF agent to receive the parliamentary grant directed him to deposit the money in the Bank of England where it was to "remain subject to the drafts and bills of exchange of the trustees of the general loan office." *Statutes at Large, Pa.*, V, 461.

fidence I could wish, that what appears right and reasonable to me, may easily be made appear the same to others.

I have an equal Esteem with you for our Friend Mr. Davy,[6] but doubt my being able to do him any Service in the Affair you Mention. Those kind of Things are generally promis'd long before they fall. You cannot conceive the Swarm of Expectants there are lying in wait for all Offices even the least valuable, and what powerful Interest is made for them. The Member of Parliament is oblig'd to a Number of People for their Votes; each of these has a Number of Sons or Cousins or other Relations, for whom the Member must get little Places in the Army, the Navy, the Excise or the Customs; and to a Member nothing must be deny'd that is not ask'd for by another Member. I shall however have an Opportunity in a few Days of trying what may be done, and will advise you if I have any Prospect of Success.

As soon as the Event of these Bills is known, I shall beg leave to turn my Face homeward, as I grow weary of so long a Banishment, and anxiously desire once more the happy Society of my Friends and Family in Philadelphia. With sincere Esteem I am, Dear Friend, Yours affectionately   B F

To Jane Mecom   ALS: American Philosophical Society

Dear Sister,   London, Jan. 9. 1760

I received a Letter or two from you, in which I perceive you have misunderstood and taken unkindly something I said to you in a former jocular one of mine concerning CHARITY.[7] I forget what it was exactly, but I am sure I neither express nor meant any personal Censure on you or any body. If anything, it was a general Reflection on our Sect; we zealous Presbyterians being too apt to think ourselves alone in the right, and that besides all the Heathens, Mahometans and Papists, whom we give to Satan in a Lump, other Sects of Christian Protestants that do not agree

6. Possibly the Hugh Davey who died June 15, 1773, aged 68, inspector of lumber at the port of Philadelphia. *Pa. Gaz.*, June 30, 1773. Galloway was apparently trying to get some appointment for his friend.

7. For BF's "jocular" letter on charity, Sept. 16, 1758, see above, VIII, 152–5. His sister's replies have not been found.

with us, will hardly escape Perdition. And I might recommend it to you to be more charitable in that respect than many others are; not aiming at any Reproof, as you term it; for if I were dispos'd to reprove you, it should be for your only Fault, that of supposing and spying Affronts, and catching at them where they are not. But as you seem sensible of this yourself, I need not mention it; and as it is a Fault that carries with it its own sufficient Punishment, by the Uneasiness and Fretting it produces, I shall not add Weight to it. Besides, I am sure your own good Sense, join'd to your natural good Humour will in time get the better of it.

I am glad that Cousin Benny could advance you the Legacy, since it suited you best to receive it immediately.[8] Your Resolution to forbear buying the Cloak you wanted, was a prudent one; but when I read it, I concluded you should not however be without one, and so desired a Friend to buy one for you.[9] The Cloth ones, it seems, are quite out of Fashion here, and so will probably soon be out with you; I have therefore got you a very decent one of another kind, which I shall send you by the next convenient Opportunity.

It is remarkable that so many Breaches should be made by Death in our Family in so short a Space.[1] Out of Seventeen Children that our Father had, thirteen liv'd to grow up and settle in the World. I remember these thirteen (some of us then very young) all at one Table, when an Entertainment was made in our House on Occasion of the Return of our Brother Josiah, who had been absent in the East-Indies, and unheard of for nine Years. Of these thirteen, there now remains but three.[2] As our Number diminishes, let our Affection to each other rather increase: for besides its being our Duty, tis our Interest, since the more affectionate Relations are to one another, the more they are respected by the rest of the World.

8. For Jane Mecom's legacy of £11 8s. 4d. sterling from her English cousin, Mary Franklin Fisher (A.5.2.1.1), see above, VIII, 414–15. "Cousin Benny" was BF's nephew, Benjamin Mecom.

9. Probably BF's landlady, Mrs. Margaret Stevenson, who often undertook BF's shopping for American feminine relatives.

1. The most recent death in the Franklin family was that of BF's half-sister, Elizabeth Douse (C.1), on Aug. 25, 1759. His sister, Lydia Scott (C.16) had died during 1758 and his brother, John (C.8), on Jan. 30, 1756.

2. Peter (C.9), BF, and Jane (C.17).

My Love to Brother Mecom[3] and your Children. I shall hardly have time to write to Benny by this Conveyance. Acquaint him that I received his Letter of Sept. 10,[4] and am glad to hear he is in so prosperous a Way, as not to regret his leaving Antigua.[5] I am, my dear Sister, Your ever affectionate Brother

B FRANKLIN

March 26. The above was wrote at the time it is dated; but on reading it over, I apprehended that something I had said in it about Presbyterians, and Affronts, might possibly give more Offence; and so I threw it by, concluding not to send it. However, Mr. Bailey[6] calling on me, and having no other Letter ready nor time at present to write one, I venture to send it, and beg you will excuse what you find amiss in it. I send also by Mr. Bailey the Cloak mention'd in it, and also a Piece of Linnen, which I beg you to accept of from Your loving Brother   B F.

I received your Letter, and Benny's and Peter's by Mr. Baily,[7] which I shall answer per next Opportunity.

From Mary Stevenson   ALS: American Philosophical Society

Dear Sir   Wanstead, Janr 14. 1760
Permit me to address you with the Compliment of the Season; not merely as a Compliment, but with a fervent sincerity. May this Year give you a happy sight of your Native Country, and of those dear Relations you left in it; and if there is anything else wanting to compleat your Felicity, May that be added! May you

3. Edward Mecom, Jane's husband.
4. Not found.
5. After spending four years as a printer in Antigua, 1752–56, Benjamin Mecom had set up a printing office in Boston. During 1758–59 BF sent him printing equipment, stationery, paper, and books to sell on commission and on his own account. "Account of Expences," pp. 16, 32, 35, 37, 43; *PMHB,* LV (1931), 111, 115, 121. But his prosperity at Boston did not endure and by the end of 1762 he had resumed his restless changes of location. See above, IV, 355–6 n.
6. Jacob Bailey (1731–1818), A.B., Harvard, 1755, had been in England to receive ordination in the Anglican Church. Upon his return to America he served as a missionary on the Maine frontier. *DAB.*
7. None of these letters have been found.

enjoy a long succession of Years, fraught with all the Blessings you desire!

I thank you, dear Sir, for the present you intend me.[8] Your kind Remembrance of me upon every occasion demands my utmost Gratitude. I am extremely happy in finding I am still so much the object of your Regard; and I hope I shall continue to be so, for I shall never cease to be with the highest Esteem your grateful and affectionate Humble Servant   M STEVENSON

Addressed: To   Benj Franklin Esqr

Endorsed: Miss Stevenson

Minute of the Associates of the Late Dr. Bray

MS: University of Virginia Library

At a meeting of the Associates of the late Dr. Bray called for Jan. 17, 1760, to enable the Society to avail itself of Franklin's advice (see above, pp. 12–13), he recommended New York, Williamsburg, and Newport as the best places to establish the three Negro schools which the Society intended to found in America in addition to the one already started in Philadelphia, and he suggested the men mentioned in this document to superintend them.[9] While none of Franklin's letters to the persons named have been found, a reply from William Hunter to the Associates, dated June 1760, expresses his pleasure at receiving a commission "to open a Negroe School."[1] For the success of the schools in the three localities mentioned, see Edgar L. Pennington, "Thomas Bray's Associates and their Work among the Negroes," *American Antiquaries Society, Proceedings,* new series, XLVIII (1938), 311–403.

AGREED,   January 17. 1760

That Mr. Franklin be desired to write to the aforesaid Gentlemen (viz. Dr. Johnson, Mr. Barclay, and Mr. Auchmutey, at New-York, Mr. Hunter, Mr. Dawson, and the Minister of the Church

8. Possibly a silver inkstand made by Edward Aldridge and John Stamper of London in 1758 or 1759 and inscribed: "The Gift of Benjamin Franklin to Mary Stevenson." In 1936 it was in the possession of Mrs. Mary Hewson Bradford Laning. It is described and illustrated in R. T. H. Halsey, comp., *Benjamin Franklin and His Circle a Catalogue of an Exhibition* (Metropolitan Museum of Art, N.Y., 1936), pp. 140, 141.

9. Minutes of the Associates of the late Rev. Dr. Bray, p. 130; S.P.C.K. House, London.

1. *Ibid.,* p. 142.

at Williamsburgh, and Mr. Pollen at Newport)[2] to request the Favour of their kind Assistance in establishing these Schools; that they would occasionally, and as often as they may judge convenient, visit and inspect them, and from time to time transmit to the Associates an Account of their Proceedings and the Progress the Children make, and the Reception the Design meets with from the Inhabitants in general.

The above is an Extract of the Minutes of the Associates of Dr. Bray, relating to the Erecting Schools for Negro Children, at New-York, Williamsburg and Newport Rhodeisland—mention'd in a former Letter.[3]

To Mary Stevenson   ALS: American Philosophical Society

Feb. 14. 60.

I see I must overcome the Indolence so natural to old Men, and write now and then to my dear good Girl, or I shall seldom have the Pleasure of a Line from her; and indeed it is scarce reasonable in me to expect it.

2. These men were: New York: Dr. Samuel Johnson (above, III, 477 n), now president of King's College (Columbia); he is not to be confused with the well-known English Dr. Johnson, who became a member of the Bray Associates soon after this meeting; Henry Barclay (c. 1712–1764), B.A., Yale, 1734; Anglican missionary at Albany, 1738–46; and thereafter rector of Trinity Church, N.Y. (Dexter, *Biog. Sketches*, I, 503–6); and Samuel Auchmuty (1722–1777), A.B., Harvard, 1745; assistant rector of Trinity Church, later succeeding Barclay as rector (*Sibley's Harvard Graduates*, XI, 115–27). Williamsburg: William Hunter (above, V, 18 n), BF's colleague as deputy postmaster general; Thomas Dawson (1713–1761), Anglican commissary of Va. and president of the College of William and Mary, 1755–61 (Frederick L. Weis, *The Colonial Clergy of Virginia, North Carolina, and South Carolina*, Boston, 1955, p. 15); and William Yates (1720–1764), pastor of Abingdon Parish, Gloucester Co., Va., 1750–59, and of Bruton Parish, Williamsburg, 1759–64, president of William and Mary, 1761–64 (*ibid.*, p. 56). Newport: Thomas Pollen, B.A., Oxon., 1721; rector of Trinity Church, Newport, 1754–60 (Frederick L. Weis, *The Colonial Clergy and Colonial Churches of New England*, Lancaster, Mass., 1936, p. 166).

3. This notation is in BF's hand. It is not known to whom he sent this extract, but the present location of the MS suggests that the recipient was one of the three Virginians invited to assist. No "former Letter" on the subject to any of the men mentioned has been found.

I receiv'd your kind Congratulations on occasion of the new Year;[4] and though you had not mine in writing, be assured that I did and do daily wish you every kind of Happiness, and of the longest Continuance.

Your good Mama will have the Pleasure of seeing and conversing with you to day. I should be extreamly glad to partake of that Pleasure, by accompanying her to Wanstead; but Business will not permit.[5]

Present my respectful Compliments to the good Ladies your Aunts,[6] and believe me to be, with the sincerest Esteem and Regard Dear Polly, Your affectionate Friend   B FRANKLIN

Miss Stevenson,

Endorsed: Feb 14—60

From Francis Eyre:[7] Bill and Receipt

DS (two copies): Historical Society of Pennsylvania

On February 16 Franklin's legal adviser Francis Eyre called upon him to receive "Instructions to sollicit the Confirmation of nineteen

4. See above, p. 19.

5. BF was probably busy preparing instructions for his lawyer, Francis Eyre, to use in soliciting confirmation of the Pa. acts. Eyre attended BF to receive these instructions on the 16th; see immediately below.

6. Mrs. Mary Tickell and Mrs. Rooke.

7. Francis Eyre (1722–1797), of Colesborne, Gloucestershire, was articled to a Truro attorney in 1737 and qualified in 1744, later practicing in London. He specialized in colonial and mercantile business. Acquiring a considerable fortune through part ownership of privateering ships in the Seven Years' War, he invested heavily in estates in Jamaica as well as in England. He was an M.P. 1774–75, 1780–84, supporting the North ministry. Namier and Brooke, *House of Commons, 1754–1790,* II, 409–10. Upon the death of Ferdinand John Paris (Dec. 16, 1759), Eyre, who had lived in his house, was retained by the executrix of his estate. This connection with his former agent caused Thomas Penn to suspect that BF had hired Eyre "to get some secrets," presumably by consulting the proprietary papers in the possession of Paris' estate. While granting that Eyre made "a deal of shew in business," Penn thought him "of no great depth" and told Richard Peters that when he "made enquirys after an Agent" Eyre was "not foremost in the opinion of any of those I consulted." Penn to James Hamilton, March 8, 1760, to Richard Peters, March 8, July 12, 1760, Penn Papers, Hist. Soc. Pa.

Pennsylvania Acts of Assembly" passed during 1758 and 1759. The Proprietors opposed eleven of the measures, including the two most important, the £100,000 Supply Act of 1759 and an act authorizing Franklin, as agent, to apply for and receive Pennsylvania's share of the funds voted by Parliament to be distributed among the colonies in repayment of war expenses. Preparation of the Assembly's case and attendance at hearings before the Board of Trade and the Privy Council Committee occupied most of the time and attention of Franklin and Eyre until the Privy Council order of September 2 brought the issues to a close.

Late in the autumn Eyre rendered his bill. In accordance with British practice it is a minutely detailed statement, showing by dates the solicitor's expenditures on behalf of his client and his own charges for every document prepared, conference or hearing attended, or other service. The bill occupies four closely written pages and contains a total of 144 entries of services performed and expenses incurred. The total charge was £470 8s. 8d., of which Franklin had advanced at various times sums amounting to £152 10s.[8] Eyre's receipt for the final £317 18s., dated Dec. 2, 1760, concludes the document.[9] It will not be reproduced here in full, but some of its contents may usefully be described. A summary of the expenditures under major heads will follow to show where the money went.

The two barristers retained to represent Franklin and Robert Charles, the Pennsylvania agents, at the hearings were William de Grey[1] and Richard Jackson.[2] They did not receive single fees covering their entire services, but instead specific fees for each separate participating action: 10 guineas to de Grey as a retainer, 5 guineas to Jackson; 15 guineas apiece for the initial briefing and instruction; 5 guineas each for every subsequent consultation; and 10 guineas for each day's attendance at a hearing before the Board of Trade or the Privy Council Committee. In addition, de Grey's "Clerk and Man" and Jackson's "Man" received

8. "Account of Expences," pp. 52, 53. Eddy, in *PMHB*, LV (1931), 127, gives the total incorrectly.

9. "Account of Expences," p. 57; *PMHB*, LV (1931), 129. In the final payment the 8d. was ignored.

1. William de Grey (1719–1781), Trinity Hall, Cambridge, 1737; Middle Temple, 1738; called to the bar, 1742; M.P., 1761–71; solicitor to the Queen, 1761–63; solicitor general, 1763–66; attorney general, 1766–71; lord chief justice of the Common Pleas, 1771–80; knighted, 1771; raised to the peerage as Baron Walsingham, 1780. *DNB;* Namier and Brooke, *House of Commons,* II, 308–9.

2. See above, V, 148 n, and Namier and Brooke, *House of Commons,* II, 669–72.

small gratuities on each occasion proportioned to their masters' fees. Eyre himself charged from 6s. 8d.[3] for a minor errand to the Board of Trade, to 2 guineas for his and his clerk's attendance at a formal hearing, and £31 6s. 8d. for drawing the brief to be used by the barristers in support of the acts. Many documents, including some in the files of the Board of Trade, had to be copied, and these became a major item of expense. No branch of the British government conducted business without fees, which, in fact, were a principal source of income to the clerical staffs, and in a case such as this, supplemental gratuities were very much in order if the parties expected to receive considerate treatment in the future. In sum, the prosecution of business before governmental agencies, however legitimate, was an expensive business. The expenditures shown on Eyre's detailed bill may be grouped and summarized as follows:

	£	s.	d.
Francis Eyre (drafting legal papers, conferring formally or informally with the barristers, securing information at the Board of Trade, attending hearings, etc.)	87	11	2
Fair copies of documents required in the case	68	4	0
Fees to William de Grey	105	0	0
Gratuities to de Grey's clerk and man	4	7	6
Fees to Richard Jackson	99	15	0
Gratuities to Jackson's man	2	5	0
Doorkeeper's fees, Plantation Office (Board of Trade)	4	4	0
Bill at the Plantation Office	13	19	0
"To the Clerks for their Extraordinary Trouble"	2	2	0
Doorkeeper's fees, Cockpit (Privy Council Office)	3	3	0
Council Office bill	53	13	0
Privy Council clerks, extra	2	2	0
Mr. Cooke, the short-hand writer, for his attendance	10	10	0
Warrant and gratuity at the Treasury	13	13	0
Total due	£470	8	8
Paid on account	152	10	0
Balance due	£317	18	8

"Received the 2d Day of December 1760, of Benja. Franklyn Esqr. three hundred and seventeen Pounds eighteen Shillings, for which I have given another Receit on a Duplicate of this Bill, I say received in full of all Demands, by me   FRAS EYRE

£317. 18. 0"

3. A traditional amount (one third of a pound), which represented the value of a noble or angel, a gold coin issued until 1634.

To Deborah Franklin

ALS: American Philosophical Society; transcript: Harvard College Library (Sparks)

My dear Child,   London Feb. 21. 1760

Since I wrote you last, I have receiv'd yours of Nov. 7. and 29, Dec. 17. and Jan. 4. the last yesterday by Capt. Monck.[4] I rejoice to hear you and Sally and Mother[5] are well. I have lately been much indispos'd with an Epidemical Cold, that has lain greatly in my Head; but being just now cupp'd by Dr. Fothergill's Advice,[6] and parting with 8 Ounces of Blood from the Back of my Head, I find myself better, but cannot write much. I shall only acknowledge the Receipt of the Apples; those in the Boxes turn'd out much better than those in the Barrels; and amongst the Boxes, Billy's rather the best. I send you per Capt. Bolitho, two Saucepans, which instead of being tin'd within, are plated with Silver, that will not melt off like the Tin. The biggest cost me 2 Guineas, the smallest 17s. I flatter my self they will please you.[7] O that I were with you, or you with Your affectionate Husband

B FRANKLIN

P.S. Feb. 26. I continue mending, but not quite hearty yet. I was blooded on Sunday, 16 Ounces, which was of great Service; but that and Physic has left me a little weak. I bought 3 Saucepans, but keep the smallest to use here. I write to Sally per the Beulah, and send her some Goods.[8] Mrs. Garrigue's Things will go in Capt. Gibbon, I mention'd them in a former Letter.[9] Mr. Bland[1] buys and ships them.

Addressed: To / Mrs Franklin / Philadelphia

4. None of these letters has been found.

5. DF's mother, Sarah Read.

6. For Dr. John Fothergill, see above, IV, 126–7 n.

7. BF bought these saucepans in Sheffield, either on his way to, or his return from Scotland in the fall of 1759; see below, p. 27. The *Myrtilla,* Capt. John Bolitho, left Portsmouth on March 19, 1760, and arrived in Philadelphia on May 4, 1760. *Pa. Gaz.,* May 8, 1760.

8. *Pa. Gaz.,* June 5, 1760, records the arrival of the *Beulah,* Capt. James Gibbon.

9. Mrs. Mary Garrigues (above, VII, 274 n), daughter of BF's old friend, James Ralph. The letter mentioned here has not been found.

1. Elias Bland, London Quaker merchant (above, III, 141 n).

To Joseph Galloway

ALS: Yale University Library

Dear Sir, London, Feb. 26. 1760

The above is a Copy of mine per Capt. House[2] Since which I have receiv'd your Favour of Jan. 8. but one you mention to have wrote of Dec. 2. is not come to hand.[3] Nothing material has pass'd in our Affairs since my last,[4] the Proprietor not having yet presented the Laws.[5] They are at present under Consideration of our Council on both sides.[6] You desire some Information relating to the Stocks. They are now about 20 per Cent. below Par, or what it is suppos'd they will be on a Peace. For Instance £100 Stock that bears 3 per Cent. Interest, payable at the Bank half yearly, may now be bought for £80 or thereabouts; and on a Peace it is thought the same will sell for the full £100 and perhaps something more. I have laid out most of the Money I had here in the Stocks,[7] in hopes of this Advantage, some Interest, tho' low, arising in the meantime and a Peace it is thought we must have next Year. If you incline to employ any Money in the same Way, I shall readily serve you, on Request, in transacting the Affair.[8] My Son joins his best Wishes, with those of Dear Sir, Your affectionate Friend and humble Servant B FRANKLIN

2. See above, pp. 15–17. 3. Neither of these letters has been found.

4. Presumably that of Jan. 9, 1760, mentioned in the first sentence.

5. On March 13, 1760, Thomas Penn's agent, Henry Wilmot (above, p. 16 n), presented to the King in Council eighteen acts passed by the Pa. Assembly during 1758–59. Earlier, on Feb. 16, 1760, BF himself had presented the act passed by the Assembly on Sept. 29, 1759 (above, VIII, 442 n), appointing him agent to receive the province's share of the parliamentary grant for 1758. *Statutes at Large, Pa.,* V, 660. For the Penn's opposition to eleven of these nineteen acts, see below, pp. 125–130.

6. BF's solicitor was Francis Eyre during the hearings on the nineteen Pa. acts and his counsel were Richard Jackson and William de Grey; the proprietors' solicitor was Henry Wilmot and their counsel were the attorney and solicitor general, Sir Charles Pratt and Charles Yorke. See below, p. 128 n.

7. On March 15, 1759, BF bought £1575 of the 3 percent annuities of 1759. Apparently this was all that he purchased for his own account during his first mission, although on April 12, 1759, he bought 15 lottery tickets associated with the stock at £10 each, and at various times also purchased stock for Isaac Norris and for the province and transferred some of his own holdings to Norris. "Account of Expences," pp. 25, 26, 28, 42, 44, 49, 50, 52, 53, 58, 60, 62, 63: *PMHB,* LV (1931), 117, 118–19, 125, 126–7, 129, 130, 131, 132.

8. Galloway seems not to have availed himself of this offer.

To Deborah Franklin

ALS: American Philosophical Society

My dear Child,   London, Feb. 27. 1760.

Mr. Lemar[9] doing me the Favour to call on me, and acquaint me with his going to Philadelphia, I write this Line to acquaint you that I am now quite well of my late Indisposition, which I mention'd in former Letters.[1] By Capt. Bolitho I send you two Saucepans, plated inside with Silver instead of tinning. I bought them at Sheffield, because I thought they would please you; and if you are not much taken with them, I shall be greatly disappointed. I got three, but keep the smallest here to make my Watergruel, and send you the largest and middlemost. The Wine being now fine, proves excellent: The Apples are a great Comfort to me. My Love to all. Please to take Care of and forward the enclos'd.[2] I have sent Sally a Cask of Sheffield Goods instead of the Stationary she wrote for to Mr. Hall; which I imagine may answer better.[3] I am, my dearest Debby Your ever-loving Husband

B FRANKLIN

Addressed: To | Mrs Franklin | Philadelphia | per favour of | Mr Lemar.

From Isaac Norris

Letterbook copy: Historical Society of Pennsylvania

Dear Friend B Franklin   Philada Febry 27. 1760

I am just come from the House to my Brother's where I met a Gentleman setting out for NY[4] who complements me with staying for this Letter which will probably reach the Albany Sloop of

9. Not identified.

1. See above, p. 25, for BF's "Indisposition" and for the other matters mentioned in this letter.

2. Not identified.

3. For Sally Franklin's previous small ventures in business enterprise, beginning when she was only eight years old, see above, IV, 196, 224, 323, 326; VI, 277–8. Now sixteen, she had apparently ordered some stationery to sell, but her father had substituted a cask of Sheffield goods, and sent it in care of his partner David Hall.

4. In the margin: "dd T. Lloyd" for "delivered to Thomas Lloyd." See above, VI, 380 n.

War to be dispatched by General Amherst, as he writes our Governor in ten Days from the 21st Instant. This Vessel brot Secretary Pitts Letter with the Plan of Operations for the ensuing Campaigne in N America on the same Terms as last Year.[5]

The Governor did not lay this Letter and General Amhersts Two Letters accompanying it before us 'till two or three Hours ago, thô he received them last Week so that I cannot send you the Resolves of the House for want of Time but, by what has been said by several Members I think, there is no Doubt we shall raise the same Number of Men that we supplied last year in hopes the present Ministry will not sacrifice their American Possessions to a foreign Interest in a future Peace.[6]

This farther Grant will load us with a great Debt and it would have been some Direction to our future Supplies to have received an Account of the proportion of the Parliamentary Grant allotted to our Province,[7] but this Crisis in America demands our utmost Strength and we contribute it freely for our own Security and in Aid of the vast Expences of our Mother Country in this just and necessary War.

I recd your Two Letters of the 10th November and 8th. of De-

5. On Feb. 21, 1760, General Amherst (above, VIII, 328 n) wrote Governor Hamilton two letters urging him to use his "utmost Endeavours" to enlist the full support of the Pa. Assembly for the ensuing campaign. These, and William Pitt's letter to Hamilton of Jan. 7, 1760, which Amherst enclosed and in part paraphrased, were laid before the Assembly on Feb. 27, 1760. 8 *Pa. Arch.,* VI, 5102–9. The *Albany,* Capt. Jarvis, sailed from N.Y. during the third week of March convoying troops to Charleston, S.C. She arrived there on April 1 and was to sail directly for England. *N.-Y. Mercury,* March 17, April 14, 1760; *Pa. Gaz.,* April 17, 1760; John R. Alden, *John Stuart and the Southern Colonial Frontier* (Ann Arbor, 1944), pp. 106–7.

6. For the men and money raised by the Assembly for the 1760 campaign, see next page. In the margin there is this notation: "see Mar. 1st. 1760 entered postea pag. 113."

7. Pa.'s share of the £200,000 voted by Parliament to reimburse the colonies for their war expenditures in 1758 (see above, VIII, 333) was £26,902 8s. After deducting various fees and gratuities paid to officials at the Exchequer and his commission for receiving the money and depositing it in the Bank of England, BF calculated, Nov. 4, 1760, that "the neat sum in the bank, belonging to the Province" was £26,648 4s. 6d. Pa. appears to have received about £30 less than this, however, because in rounding off a figure to simplify his calculations, BF credited the province with £17 5s. 2d. too much and he also failed to deduct certain charges by the solicitor. See below, pp. 241–2.

cember last[8] and Now inclose a First Bill of Exchange.[9] John Hunter on Messrs Thomlinson Hanbury Colebrooke & Nisbett No 3,638 for £100 Sterl which I request you to receive for my Account.[1] I am &c.

Endorsed: Via N Y. by the Albany Sloop of War
B F received this Letter ackd. June 14th 1760.[2]

From Isaac Norris

Letterbook copy: Historical Society of Pennsylvania

Dear Friend B Franklin   March 1st. 1760
    I wrote on the 27th of February last[3] by a Gentleman to N York. This will inform you that the Assembly have resolved to grant £100,000 for the raising paying and cloathing 2,700 Men to Act in Conjunction with his Majestys Forces during the ensuing Campaign and have got their Bill into the Hands of a Committee for those Purposes.

    As we shall follow the Plan of the Law enacted last Year we hope to get it with the Governor very soon,[4] and reserve a Bill for settling the Quotas for each County to the latter End of the Session at which Time we hope to be furnished with the Duplicates of the last Year's Taxation throughout the Province, but as this difficult Work of proportioning the several Counties may be imperfect on the first Essay the House agree generally to continue it for One Year only.[5]

8. Neither letter has been found.
9. In the margin: "First Bill Excha. No. 3638. £100. o. o."
1. BF received this bill on April 22, 1760. "Account of Expences," p. 57; *PMHB*, LV (1931), 129.
2. No letter of this date from BF to Norris has been found.
3. See immediately above.
4. On Feb. 27, 1760, the Pa. Assembly resolved to raise 2700 men and the next day voted to grant £100,000 to levy, pay, and clothe them. On March 1 a committee was appointed to prepare the necessary bill; it was reported on March 4, passed the House on March 8, and was sent to Governor Hamilton the same day. After some demur he signed it on April 12. The measure was modeled on the Supply Act of April 17, 1759 (above, VIII, 326–7 n); 8 *Pa. Arch.*, VI, 5109–33; *Pa. Col. Recs.*, VIII, 460–3, 472–84.
5. On March 5, 1760, the Assembly appointed a committee "to prepare and bring in a Bill for ascertaining the proportional Sum to be yearly paid

I send inclosed a Second Bill of Exchange John Hunter on Messrs. Thomlinson &c. No. 3638 for a Hundred Pounds Sterling which please to receive.[6] I am Your Assured Friend   I N

Carolina appears to be in great Distress and under the apprehensions of an Indian War.[7] I send inclosed at your Request a Power of Attorney to which Our Friend Charles Beatty[8] is an Evidence and who will be on the Spot to prove it if he has a prosperous Voyage which I heartily wish him.   I N

per favr of Ch Beatty—per Captn Grant[9]

---

by the several Counties" toward sinking the £100,000 voted on February 28. On March 25 the committee presented "a Draught for that Purpose" which was debated several times and on April 12 a new committee was appointed to meet on May 19 "to examine and consider the Returns of Assessments from the several Counties, and to make an Essay towards ascertaining, in the most equitable Manner, the Sum to be raised annually by each. . . ." On September 25 this committee presented a report, proposing quotas for each county, but the Assembly took no further action before its final adjournment. 8 *Pa. Arch.,* VI, 5114, 5118–19, 5121, 5133–4, 5141.

6. For this bill, see the letter immediately above.

7. *Pa. Gaz.* reported, Feb. 28, 1760, that "open Hostilities" had broken out between disaffected Cherokee and the government of South Carolina over incidents reaching back to the expedition against Fort Duquesne in 1758 (above, VIII, 76–7 n). On the return journey the Cherokee had stolen horses and fought several small engagements with frontiersmen in Bedford Co., Va., where they incurred losses. In April 1759 they retaliated by killing about a score of settlers in the back country of South Carolina, whereupon Gov. William H. Lyttelton cut off trade with them and got his Assembly to vote 1500 men for a punitive expedition. Some of their chieftains concluded a peace treaty, Dec. 26, 1759, but this did not prevent an Indian offensive in January 1760, which took the lives of 40 to 50 settlers, and depopulated the South Carolina upcountry. The Cherokee captured Fort Loudoun (in present-day Tennessee), but were finally subdued in the fall of 1761 by two expeditions of regulars sent by General Amherst from the north. John Richard Alden, *John Stuart and the Southern Colonial Frontier* (Ann Arbor, 1944), pp. 78–88.

8. Charles Clinton Beatty (*c.* 1715–1772), a popular Presbyterian clergyman, had been chaplain of the forces under BF, building forts in Northampton Co., Pa., during the winter of 1756; see above, VI, 358, 382; *Autobiog.* (APS-Yale edit.), p. 235. He was now sailing to England and Ireland to raise money for the support of his poor colleagues and their families. See below, p. 174.

9. *Pa. Gaz.,* March 6, 1760, reported the clearance of the *Rachel,* Capt. Thomas Grant, for Liverpool.

[*Endorsed:*] B Franklin received this Letter ackd June 14th 1760[1]
Omitted entry in the proper Place

[Enclosure]
To all People to whom these Presents shall come I Isaac Norris
of the City and County of Philadelphia in the Province of Pensylvania in N America Esquire send greeting Know ye that I the said
Is Norris have made and ordained and by these Presents do make
ordain and in my Place and Stead put and constitute Benjamin
Franklin at present residing in the City of London Esquire to be
my true and lawful Attorney for me and in my Name and to and
for my proper Use to demand and receive of and from all and
every person and persons of what Degree or Quality soever whom
it now doth shall or may concern all and every such Sum and
Sums of mony Dividends Payments and Profits which now are
and which shall hereafter become due and payable to me for and
respect of all or any Annuities Yearly or other payments payable
and belonging to me for and in Respect of all and every or any
such Capital Stock or Stocks which I now have or hereafter shall
have in the Bank of England or in any other Fund or Stock whatever. ALSO for me and in my Name to accept of all such Capital
Stock or Stocks which I have already bought or contracted to buy
or shall hereafter buy or contract to buy of any person or persons
whatsoever upon the transferring thereof according to the usual
Manner of transferring the said Stock or Stocks and to pay such
Sum or Sums of Mony or Consideration for the Purchase of all
such Capital Stock or Stocks upon the transferring thereof from
Time to Time as I shall in that Behalf order. AND upon receipt of
the premises or any part thereof for me and in my Name from
Time to Time to make and give sufficient Acquittances and Discharges. And I do hereby give and grant unto my said Attorney
full Power and Authority to do and perform all Matters and
Things relating to the Premises as fully as I my self might or could
do was I personally present. And I do hereby ratify and confirm
all and whatsoever my said Attorney shall legally do or procure to
be done in and touching the Premises.[2] IN WITNESS whereof I
the said Isaac Norris have hereunto set my Hand and Seal the

1. No letter from BF to Norris of this date has been found.
2. For BF's investments on Norris' behalf, see above, VIII, 147–8.

First Day of March in the Year of Our Lord One thousand Seven Hundred and Sixty. I NORRIS LS

Sealed and delivered in the presence of us
  CHARLES BEATTY
  JAMES JOHNSTON

Copia

Endorsed: Mar. 1. 1760 Copy of my Power of Attorn. to B Franklin

To Deborah Franklin ALS: American Philosophical Society

My dear Child, London, March 5. 1760

I receiv'd the Enclos'd some time since from Mr. Strahan.[3] I afterwards spent an Evening in Conversation with him on the Subject. He was very urgent with me to stay in England and prevail with you to remove hither with Sally. He propos'd several advantageous Schemes to me which appear'd reasonably founded. His Family is a very agreable one; Mrs. Strahan a sensible [and][4] good Woman, the Children of amiable [char]acters and particularly the young Man, [who is] sober, ingenious and industrious, and a [desirable] Person. In Point of Circumstances [there can] be no Objection, Mr. Strahan being [in so thriving] a Way,[5] as to lay up a Thousand [Pounds] every Year from the Profits of his Business, after maintaining his Family and paying all Charges.

3. Not found, but from what follows, clearly a formal proposal for the marriage of Sarah Franklin and William Strahan, Jr. (above, V, 439 n), and for the permanent settlement of the Franklin family in England. Both fathers had contemplated the match since Sarah was seven and William ten; see above, III, 479–80; VI, 220; VII, 69, 115, 297.

4. The MS is torn; missing words or parts of words are supplied conjecturally in brackets. With one exception, noted below, they agree with the insertions printed without brackets by Sparks (*Works*, VII, 194–5). Bigelow followed Sparks exactly (*Works*, III, 44–5); Smyth used brackets and deviated from Sparks where the present editors have, but in a different way (*Writings*, IV, 9–10).

5. Sparks, and Bigelow after him, printed "Mr. Strahan being in such a way," thereby ignoring the plainly written "iving" which remains in the MS. Smyth suggested "Mr. Strahan being [now] living a Way," which seems less satisfactory than the suggestion made here.

I gave him, however, two Reasons why I could not think of removing hither. One, my Affection to Pensilvania, and long established Friendships and other Connections there: The other, your invincible Aversion to crossing the Seas. And without removing hither, I could not think of parting with my Daughter to such a Distance. I thank'd him for the Regard shown us in the Proposal; but gave him no Expectation that I should forward the Letters. So you are at Liberty to answer or not, as you think proper. Let me however, know your Sentiments.[6] You need not deliver the Letter to Sally, if you do not think it proper.

My best Respects to Mr. Hughes, Mr. Bartram,[7] and all enquiring Friends. I am, Your ever loving Husband   B [FRANKLIN]

PS. I have wrote several Letters to you lately.[8] But can now hardly tell by what Ships.

Addressed: To / Mrs Franklin / Philadelphia / per favour of / Mr Drinker[9]

From David Hall

Duplicate: American Philosophical Society

Sir,   Philada. March 5. 1760

By the Captains Friend and Lowther to London and Captain Rankin to Bristol, I sent you the first, second and third Copies of a Bill of Exchange for £200 Sterling; some of which, if not all, must have got to your Hands long before this reaches you.[1] I am not sure whether I wrote you the Exchange of that Bill; but in case I did not, it was Fifty-two.

6. No letter from DF in response has been found; her steadfast refusal to cross the ocean would have been a barrier to Strahan's plan, whatever she might have thought of the proposed match.

7. John Hughes (above, VI, 284–5 n) and John Bartram, the botanist (above, II, 378 n).

8. For BF's letters of Feb. 21 and 27, 1760, see above, pp. 25, 27.

9. Henry Drinker (1734–1809), Quaker merchant and partner in the Philadelphia firm of James and Drinker. *PMHB*, XIV (1890), 41–5.

1. BF recorded the receipt of this bill, drawn by William Plumsted (above, II, 153) on the London merchants, Nesbitt & Colebrook, on Jan. 31, 1760. It arrived in the *James and Mary*, Capt. James Friend. "Account of Expences," p. 51; *PMHB*, LV (1931), 126; see also VIII, 448. *Pa. Gaz.*, Feb. 14, 1760, records the clearance of the *America*, Capt. James Lowther, and the *Prince George*, Capt. Moses Rankin.

Inclosed I now send you the first Copy of another Bill of Exchange for £200 Sterling more;[2] which, with what I have before remitted you, since you left Philadelphia, makes in all Nineteen Hundred Forty-nine Pounds, Twelve Shillings, and Five Pence Sterling.[3] For the Receipt of this last, you will please advise me, as usual, and give me Credit for it, when paid. The Exchange of this last Fifty-four.

I have wrote you so often lately, and hear so seldom from you, that I have nothing new or material to say; but must own that I was a good Deal surprised, on not receiving a single Line from you by the November or December Mails into New-York, nor by the Friendship, Captain McClelland, who arrived here from London Monday last, was a Week[4]. Your Reason for so long Silence, I am at a Loss to conceive. Wish the Fount of Brevier for the News Advertisements, (if we are to have one) was come; the old Letter is shockingly bad, and I don't care to use the Bourjois,[5] for the Reason I have several times given you, that it drives out so much.[6] Wish you would send a Receipt for all the Bills sent you

2. This bill, drawn by Scott & McMichael, merchants of Philadelphia, on George and James Portis, merchants of London, and a bill for £100, involving the same parties, which Hall sent BF on April 18, 1760 (below, p. 100), were protested. BF was entitled to 20 percent damages from the drawers of the protested bills, and on Aug. 26, 1760, Hall sent him a "fresh Draught" for £360 (below, p. 187). Believing, however, that Scott & McMichael had been "hardly us'd" by the Portises, BF refused to accept the damages; Hall heartily concurred, Scott & McMichael being in his opinion "very honest Men, and most genteel Dealers." See below, pp. 177–8, 235. BF's memorandum of this transaction is recorded in "Account of Expences," p. 56, and in *PMHB*, LV (1931), 128–9.

3. For a list of Hall's remittances, see above, VII, 235–6.

4. On March 28, 1760, BF acknowledged letters from Hall of Dec. 15, 1759 (above, VIII, 448–9), and Feb. 8, 1760 (not found). From Hall's letter of April 18 (below, p. 100) it would appear that BF last wrote him in August 1759.

5. On Feb. 22, 1760, BF recorded paying William Caslon £43 2s. 6d. "for Brevier for my printing house." "Account of Expences," p. 52. (Eddy in *PMHB*, LV (1931), 127, inaccurately gives the sum as £42 2s. 6d.) The Brevier type was shipped in the *Beulah*, Capt. James Gibbon, which arrived in Philadelphia about June 1, 1760. On July 2, 1760, Hall acknowledged the receipt of the type. See below, pp. 39, 179, and *Pa. Ga{.*, June 5, 1760.

6. That is, it uses too much space.

on a separate Piece of Paper, in your next Letter, and am Yours
most sincerely   D. HALL
To Mr. Franklin.
By the Wolfe, Capt. McKinly, to Dublin[7]

From David Hall   ALS: American Philosophical Society

Sir,   Philada. March 6. 1760.
This serves to confirm the above,[8] and to inclose the second
Copy of the above mentioned Bill from Yours, &c.   D. HALL
To Mr. Franklin
By the Rachel, Capt. Grant, to Liverpool.[9]

To Deborah Franklin   ALS: American Philosphical Society

                          London, Pennsilva. Coffee House
My dear Child,   March 18. 1760
    Being just told by Mr. Wickoff,[1] that he goes tomorrow for
Philadelphia, I write this Line here to let you know I am pretty
well recover'd of a slight Illness I lately had, the same that affected me when I came down first from Gnadenhut, if you remember it, a Pain and Giddiness in my Head,[2] I have been cupp'd,

    7. *Pa. Gaz.*, March 6, 1760, records the clearance of the *Wolfe,* Capt. Allen
M'Kinly.
    8. The duplicate of Hall's letter of March 5 (printed immediately above)
is on the same sheet as this brief note.
    9. *Pa. Gaz.*, March 6, 1760, records the clearance of the *Rachel,* Capt.
Thomas Grant.
    1. In *Pa. Gaz.* as late as Nov. 15, 1759, John and Peter Wikoff were jointly
advertising European and India goods for sale at their store in Front St.,
Philadelphia, at the corner of Black Horse Alley. In the issue of June 26,
1760, John Wikoff began to advertise similar goods under his own name at
John Relfe's former store in Second St., and on Dec. 11, 1760, Peter Wikoff
began advertising from the former location and requested all persons indebted "to the late Partnership of John and Peter Wikoff" to pay him. Both
men are listed as members of the Mount Regale Fishing Co. of Philadelphia,
1762–63. *PMHB*, XXVII (1903), 89.
    2. Gnadenhütten (now Weissport, Pa.) was a Moravian settlement in North-
ampton Co. at which BF supervised the building of Ft. Allen in January 1756;

blooded, physick'd and at last blister'd for it; and it seems now quite remov'd; but by those Operations and very spare Living, I am grown a little thin, which I do not dislike. I hope this will find you well, and Mother and Sally. I purpose a little Journey of a few Days during the Easter Holidays.[3] My Love to all enquiring Friends. I am, as ever, dear Debby Your affectionate Husband

B FRANKLIN

Addressed: To / Mrs Franklin / Philadelphia / per favour of / Mr Wikoff

Deed of Trust for the Loganian Library

Transcript: Commissioner of Records, City of Philadelphia; abstract: American Philosophical Society[4]

On Aug. 28, 1754, William Logan and James Logan, sons of James Logan, deceased (above, I, 191 n), his son-in-law John Smith, and Hannah Smith, his surviving daughter, together with Israel Pemberton, William Allen, Richard Peters, and Benjamin Franklin, executed a deed of trust establishing the Loganian Library, thereby carrying out the intentions of the elder James Logan, left unfulfilled at the time of his death. An extended abstract of this document was printed above, V, 423–6. The original manuscript is now in the possession of the Library Company of Philadelphia (which by act of the Pennsylvania Assembly, approved March 31, 1792, acquired possession of the Loganian Library), but the deed of 1754 was never "acknowledged and Recorded in the Office for Recording of Deeds in the Province of Pennsylvania," as it stipulated should be done.

For a reason now not entirely clear a new deed of trust was prepared, dated March 25, 1760. There are some differences in the arrangement of the subject matter and many minor variations in phraseology, but no

---

see above, VI, 307–8, 365–8. On his dizzy spells after that experience, see above, VI, 429.

3. There is no record of such a trip; BF was probably too busy preparing for the Board of Trade hearings on the Pa. acts of 1758–59 to leave London at this time.

4. The second document, among the Bache Papers, is in an unknown hand, but bears an endorsement on the last page in BF's hand: "Extract Deed Loganian Library." It is not, however, a copy of any part of the original, but a short abstract or précis of the whole.

significant changes from the terms and conditions of the deed of 1754. Hence a new abstract here is unnecessary.

According to the recorded copy, the new deed was "contained in five Sheets of Parchment" and was signed and sealed by all the parties. Witnesses for all but Franklin were Edward Jones and Robert Greenway. Those for Franklin, who must have acted at a much later time, were Edward Shippen and William Bache.[5] Probably his signing and sealing was delayed until Sept. 9, 1789, on which date he formally acknowledged his act before Shippen, then president of the Court of Common Pleas. On Sept. 19, 1792, James Logan, one of the other parties, appeared before Shippen, now one of the justices of the Pennsylvania Supreme Court, and made affirmation that he had been present and saw William Logan, John and Hannah Smith, Israel Pemberton, William Allen, and Richard Peters sign and seal the document, and he acknowledged his own act. With these formalities completed, the deed was at last recorded in Deed Book D 34 of the Department of Records, Philadelphia, on March 20, 1792. This belated action came just eleven days before the passage of the bill transferring the Loganian Library to the Library Company of Philadelphia.

To Deborah Franklin ALS: American Philosophical Society

My dear Child, London [March 28? 1760][6]
Yesterday I receiv'd your [Letter] of Feb. 10.[7] in which you mention that it was some Months since you heard from me. During my Journey I wrote several times to you, particularly from

5. William Bache (D.3.2), BF's grandson, born in 1773, was still only sixteen if BF delayed signing until 1789.

6. The upper corner of the MS is torn and most of the date line is lost. The date is established by reference to the receipt "yesterday" of DF's letter of February 10. Philadelphia experienced a long freeze-up during the winter of 1760, no ships being able to sail from early January until on February 14 *Pa. Gaz.* reported 31 vessels as having cleared. Among these was the snow *America,* Capt. James Lowther, for London; it was reported in *London Chron.,* March 25–27, as having arrived at Dover. BF's letter to David Hall, March 28 (immediately below) acknowledges receipt of a letter of February 8, which must have come on the same vessel. BF probably received both letters on the 27th and answered both the next day. Reference in the final paragraph to the Board of Trade hearing, originally scheduled for April 18, as being "less than a Month away" confirms March 28 as being at least the approximately correct date of this letter.

7. Not found.

Liverpole and Glasgow;[8] and since my Return some very long Letters that might have been with you before your last to me, but I suppose the severe Winter on your Coast, among other Delays, has kept the Vessels out. One Pacquet, Bonnel, was blown quite back to England.[9]

I am sorry for the Death of your black Boy, as you seem to have had a regard for him.[1] You must have suffer'd a good deal in the Fatigue of Nursing him in such a Distemper. That Flower[2] has wrote me a very idle Letter, desiring me not to furnish the Woman pretending to be his Wife with anything on his Account: and says the Letters she shows are a Forgery. But I have one she left with me, in which he acknowledges her to be his Wife, and the Children his, and I am sure it is his Hand-Writing, by comparing it with this he has now wrote me and a former one. So he must be a very bad Man, and I am glad I never knew him. She was sick and perishing with her Children in the Beginning of the Winter, and has had of me in all about 4 Guineas.[3] What is become of her now I know not. She seem'd a very helpless silly Body, and I found her in some Falshoods that disgusted me, but I pity'd the poor Children, the more as they were descended, tho' remotely, from our good old Friends[4] whom you remember.

8. BF's letter from Liverpool, Aug. 29, 1759 (above, VIII, 430–2) is the only one that has been found.

9. For BF's letters to DF, written after his return from Scotland (Nov. 2, 1759), see above, pp. 25, 27, 32–3. Since the earliest of these is Feb. 21, 1760, and since they are all short, probably none of the "very long Letters" to which he here refers have been found. In his letter of March 5 (above, p. 34) David Hall also complained of BF's long silence. The *Harriot*, Capt. Bonnell, left Falmouth on Nov. 23, 1759, was dismasted three weeks later off the banks of Newfoundland, and limped back into Fowey, England, during the first week of January 1760. *Pa. Gaz.*, Feb. 21, 1760; *London Chron.*, Jan. 10–12, 12–15, 1760.

1. Probably Othello, whom DF was thinking of sending to the Bray Associates school in Philadelphia; see above, VIII, 425.

2. For Henry Flower, the Philadelphia watchmaker, and for BF's assistance to his wife, see above, VIII, 424. His "very idle Letter" and the "former one," both mentioned in this paragraph, have not been found.

3. Loans to Mrs. Flower of 3 guineas on Aug. 4, 1759, and of 10*s*. 6*d*., undated, are recorded in "Account of Expences," p. 45; *PMHB*, LV (1931), 125.

4. A Henry Flower (d. 1736), was one of the early postmasters of Philadelphia; see above, II, 158. An Enoch Flower was admitted a member of the Library Co., April 14, 1746; *PMHB*, XXXVIII (1914), 373–4.

I have now the Pleasure to acquaint you, that our Business draws near a Conclusion, and that in less than a Month we shall have a Hearing, after which I shall be able to fix a Time for my Return. My Love to all, from, Dear Debby Your affectionate Husband　　　　　　　　　　　　　　　　　　　B FRANKLIN

Billy presents his Duty.

To David Hall

ALS: Historical Society of Pennsylvania

Dear Mr. Hall,　　　　　　　　　　London, March 28. 1760

I receiv'd yours of Dec. 15. with the Bill for £200 drawn by W Plumsted on Nesbit & Cheesbrook. Also yours of Feb. 8.[5]

The Brevier went in Capt. Gibbon, and I hope will get safe to hand.[6] I order'd the Fount all Roman, as it will hold out better in the same Quantity of Work, having but half the Chance of Wanting Sorts,[7] that the same Weight of Rom. and Ital. would have; and the old Italic is not so much worn as the Roman, and so may serve a little longer.

I am oblig'd to Mr. Colden[8] for his useful Correspondence with you, which you mention to me.

I am amaz'd at the great Price of Wood among you, and the high Rents I hear are given for Houses.[9] The first I suppose must be owing to the Want of Hands to cut it; the last to the Encrease of Trade and Business, and Number of Inhabitants.

I think you have done very well with the Almanacks. I see there

5. See above, VIII, 448–9, for Hall's letter of Dec. 15, 1759; for Plumsted's bill, see this volume, p. 33 n; Hall's letter of Feb. 8, 1760, has not been found. The firm name was Nesbit and Colebrooke; BF inadvertently wrote "Cheesbrook."

6. For BF's purchase and shipment of Brevier type to Hall, see above, p. 34 n. Arrival of the *Beulah*, Capt. James Gibbon, was reported in *Pa. Gaz.*, June 5, 1760.

7. Characters or pieces in a font of type.

8. Probably Alexander Colden (above, VI, 113 n), N.Y. postmaster. This correspondence may have related to the prompt sending to Hall of London newspapers received by packet.

9. In a letter to BF of June 4, 1759, Isaac Norris had observed that the war had driven up the price of houses in Philadelphia; see above, VIII, 391.

are others advertis'd: but doubt not Poor Richard will hold his Ground.[1]

I begin to see a Prospect of returning home this Summer, as I think our Affairs here will now soon be brought to a Conclusion.[2] It will be a great Pleasure to me to see you and my other Friends, and to find all well.

There are abundant Rumours just now of a Peace; but it is thought it can hardly take Place till next Winter.[3]

My Love to Cousin Molly and your Children.[4] I am, Yours affectionately   B FRANKLIN

Addressed: To | Mr David Hall | Printer | Philadelphia

Endorsed: B. Franklin March 28. 1760.

From David Hall   Letterbook copy: American Philosophical Society

Sir,   Philada. March 31. 1760

In my two last to you, of the 5th and 6th Instant,[5] by the Captains Grant and McKinly, to Liverpool and Dublin, were inclosed the first and second Copies of a Bill of Exchange for £200 Ster-

1. In a letter of Dec. 15, 1759, Hall mentions sending BF *Poor Richard's Almanack* for 1760 and the *Pocket Almanack* for 1760; see above, VIII, 448. In the fall of 1759 *Pa. Gaẓ.* advertised, among others, *Father Abraham's Almanack, The Pennsylvania Almanac* by Thomas Thomas, *The American Almanac* by John Jerman—all printed by William Dunlap—and *The Universal American Almanack* printed by William Bradford. *Pa. Gaẓ.*, Oct. 18, Nov. 15, 1759.

2. A hearing before the Board of Trade on the Pa. acts passed in 1758–59 was scheduled for April 18, 1760, but owing to numerous complications, BF's "long Litigation" with the proprietors was not finished until the end of the summer. See below, pp. 125–73, 196–211.

3. The rumors were probably inspired by an Anglo-Prussian declaration, Nov. 25, 1759, proposing a peace conference to France, Russia, and Austria. Three months later these three powers responded with a counter-declaration which led to "interminable diplomatic maneuvers" but nothing else. Britain and France did not sign a definitive peace treaty until Feb. 10, 1763. Gipson, *British Empire*, VIII, 204–7, 309.

4. "Cousin Molly" was Mary Leacock Hall (F.2.2.3), DF's second cousin. The Hall children were William (1752–1834), Deborah (1754–1770), and David, Jr. (1755–1821).

5. See above, pp. 33–5.

ling; and, in case of Miscarriages, I now send you the third Copy of the same Bill, and am, Sir, Yours, &c.   D. HALL

To Mr. Franklin.

By the Roebuck, Capt. Jones, to Holyhead.[6]

To [Alexander] Colden[7]   Draft: American Philosophical Society

Mr. Colden

Dear Sir,   London, April 8. 1760

I have ordered into your Care from Liverpool 9 Casks and a Bale, which I request you would receive and forward to my Brother Peter Franklin, in Newport, Rhodeisland.[8] Enclos'd is the Bill of Lading. Please to pay the Freight (Eight Guineas) and charge me with it. I hope this Summer to have the Pleasure of seeing you, and of finding both the Families well for whom I have the sincerest Regard. I am, Dear Sir, Yours affectionately   BF

To Messrs. Hillary and Scot[9]   Draft: American Philosophical Society

Gentlemen   London, April 8. 1760

I receiv'd yours of the 26th past,[1] with the Invoice and Bill of Lading for the Earthen Ware.[2] I am told on Enquiry that I cannot

6. *Pa. Gaz.*, April 3, 1760, reported the clearance of the *Roebuck*, Capt. Robert Braden, for Holyhead, Wales.

7. For Alexander Colden, postmaster at N.Y., see above, VI, 113 n. It seems unlikely that BF would have asked the father, Cadwallader Colden (above, II, 386 n), who spent most of his time at his estate, Coldengham, up the Hudson, to execute the mercantile commission here described.

8. The casks probably contained the earthenware shipped for BF by Messrs. Hillary & Scot of Liverpool (see the following document). Since Kendal is a woolen manufacturing center in Westmorland County, the bale mentioned in the next document as coming from there probably contained cloth BF had ordered while passing through on his journey to Scotland late in the previous summer. Peter Franklin's Ledger, 1739–64 (APS) shows in various accounts of 1760, and especially of 1761 and 1762, considerable sales of crockery, china, glassware, and worsted.

9. Presumably a Liverpool mercantile firm.

1. Not found.

2. For the shipment of this and of the "Bale from Kendal," see the document immediately above.

insure here to more Advantage than with you; so desire you would get Insurance made for £50 which will include the Bale from Kendal; and draw on me for the whole Amount, deducting only the Allowance, (if any is customary with your Potter) for prompt Pay[ment] and your Draft shall be paid on sight. If the Ship is not gone, please to send a Copy of the Invoice with the Goods, to Peter Franklin of Rhodeisland. I am, Gentlemen, Your obliged Friend and humble Servant   B FRANKLIN

Messrs Hillary & Scot

To ————³   Draft: American Philosophical Society

Dear Sir   London April 8. 1760

I received your Favour of the 31st of last Month,⁴ the answering of which I delayed and [I] should be glad to accompany you from London, in your next Return to Derbyshire; but doubt it will not be in my Power. I am sorry I cannot be certain as to the time of my going into Derbyshire. For on the very day you pur-

3. The editors can only guess at the identity of the addressee. On his way to Scotland in August 1759 BF "spent some time in Derbyshire among the Gentry there" and his present correspondent was probably one of the men he met then. The addressee seems to have been someone with scientific or technological interests because of BF's expressed hope of profiting from his acquaintance's "Instructions." Before leaving England in the Summer of 1762 BF is known to have become friendly with two such Derbyshire men: John Whitehurst (1713–1788) of Derby, horologer and maker of philosophical instruments, later author of a popular geological treatise, *Inquiry into the Original State and Formation of the Earth* (London, 1778), and F.R.S.; and Anthony Tissington of Swanwick, near Alfreton, apparently concerned with the management of mines, for whom BF signed a certificate of nomination to the Royal Society, June 19, 1766 (see above, VIII, 358). Derbyshire Archeological and Natural History Society *Journal*, XLVI (1924–25), 7–11; LXXX (1960), 82, 87–8. The earliest surviving documentation of BF's acquaintance with either man is a letter from Whitehurst dated March 28, 1762, and that with Tissington about a year later, when Whitehurst sent BF greetings from their mutual friend, but the tenor of these letters shows that cordial relations with both had been established for some time. No other resident of Derbyshire in 1760 can be suggested who fits so well the present requirements, hence it seems likely that this letter was addressed either to Whitehurst or to Tissington, but to which one remains a matter of conjecture.

4. Not found.

pose coming to Town, viz. the 18th of this Month, our Province Affairs are to have Hearing before the Board of Trade.[5]

For being engag'd in some publick Business relating to our Colonies, which will probably have several Hearings before the Lords of Trade and the Council, the first of which is fix'd to the 18th Instant, and the rest uncertain—it is impossible for me to foresee when I shall be quite at Liberty; but as soon as I am, I promise myself the Pleasure of visiting you, and the Advantage of your Instructions, if my Leisure does not happen at a time inconvenient to you.

My Son joins in best Wishes for you and your's, with, Dear Sir, Your most obedient humble Servant B FRANKLIN

From Isaac Norris

Letterbook copy: Historical Society of Pennsylvania

Dear Friend B Franklin 15th. Aprl. 1760

It is so long since we received any Accounts of our Publick Affairs in England, that I hope the old Saying "that No News is good News," may be our Case,[6] with respect to the Bills Pass'd by Governor Denny the last Year, should the ReEmitting Act (of which I own I was very Apprehensive) be repealed it would now throw us into extream Confusion.[7] As for the Supply Bill[8] I never fear'd it, and now less than ever, since Governor Hamilton has not venturd to refuse Our last Act passd a few Days Ago for Granting £100,000, and £2700 [sic] Men, in which the Proprietary Estate is taxed as in the Law past by Governor Denny. It is True Governor Hamilton gave his Assent to it with an Ill Grace as will appear by the inclos'd Paper of Amendments and his Message to which I refer.[9] The Verbal Message of the 8th April Instant

5. For the hearings before the Board of Trade on the confirmation of the acts passed by the Pa. Assembly, see below, pp. 125–31.

6. BF's most recent letter to Norris was apparently that of Dec. 8, 1759 (not found); see above, pp. 28–9.

7. For the act re-emitting the Pa. bills of credit, signed by Governor Denny on June 20, 1759, see above, VIII, 419 n.

8. That of April 17, 1759; see above, VIII, 326–7 n.

9. After presenting the £100,000 supply bill to Governor Hamilton on March 8, 1760 (see above, p. 29 n), the Pa. Assembly adjourned until March

refers to An Anecdote which I will hint to You, as I apprehend it.[1] When the House Resolved on the Sum of £1,500 to defray the Expences of the Agency in soliciting the Affairs of this Province at the Court of G.B, on the 3d. February, and 1st April 1757, I need not inform You they ordered Immediate Payment for £750 Sterling, part of that Sum Out of the L. Office,[2] but when the Re-emitting Act expird,[3] and the Annual Sinking of the Money, let out Upon Loan brought the Int[erest] Mony to a Meer Triffle, the House became very sensible that They shou'd soon be in the Condition the Proprietors had long labourd to bring upon the

17, but because of bad weather and a fit of gout which immobilized Speaker Norris, it did not resume its business until March 24, meeting then and for the next several days in Charles Norris' house. On March 25 Richard Peters delivered the bill to the House with a series of amendments proposed by Hamilton and his council on March 18. These were designed to assure the governor's participation in the disposition of the public revenue and to protect the Proprietors by having commissioners appointed to hear appeals from the popularly elected assessors. The House at once unanimously rejected these changes and then returned the bill to the governor on April 1. The next day Hamilton sent the House a message defending his amendments and desiring the House to reconsider them. Having done so, the House informed Hamilton on April 5 that it saw "no Reason to recede" from its bill and desired him to pass it as it stood. This the governor with the advice of his council decided to do on April 8, notifying the House of his intentions on April 10 and complaining of the "Hardships" imposed upon him by the bill and observing that the Proprietors might be "greatly injured" by it and the "legal Powers of Government . . . very much prejudiced and wounded." Nevertheless, Hamilton signed the bill on April 12, 1760. 8 *Pa. Arch.*, VI, 5115–18, 5121–9, 5132; *Pa. Col. Recs.*, VIII, 460–3, 480. Norris to Sampson Lloyd, March 31, 1760, Hist. Soc. Pa.

1. Hamilton's verbal message of April 8, 1760, delivered to the House by Peters, stated that since the supply bill authorized the trustees of the provincial Loan Office "to pay and discharge all such Certificates and Draughts as have been heretofore made, by Order of Assembly to the Provincial Treasurer, for Services done the Public, which yet remain unpaid," he wanted to be informed "what the Sum total of those Certificates and Draughts may amount to, and likewise the Services for which they were made and given." The next day the House furnished the governor "with the List of Certificates and Draughts of Assembly on the Provincial Treasurer" and he "was pleased to say, it was very well." 8 *Pa. Arch.*, VI, 5126–7.

2. See above, VII, 166–7.

3. That of March 7, 1746 (N. S.), which directed the trustees of the provincial Loan Office to re-emit until Oct. 15, 1756, all the bills of credit which they received. *Statutes at Large, Pa.*, V, 7–15.

Province That the People shou'd have no Power over their own Mony. They therefore on the 20th. March 1759, gave a Certificate for the whole Sum of £1500, "To be Paid out of the Next Supplies to be Granted for discharging of the Publick Debts, and other Purposes for the King's Use,"[4] and they were very Justifiable in ordering that Certificate to be signed, As the Members were at that Time apprehensive they shoud be Necessitated to pass their Supply Bill with an Exclusion of the Proprietary Estate, (and I say the More upon this Occasion As I had some Concern in Procuring that Certificate.) Thô I must Confess that as it has since turn'd out there seems some hardship in making the Proprietors pay a Part of that Charge, Governor Denny or his Council got, from one of Our Members, who did not well understand it, a hint (as we suppose) of this Transaction and therefore on the sending Up the former Supply Bill, He sent a Message by the Secretary to Enquire what Orders upon the Treasurer remain Unpaid which were comprehended in that Clause of the Bill then offer'd to him.[5] We made the Secretary explain himself with Precision, and when he insisted on his Message and confind it to the Orders on the Treasurer which then remaind Unpaid We told him, That there were none and Governor Denny afterwards Past the Bill, (which One of our Country Members said, "was like swallowing a Chesnut with the Bur on").[6] But since that Bill Past, Our Votes have been made Publick,[7] and it there appears that a Certificate was signd in the House, on the 20th March 1759, for the Aforesaid Sum of £1500 Sterling To be Paid as I have informd You above. This Probably produced the Message of the 8th. April, Inst. But behold There was No part of That Mony Unpaid or to be paid Out of the last Supply Bill, and Governor Hamilton had No Right to Enquire any further, so that for any Thing I can find they must remain in Statû Quo prius, "till our Accounts come to be made

4. See *Votes*, 1758–59, p. 45, and above, VIII, 405.

5. Peters delivered this message on March 28, 1759. See *Votes*, 1758–59, p. 50.

6. The certificate of March 20, 1759, was an acknowledgement of a debt due, which "ought to be paid out of the next Supplies to be granted," and was not in form or in intent an order "on the Treasurer which then remained Unpaid." The Assembly was therefore technically justified in failing to tell the secretary about it.

7. *Pa. Gaz.*, Nov. 29, 1759, advertised *Votes*, 1758–59, as "just published."

Publick."[8] This situation of that Affair, I presume, has Induced the Members, to whom I repeatedly mentiond the Necessity of Making A New Order for the Remainder of the £1500 Sterling to let it lye As it now does Upon the Resolves of February and April 1757, and 20th. March 1759, But this ought Not, and will not Alter your Conduct of Useing what I have remitted, As the Publick Occasions shall require for their Service. Bills of Exchange have Risen for some Time from 5 to 7½ per Cent but I Apprehend These new Contractors will be Under a Necessity of Lowering them a Little, if the Campaign shou'd be Carried on Vigourously in America This Year. If that shou'd be the Case, I shall Continue to Remit a few More Bills of Exchange, if I receive some Payments the People Indebted to me gave me Reason to expect, but in the Mean Time, what Apology Can I make for the Trouble it gives You in Negotiating My Concerns There in Mony Matters. This incloses a 3d Bill of Exchange John Hunter, on Messrs. Tomlinson & Co. No. 3638 for £100,[9] and I must request the favour that You will be Pleasd to pay to my Kinsman Samsn Lloyd[1] of Birmingham, for a few Goods he shipd for my Account Viâ, Bristol, the greatest part of which is Arriv'd and the rest came to Bristol too late to be put on board. The whole Amounts to about £51 or 2, of which he will, in pursuance of my Letter to him, Produce the Account, which cou'd not be exactly sent to me for want of some small Charges on the Goods. I hope the Passing of the Last Supply Bill will near finish Our Squables with the Proprietors on that Head, and we also hope the Death of F.J. Paris[2] will be no loss to this Province which has felt the Effects of his great Pains and

8. The account of expenditures under the Supply Act of April 17, 1759, appeared in *Votes*, 1759–60, advertised as "Lately published" in *Pa. Gaz.*, Nov. 27, 1760. This contained a record of the £2362 10*s.* currency paid to Norris, June 14, 1759, it having been "advanced by him to Benjamin Franklin, Esq; Agent." 8 *Pa. Arch.*, VI, 5154.

9. For this bill, see above, p. 29 n.

1. Sampson Lloyd (1699–1779), Norris' second cousin, was an ironmaster at Birmingham and co-founder (1765) of the banking firm, Taylor & Lloyd (later Lloyds Bank). He had sent Norris glass, ironware, and nails and was advised in a letter of March 31, 1760, that BF would pay for them. Norris to Lloyd, March 31, 1760, Hist. Soc. Pa. For the Lloyd family in England, see Samuel Lloyd, *The Lloyds of Birmingham* (3d edit., London, 1909) and Arthur Raistrick, *Quakers in Science and Industry* (N.Y., 1950).

2. On Dec. 16, 1759.

Active Industry for Many Years Past, to do us all the Mischief in his Power. I am Your Assured Friend   I N

The House have appointed a Committee to Consider the Governors Message, and report Their Opinion at the next Sitting.[3]

Copy.

[*Endorsed:*] B F received this Lettr. ackd June 14th. 1760[4]

The Interest of Great Britain Considered

The Interest of Great Britain Considered, With Regard to her Colonies, And the Acquisitions of Canada and Guadaloupe. To which are added, Observations concerning the Increase of Mankind, Peopling of Countries, &c. London: Printed for T. Becket, at Tully's Head, near Surry-Street in the Strand. MDCCLX. (Yale University Library); draft (five scattered pages only): American Philosophical Society.[5]

Even before the end of 1759, British victories, especially those in North America and the West Indies, and the obvious decline of French strength had led many observers to believe that the war was drawing to a close. Active discussion, therefore, soon began in Great Britain about proper terms for a peace settlement. Sharp differences of opinion emerged as to which of the British conquests the ministry should insist on keeping, both to secure the safety of the nation's existing overseas possessions and to enhance the trade and prosperity of the mother country and the empire as a whole. Very quickly these conflicting views produced a full-scale pamphlet war. Abortive peace negotiations took place in 1761, but the definitive treaty ending the armed conflict was delayed until February 1763. Meanwhile the battle of words went on until at least sixty-five

3. Hamilton had sent two messages to the Assembly, April 2 and 10, highly critical of the supply bill, but in the second one agreed to pass it because of "the Necessity of the Times." The House thereupon appointed a committee to consider these messages and report at the next sitting. The Assembly adjourned April 12, but when it met in September for its final sitting this committee made no report. 8 *Pa. Arch.,* VI, 5122–5, 5127–9, 5134–57.

4. No letter from BF to Norris of this date has been found.

5. Six pages of draft are placed together in Franklin Papers, L (ii), 13. The first of these (numbered at the bottom "7") is not part of this pamphlet, however, but a fragment of a proposed tract of 1766 relating to the Stamp Act. The other five pages (numbered 43, 45, 53, 58, 67) are parts of BF's draft of the present work. In an errata note at the end of the printed text BF supplied three corrections; these have been incorporated silently in this reprinting.

pamphlets had been published on this one topic, besides uncounted articles and letters in the newspapers.[6]

From the start the main issue between the writers was whether Britain should retain the whole of Canada (Louisbourg had fallen in 1758, Quebec in 1759, and the surrender of the principal remaining enemy force at Montreal in the next campaign was confidently expected), or should merely restrain the French on the North American continent at a safe distance from the existing British colonies and keep instead the rich sugar-producing island of Guadeloupe (also captured in 1759). It was generally recognized that Britain could not expect to keep all of Canada and the island too. Despite their numbers and vigor, the pamphleteers probably had very little influence on the decisions of the responsible ministers or on the opinions of leaders of the various political factions; for their own reasons these men finally agreed, with dissent only on details, to take Canada and all other French mainland territory east of the Mississippi and to return Guadeloupe and Martinique (captured in 1762). The so-called "Neutral Islands," chiefly Grenada, the Grenadines, and Tobago, ownership of which had long been disputed, remained in British possession.[7]

The attitudes and arguments of the writers were greatly influenced by the economic theories they held as individuals and those of the readers they hoped to persuade. This was the late age of English mercantilism, when many men were changing their views on the chief values

6. The most complete bibliography of these pamphlets is in Clarence W. Alvord, *The Mississippi Valley in British Politics* (Cleveland, 1917), II, 253–64.

7. The pamphlet war and its relations to the peace settlement are most usefully discussed in the following works: William L. Grant, "Canada versus Guadeloupe, an Episode of the Seven Years' War," *Amer. Hist. Rev.*, XVII (1911–12), 735–53; a general review of the controversy with brief analyses of some of the most important pamphlets. Alvord, *Mississippi Valley*, I, 45–75; strong on the differing political theories influencing the principal writers, but assigning to the public discussion too much effect upon the attitude of the politicians and incorrectly attributing major authorship of the present pamphlet to Richard Jackson. Sir Lewis Namier, *England in the Age of the American Revolution* (2d edit., N.Y., 1961), pp. 273–82, and Jack M. Sosin, *Whitehall and the Wilderness The Middle West in British Colonial Policy, 1760–1775* (Lincoln, Neb., 1961), pp. 5–26; valuable correctives to Alvord on the influence of the writers and helpful on the positions taken by political leaders, but less useful on the pamphlet controversy itself and the economic theories involved. Gerald Stourzh, *Benjamin Franklin and American Foreign Policy* (Chicago, 1953), pp. 66–82; the outstanding treatment of BF's political ideas as revealed in the present pamphlet and of his expansionism and "grandiose vision of the American future."

THE

INTEREST

OF

GREAT BRITAIN

CONSIDERED,

With Regard to her

COLONIES,

AND THE ACQUISITIONS OF

CANADA and GUADALOUPE.

To which are added,

OBSERVATIONS concerning the Increase of
Mankind, Peopling of Countries, &c.

LONDON:
Printed for T. BECKET, at Tully's Head, near
Surry-Street in the Strand.
MDCCLX.

the mother country could derive from the possession of colonies. Virtually everyone agreed that colonies were not worth having at all if they did not somehow contribute significantly to the wealth of the parent state, but there had for some time been less unanimity as to how that contribution might best be made.

Those who adhered to the older view took as their ideal that of the self-sufficing colonial empire in which overseas possessions, differing widely in climate and topography from the homeland, could contribute the raw materials and other products not otherwise available except by purchase from foreign lands. If colonies could produce more of these commodities than could be consumed in the mother country, so much the better, for under proper controls the surpluses could be sold abroad to the benefit of the nation's foreign exchange. Great Britain's colonial possessions came closest to meeting this ideal: her tropical possessions in the West Indies and her southern continental colonies supplied such "exotic" staples as sugar and molasses, indigo and other dyestuffs, rice, and tobacco; from Newfoundland and elsewhere in northern coastal waters came quantities of fish, particularly useful for export to the Catholic countries of southern Europe; from various parts of the North American continent came furs and deerskins, lumber, and also large quantities of hemp, and naval stores to free Britain's merchant marine and the Royal Navy from dependence on Scandinavia; from the middle Atlantic area, the so-called "bread colonies," surplus foodstuffs could be supplied to the "staple colonies," permitting them to concentrate their agriculture on the valuable commodities only they could produce; ports on the west coast of Africa supplied the Negro manpower to operate the plantations of the South and the islands. In the minds of many mercantilists of the older school the most highly esteemed of all these colonial areas was that of the sugar islands of the West Indies. The writers of the 1760s who held to this view, therefore, were eager to add the fertile island of Guadeloupe to the British possessions in that region.

The great expansion in manufacturing activities taking place in England in the eighteenth century, especially important in the Midlands, was, however, leading many Englishmen to value colonies less as sources of raw materials than as markets for the sale of British products. An island in the Caribbean, with only a relatively small white population of planters and their overseers and large numbers of lightly clad Negro slaves, offered far fewer possibilities for the sale of British textiles, metal products, and other manufactured goods than did the middle and northern colonies of the continent, rapidly filling with independent farming families and prosperous merchants, all needing to buy warm clothing and useful household goods, and eager to acquire the articles of comfort and even of luxury that only the mother country could supply. As British exports to the North American continent increased at an amazing rate during the middle decades of the eighteenth century, more and more businessmen and economists came to believe that, valuable as the sugar and tobacco colonies undoubtedly still were as sources of raw materials, the northern colonies with their expanding consumption of British goods were even more important as market areas. Any threat to their continued growth, such as the French created by their "incursions" in the north and west, was a real danger to existing and prospective British markets. Hence the elimination of that threat by the retention of Canada seemed more important than the addition of one more sugar island, however fertile it might be.

When Franklin joined in the debate he was not personally concerned with the economic aims of either group of English mercantilists; as a colonial he was, of course, less interested in promoting a particular branch of British trade than in protecting the lives and property of his fellow colonists from such losses as the French and their Indian allies had inflicted on them in recent years. Yet, posing as an Englishman in his anonymous writings and directly addressing British readers, he quite understandably wrote for the most part as a thoroughgoing mercantilist and used the arguments of the more recent economic school whose theories supported the decision he hoped would be made.

His first contribution to the public discussion was the relatively short "Humourous Reasons for Restoring Canada," in the *London Chronicle*, Dec. 25–27, 1759 (above, VIII, 449–52); his next and most important treatment of the subject was *The Interest of Great Britain Considered*, often called "The Canada Pamphlet," which the *London Chronicle*, April 15–17, 1760, announced as "This Day" published. This work is closely connected in the public debate with two other pamphlets. In the middle of December 1759, one week before his piece on "Humourous Reasons" was printed, there appeared *A Letter Addressed to Two Great Men*.[8] The author was almost certainly John Douglas (1721–1807), vicar of High Ercall, Shropshire, protégé of the Earl of Bath, and many years later Bishop of Salisbury. He argued strongly in favor of imposing

8. *A Letter Addressed to Two Great Men, on the Prospect of Peace; And on the Terms necessary to be insisted upon in the Negociation.* London: Printed for A. Millar, in the Strand. MDCCLX. While the titlepage is thus dated 1760, an advertisement in *London Chron.*, Dec. 15–18, 1759, uses the words "This week will be published," and one in the issue of Dec. 18–20, says "This day is published." The "Two Great Men" were the Duke of Newcastle and William Pitt.

severe terms on the "perfidious" French and of making the cession of Canada to Great Britain an indispensable condition of the peace treaty: "In a Word, you must keep Canada, otherways you lay the Foundation of another War."[9] This pamphlet produced prompt replies, of which the one of immediate concern here was entitled *Remarks on the Letter Address'd to Two Great Men. In a Letter to the Author of that Piece.* Its writer is generally believed to have been William Burke, a reputed "kinsman" of Edmund Burke, and the author of at least one other pamphlet in this controversy.[1] He had recently been appointed secretary and register of Guadeloupe and so had a personal interest in its retention by Great Britain. He vigorously, but politely, attacked the author of *A Letter,* opposed the retention of Canada, and urged the importance of Guadeloupe as a valuable addition to Britain's sugar-producing colonies. This pamphlet appeared about a month after *A Letter,*[2] and induced Franklin to enter the lists in support of the retention of Canada. He took somewhat more time than Burke had done and three months passed before his response appeared. It may be regarded as one of his most important publications in pamphlet form.

There has been considerable controversy over the authorship of *The Interest of Great Britain Considered.* At the time, Franklin was generally considered the author; later, credit was often given to Richard Jackson, writing perhaps at Franklin's instigation as had happened earlier with *An Historical Review of the Constitution and Government of Pensylvania;* in recent years Franklin's authorship has been reestablished in the minds of all but a few doubters, though, as Franklin himself seems to have acknowledged, he received some help from his friend and ally Jackson. With this attribution to Franklin the present editors fully concur.[3]

9. *Letter to Two Great Men,* p. 30.

1. William Burke (1729–1798), lawyer, called to the bar from the Middle Temple, 1755; secretary and register of Guadeloupe, 1759–63; under secretary of state, 1765–67; M.P., 1766–74; deputy paymaster of the forces in India, 1782–93. Though there probably was no blood relationship between him and Edmund Burke, the two men were close friends and political associates throughout life. William's career shows that he was an opportunist, politically and financially, with none of those personal qualities which enabled Edmund to attain distinction in public affairs. Namier and Brooke, *House of Commons,* II, 153–8.

2. The *Remarks* bear no date on the titlepage of the first edition, but *London Chron.,* Jan. 19–22, 1760, advertised it as "This Day" published.

3. The most thorough and convincing study of the problem is Verner W. Crane, "Certain Writings of Benjamin Franklin on the British Empire and the American Colonies," Bibliographical Soc. of America *Papers,* XXVIII (1934), 1–27, esp. 5–12. Also important are I. Minis Hays, "On the Author-

Writing to Lord Kames, May 3, 1760, about two weeks after the pamphlet was published, Franklin said that he had been occupied during the intervals of a recent illness "in writing something of the present Situation of our Affairs in America, in order to give more correct Notions of the British Interest with regard to the Colonies, than those I found many sensible Men possess'd of. Inclos'd you have the Production, such as it is."[4] This reference could only be to the Canada Pamphlet; no other writing of Franklin's in this period fits the description. From this quiet assertion of authorship he never deviated, and at no time in his life is he known to have taken credit falsely for another person's writings.

When Benjamin Vaughan was preparing his 1779 edition of Franklin's works he wrote numerous letters to his friend, then in France, asking questions and sending unbound sheets as they came from the printer. On April 9, 1779, Vaughan sent a large packet of sheets and in the accompanying letter discussed specifically his treatment of the Canada Pamphlet: by dividing the whole into sections with appropriate headings and so "making the piece more luminous as to the parts," Vaughan believed he had "only done you infinitely more credit."[5] Franklin replied May 5, saying on this matter only "I leave the whole Management of that Edition in your Hands with great Confidence, as I am sure my Pieces will be improv'd by your Attention to the Matters you mention."[6] If he had not written the pamphlet himself, this would have been the time and place to say so. In the "Addenda et Corrigenda" at the end of the published volume, Vaughan inserted a note to be read at the end of the Canada Pamphlet: "Dr. Franklin has often been heard to say, that in writing this pamphlet, he received considerable assistance from a learned friend who was not willing to be named. Ed."[7]

---

ship of the Anonymous Pamphlet Published in London in 1760 Entitled 'The Interest of Great Britain Considered with Regard to Her Colonies and the Acquisition of Canada and Guadeloupe,'" APS *Proc.*, LXIII (1924), 1–9; and Van Doren, *Franklin-Jackson*, pp. 8–16. For a complete review of the case for BF's authorship these three treatments should be read in conjunction with the present discussion, which does not repeat all the details of evidence given by one or another of these writers. In his examination Van Doren prints the full text of Maseres' letter and Vaughan's reply, both described below.

4. See below, p. 103.

5. Vaughan to BF, April 9, 1779, APS.

6. BF to Vaughan, May 5, 1779 (draft), Lib. Cong.

7. *Political, Miscellaneous, and Philosophical Pieces;* . . . *Written by Benj. Franklin, LL.D. and F.R.S.* (London, 1779), p. [568].

The "learned friend" most certainly was Richard Jackson, but his "considerable assistance" might well have been no more than the supplying of some useful material, and need not have extended to include any of the actual composition. One Englishman, however, was sure that Vaughan had done Jackson an injustice. On Jan. 27, 1780, soon after the book appeared, Francis Maseres,[8] cursitor baron of the Exchequer, wrote the editor and compiler that Franklin had written only parts of the Canada Pamphlet. He sent along his own copy of Vaughan's book with vertical lines marked in the margins to show the parts "which were written by Dr. Franklin." On the inner pages of the folded sheet containing this letter is a copy of "A memorandum, found in Baron Maseres copy of the book," and Vaughan's draft reply. The memorandum begins with the unequivocal statement that "This pamphlet was the joint production of Mr. Jackson and Dr. Franklin." On the address page of the same sheet is a list of the passages Maseres had marked as the only ones (besides all the footnotes) that Franklin had written. Vaughan replied thanking Maseres and adding that, as to taking notice of this information in a possible second edition, the affair of the pamphlet "has now become too delicate for the Editor to again to [sic] intermeddle in it. He observes that Mr. Jackson's present claim goes to about ⅔ of the pamphlet."[9]

Maseres cited no authority for his assertion of Jackson's principal authorship of a pamphlet published nearly twenty years earlier, and no evidence has appeared since 1780 to support his identification of the parts he said were written by each of the two men. No statement by Jackson himself has been found which even suggests that he shared in the composition.[1] Nevertheless, numerous writers, bibliographers, and

8. Francis Maseres (1731–1824), F.R.S., F.S.A., lawyer, political and legal writer, mathematician; B.A. Cambridge, 1752; called to the bar from the Inner Temple, 1758. He was attorney general of Quebec, 1766–69; cursitor baron of the Exchequer from 1773 to his death; deputy recorder of London, 1779–83. *DNB; Gent. Mag.*, XCIV (1824), pt. I, 569–73.

9. Maseres to Vaughan, Jan. 27, 1780, APS; Vaughan's undated draft reply, and memoranda as indicated above, Lib. Cong.

1. Maseres' attribution of particular passages to Jackson is puzzling because he was so specific. He and Jackson had long been neighbors in London and since 1774 both had been benchers of the Inner Temple and so members of its governing body. Undoubtedly they were close friends, and Maseres must have thought he had excellent authority for his detailed attributions. Quite possibly Jackson himself had marked the passages in the copy of the pamphlet his friend sent to Vaughan, doing it either to show authorship as he remembered it or for some other reason not now known. In the light of the documentary evidence considered below, however, the present editors are com-

cataloguers, though not all, have accepted Maseres' statement at face value, some even going so far as to attribute authorship of the whole to Jackson, without crediting Franklin with any share. Within the twentieth century, however, two important pieces of evidence have been discovered to refute Maseres' identification and to reestablish the belief that Franklin was at least the principal author and probably the only one.

In 1924 I. Minis Hays, who had edited the *Calendar of the Papers of Benjamin Franklin in the Library of the American Philosophical Society*, published sixteen years earlier, pointed out that in this collection there were several scattered pages of draft of the Canada Pamphlet in Franklin's hand.[2] Examination of these pages not only confirms the identification but makes clear that they are part of a draft set down in the actual process of composition. Several of the many changes and corrections are of the sort that would never have appeared if Franklin had been engaged in the improbable task of copying and then revising a draft already written by Jackson.[3] Furthermore, of the five pages in Franklin's draft four are entirely of passages which Maseres assigned to Jackson and the first lines of the remaining one are also part of what he thought Jackson wrote. To show how unreliable Maseres' identification was, the parts he did not attribute to Franklin and hence ascribed to Jackson are listed here in the left-hand column and those we know from the draft Franklin certainly composed are in the right. Page and line references are to the text as printed below. The page numbers of the draft are indicated in brackets. Footnotes are not considered in this comparison, since Maseres conceded that Franklin wrote them all.[4]

---

pelled to believe either that Jackson's memory was at fault or that Maseres misunderstood the purport of the markings in this copy.

2. APS *Proc.*, LXIII (1924), 7–8. As indicated in the first footnote to this headnote, the first of the six draft pages calendared and filed together does not belong to the Canada Pamphlet as Hays thought it did.

3. For example: "Let him compare those Countries with others on this same Island, where [those Advan *struck out*] Manufactures have not yet extended themselves." "Whatever Charges arise on the [Value of *struck out*] Carriage of Goods, are added to the Value and all paid by the Consumer." "I shall select one as a Sample, being that from the Colony of Rhode Island; [which *struck out*] a Colony that of all the others receives the least Addition from Strangers."

4. On p. 58 of BF's draft, following "Rhode Island," is an asterisk, and in the margin another followed: "Here put that Acct. by Way of Note." Similarly a dagger follows "Pensilvania" and in the margin: "Here a Note with that Acct." Compare pp. 87, 88, below.

Ascribed to Jackson by Maseres	*Surviving draft in Franklin's hand*
From beginning to p. 61, l. 7: "or useless."	
p. 61, l. 11, to p. 65, ls. 23–4: "Supposing then . . . of government."	
p. 65, l. 27, to l. 30: "And two . . . of a neighbour."	
p. 65, l. 32, to p. 66, l. 12: "Happy it prov'd . . . and bloodshed."	
p. 71, l. 11, to p. 74, l. 26: "But to leave . . . *to be apprehended.*'"	
p. 77, l. 12, to p. 78, l. 34: "In short . . . trade increases."	
	[43] p. 79, l. 26, to p. 80, l. 3: "what a difference . . . to extend their"
p. 79, l. 7, to p. 86, l. 20: "Were the inhabitants . . . is not so great."	[45] p. 80, l. 16, to l. 31: "favourable to . . . I say, if"
	[53] p. 85, l. 18, to ls. 37–8: "it is not true . . . private property is"
p. 87, l. 3, to l. 12: "However this may be . . . from that kingdom."	
p. 87, l. 18, to l. 26: "Our trade . . . as in numbers."5	[58] p. 87, l. 24, to p. 88, l. 5 "increasing with . . . inhabitants, and"
p. 90, l. 3, to p. 93, ls. 8–9: "Thus much . . . overturned it."	[67] p. 92, l. 9, to l. 21: "Yet with all . . . that policy which"
p. 95, l. 31, "In Guadaloupe," to the end of the pamphlet.	

5. To do Maseres justice it should be said that in this instance he was admittedly uncertain whether a passage he attributed to BF began where he indicated or farther back at the start of the paragraph.

In 1934 Verner W. Crane produced further documentary evidence to support the belief that Franklin wrote the major part, if not the whole, of the pamphlet. In the Historical Society of Pennsylvania is Franklin's own copy of *Remarks on the Letter Address'd to Two Great Men,* the work to which *The Interest of Great Britain Considered* was a direct reply. Underscoring or marginal lines mark several passages which the Canada Pamphlet specifically rebuts, frequently with quotations or paraphrases from the *Remarks.* Elsewhere there are a number of marginal notations in Franklin's hand. While a later binder unfortunately trimmed the pages so closely that some of these notes cannot be reconstructed, Crane amply demonstrated the close connection of these marginalia with the ideas developed in the Canada Pamphlet. "Enough remain," as he put it, "to indicate clearly that here is the first sketch for Franklin's reply." He concluded, and the present editors agree, that the only part of the pamphlet that Jackson may have written—a "dubious possibility" at best—is the relatively short section on the trade with Russia and the medieval trade routes from Asia.[6] These are topics not dealt with in the *Remarks* or in the surviving pages of the draft. It appears to the editors more probable, however, that the "considerable assistance" of Jackson, which Vaughan said Franklin often acknowledged orally, did not refer to any actual composition, but rather to the supplying of information on topics not already familiar to Franklin. In that case, it would be a reasonable guess that Jackson's chief contribution was the data on which Franklin based this short passage on Russian and Asiatic trade.

At the end of the pamphlet Franklin reprinted almost the whole of his "Observations concerning the Increase of Mankind," written in 1751 (above, IV, 227–34, and not reproduced here)[7] to support his arguments on the steadily increasing value of the continental colonies as markets for British manufactures, and he concluded with two pages of comparative statistics on British exports to North America and the West Indies.

6. Bibliog. Soc. of America *Papers,* XXVIII, 10–12. It is entirely possible, of course, that BF acquired a knowledge of Russian and Asiatic trade routes from his own extensive reading of travel literature and that Jackson's help was confined to preliminary advice and suggestions, given orally, and to reading and criticism of the draft.

7. BF called it "an Extract" and for this British audience carefully omitted (though with rows of asterisks): paragraph no. 11 on the consequence that might follow if British manufactures rose too high in price because of American demands; the last half of paragraph 23 on the Pa. Germans as "Palatine Boors"; and all of paragraph 24 in favor of "White People" and the exclusion of all "Blacks and Tawneys" from America.

This pamphlet was Franklin's first large-scale attempt to influence the British on a matter of major public policy. It shows him, though a colonial, thinking in terms of broad imperial interests. While he discusses the argument that the retention of Canada might lead in time to the independence of the older colonies, he does so only to refute the charge, and he urges that fair and considerate treatment by Great Britain would effectively prevent any move toward separation. "The waves do not rise, but when the winds blow." There is no reason to believe that Franklin was insincere in his treatment of this topic; on the contrary, the heavy stress he places here on the promotion of trade between the mother country and the colonies as an enduring bond between them shows him as being at this time an ardent supporter of the connection and an advocate of increasing, not diminishing, its economic base.

THE INTEREST OF GREAT BRITAIN
With Regard to her COLONIES.

I have perused with no small pleasure the *Letter addressed to Two Great Men,* and the *Remarks* on that letter. It is not merely from the beauty, the force and perspicuity of expression, or the general elegance of manner conspicuous in both pamphlets, that my pleasure chiefly arises; it is rather from this, that I have lived to see subjects of the greatest importance to this nation publickly discussed without party views, or party heat, with decency and politeness, and with no other warmth than what a zeal for the honour and happiness of our king and country may inspire; and this by writers whose understanding (however they may differ from each other) appears not unequal to their candour and the uprightness of their intention.

But, as great abilities have not always the best information, there are, I apprehend, in the *Remarks* some opinions not well founded, and some mistakes of so important a nature, as to render a few observations on them necessary for the better information of the publick.

The author of the *Letter,* who must be every way best able to support his own sentiments, will, I hope, excuse me, if I seem officiously to interfere; when he considers, that the spirit of patriotism, like other qualities good and bad, is catching; and that his long silence since the *Remarks* appeared has made us despair of seeing the subject farther discussed by his masterly hand. The ingenious and candid remarker, too, who must have been misled himself before he employed his skill and address to mislead others, will certainly, since he declares he *aims at no seduction,** be disposed to excuse even the weakest effort to prevent it.

And surely if the general opinions that possess the minds of the people may possibly be of consequence in publick affairs, it must be fit to set those opinions right. If there is danger, as the remarker supposes, that "extravagant expectations" may embarass "a virtuous and able ministry," and "render the negotiation for peace a work of infinite difficulty;"† there is no less danger that expectations too low, thro' want of proper information, may have a contrary effect, may make even a virtuous and able ministry less anxious, and less attentive to the obtaining points, in which the honour and interest of the nation are essentially concerned; and the people less hearty in supporting such a ministry and its measures.

The people of this nation are indeed respectable, not for their numbers only, but for their understanding and their publick spirit: they manifest the first, by their universal approbation of the late prudent and vigorous measures, and the confidence they so justly repose in a wise and good prince, and an honest and able administration; the latter they have demonstrated by the immense supplies granted in parliament unanimously, and paid through the whole kingdom with chearfulness. And since to this spirit and these supplies our "victories and successes"‡ have in great measure been owing, is it quite right, is it generous to say, with the *remarker,* that the people "had no share in acquiring them?" The mere mob he cannot mean, even where he speaks of the *madness of the people;* for the madness of the mob must be too feeble and impotent, arm'd as the government of this country at present is, to "over-rule,"§ even in the slightest instances, the "virtue and moderation" of a firm and steady ministry.

While the war continues, its final event is quite uncertain. The Victorious of this year may be the Vanquish'd of the next. It may therefore be too early to say, what advantages we ought absolutely to insist on, and make the *sine quibus non* of a peace. If the necessity of our affairs should oblige us to accept of terms less advantageous than our present successes seem to promise us, an

*Remarks, p. 6.   †Remarks, p. 7.   ‡Remarks, p. 7.
§Remarks, p. 7.

intelligent people as ours is, must see that necessity, and will acquiesce. But as a peace, when it is made, may be made hastily; and as the unhappy continuance of the war affords us time to consider, among several advantages gain'd or to be gain'd, which of them may be most for our interest to retain, if some and not all may possibly be retained; I do not blame the public disquisition of these points, as premature or useless. Light often arises from a collision of opinions, as fire from flint and steel; and if we can obtain the benefit of the *light*, without danger from the *heat* sometimes produc'd by controversy, why should we discourage it?

Supposing then, that heaven may still continue to bless his Majesty's arms, and that the event of this just war may put it in our power to retain some of our conquests at the making of a peace; let us consider whether we are to confine ourselves to those possessions only that were "the *objects* for which we began the war."* This the *remarker* seems to think right, when the question relates to 'Canada, properly so called,' it having never been 'mentioned as one of those objects in any of our memorials or declarations, or in any national or public act whatsoever.' But the gentleman himself will probably agree, that if the cession of Canada would be a real advantage to us, we may demand it under his second head, as an "*indemnification* for the charges incurred" in recovering our just rights; otherwise according to his own principles the demand of Guadaloupe can have no foundation.

That "our claims before the war were large enough for possession and for security too,"† tho' it seems a clear point with the ingenious remarker, is, I own, not so with me. I am rather of the contrary opinion, and shall presently give my reasons. But first let me observe, that we did not make those claims because they were large enough for security, but because we could rightfully claim no more. Advantages gain'd in the course of this war, may increase the extent of our rights. Our claims before the war contain'd some security; but that is no reason why we should neglect acquiring more when the demand of more is become reasonable. It may be reasonable in the case of America to ask for the security recommended by the author of the letter, tho'‡ it would be preposterous

*Remarks, p. 19. †Ibid. ‡P. 30 of the *Letter*, and p. 21 of the *Remarks*.

to do it in many other cases: his propos'd demand is founded on the little value of Canada to the French; the right we have to ask, and the power we may have to insist on an indemnification for our expences; the difficulty the French themselves will be under of restraining their restless subjects in America from encroaching on our limits and disturbing our trade; and the difficulty on our parts of preventing encroachments that may possibly exist many years without coming to our knowledge. But the remarker "does not see why the arguments employ'd concerning a security for a peaceable behaviour in Canada, would not be equally cogent for calling for the same security in Europe." * On a little farther reflection, he must I think be sensible, that the circumstances of the two cases are widely different. Here we are separated by the best and clearest of boundaries, the ocean, and we have people in or near every part of our territory. Any attempt to encroach upon us, by building a fort, even in the obscurest corner of these islands, must therefore be known and prevented immediately. The aggressors also must be known, and the nation they belong to would be accountable for their aggression. In America it is quite otherwise. A vast wilderness thinly or scarce at all peopled, conceals with ease the march of troops and workmen. Important passes may be seiz'd within our limits and forts built in a month, at a small expence, that may cost us an age, and a million to remove. Dear experience has taught us this. But what is still worse, the wide extended forests between our settlements and theirs, are inhabited by barbarous tribes of savages that delight in war and take pride in murder, subjects properly neither of the French nor English, but strongly attach'd to the former by the art and indefatigable industry of priests, similarity of superstitions, and frequent family alliances. These are easily, and have been continually, instigated to fall upon and massacre our planters, even in times of full peace between the two crowns, to the certain diminution of our people and the contraction of our settlements.† And tho' it is known they

*Remarks, p. 24.

†A very intelligent writer of that country, Dr. Clark,[8] in his *Observations on the late and present Conduct of the French*, &c. printed at Boston 1755, says, [*Textual note continued on next page.*]

8. On Dr. William Clarke, Boston physician and political writer, see above, V, 250 n. BF's "Observations Concerning the Increase of Mankind" was first

are supply'd by the French and carry their prisoners to them, we can by complaining obtain no redress, as the governors of Canada have a ready excuse, that the Indians are an independent people, over whom they have no power, and for whose actions they are therefore not accountable. Surely circumstances so widely different, may reasonably authorise different demands of security in America, from such as are usual or necessary in Europe.

The *remarker,* however, thinks, that our real dependance for keeping "France or any other nation true to her engagements, must not be in demanding securities which no nation whilst *inde-*

'The Indians in the French interest are, upon all proper opportunities, instigated by their priests, who have generally the chief management of their public councils, to acts of hostility against the English, even in time of profound peace between the two crowns. Of this there are many undeniable instances: The war between the Indians and the colonies of the Massachusetts Bay and New Hampshire, in 1723, by which those colonies suffered so much damage, was begun by the instigation of the French; their supplies were from them, and there are now original letters of several Jesuits to be produced, whereby it evidently appears, that they were continually animating the Indians, when almost tired with the war, to a farther prosecution of it. The French not only excited the Indians, and supported them, but joined their own forces with them in all the late hostilities that have been committed within his Majesty's province of Nova Scotia. And from an intercepted letter this year from the Jesuit at Penobscot, and from other information, it is certain that they have been using their utmost endeavours to excite the Indians to new acts of hostility against his Majesty's colony of the Massachusetts Bay, and some have been committed. The French not only excite the Indians to acts of hostility, but reward them for it, by buying the English prisoners of them; for the ransom of each of which they afterwards demand of us the price that is usually given for a slave in these colonies. They do this under the specious pretence of rescuing the poor prisoners from the cruelties and barbarities of the savages; but in reality to encourage them to continue their depredations, as they can by this means get more by hunting the English than by hunting wild-beasts; and the French at the same time are thereby enabled to keep up a large body of Indians entirely at the expence of the English.'

printed as an appendix to the pamphlet here quoted. For this and later quotations from Clarke BF was using the London reprint of 1755. This passage is taken, with minor changes, from pp. 11–12; in the original Boston edition, pp. 12–14.

63

pendent can give, but on our own strength and our own vigilance."*
No nation that has carried on a war with disadvantage, and is
unable to continue it, can be said, under such circumstances, to be
independent; and while either side thinks itself in a condition to
demand an indemnification, there is no man in his senses, but will,
caeteris paribus prefer an indemnification that is a cheaper and
more effectual security than any other he can think of. Nations in
this situation demand and cede countries by almost every treaty
of peace that is made. The French part of the island of St. Christophers was added to Great Britain in circumstances altogether
similar to those in which a few months may probably place the
country of Canada.⁹ Farther security has always been deemed a
motive with a conqueror to be less moderate; and even the vanquish'd insist upon security as a reason for demanding what they
acknowledge they could not otherwise properly ask. The security
of the frontier of France on the side of the Netherlands, was always considered, in the negotiation that began at Gertruyden-
burgh,¹ and ended with that war. For the same reason they demanded and had Cape Breton.² But a war concluded to the advantage of France has always added something to the power,
either of France or the house of Bourbon. Even that of 1733, which
she commenced with declarations of her having no ambitious
views, and which finished by a treaty at which the ministers of
France repeatedly declared that she desired nothing for herself, in
effect gained for her Lorrain, an indemnification ten times the value
of all her North American possessions.³

*Remarks, p. 25.

9. Both England and France had colonized parts of St. Christopher (St.
Kitts) in the Leeward Islands during the seventeenth century. When war
began in 1702 the English drove out the French but were later attacked in
turn and many of their plantations were destroyed. In the Treaty of Utrecht,
1713, France ceded her parts of the island. Ruth Bourne, *Queen Anne's Navy
in the West Indies* (New Haven, 1939), pp. 29, 189–93, 265.
1. Abortive negotiations took place at this Dutch town, June–July 1710,
designed to end the War of the Spanish Succession.
2. The French were allowed to retain Cape Breton while ceding to Great
Britain the rest of Acadia (Nova Scotia) in the Treaty of Utrecht, 1713.
3. In the War of the Polish Succession, 1733–35, Louis XV sided with the
Poles against Russia and Austria. The Poles were defeated but France successfully occupied the Duchy of Lorraine. After the war it became closely

In short, security and quiet of princes and states have ever been deemed sufficient reasons, when supported by power, for disposing of rights; and such disposition has never been looked on as want of moderation. It has always been the foundation of the most general treaties. The security of Germany was the argument for yielding considerable possessions there to the Swedes: and the security of Europe divided the Spanish monarchy, by the partition treaty, made between powers who had no *other* right to dispose of any part of it.[4] There can be no cession that is not supposed at least, to increase the power of the party to whom it is made. It is enough that he has a right to ask it, and that he does it not merely to serve the purposes of a dangerous ambition. Canada in the hands of Britain, will endanger the kingdom of France as little as any other cession; and from its situation and circumstances cannot be hurtful to any other state. Rather, if peace be an advantage, this cession may be such to all Europe. The present war teaches us, that disputes arising in America, may be an occasion of embroiling nations who have no concerns there. If the French remain in Canada and Louisiana, fix the boundaries as you will between us and them, we must border on each other for more than 1500 miles. The people that inhabit the frontiers, are generally the refuse of both nations, often of the worst morals and the least discretion, remote from the eye, the prudence, and the restraint of government. Injuries are therefore frequently, in some part or other of so long a frontier, committed on both sides, resentment provoked, the colonies first engaged, and then the mother countries. And two great nations can scarce be at war in Europe, but some other prince or state thinks it a convenient opportunity, to revive some ancient claim, seize some advantage, obtain some territory, or enlarge some power at the expence of a neighbour. The flames of war once kindled, often spread far and wide, and the mischief is infinite. Happy it prov'd to both nations, that the

---

linked to France and, six years after BF wrote, was formally incorporated into the kingdom.

4. Probably a reference to the Partition Treaty of 1700 between England, France, and the Dutch, by which the possessions of the childless King Charles II of Spain were to be divided between the Hapsburg Archduke Charles and the French dauphin; the Duke of Lorraine was to receive Milan in exchange for Lorraine to be given to France. The court of Charles II had other plans and the War of the Spanish Succession soon followed.

Dutch were prevailed on finally to cede the New Netherlands (now the province of New York) to us at the peace of 1674;[5] a peace that has ever since continued between us, but must have been frequently disturbed, if they had retained the possession of that country, bordering several hundred miles on our colonies of Pensilvania westward, Connecticut and the Massachusetts eastward. Nor is it to be wondred at that people of different language, religion, and manners, should in those remote parts engage in frequent quarrels, when we find, that even the people of our own colonies have frequently been so exasperated against each other in their disputes about boundaries, as to proceed to open violence and bloodshed.

But the *remarker* thinks we shall be sufficiently secure in America, if we "raise English forts at such passes as may at once make us respectable to the French and to the Indian nations."* The security desirable in America, may be considered as of three kinds; 1. A security of possession, that the French shall not drive us out of the country. 2. A security of our planters from the inroads of savages, and the murders committed by them. 3. A security that the British nation shall not be oblig'd on every new war to repeat the immense expence occasion'd by this, to defend its possessions in America. Forts in the most important passes, may, I acknowledge be of use to obtain the first kind of security: but as those situations are far advanc'd beyond the inhabitants, the expence of maintaining and supplying the garrisons, will be very great even in time of full peace, and immense on every interruption of it; as it is easy for skulking parties of the enemy in such long roads thro' the woods, to intercept and cut off our convoys, unless guarded continually by great bodies of men. The second kind of security, will not be obtained by such forts, unless they were connected by a wall like that of China, from one end of our settlements to the other. If the Indians when at war, march'd like the Europeans, with great armies, heavy cannon, baggage and carriages, the passes thro' which alone such armies could penetrate our country or receive their supplies, being secur'd, all might be sufficiently

*Remarks, p. 25.

5. The English captured New Netherland in 1664; the Dutch recaptured it in 1673 during the Third Anglo-Dutch War, but ceded it at the Treaty of Westminster which concluded that war in 1674.

secure; but the case is widely different. They go to war, as they call it, in small parties, from fifty men down to five. Their hunting life has made them acquainted with the whole country, and scarce any part of it is impracticable to such a party. They can travel thro' the woods even by night, and know how to conceal their tracks. They pass easily between your forts undiscover'd; and privately approach the settlements of your frontier inhabitants. They need no convoys of provisions to follow them; for whether they are shifting from place to place in the woods, or lying in wait for an opportunity to strike a blow, every thicket and every stream furnishes so small a number with sufficient subsistence. When they have surpriz'd separately, and murder'd and scalp'd a dozen families, they are gone with inconceivable expedition thro' unknown ways, and 'tis very rare that pursuers have any chance of coming up with them.* In short, long experience has taught

*'Although the Indians live scattered, as a hunter's life requires, they may be collected together from almost any distance, as they can find their subsistence from their gun in their travelling. But let the number of the Indians be what it will, they are not formidable merely on account of their numbers; there are many other circumstances that give them a great advantage over the English. The English inhabitants, though numerous, are extended over a large tract of land, 500 leagues in length on the sea-shore; and although some of their trading towns are thick settled, their settlements in the country towns must be at a distance from each other: besides, that in a new country where lands are cheap, people are fond of acquiring large tracts to themselves; and therefore in the out settlements, they must be more remote: and as the people that move out are generally poor, they sit down either where they can easiest procure land, or soonest raise a subsistence. Add to this, that the English have fixed settled habitations, the easiest and shortest passages to which the Indians, by constantly hunting in the woods, are perfectly well acquainted with; whereas the English know little or nothing of the Indian country nor of the passages thro' the woods that lead to it. The Indian way of making war is by sudden attacks upon exposed places; and as soon as they have done mischief, they retire and either go home by the same or some different rout, as they think safest; or go to some other place at a distance to renew their stroke. If a sufficient party should happily be ready to pursue them, it is a great chance, whether in a country consisting of woods and swamps which the English are not acquainted with, the enemy do not lie in ambush for them in some convenient place, and from thence destroy them. If this should not be

67

our planters, that they cannot rely upon forts as a security against Indians: The inhabitants of Hackney might as well rely upon the tower of London to secure them against highwaymen and house-breakers. As to the third kind of security, that we shall not in a few years, have all we have now done to do over again in America; and be oblig'd to employ the same number of troops, and ships, at the same immense expence to defend our possessions

---

the case, but the English should pursue them, as soon as they have gained the rivers, by means of their canoes, to the use of which they are brought up from their infancy, they presently get out of their reach: further, if a body of men were to march into their country to the places where they are settled, they can, upon the least notice, without great disadvantage, quit their present habitations, and betake themselves to new ones.' Clark's *Observations, p.* 13.[6]

'It has been already remarked, that the tribes of the Indians living upon the lakes and rivers that run upon the back of the English settlements in North America, are very numerous, and can furnish a great number of fighting men, all perfectly well acquainted with the use of arms as soon as capable of carrying them, as they get the whole of their subsistence from hunting; and that this army, large as it may be, can be maintained by the French without any expence. From their numbers, their situation, and the rivers that run into the English settlements, it is easy to conceive that they can at any time make an attack upon, and constantly annoy as many of the exposed English settlements as they please, and those at any distance from each other. The effects of such incursions have been too severely felt by many of the British colonies, not to be very well known. The entire breaking up places that had been for a considerable time settled at a great expence, both of labour and money; burning the houses, destroying the stock, killing and making prisoners great numbers of the inhabitants, with all the cruel usage they meet with in their captivity, is only a part of the scene. All other places that are exposed are kept in continual terror; the lands lie waste and uncultivated from the danger that attends those that shall presume to work upon them: besides the immense charge the governments must be at in a very ineffectual manner to defend their extended frontiers; and all this from the influence the French have had over, but comparatively, a few of the Indians. To the same or greater evils still will every one of the colonies be exposed, whenever the same influence shall be extended to the whole body of them.' *Ibid. p.* 20.[7]

6. Boston edition, pp. 14–16; London reprint, pp. 13–14.
7. Boston edition, pp. 22–4; London reprint, pp. 20–1.

there, while we are in proportion weaken'd here: such forts I think cannot prevent this. During a peace, it is not to be doubted the French, who are adroit at fortifying, will likewise erect forts in the most advantageous places of the country we leave them, which will make it more difficult than ever to be reduc'd in case of another war. We know by the experience of this war, how extremely difficult it is to march an army thro' the American woods, with its necessary cannon and stores, sufficient to reduce a very slight fort. The accounts at the treasury will tell you what amazing sums we have necessarily spent in the expeditions against two very trifling forts, Duquesne and Crown Point. While the French retain their influence over the Indians, they can easily keep our long extended frontier in continual alarm, by a very few of those people; and with a small number of regulars and militia, in such a country, we find they can keep an army of ours in full employ for several years. We therefore shall not need to be told by our colonies, that if we leave Canada, however circumscrib'd, to the French, *"we have done nothing;"** we shall soon be made sensible ourselves of this truth, and to our cost.[8]

I would not be understood to deny that even if we subdue and retain Canada, some few forts may be of use to secure the goods of the traders, and protect the commerce, in case of any sudden misunderstanding with any tribe of Indians: but these forts will be best under the care of the colonies interested in the Indian trade, and garrison'd by their provincial forces, and at their own expence. Their own interest will then induce the American governments to take care of such forts in proportion to their importance; and see that the officers keep their corps full and mind their duty. But any troops of ours plac'd there and accountable here, would, in such remote and obscure places and at so great a

---

*Remarks, p. 26.

8. The author of *A Letter Addressed to Two Great Men* had written, pp. 29–30: "But though Care should be taken to keep all those Places just mentioned [Louisbourg, Quebec, Nova Scotia to the Bay of Fundy and the River St. John, Crown Point, Niagara, Fort Duquesne, and the country near the Ohio]; something more must be done, or our American Colonies will tell you, you have done Nothing." The Remarker, p. 26, quoted this sentence and replied: "On what Authority this is so positively asserted to be the Language of our American Colonies, you have not told us. I hope and believe that you have been misinformed."

distance from the eye and inspection of superiors, soon become of little consequence, even tho' the French were left in possession of Canada. If the four independent companies maintained by the Crown in New York more than forty years, at a great expence, consisted, for most part of the time, of faggots[9] chiefly; if their officers enjoy'd their places as *sine cures,* and were only, as a writer* of that country stiles them, a kind of *military monks;* if this was the state of troops posted in a populous country, where the imposition could not be so well conceal'd; what may we expect will be the case of those that shall be posted two, three or four hundred miles from the inhabitants, in such obscure and remote places as Crown Point, Oswego, Duquesne, or Niagara? they would scarce be even faggots; they would dwindle to meer names upon paper, and appear no where but upon the muster rolls.

Now all the kinds of security we have mention'd are obtain'd by subduing and retaining Canada. Our present possessions in America, are secur'd; our planters will no longer be massacred by the Indians, who depending absolutely on us for what are now become the necessaries of life to them, guns, powder, hatchets, knives, and cloathing; and having no other Europeans near, that can either supply them, or instigate them against us; there is no doubt of their being always dispos'd, if we treat them with common justice, to live in perpetual peace with us. And with regard

*Douglass.[1]

9. A person hired to take the place of another at the muster of a company.

1. William Douglass, *A Summary, Historical and Political, of the First Planting, Progressive Improvements, and Present State of the British Settlements in North-America.* This work first appeared serially in Boston, 1747–52, was reprinted in two bound volumes, 1749 and 1753, and twice reprinted in London, 1755 and 1760. BF was doubtless using the London edition of 1755. As a boy he had known Dr. Douglass, who was one of his brother James's friends and associates in the *New-England Courant* and had had later dealings with him (see above, I, 8; IV, 236, 338, 414, 416; V, 191, 454). The passage referred to here reads (II, 243): "Why do we not send military officers amongst the Indians to instruct them in the European arts of war. The French with good success follow this practice. Some say that the officers of the four independent companies of fusileers in New-York live like military monks in idleness and luxury." For an account of these units of the British Army, see Stanley M. Pargellis, "The Four Independent Companies of New York," *Essays in Colonial History Presented to Charles McLean Andrews by his Students* (New Haven, 1931), pp. 96–123.

to France, she cannot in case of another war, put us to the immense expence of defending that long extended frontier; we shall then, as it were, have our backs against a wall in America, the sea-coast will be easily protected by our superior naval power; and here "our own watchfulness and our own strength" will be properly, and cannot but be successfully employed.[2] In this situation the force now employ'd in that part of the world, may be spar'd for any other service here or elsewhere; so that both the offensive and defensive strength of the British empire on the whole will be greatly increased.

But to leave the French in possession of Canada when it is in our power to remove them, and depend, as the remarker proposes, on our own *"strength and watchfulness"** to prevent the mischiefs that may attend it, seems neither safe nor prudent. Happy as we now are, under the best of kings, and in the prospect of a succession promising every felicity a nation was ever bless'd with: happy too in the wisdom and vigour of every part of the administration, particularly that part whose peculiar province is the British plantations, a province every true Englishman sees with pleasure under the principal direction of a nobleman, as much distinguish'd by his great capacity, as by his unwearied and disinterested application to this important department;[3] we cannot, we ought not to promise ourselves the uninterrupted continuance of those blessings. The safety of a considerable part of the state, and the interest of the whole are not to be trusted to the wisdom and vigor of future administrations, when a security is to be had more effectual, more constant, and much less expensive. They who can be moved by the apprehension of dangers so remote as that of the future independence of our colonies (a point I shall hereafter consider)

*P. 25.

2. "Every wise Nation will rely on its own Watchfulness, and its own Strength, to maintain the Terms they oblige their Enemy to give them, and whoever expects any other Dependence, will find himself the Dupe." *Remarks*, pp. 25–6.

3. George Montagu Dunk, 2d Earl of Halifax (1716–1771), was president of the Board of Trade, 1748–61 (see above, VIII, 67 n). Through his insistence the office was raised in importance during his tenure and in 1757 he was admitted to the cabinet. Because of his assiduity and energy he was sometimes called "Father of the Colonies." *DNB*. The reasons for the Pa. agent's desire to compliment Halifax publicly in this manner are obvious.

seem scarcely consistent with themselves when they suppose we may rely on the wisdom and vigour of an administration for their safety.

I should indeed think it less material whether Canada were ceded to us or not, if I had in view only the *security of possession* in our colonies. I entirely agree with the Remarker, that we are in North America "a far greater continental as well as naval power;"[4] and that only cowardice or ignorance can subject our colonies there to a French conquest. But for the same reason I disagree with him widely upon another point. I do not think that our "blood and treasure has been expended," as he intimates, "*in the cause of the colonies,*" and that we are "making conquests *for them:*"* yet I believe this is too common an error. I do not say they are altogether unconcerned in the event. The inhabitants of them are, in common with the other subjects of Great Britain, anxious for the glory of her crown, the extent of her power and commerce, the welfare and future repose of the whole British people. They could not therefore but take a large share in the affronts offered to Britain, and have been animated with a truely British *spirit* to exert themselves beyond their strength, and against their evident interest. Yet so unfortunate have they been, that their virtue has made against them; for upon no better foundation than this, have they been supposed the authors of a war carried on *for their advantage only*. It is a great mistake to imagine that the American country in question between Great Britain and France, is claimed as the property of any individuals or publick body in America, or that the possession of it by Great Britain, is likely, in any lucrative view, to redound at all to the advantage of any person there. On the other hand, the bulk of the inhabitants of North America are land-owners, whose lands are inferior in value to those of Britain, only by the want of an equal number of people. It is true the accession of the large territory claimed before the war began, especially if that be secured by the possession of Canada, will tend to the increase of the British subjects faster than if they had been confin'd within the mountains: yet the increase within the mountains only, would evidently make the comparative

*Remarks, p. 26.

4. *Remarks,* pp. 27–8.

population equal to that of Great Britain much sooner than it can be expected when our people are spread over a country six times as large. I think this is the only point of light in which this question is to be viewed, and is the only one in which any of the colonies are concerned. No colony, no possessor of lands in any colony, therefore wishes for conquests, or can be benefited by them, otherwise than as they may be a means of securing peace on their borders. No considerable advantage has resulted to the colonies by the conquests of this war, or can result from confirming them by the peace, but what they must enjoy in common with the rest of the British people; with this evident drawback from their share of these advantages, that they will necessarily lessen, or at least prevent the increase of the value of what makes the principal part of their private property. A people spread thro' the whole tract of country on this side the Mississipi, and secured by Canada in our hands, would probably for some centuries find employment in agriculture, and thereby free us at home effectually from our fears of American manufactures. Unprejudic'd men well know that all the penal and prohibitory laws that ever were thought on, will not be sufficient to prevent manufactures in a country whose inhabitants surpass the number that can subsist by the husbandry of it. That this will be the case in America soon, if our people remain confined within the mountains, and almost as soon should it be unsafe for them to live beyond, tho' the country be ceded to us, no man acquainted with political and commercial history can doubt. Manufactures are founded in poverty. It is the multitude of poor without land in a country, and who must work for others at low wages or starve, that enables undertakers to carry on a manufacture, and afford it cheap enough to prevent the importation of the same kind from abroad, and to bear the expence of its own exportation. But no man who can have a piece of land of his own, sufficient by his labour to subsist his family in plenty, is poor enough to be a manufacturer and work for a master. Hence while there is land enough in America for our people, there can never be manufactures to any amount or value. It is a striking observation of a very *able pen*,[5] that the natural livelihood of the thin in-

5. The editors have not identified precisely the "*able pen*" BF had in mind, but the ideas here expressed were current by the middle of the eighteenth century. See for example, David Hume, "Of Commerce," *Essays Moral,*

habitants of a forest country, is hunting; that of a greater number, pasturage; that of a middling population, agriculture; and that of the greatest, manufactures; which last must subsist the bulk of the people in a full country, or they must be subsisted by charity, or perish. The extended population, therefore, that is most advantageous to Great Britain, will be best effected, because only effectually secur'd by our possession of Canada. So far as the being of our present colonies in North America is concerned, I think indeed with the *remarker*, that the French there are not *"an enemy to be apprehended,"** but the expression is too vague to be applicable to the present, or indeed to any other case. Algiers, Tunis and Tripoli, unequal as they are to this nation in power and numbers of people, are enemies to be still apprehended; and the Highlanders of Scotland have been so for many ages by the greatest princes of Scotland and Britain. The wild Irish were able to give a great deal of disturbance even to Queen Elizabeth, and cost her more blood and treasure than her war with Spain. Canada in the hands of France has always stinted the growth of our colonies: In the course of this war, and indeed before it, has disturb'd and vex'd even the best and strongest of them, has found means to murder thousands of their people and unsettle a great part of their country. Much more able will it be to starve the growth of an infant settlement. Canada has also found means to make this nation spend two or three millions a year in America; and a people, how small soever, that in their present situation, can do this as often as we have a war with them, is methinks, *"an enemy to be apprehended."*

Our North American colonies are to be considered as the frontier of the British empire on that side. The frontier of any dominion being attack'd, it becomes not merely *"the cause"* of the people immediately affected, (the inhabitants of that frontier) but properly *"the cause"* of the whole body. Where the frontier people owe and pay obedience, there they have a right to look for protection. No political proposition is better established than this. It is therefore

*Remarks, p. 27.

Political, and Literary, T. H. Green and T. H. Grose, eds. (London, 1898), I, 289–99; and Gustave Schelle, ed., *Oeuvres de Turgot et documents le concernant* (Paris, 1913), I, 279–83. BF had already suggested some of this line of thought in "Observations concerning the Increase of Mankind," above, IV, 228.

invidious to represent the "blood and treasure" spent in this war, as spent in "the cause of the colonies" only, and that they are "absurd and ungrateful" if they think we have done nothing unless we "make conquests for them," and reduce Canada to gratify their "vain ambition," &c.[6] It will not be a conquest for them, nor gratify any vain ambition of theirs. It will be a conquest for the whole, and all our people will, in the increase of trade and the ease of taxes, find the advantage of it. Should we be obliged at any time to make a war for the protection of our commerce, and to secure the exportation of our manufactures, would it be fair to represent such a war merely as blood and treasure spent in the cause of the weavers of Yorkshire, Norwich, or the West, the cutlers of Sheffield, or the button-makers of Birmingham?[7] I hope it will appear before I end these sheets, that if ever there was a *national war,* this is truly such a one: a war in which the interest of the *whole* nation is directly and fundamentally concerned.

Those who would be thought deeply skilled in human nature, affect to discover self-interested views every where at the bottom of the fairest, the most generous conduct. Suspicions and charges of this kind, meet with ready reception and belief in the minds even of the multitude; and therefore less acuteness and address than the *remarker* is possessed of, would be sufficient to persuade the nation generally, that all the zeal and spirit manifested and exerted by the colonies in this war, was only in "their own cause" to "make conquests for themselves," to engage us to make more for them, to gratify their own "vain ambition." But should they now humbly address the mother country in the terms and the sentiments of the *remarker,* return her their grateful acknowledgments for the blood and treasure she had spent in *"their cause,"* confess that enough had been done *"for them;"* allow that "English forts raised in proper passes, will, with the wisdom and vigour of her administration" be a sufficient future protection; express their desires that their people may be confined within the mountains, lest if they are suffered to spread and extend themselves in the fertile and pleasant country on the other side, they should *"in-*

6. *Remarks,* pp. 26–7.

7. BF had met some of these Birmingham button makers among his wife's relatives in 1758 (see above, VIII, 133–46) and on his journey to Scotland in 1759 had seen something of other English manufacturing towns.

crease infinitely from all causes, " "live wholly on their own labour" and become independent; beg therefore that the French may be suffered to remain in possession of Canada, as their neighbourhood may be useful to prevent our increase; and the removing them may "in its consequences be even dangerous."* I say, should such an address from the colonies make its appearance here, though, according to the *remarker,* it would be a most just and reasonable one; would it not, might it not with more justice be answered; We understand you, gentlemen, perfectly well: you have only your own interest in view: you want to have the people confined within your present limits, that in a few years the lands you are possessed of may increase tenfold in value! you want to reduce the price of labour by increasing numbers on the same territory, that you may be able to set up manufactures and vie with your mother country! you would have your people kept in a body, that you may be more able to dispute the commands of the crown, and obtain an independency. You would have the French left in Canada, to exercise your military virtue, and make you a warlike people, that you may have more confidence to embark in schemes of disobedience, and greater ability to support them! You have tasted too, the sweets of TWO or THREE MILLIONS Sterling *per annum* spent among you by our fleets and forces, and you are unwilling to be without a pretence for kindling up another war, and thereby occasioning a repetition of the same delightful doses! But gentlemen, allow us to understand our interest a little likewise: we shall remove the French from Canada that you may live in peace, and we be no more drained by your quarrels. You shall have land enough to cultivate, that you may have neither necessity nor inclination to go into manufactures, and we will manufacture for you and govern you.

A reader of the remarks may be apt to say; if this writer would have us restore Canada on principles of moderation, how can we consistent with those principles, retain Guadaloup, which he represents of so much greater value! I will endeavour to explain this, because by doing it I shall have an opportunity of showing the truth and good sense of the answer to the interested application I have just supposed. The author then is only *apparently* and not

*Remarks, p. 50, 51.

really inconsistent with himself. If we can obtain the credit of moderation by restoring Canada, it is well: but we should, however, restore it at all events; because it would not only be of no use to us, but "the possession of it (in his opinion) may in its consequence be dangerous."* As how? Why, plainly, (at length it comes out) if the French are not left there to check the growth of our colonies, "they will extend themselves almost without bounds into the in-land parts, and increase infinitely from all causes; becoming a numerous, hardy, *independent* people, possessed of a strong country, communicating little or not at all with England, living wholly on their own labour, and in process of time knowing little and enquiring little about the mother country." In short, according to this writer, our present colonies are large enough and numerous enough, and the French ought to be left in North America to prevent their increase, lest they become not only *useless* but *dangerous* to Britain.

I agree with the gentleman, that with Canada in our possession, our people in America will increase amazingly. I know, that their common rate of increase, where they are not molested by the enemy, is doubling their numbers every twenty five years by natural generation only, exclusive of the accession of foreigners.† I think this increase continuing, would probably in a century more, make the number of British subjects on that side the water more numerous than they now are on this; but I am far from entertaining on that account, any fears of their becoming either *useless* or *dangerous* to us; and I look on those fears, to be merely imaginary and without any probable foundation. The *remarker* is reserv'd in

---

*Remarks, p. 50, 51.

†The reason of this greater increase in America than in Europe, is, that in old settled countries, all trades, farms, offices, and employments are full, and many people refrain marrying till they see an opening, in which they can settle themselves, with a reasonable prospect of maintaining a family: but in America, it being easy to obtain land which with moderate labour will afford subsistence and something to spare, people marry more readily and earlier in life, whence arises a numerous offspring and the swift population of those countries. 'Tis a common error that we cannot fill our provinces or increase the number of them, without draining this nation of its people. The increment alone of our present colonies is sufficient for both those purposes.

77

giving his reasons, as in his opinion this "is not a fit subject for discussion." I shall give mine, because I conceive it a subject necessary to be discuss'd; and the rather, as those fears how groundless and chimerical soever, may by possessing the multitude, possibly induce the ablest ministry to conform to them against their own judgment, and thereby prevent the assuring to the British name and nation a stability and permanency that no man acquainted with history durst have hoped for, 'till our American possessions opened the pleasing prospect.

The remarker thinks that our people in America, "finding no check from Canada would extend themselves almost without bounds into the inland parts, and increase infinitely from all causes." The very reason he assigns for their so extending, and which is indeed the true one, their being "invited to it by the pleasantness, fertility and plenty of the country," may satisfy us, that this extension will continue to proceed as long as there remains any pleasant fertile country within their reach. And if we even suppose them confin'd by the waters of the Mississipi westward, and by those of St. Laurence and the lakes to the northward, yet still we shall leave them room enough to increase even in the *sparse* manner of settling now practis'd there, till they amount to perhaps a hundred millions of souls. This must take some centuries to fulfil, and in the mean time, this nation must necessarily supply them with the manufactures they consume, because the new settlers will be employ'd in agriculture, and the new settlements will so continually draw off the spare hands from the old, that our present colonies will not, during the period we have mention'd find themselves in a condition to manufacture even for their own inhabitants, to any considerable degree, much less for those who are settling behind them. Thus our *trade* must, till that country becomes as fully peopled as England, that is for centuries to come, be continually increasing, and with it our naval power; because the ocean is between us and them, and our ships and seamen must increase as that trade increases.

The human body and the political differ in this, that the first is limited by nature to a certain stature, which, when attain'd, it cannot, ordinarily, exceed; the other by better government and more prudent police, as well as by change of manners and other circumstances, often takes fresh starts of growth, after being long at a

78

stand; and may add tenfold to the dimensions it had for ages been confined to. The mother being of full stature, is in a few years equal'd by a growing daughter: but in the case of a mother country and her colonies, it is quite different. The growth of the children tends to encrease the growth of the mother, and so the difference and superiority is longer preserv'd.

Were the inhabitants of this island limited to their present number by any thing in nature, or by unchangeable circumstances, the equality of population between the two countries might indeed sooner come to pass: but sure experience in those parts of the island where manufactures have been introduc'd, teaches us, that people increase and multiply in proportion as the means and facility of gaining a livelihood increase; and that this island, if they could be employed, is capable of supporting ten times its present number of people. In proportion therefore, as the demand increases for the manufactures of Britain, by the increase of people in her colonies, the numbers of her people at home will increase, and with them the strength as well as the wealth of the nation. For satisfaction in this point let the reader compare in his mind the number and force of our present fleets, with our fleet in Queen Elizabeth's time* before we had colonies. Let him compare the antient with the present state of our towns and ports on our western coast, Manchester, Liverpool, Kendal, Lancaster, Glasgow, and the countries round them, that trade with and manufacture for our colonies, not to mention Leeds, Halifax, Sheffield and Birmingham, and consider what a difference there is in the numbers of people, buildings, rents, and the value of land and of the produce of land, even if he goes back no farther than is within man's memory. Let him compare those countries with others on this same island, where manufactures have not yet extended themselves, observe the present difference, and reflect how much greater our strength may be, if numbers give strength, when our manufacturers shall occupy every part of the island where they can possibly be subsisted.

But, say the objectors, "there is a certain distance from the sea, in America, beyond which the expence of carriage will put a stop to the sale and consumption of your manufactures; and this, with

---

*Viz. 40 sail, none of more than 40 guns.

79

the difficulty of making returns for them, will oblige the inhabitants to manufacture for themselves; of course, if you suffer your people to extend their settlements beyond that distance, your people become useless to you:" and this distance is limited by some to 200 miles, by others to the Apalachian mountains. Not to insist on a very plain truth, that no part of a dominion, from whence a government may on occasion draw supplies and aids both of men of money, tho' at too great a distance to be supply'd with manufactures from some other part, is therefore to be deem'd useless to the whole; I shall endeavour to show that these imaginary limits of utility, even in point of commerce are much too narrow.

The inland parts of the continent of Europe are much farther from the sea than the limits of settlement proposed for America. Germany is full of tradesmen and artificers of all kinds, and the governments there, are not all of them always favourable to the commerce of Britain, yet it is a well-known fact, that our manufactures find their way even into the heart of Germany. Ask the great manufacturers and merchants of the Leeds, Sheffield, Birmingham, Manchester and Norwich goods, and they will tell you, that some of them send their riders frequently thro' France or Spain and Italy, up to Vienna and back thro' the middle and northern parts of Germany, to show samples of their wares and collect orders, which they receive by almost every mail, to a vast amount. Whatever charges arise on the carriage of goods, are added to the value, and all paid by the consumer. If these nations over whom we have no government, over whose consumption we can have no influence, but what arises from the cheapness and goodness of our wares; whose trade, manufactures, or commercial connections are not subject to the controul of our laws, as those of our colonies certainly are in some degree: I say, if these nations purchase and consume such quantities of our goods, notwithstanding the remoteness of their situation from the sea; how much less likely is it that the settlers in America, who must for ages be employ'd in agriculture chiefly, should make cheaper for themselves the goods our manufacturers at present supply them with; even if we suppose the carriage five, six or seven hundred miles from the sea as difficult and expensive as the like distance into Germany: whereas in the latter, the natural distances are frequently doubled by political obstructions, I mean the intermix'd territories and clashing interests of princes. But when we consider that the inland parts of America are penetrated by great navigable rivers; that there are a number of great lakes, communicating with each other, with those rivers and with the sea, very small portages here and there excepted;* that the sea coasts (if one may be allow'd the expression) of those lakes only, amount at least to 2700 miles, ex-clusive of the rivers running into them; many of which are naviga-ble to a great extent for boats and canoes, thro' vast tracts of country; how little likely is it that the expence on the carriage of our goods into those countries, should prevent the use of them. If the poor Indians in those remote parts are now able to pay for the linnen, woolen and iron wares they are at present furnish'd with by the French and English traders, tho' Indians have nothing but what they get by hunting, and the goods are loaded with all the impositions fraud and knavery can contrive to inhance their value; will not industrious English farmers, hereafter settled in those countries, be much better able to pay for what shall be brought them in the way of fair commerce?

If it is asked, what can such farmers raise, wherewith to pay for the manufactures they may want from us? I answer, that the inland parts of America in question are well-known to be fitted for the production of hemp, flax, potash, and above all silk; the southern parts, may produce olive oil, raisins, currans, indigo, and cochineal. Not to mention horses and black cattle, which may easily be driven to the maritime markets, and at the same time assist in conveying other commodities. That the commodities first mention'd, may easily by water or land carriage be brought to the sea ports from interior America, will not seem incredible, when

---

*From New York into lake Ontario, the land carriage of the several portages altogether, amounts to but about 27 miles. From lake Ontario into lake Erie, the land carriage at Niagara is but about 12 miles. All the lakes above Niagara communicate by navigable straits, so that no land carriage is necessary, to go out of one into another. From Presqu' isle on lake Erie, there are but 15 miles land-carriage, and that a good waggon road, to Beef River a branch of the Ohio, which brings you into a navigation of many thousand miles inland, if you take together the Ohio, the Mississipi, and all the great rivers and branches that run into them.

we reflect, that hemp formerly came from the Ukraine and most southern parts of Russia to Wologda, and down the Dwina to Archangel, and thence by a perilous navigation round the North Cape to England and other parts of Europe.[8] It now comes from the same country up the Dnieper and down the Duna with much land carriage.[9] Great part of the Russia iron, no high-priced commodity, is brought 3000 miles by land and water from the heart of Siberia. Furs, [the produce too of America][1] are brought to Amsterdam from all parts of Siberia, even the most remote, Kamschatka.[2] The same country furnishes me with another instance of extended inland commerce. It is found worth while to keep up a mercantile communication between Peking in China and Petersburgh. And none of these instances of inland commerce exceed those of the courses by which, at several periods, the whole trade of the East was carried on. Before the prosperity of the Mamaluke dominion in Egypt fixed the staple for the riches of the East at Cairo and Alexandria, whither they were brought from the Red Sea, great part of those commodities were carried to the cities of Cashgar and Balk.[3] This gave birth to those towns, that still subsist upon the remains of their ancient opulence, amidst a people and country equally wild. From thence those goods were carried down the Amû, the ancient Oxus, to the Caspian Sea, and up the Wolga to Astrachan, from whence they were carried over to, and down the Don to the mouth of that river, and thence again the Venetians directly, and the Genoese and Venetians indirectly by way of Kaffa and Trebisonde, dispers'd them thro' the Mediterranean and

8. Vologda, about 250 miles north-northeast of Moscow, is on the Sukhona River, a tributary of the Dvina, which empties into the White Sea at Archangel.

9. Carried from the Ukraine up the Dnieper, the hemp was probably taken overland from Orska to Vitebsk on the Duna River (also called the West Dvina or the Daugava) and then downstream to Riga on the Gulf of Riga, an arm of the Baltic. Riga was for many generations famous for its commerce in hemp.

1. Brackets in the original.

2. The peninsula of Kamchatka extends southward from the northeastern part of Siberia.

3. Kashgar (Chinese K'oshih or Shufu) is in western Sinkiang. Balkh (now Wazirabad) is in northern Afghanistan, about forty miles from the Amu River.

82

some other parts of Europe.[4] Another part of those goods was carried over-land from the Wolga to the rivers Duna and Neva;[5] from both they were carried to the city of Wisbuy in the Baltick, so eminent for its sea-laws;[6] and from the city of Ladoga on the Neva, we are told they were even carried by the Dwina to Archangel, and from thence round the North Cape.

If iron and hemp will bear the charge of carriage from this inland country, other metals will as well as iron; and certainly silk, since 3*d. per lb.* is not above 1 *per cent.* on the value, and amounts to £28 *per* ton.

If the growths of a country find their way out of it, the manufactures of the countries where they go will infallibly find their way into it. They who understand the oeconomy and principles of manufactures, know, that it is impossible to establish them in places not populous; and even in those that are populous, hardly possible to establish them to the prejudice of the places already in possession of them. Several attempts have been made in France and Spain, countenanced by the government, to draw from us and establish in those countries, our hard-ware and woolen manufactures, but without success. The reasons are various. A manufacture is part of a great system of commerce, which takes in conveniencies of various kinds, methods of providing materials of all sorts, machines for expediting and facilitating labour, all the channels of correspondence for vending the wares, the credit and confidence necessary to found and support this correspondence, the mutual aid of different artizans, and a thousand other particulars, which time and long experience have gradually established. A part of such a system cannot support itself without the whole, and before

4. The Amu Dar'ya flows into the Aral Sea, whence goods were transported overland to the Caspian Sea, into which the Volga flows. From Astrakhan they may have been carried up the river to Tsaritsyn (later Stalingrad, now Volgograd), then overland to the nearest point on the Don, then down that river to Rostov or Azov near the mouth, finally via the Sea of Azov and the Black Sea to the Mediterranean. Alternatively, they were carried to Kaffa (Caffa, Theodosia, the modern Feodosiya) on the southeast coast of the Crimean Peninsula or to Trevizond (Trabzon) on the eastern Black Sea coast of Asia Minor for transportation to Genoa and Venice.

5. The Neva drains Lake Ladoga, emptying into the Gulf of Finland at what is now Leningrad.

6. Visby is the principal city on the island of Gotland in the Baltic.

the whole can be obtained the part perishes. Manufactures where they are in perfection, are carried on by a multiplicity of hands, each of which is expert only in his own part, no one of them a master of the whole; and if by any means spirited away to a foreign country, he is lost without his fellows. Then it is a matter of the extremest difficulty to persuade a compleat set of workmen, skilled in all parts of a manufactory to leave their country together and settle in a foreign land. Some of the idle and drunken may be enticed away, but these only disappoint their employers, and serve to discourage the undertaking. If by royal munificence, and an expence that the profits of the trade alone would not bear a compleat set of good and skilful hands are collected and carried over, they find so much of the system imperfect, so many things wanting to carry on the trade to advantage, so many difficulties to overcome, and the knot of hands so easily broken, by death, dissatisfaction and desertion, that they and their employers are discouraged together, and the project vanishes into smoke.[7] Hence it happens, that established manufactures are hardly ever lost, but by foreign conquest, or by some eminent interior fault in manners or government; a bad police oppressing and discouraging the workmen, or religious persecutions driving the sober and industrious out of the country. There is in short, scarce a single instance in history of the contrary, where manufactures have once taken firm root. They sometimes start up in a new place, but are generally supported like exotic plants at more expence than they are worth for any thing but curiosity, until these new seats become the refuge of the manufacturers driven from the old ones. The conquest of Constantinople and final reduction of the Greek empire, dispersed many curious manufacturers into different parts of Christendom. The former conquests of its provinces had before done the same. The loss of liberty in Verona, Milan, Florence, Pisa, Pistoia, and other great cities of Italy, drove the manufacturers of woolen cloth into Spain and Flanders. The latter first lost their trade and manufacturers to Antwerp and the cities of Brabant, from whence by persecution for religion they were sent into Holland and England. The civil wars during the minority of

7. BF may have had in mind the experience of his brother John and others in trying to establish glass works in Germantown, Braintree, Mass., in 1750, importing German workmen. See above, IV, 65 n; V, 119 n.

Charles the first of Spain, which ended in the loss of the liberty of their great towns, ended too in the loss of the manufactures of Toledo, Segovia, Salamanca, Medina del campo, &c. The revocation of the edict of Nantes, communicated, to all the Protestant parts of Europe, the paper, silk, and other valuable manufactures of France, almost peculiar at that time to that country, and till then in vain attempted elsewhere.

To be convinc'd that it is not soil and climate, or even freedom from taxes, that determines the residence of manufacturers, we need only turn our eyes on Holland, where a multitude of manufactures are still carried on (perhaps more than on the same extent of territory any where in Europe) and sold on terms upon which they cannot be had in any other part of the world. And this too is true of those growths, which by their nature and the labour required to raise them, come the nearest to manufactures.

As to the common-place objection to the North American settlements, that they are in the same climate and their produce the same as that of England; in the first place it is not true; it is particularly not so of the countries now likely to be added to our settlements; and of our present colonies, the products, lumber, tobacco, rice and indigo, great articles of commerce do not interfere with the products of England: in the next place, a man must know very little of the trade of the world, who does not know, that the greater part of it is carried on between countries whose climate differs very little. Even the trade between the different parts of these British islands, is greatly superior to that between England and all the West-India islands put together.

If I have been successful in proving that a considerable commerce may and will subsist between us and our future most inland settlements in North America, notwithstanding their distance, I have more than half proved no other inconveniency will arise from their distance. Many men in such a country, must *"know,"* must *"think,"* and must *"care"* about the country they chiefly trade with. The juridical and other connections of government are yet a faster hold than even commercial ties, and spread directly and indirectly far and wide. Business to be solicited and causes depending, create a great intercourse even where private property is not divided in different countries, yet this division will always subsist where different countries are ruled by the same government. Where a man has landed property both in the mother country and a province, he will almost always live in the mother country: this, though there were no trade, is singly a sufficient gain. It is said, that Ireland pays near a million Sterling annually to its absentees in England: The ballance of trade from Spain or even Portugal is scarcely equal to this.

Let it not be said we have no absentees from North-America. There are many to the writer's knowledge; and if there are at present but few of them that distinguish themselves here by great expence, it is owing to the mediocrity of fortune among the inhabitants of the Northern colonies; and a more equal division of landed property, than in the West-India islands, so that there are as yet but few large estates. But if those who have such estates, reside upon and take care of them themselves, are they worse subjects than they would be if they lived idly in England? Great merit is assumed for the gentlemen of the West-Indies,* on the score of their residing and spending their money in England. I would not depreciate that merit; it is considerable, for they might, if they pleased spend their money in France: but the difference between their spending it *here* and *at home* is not so great. What do they spend it in when they are here, but the produce and manufactures of this country; and would they not do the same if they were at home? Is it of any great importance to the English farmer, whether the West-India gentleman comes to London and eats his beef, pork, and tongues, fresh, or has them brought to him in the West-Indies salted; whether he eats his English cheese and butter or drinks his English ale at London or in Barbadoes? Is the clothier's, or the mercer's, or the cutler's, or the toy-man's profit less, for their goods being worn and consumed by the same persons residing on the other side of the ocean? Would not the profits of the merchant and mariner be rather greater, and some addition made to our navigation, ships and seamen? If the North-American gentleman stays in his own country, and lives there in that degree of luxury and expence with regard to the use of British manufactures, that his fortune entitles him to; may not his example (from the imitation of superiors so natural to mankind) spread the use of those manufactures among hundreds of families around him, and

*Remarks, p. 47, 48, &c.

86

occasion a much greater demand for them, than it would do if he should remove and live in London?

However this may be, if in our views of immediate advantage, it seems preferable that the gentlemen of large fortunes in North America should reside much in England, 'tis what may surely be expected as fast as such fortunes are acquired there. Their having "colleges of their own for the education of their youth,"[8] will not prevent it: A little knowledge and learning acquired, increases the appetite for more, and will make the conversation of the learned on this side the water more strongly desired. Ireland has its university likewise; yet this does not prevent the immense pecuniary benefit we receive from that kingdom. And there will always be in the conveniencies of life, the politeness, the pleasures, the magnificence of the reigning country, many other attractions besides those of learning, to draw men of substance there, where they can, apparently at least, have the best bargain of happiness for their money.

Our trade to the West-India islands is undoubtedly a valuable one: but whatever is the amount of it, it has long been at a stand. Limited as our sugar planters are by the scantiness of territory, they cannot increase much beyond their present number; and this is an evil, as I shall show hereafter, that will be little helped by our keeping Guadaloupe. The trade to our Northern Colonies, is not only greater, but yearly increasing with the increase of people: and even in a greater proportion, as the people increase in wealth and the ability of spending as well as in numbers. I have already said, that our people in the Northern Colonies double in about 25 years, exclusive of the accession of strangers. That I speak within bounds, I appeal to the authentic accounts frequently required by the board of trade, and transmitted to that board by the respective governors; of which accounts I shall select one as a sample, being that from the colony of Rhode-Island;* a colony that of all the others receives the least addition from strangers. For the increase of our trade to those colonies, I refer to the ac-

*Copy of the Report of Governor Hopkins to the Board of Trade, on the Numbers of People in Rhode-Island.

In obedience to your lordships' commands, I have caused the within account to be taken by officers under oath. By it there appears to be in

8. Remarks, p. 50.

counts frequently laid before Parliament, by the officers of the customs, and to the custom-house books: from which I have also selected one account, that of the trade from England (exclusive of Scotland) to Pensilvania;* a colony most remarkable for the plain frugal manner of living of its inhabitants, and the most suspected of carrying on manufactures on account of the number of German artizans, who are known to have transplanted themselves into that country, though even these, in truth, when they come there, generally apply themselves to agriculture as the surest support and most advantageous employment. By this account it appears, that the exports to that province have in 28 years, increased nearly in the proportion of 17 to 1; whereas the people themselves, who by other authentic accounts appear to double their numbers

---

this colony at this time 35,939 white persons, and 4697 blacks, chiefly negroes.

In the year 1730, by order of the then lords commissioners of trade and plantations, an account was taken of the number of people in this colony, and then there appeared to be 15,302 white persons, and 2633 blacks.

Again in the year 1748, by like order, an account was taken of the number of people in this colony, by which it appears there were at that time 29,755 white persons, and 4373 blacks.

STEPHEN HOPKINS

Colony of Rhode-Island,
  Dec. 24. 1755.

  *An Account of the Value of the Exports from England to Pensylvania, in one Year, taken at different Periods, viz.

In 1723 they amounted only to	£ 15,992 : 19 : 4
1730 they were	48,592 : 7 : 5
1737	56,690 : 6 : 7
1742	75,295 : 3 : 4
1747	82,404 : 17 : 7
1752	201,666 : 19 : 11
1757	268,426 : 6 : 6

N.B. The accounts for 1758 and 1759 are not yet compleated; but those acquainted with the North American trade, know, that the increase in those two years, has been in a still greater proportion; last year being supposed to exceed any former year by a third; and this owing to the increased ability of the people to spend, from the greater quantities of money circulating among them by the war.

88

(the strangers who settle there included) in about 16 years, cannot in the 28 years have increased in a greater proportion than as 4 to 1: the additional demand then, and consumption of goods from England, of 13 parts in 17 more than the additional number would require, must be owing to this, that the people having by their industry mended their circumstances, are enabled to indulge themselves in finer cloaths, better furniture, and a more general use of all our manufactures than heretofore. In fact, the occasion for English goods in North America, and the inclination to have and use them, is, and must be for ages to come, much greater than the ability of the people to pay for them; they must therefore, as they now do, deny themselves many things they would otherwise chuse to have, or increase their industry to obtain them; and thus, if they should at any time manufacture some coarse article, which on account of its bulk or some other circumstance, cannot so well be brought to them from Britain, it only enables them the better to pay for finer goods that otherwise they could not indulge themselves in: So that the exports thither are not diminished by such manufacture but rather increased. The single article of manufacture in these colonies mentioned by the *remarker,* is *hats* made in New-England. It is true there have been ever since the first settlement of that country, a few hatters there, drawn thither probably at first by the facility of getting beaver, while the woods were but little clear'd, and there was plenty of those animals. The case is greatly alter'd now. The beaver skins are not now to be had in New England, but from very remote places and at great prices. The trade is accordingly declining there, so that, far from being able to make hats in any quantity for exportation, they cannot supply their home demand; and it is well known that some thousand dozens are sent thither yearly from London, and sold there cheaper than the inhabitants can make them of equal goodness. In fact, the colonies are so little suited for establishing of manufactures, that they are continually losing the few branches they accidentally gain. The working brasiers, cutlers, and pewterers, as well as hatters, who have happened to go over from time to time and settle in the colonies, gradually drop the working part of their business, and import their respective goods from England, whence they can have them cheaper and better than they can make them. They continue their shops indeed, in the same way of dealing, but

89

become *sellers* of brasiery, cutlery, pewter, hats, &c. brought from England, instead of being *makers* of those goods.

Thus much as to the apprehension of our colonies becoming *useless* to us. I shall next consider the other supposition, that their growth may render them *dangerous*. Of this I own, I have not the least conception, when I consider that we have already fourteen separate governments on the maritime coast of the continent,[9] and if we extend our settlements shall probably have as many more behind them on the inland side. Those we now have, are not only under different governors, but have different forms of government, different laws, different interests, and some of them different religious persuasions and different manners. Their jealousy of each other is so great that however necessary an union of the colonies has long been, for their common defence and security against their enemies, and how sensible soever each colony has been of that necessity, yet they have never been able to effect such an union among themselves, nor even to agree in requesting the mother country to establish it for them.[1] Nothing but the immediate command of the crown has been able to produce even the imperfect union but lately seen there, of the forces of some colonies. If they could not agree to unite for their defence against the French and Indians, who were perpetually harassing their settlements, burning their villages, and murdering their people; can it reasonably be supposed there is any danger of their uniting against their own nation, which protects and encourages them, with which they have so many connections and ties of blood, interest and affection, and which 'tis well known they all love much more than they love one another? In short, there are so many causes that must operate to prevent it, that I will venture to say, an union amongst them for such a purpose is not merely improbable, it is impossible; and if the union of the whole is impossible, the attempt of a part must be madness: as those colonies that did not join the rebellion, would join the mother country in suppressing it.

When I say such an union is impossible, I mean without the most grievous tyranny and oppression. People who have property in a country which they may lose, and privileges which they may endanger; are generally dispos'd to be quiet; and even to bear

9. Nova Scotia and the thirteen that declared their independence in 1776.
1. On the Albany Plan of Union, 1754, see above, v, *passim.*

90

much, rather than hazard all. While the government is mild and just, while important civil and religious rights are secure, such subjects will be dutiful and obedient. The waves do not rise, but when the winds blow.[2] What such an administration as the Duke of Alva's in the Netherlands, might produce, I know not; but this I think I have a right to deem impossible.[3] And yet there were two very manifest differences between that case, and ours, and both are in our favour. The first, that Spain had already united the seventeen provinces under one visible government, tho' the states continued independent: The second, that the inhabitants of those provinces were of a nation, not only different from, but utterly unlike the Spaniards. Had the Netherlands been peopled from Spain, the worst of oppression had probably not provoked them to wish a separation of government. It might and probably would have ruined the country, but would never have produced an independent sovereignty. In fact, neither the very worst of governments, the worst of politicks in the last century, nor the total abolition of their remaining liberty, in the provinces of Spain itself, in the present, have produced any independency that could be supported. The same may be observed of France. And let it not be said that the neighbourhood of these to the seat of government has prevented a separation. While our strength at sea continues, the banks of the Ohio, (in point of easy and expeditious conveyance of troops) are nearer to London, than the remote parts of France and Spain to their respective capitals; and much nearer than Connaught and Ulster were in the days of Queen Elizabeth. No body foretels the dissolution of the Russian monarchy from its extent, yet I will venture to say, the eastern parts of it are already much more inaccessible from Petersburgh, than the country on the Mississipi is from London; I mean more men, in less time, might be conveyed the latter than the former distance.

2. BF used these words eight years later as the motto of his "Causes of the American Discontents before 1768."

3. The arbitrary and oppressive rule of the Duke of Alva, 1567–73, was a major factor in the revolt of the Netherlands against Philip II, which persisted intermittently until the Treaty of Westphalia, 1648, recognized the independence of the United Provinces. Intervention by England on the side of the Dutch, 1585, was a contributing factor to the war with Spain, 1588–1604, in which the Spanish Armada was destroyed, 1588.

The rivers Oby, Jenesea and Lena,[4] do not facilitate the communication half so well by their course, nor are they half so practicable as the American rivers. To this I shall only add the observation of Machiavel, in his *Prince,* that a government seldom long preserves its dominion over those who are foreigners to it; who on the other hand fall with great ease, and continue inseparably annex'd to the government of their own nation, which he proves by the fate of the English *conquests* in France.

Yet with all these disadvantages, so difficult is it to overturn an established government, that it was not without the assistance of France and England, that the United Provinces supported themselves: which teaches us, that if the visionary danger of independence in our colonies is to be feared, nothing is more likely to render it substantial than the neighbourhood of foreigners at enmity with the sovereign government, capable of giving either aid or an asylum, as the event shall require. Yet against even these disadvantages, did Spain preserve almost ten provinces, merely thro' their want of union, which indeed could never have taken place among the others, but for causes, some of which are in our case impossible, and others it is impious to suppose possible.

The Romans well understood that policy which teaches the security arising to the chief government from separate states among the governed, when they restored the liberties of the states of Greece, (oppressed but united under Macedon,) by an edict that every state should live under its own laws.* They did not even name a governor. *Independence of each other, and separate interests,* tho' among a people united by common manners, language, and I may say religion, inferior neither in wisdom, bravery, nor their love of liberty, to the Romans themselves, was all the security the sovereigns wished for their sovereignty. It is true, they did

---

Omnes Graecorum civitates, quae in Europa, quaeque in Asia essent, libertatem ac suas leges haberent, &c.   Liv. lib. 33. c. 30.

4. The three major rivers of Siberia, which flow generally northward to the Arctic Ocean. The Ob on the west, nearest to the Ural Mountains, empties into the Gulf of Ob; it is 2260 miles long. The Yenisey, somewhat west of center, is nearly 3000 miles in length. The Lena, in eastern Siberia, is 2860 miles long. Although all are navigable during the summer season for great distances, they are able to contribute very little to east-west communication with European Russia because of their direction.

not call themselves sovereigns; they set no value on the title; they were contented with possessing the thing; and possess it they did, even without a standing army. What can be a stronger proof of the security of their possession? And yet by a policy similar to this throughout, was the Roman world subdued and held: a world compos'd of above an hundred languages and sets of manners different from those of their masters.* Yet this dominion was unshakeable, till the loss of liberty and corruption of manners overturned it.

But what is the prudent policy inculcated by the *remarker*, to obtain this end, security of dominion over our colonies: It is, to leave the French in Canada, to *"check"* their growth, for otherwise our people may "increase infinitely from all causes."† We have already seen in what manner the French and their Indians *check the growth* of our colonies. 'Tis a modest word, this, *check*, for massacring men, women and children. The writer would, if he could, hide from himself as well as from the public, the horror arising from such a proposal, by couching it in general terms: 'tis no wonder he thought it a "subject not fit for discussion" in his letter, tho' he recommends it as "a point that should be the constant object of the minister's attention!" But if Canada is restored on this principle, will not Britain be guilty of all the blood to be shed, all the murders to be committed in order to check this dreaded growth of our own people? Will not this be telling the

*When the Romans had subdu'd Macedon and Illyricum, they were both form'd into republicks by a decree of the senate, and Macedon was thought safe from the danger of a revolution, by being divided, into a division common among the Romans, as we learn from the tetrarchs in scripture. *Omnium primum liberos esse placebat Macedonas atque Illyrios; ut omnibus gentibus appareret, arma populi Romani non liberis servitutem, sed contra servientibus libertatem afferre. Ut et in libertate gentes quae essent, tutam eam sibi perpetuamque sub tutela populi Romani esse: et quae sub regibus viverent, et in presens tempus mitiores eos jusioresque respectu populi Romani habere se; et si quando bellum cum populo Romano regibus fuisset suis, excitum ejus victoriam Romanis, sibi libertatem allaturum crederent. . . . In quatuor regiones describi Macedoniam, ut suum quaeque concilium haberet, placuit: et dimidium tributi quam quod regibus ferre soliti erant, populo Romano pendere.* Similia his et in Illyricum mandata.   Liv. lib. 45. c. 18.

†Remarks, p. 50, 51.

French in plain terms, that the horrid barbarities they perpetrate with their Indians on our colonists, are agreeable to us; and that they need not apprehend the resentment of a government with whose views they so happily concur? Will not the colonies view it in this light? Will they have reason to consider themselves any longer as subjects and children, when they find their cruel enemies halloo'd upon them by the country from whence they sprung, the government that owes them protection as it requires their obedience? Is not this the most likely means of driving them into the arms of the French, who can invite them by an offer of that security their own government chuses not to afford them? I would not be thought to insinuate that the *remarker* wants humanity. I know how little many good-natured persons are affected by the distresses of people at a distance and whom they do not know. There are even those, who, being present, can sympathize sincerely with the grief of a lady on the sudden death of her favourite bird, and yet can read of the sinking of a city in Syria with very little concern. If it be, after all, thought necessary to *check* the growth of our colonies, give me leave to propose a method less cruel.[5] It is a method of which we have an example in scripture. The murder of husbands, of wives, of brothers, sisters, and children whose pleasing society has been for some time enjoyed, affects deeply the respective surviving relations: but grief for the death of a child just born is short and easily supported. The method I mean is that which was dictated by the Egyptian policy, when the "infinite increase" of the children of Israel was apprehended as dangerous to the state.* Let an act of parliament, [then] be made, enjoining the colony midwives to stifle in the birth every third or fourth child.

*And Pharoah said unto his people, behold the people of the children of Israel are more and mightier than we; come on, let us deal *wisely* with them; *lest they multiply;* and it come to pass that when there falleth out any war, they join also unto our enemies and fight against us, and so get them up out of the land. . . . And the king spake to the Hebrew midwives, &c.   *Exodus, Chap.* 1.[6]

5. In the vigor of its satire the rest of this paragraph is reminiscent of BF's proposal, printed in *Pa. Gaz.*, May 9, 1751, that the colonists collect and ship thousands of rattlesnakes to England and release them there in grateful and dutiful return for the felons the British government was transporting to America. See above, IV, 130–3.

6. Verses 9–10, 15.

By this means you may keep the colonies to their present size. And if they were under the hard alternative of submitting to one or the other of these schemes for *checking* their growth, I dare answer for them, they would prefer the latter.

But all this debate about the propriety or impropriety of keeping or restoring Canada, is possibly too early. We have taken the capital indeed, but the country is yet far from being in our possession; and perhaps never will be: for if our M———rs are persuaded by such counsellors as the *remarker*, that the French there are "not the worst of neighbours," and that if we had conquered Canada, we ought for our own sakes to restore it, as a *check* to the growth of our colonies, I am then afraid we shall never take it. For there are many ways of avoiding the completion of the conquest, that will be less exceptionable and less odious than the giving it up.

The objection I have often heard, that if we had Canada, we could not people it, without draining Britain of its inhabitants, is founded on ignorance of the nature of population in new countries. When we first began to colonize in America, it was necessary to send people, and to send seed-corn; but it is not now necessary that we should furnish, for a new colony, either one or the other. The annual increment alone of our present colonies, without diminishing their numbers, or requiring a man from hence, is sufficient in ten years to fill Canada with double the number of English that it now has of French inhabitants.* Those who are protestants among the French, will probably chuse to remain under the English government; many will chuse to remove if they can be allowed to sell their lands improvements and effects: the rest in that thin-settled country, will in less than half a century, from the crowds of English settling round and among them, be blended and incorporated with our people both in language and manners.

In Guadalupe the case is somewhat different; and though I am far from thinking† we have sugar-land enough,‡ I cannot think

*In fact, there has not gone from Britain to our colonies these 20 years past, to settle there, so many as 10 families a year; the new settlers are either the offspring of the old, or emigrants from Germany or the north of Ireland.

†Remarks, p. 30, 34.

‡It is often said we have plenty of sugar-land still unemployed in Jamaica: but those who are well acquainted with that island, know,

Guadalupe is so desirable an increase of it, as other objects the enemy would probably be infinitely more ready to part with. A country *fully inhabited* by any nation is no proper possession for another of different language, manners and religion. It is hardly ever tenable at less expence than it is worth. But the isle of Cayenne,[7] and its appendix Equinoctial-France, would indeed be an acquisition every way suitable to our situation and desires. This would hold all that migrate from Barbadoes, the Leward-Islands, or Jamaica. It would certainly recal into an English government (in which there would be room for millions) all who have before settled or purchased in Martinico, Guadalupe, Santa-Cruz or St. John's; except such as know not the value of an English government, and such I am sure are not worth recalling.

But should we keep Guadalupe, we are told it would enable us to export £300,000 in sugars. Admit it to be true, though perhaps the amazing increase of English consumption might stop most of it here, to whose profit is this to redound? to the profit of the French inhabitants of the island: except a small part that should fall to the share of the English purchasers, but whose whole purchase-money must first be added to the wealth and circulation of France.

I grant, however, much of this £300,000 would be expended in British manufactures. Perhaps, too, a few of the land-owners of Guadalupe might dwell and spend their fortunes in Britain, (though probably much fewer than of the inhabitants of North America). I admit the advantage arising to us from these circumstances, (as far as they go) in the case of Guadalupe, as well as in that of our other West India settlements. Yet even this consumption is little better than that of an allied nation would be, who should take our manufactures and supply us with sugar, and put us to no expence in defending the place of growth.

But though our own colonies expend among us almost the

---

that the remaining vacant land in it is generally situated among mountains, rocks and gullies, that make carriage impracticable, so that no profitable use can be made of it, unless the price of sugars should so greatly increase as to enable the planter to make very expensive roads, by blowing up rocks, erecting bridges, &c. every 2 or 300 yards.

7. The seat of government and principal port of French Guiana.

whole produce of our sugar,* can we or ought we to promise our-selves this will be the case of Guadalupe. One £100,000 will supply them with British manufactures; and supposing we can effectually prevent the introduction of those of France, (which is morally impossible in a country used to them) the other 200,000 will still be spent in France, in the education of their children and support of themselves; or else be laid up there, where they will always think their home to be.

Besides this consumption of British manufactures, much is said of the benefit we shall have from the situation of Guadalupe, and we are told of a trade to the Caraccas and Spanish Main. In what respect Guadalupe is better situated for this trade than Jamaica, or even any of our other islands, I am at a loss to guess. I believe it to be not so well situated for that of the windward coast, as Tobago and St. Lucia, which in this as well as other respects, would be more valuable possessions, and which, I doubt not, the peace will secure to us. Nor is it nearly so well situated for that of the rest of the Spanish Main as Jamaica. As to the greater safety of our trade by the possession of Guadalupe, experience has con-vinced us that in reducing a single island, or even more, we stop the privateering business but little. Privateers still subsist, in equal if not greater numbers, and carry the vessels into Martinico which before it was more convenient to carry into Guadalupe. Had we all the Caribbees,[8] it is true, they would in those parts be without shelter. Yet upon the whole I suppose it to be a doubtful point and well worth consideration, whether our obtaining possession of all the Caribbees, would be more than a temporary benefit, as it would necessarily soon fill the French part of Hispaniola with French inhabitants, and thereby render it five times more valuable in time of peace, and little less than impregnable in time of war; and would probably end in a few years in the uniting the whole of that great and fertile island under a French government. It is agreed on all hands, that our conquest of St. Christophers, and driving the French from thence, first furnish'd Hispaniola with skilful and substantial planters, and was consequently the first oc-casion of its present opulence. On the other hand, I will hazard an

*Remarks, p. 47.

8. That is, all the Lesser Antilles; the West India islands exclusive of Cuba, Haiti (Hispaniola), Puerto Rico, Jamaica, and the Bahamas.

opinion, that valuable as the French possessions in the West Indies are, and undeniable the advantages they derive from them, there is somewhat to be weighed in the opposite scale. They cannot at present make war with England, without exposing those advantages while divided among the numerous islands they now have, much more than they would, were they possessed of St. Domingo only; their own share of which would, if well cultivated, grow more sugar, than is now grown in all their West India islands. .I have before said I do not deny the utility of the conquest, or even of our future possession of Guadalupe, if not bought too dear. The trade of the West Indies is one of our most valuable trades. Our possessions there deserve our greatest care and attention. So do those of North America. I shall not enter into the invidious task of comparing their due estimation. It would be a very long and a very disagreeable one, to run thro' every thing material on this head. It is enough to our present point, if I have shown, that the value of North America is capable of an immense increase, by an acquisition and measures, that must necessarily have an effect the direct contrary of what we have been industriously taught to fear; and that Guadalupe is, in point of advantage, but a very small addition to our West India possessions, rendered many ways less valuable to us than it is to the French, who will probably set more value upon it than upon a country that is much more valuable to us than to them.

There is a great deal more to be said on all the parts of these subjects; but as it would carry me into a detail that I fear would tire the patience of my readers, and which I am not without apprehensions I have done already, I shall reserve what remains till I dare venture again on the indulgence of the publick.

FINIS.

In Confirmation of the Writer's Opinion concerning *Population, Manufactures, &c.* he has thought it not amiss to add an Extract from a Piece written some Years since in America, where the Facts must be well known, on which the Reasonings are founded. It is intitled OBSERVATIONS concerning the Increase of Mankind, Peopling of Countries, &c. Written in Pensilvania, 1751.

[Here follows the text of that paper, with the omissions indicated in the headnote above. It occupies nearly seven pages. The pamphlet concludes with the following:]

Since the foregoing sheets were printed off, the writer has obtained accounts of the Exports to North America, and the West India Islands, by which it appears, that there has been some increase of trade to those Islands as well as to North America, though in a much less degree. The following extract from these accounts will show the reader at one view the amount of the exports to each, in two different terms of five years; the terms taken at ten years distance from each other, to show the increase, *viz.*

First Term, from 1744 to 1748, inclusive.   *10 94 35*

	Northern Colonies.				West India Islands.		
1744	£640,114	12	4		£796,112	17	9
1745	534,316	2	5		503,669	19	9
1746	754,945	4	3		472,994	19	7
1747	726,648	5	5		856,463	18	6
1748	830,243	16	9		734,095	15	3
Total	£3,486,268	1	2	Tot.	£3,363,337	10	10
				Difference	122,930	10	4
					£3,486,268	1	2

Second Term, from 1754 to 1758, inclusive.

	Northern Colonies.				West India Islands.		
1754	1,246,615	1	11		685,675	3	0
1755	1,177,848	6	10		694,667	13	3
1756	1,428,720	18	10		733,458	16	3
1757	1,727,924	2	10		776,488	0	6
1758	1,832,948	13	10		877,571	19	11
Total	£7,414,057	4	3	Tot.	£3,767,841	12	11
				Difference,	3,646,215	11	4
					£7,414,057	4	3

In the first Term, total for West India Islands,	3,363,337	10	10
In the second Term, *ditto,*	3,767,841	12	11
Increase, only £0,404,504		2	1

In the first Term, total for Northern Colonies,	3,486,268	1	2
In the second Term, *ditto,*	7,414,057	4	3
Increase, £3,927,789		3	1

By these accounts it appears, that the Exports to the West India Islands, and to the Northern Colonies, were in the first term nearly equal; the difference being only £122,936 10s. 4d. [sic] and in the second term, the Exports to those islands had only increased £404,504 2s. 1d. Whereas the increase to the Northern Colonies is £3,927,789 3s. 1d. almost FOUR MILLIONS.

Some part of this increased demand for English goods, may be ascribed to the armies and fleets we have had both in North America and the West Indies; not so much for what is consumed by the soldiery; their clothing, stores, ammunition, &c. sent from hence on account of the government, being (as is supposed) not included in these accounts of merchandize exported; but, as the war has occasioned a great plenty of money in America, many of the inhabitants have increased their expence.

These accounts do not include any Exports from Scotland to America, which are doubtless proportionably considerable; nor the Exports from Ireland.

From David Hall Letterbook copy: American Philosophical Society

Sir,   Philada. April 18. 1760.

In my last to you, of the 31st ult.[9] by the Roebuck, Capt. Jones, to Holyhead, I inclosed you the third Copy of a Bill of Exchange for £200 Sterling. I have now sent you the first Copy of another Bill of Exchange for £100 Sterling more,[1] which, with what was before sent you, makes up Two Thousand Forty-nine Pounds, Twelve Shillings, and Five-pence Sterling, since you left this Place;[2] for which, as usual, give me Credit, and Advice of receiving. Parson Smith denies his being with Mr. Osborne, and saying any thing to my Disadvantage; but I am well satisfied what you wrote was true notwithstanding.[3] Wish the Fount of Brevier was

9. See above, pp. 40–1.
1. On the protesting of both bills mentioned here, see above, p. 34 n.
2. Hall's remittances are listed above, VII, 235–6.
3. On April 8, 1759, BF wrote that William Smith had accused Hall of charging "excessive Prices" and had applied to Thomas Osborne for a consignment of books, which he or someone else would sell at reasonable prices and so would soon have "all the Custom" in Philadelphia. See above, VIII, 319.

come, as it is much wanted;[4] have had no Letter from you later than the Beginning of last August, the Meaning of which I cannot conceive.[5] I am, Sir, Yours, &c.   D. HALL

To Mr Franklin.
By the Friendship, Capt. Falconer, to London.[6]

Exchange 52½

From David Hall   Letterbook copy: American Philosophical Society

Sir,   Philada. April 20. 1760.
    In mine to you, of the 18th Instant,[7] by the Friendship, Capt. Falconer, was inclosed the first Copy of a Bill of Exchange for £100 Sterling; which, with what I had sent you before, I told you amounted to Two Thousand Forty-nine Pounds, Twelve Shillings, and Five Pence Sterling, remitted you since you left Philadelphia, and for which I desired you would give me Credit, and to advise me of the Receipt of the Bill, as usual. In it I also acquainted you that Parson Smith denied his being with Mr. Osborne, or saying any thing to my Disadvantage; but that, notwithstanding, I was convinced what you wrote was true. I likewise told you the Fount of Brevier was much wanted; and that I had not heard from you since some Time in August last, the Reason of which I could not conceive. I have now sent you the second Copy of the above Bill, and am, Sir, Yours very sincerely   D. HALL

To Mr. Franklin.
By the Three Friends, Killner, to London.[8]

4. See above, p. 34. Hall acknowledged receipt of the type, July 2, 1760; see below, p. 179.

5. Hall acknowledged receipt of BF's August letter on Dec. 15, 1759, but it has not been found; see above, VIII, 448 n.

6. *Pa. Gaz.*, April 24, 1760, reports the clearance of the *Friendship*, Capt. Nathaniel Falconer.

7. See the document immediately above and the annotation there for matters treated in this letter.

8. *Pa. Gaz.*, April 24, 1760, records the clearance of the *Three Friends*, Capt. George Killner.

To Mary Stevenson

ALS: American Philosophical Society

Cravenstreet, May 1. 1760

I embrace most gladly my dear Friend's Proposal of a Subject for our future Correspondence; not only as it will occasion my hearing from her more frequently, but as it will lay me under a Necessity of improving my own Knowledge that I may be better able to assist in her Improvement.[9] I only fear my necessary Business and Journeys with the natural Indolence of an old Man, will make me too unpunctual a Correspondent. For this I must hope some Indulgence.

But why will you, by the Cultivation of your Mind, make yourself still more amiable, and a more desirable Companion for a Man of Understanding, when you are determin'd, as I hear, to live Single? If we enter, as you propose, into *moral* as well as natural Philosophy, I fancy, when I have fully establish'd my Authority as a Tutor, I shall take upon me to lecture you a little on that Chapter of Duty.[1] But to be serious.

Our easiest Method of Proceeding I think will be for you to read some Books, that I may recommend to you;[2] and in the Course of your Reading, whatever occurs that you do not thor-

9. No written suggestion by Polly Stevenson of such a correspondence has survived; it may have been made in conversation. She had obviously been well schooled, her mind was active, and she seems to have had a real interest in study. Beyond all this, she may have proposed to correspond with BF about moral and natural philosophy in order to win his "friendship and respect," believing that the pleasant, though "rather aimless" correspondence which she had hitherto carried on with him was not enough. Whitfield J. Bell, Jr., " 'All Clear Sunshine': New Letters of Franklin and Mary Stevenson Hewson," APS *Proc.*, C (1956), 521–36.

1. A paragraph in BF's letter of June 11, 1760 (below, pp. 121–2), might be construed as such a lecture. "The Knowledge of Nature," he wrote Polly, "may be ornamental, and it may be useful, but if to attain an eminence in that, we neglect the Knowledge and Practice of essential Duties"—and under this head he specifically mentioned being a good wife and parent—"we deserve Reprehension."

2. On May 17, 1760, BF sent Polly books on natural philosophy, probably the first volumes of the popular *Spectacle de la Nature: or, Nature Display'd being Discourses . . . to Excite the Curiosity, and Form the Minds of Youth* translated by Samuel Humphreys (8th edit., 7 vols., London, 1754–63) from the French of Noël-Antoine Pluche. The titlepage of his gift copy to her is reproduced in APS *Proc.*, C (1956), 525. In *Proposals Relating to the Education*

oughly apprehend, or that you clearly conceive and find Pleasure in, may occasion either some Questions for farther Information or some Observations that show how far you are satisfy'd and pleas'd with your Author. Those will furnish Matter for your Letters to me, and, in consequence, of mine also to you.

Let me know then, what Books you have already perus'd on the Subject intended, that I may better judge what to advise for your next Reading. And believe me ever, my dear good Girl, Your affectionate Friend and Servant   B FRANKLIN

Miss Stevenson

Endorsed: May 1—60

To Lord Kames   ALS: Scottish Record Office

My dear Lord,   London, May 3. 1760.

Your obliging Favour of January 24th.[3] found me greatly indispos'd with an obstinate Cold and Cough accompany'd with Feverish Complaints and Headachs, that lasted long and harass'd me greatly, not being subdu'd at length but by the whole Round of Cupping, Bleeding, Blistering, &c. When I had any Intervals of Ease and Clearness, I endeavour'd to comply with your Request, in writing something on the present Situation of our Affairs in America, in order to give more correct Notions of the British Interest with regard to the Colonies, than those I found many sensible Men possess'd of. Inclos'd you have the Production, such as it is.[4] I wish it may in any Degree be of Service to the Publick. I shall at least hope this from it for my own Part, that you will consider it as a Letter from me to you, and accept its Length as some Excuse for its being so long acoming.

I am now reading, with great Pleasure and Improvement, your excellent Work, the Principles of Equity.[5] It will be of the greatest Advantage to the Judges in our Colonies, not only in those which

---

of Youth in Pensilvania in 1749 BF had recommended this work before there was an English translation; see above, III, 417 n.

3. Not found.

4. *The Interest of Great Britain Considered;* above, pp. 47–100.

5. *Principles of Equity* (London and Edinburgh, [1760]).

have Courts of Chancery, but also in those which having no such Courts are obliged to mix Equity with the Common Law. It will be of the more Service to the Colony Judges, as few of them have been bred to the Law. I have sent a Book to a particular Friend, one of the Judges of the Supreme Court in Pensilvania.[6]

I will shortly send you a Copy of the Chapter you are pleas'd to mention in so obliging a Manner;[7] and shall be extreamly oblig'd in receiving a Copy of the Collection of Maxims for the Conduct of Life, which you are preparing for the Use of your Children.[8] I purpose, likewise, a little Work for the Benefit of Youth, to be call'd *The Art of Virtue.*[9] From the Title I think you will hardly conjecture what the Nature of such a Book may be. I must therefore explain it a little. Many People lead bad Lives that would gladly lead good ones, but know not *how* to make the Change. They have frequently *resolv'd* and *endeavour'd* it; but in vain, because their Endeavours have not been properly conducted. To exhort People to be good, to be just, to be temperate, &c. without *shewing* them *how* they shall *become* so, seems like the ineffectual Charity mention'd by the Apostle, which consisted in saying to

6. Probably William Coleman (above, II, 406 n), who was a justice of the Pa. Supreme Court, 1758–69.

7. BF's "Parable against Persecution" (above, VI, 114–24), with which he had apparently regaled Lord Kames during his visit at Kames in the autumn of 1759, as he had Sir Alexander and Lady Dick at Prestonfield a little earlier. Despite this promise, BF did not send the "Chapter" to Kames until Sept. 27, 1760; see below, p. 232.

8. This was undoubtedly Kames's *Introduction to the Art of Thinking* (Edinburgh, 1761). Both the first edition and the second of 1764 included BF's "Parable against Persecution," but without heading or attribution. When Kames published his *Sketches of the History of Man* (Edinburgh, 1774), he included the "Chapter" again, this time calling it a "parable against persecution" and saying that it "was communicated to me by Dr. Franklin of Philadelphia"; see above, VI, 116–18.

9. This is the earliest known reference to a project which occupied BF's attention intermittently for many years and aroused the interest and approval of several friends. In spite of their urging, he never completed and published the work, but he incorporated parts of what he apparently intended to put into it in Part II of his Autobiography, written in Passy in 1784. There he described his system of concentrating for one week at a time on each of thirteen virtues, keeping a record of his lapses, and outlined his daily schedule of activity, which he set down as an aid to observing the virtue of Order. *Autobiog.* (APS-Yale edit.), pp. 148–60.

the Hungry, the Cold, and the Naked, *be ye fed, be ye warmed, be ye clothed,* without shewing them how they should get Food, Fire or Clothing. Most People have naturally *some* Virtues, but none have naturally *all* the Virtues. To *acquire* those that are wanting, and *secure* what we acquire as well as those we have naturally, is the Subject of *an Art.* It is as properly an Art, as Painting, Navigation, or Architecture. If a Man would become a Painter, Navigator, or Architect, it is not enough that he is *advised* to be one, that he is *convinc'd* by the Arguments of his Adviser that it would be for his Advantage to be one, and that he *resolves* to be one, but he must also be taught the Principles of the Art, be shewn all the Methods of Working, and how to acquire the *Habits* of using properly all the Instruments; and thus regularly and gradually he arrives by Practice at some Perfection in the Art. If he does not proceed thus, he is apt to meet with Difficulties that discourage him, and make him drop the Pursuit. My *Art of Virtue* has also its Instruments, and teaches the Manner of Using them. Christians are directed to have *Faith in Christ,* as the effectual Means of obtaining the Change they desire. It may, when sufficiently strong, be effectual with many. A full Opinion that a Teacher is infinitely wise, good, and powerful, and that he will certainly reward and punish the Obedient and Disobedient, must give great Weight to his Precepts, and make them much more attended to by his Disciples. But all Men cannot have Faith in Christ; and many have it in so weak a Degree, that it does not produce the Effect. Our *Art of Virtue* may therefore be of great Service to those who have not Faith, and come in Aid of the weak Faith of others. Such as are naturally well-disposed, and have been carefully educated, so that good Habits have been early established, and bad ones prevented, have less Need of this Art; but all may be more or less benefited by it. It is, in short, to be adapted for universal Use. I imagine what I have now been writing will seem to savour of great Presumption; I must therefore speedily finish my little Piece, and communicate the Manuscript to you, that you may judge whether it is possible to make good such Pretensions. I shall at the same time hope for the Benefit of your Corrections.

My respectful Compliments to Lady Kaims and your amiable Children, in which my Son joins.[1] With the sincerest Esteem and

1. On Kames's children, see above, p. 9 n.

Attachment, I am, My Lord, Your Lordship's most obedient and most humble Servant   B FRANKLIN

P.S. While I remain in London I shall continue in Craven Street, Strand: if you favour me with your Correspondence when I return to America, please to direct for me in Philadelphia, and your Letters will readily find me tho' sent to any other Part of North America.

Lord Kaims

To [Peter Franklin]²

MS not found; reprinted from Benjamin Franklin, *Experiments and Observations on Electricity* (London, 1769), pp. 379–80.³

Sir,   London, May 7, 1760.
******It had, indeed, as you observe,⁴ been the opinion of some very great naturalists, that the sea is salt only from the dissolution of mineral or rock salt, which its waters happened to meet with. But this opinion takes it for granted that all water was originally fresh, of which we can have no proof. I own I am inclined to a different opinion, and rather think all the water on this globe was originally salt, and that the fresh water we find in springs and rivers, is the produce of distillation. The sun raises the vapours from the sea, which form clouds, and fall in rain upon the land, and springs and rivers are formed of that rain. As to the rock-salt found in mines, I conceive, that instead of communicating its saltness to the sea, it is itself drawn from the sea, and that of course the sea is now fresher than it was originally. This is only another effect of nature's distillery, and might be performed various ways.

2. This letter is headed in *Exper. and Obser.* "To Mr. P. F. in Newport." No correspondent of BF's with these initials is known to have been living in Newport except his one surviving brother Peter. The "Sir" in the salutation and close must have been substituted in the printed version for BF's usual "Dear Brother." The asterisks at the beginning and end undoubtedly replace passages on personal and perhaps business matters in the original letter.

3. Printed as Letter XXXV in the 1769 and 1774 editions of *Exper. and Obser.*

4. No letter from Peter Franklin on the saltiness of the ocean has been found.

It is evident from the quantities of sea-shells, and the bones and teeth of fishes found in high lands, that the sea has formerly covered them.[5] Then, either the sea has been higher than it now is, and has fallen away from those high lands; or they have been lower than they are, and were lifted up out of the water to their present height, by some internal mighty force, such as we still feel some remains of, when whole continents are moved by earthquakes. In either case it may be supposed that large hollows, or valleys among hills, might be left filled with sea-water, which evaporating, and the fluid part drying away in a course of years, would leave the salt covering the bottom; and that salt coming afterwards to be covered with earth, from the neighbouring hills, could only be found by digging through that earth. Or, as we know from their effects, that there are deep fiery caverns under the earth, and even under the sea, if at any time the sea leaks into any of them, the fluid parts of the water must evaporate from that heat, and pass off through some vulcano, while the salt remains, and by degrees, and continual accretion, becomes a great mass. Thus the cavern may at length be filled, and the volcano connected with it cease burning, as many it is said have done; and future miners penetrating such cavern, find what we call a salt mine. This is a fancy I had on visiting the salt-mines at Northwich, with my son.[6] I send you a piece of the rock-salt which he brought up with him out of the mine.******I am, Sir, &c. B. F.

Defense of the Canada Pamphlet[7]

Draft (fragment): American Philosophical Society

The London Chronicle for April 24–26 contains a long and highly favorable review of *The Interest of Great Britain Considered,* calling it a "masterly performance" which "shows the writer to be perfectly ac-

5. BF discussed this matter with Jared Eliot, July 16, 1747, and at greater length with the Swedish naturalist Peter Kalm in 1748; see above, III, 149; IV, 55. On the disarrangement of the earth's strata, see above, VII, 357.

6. Northwich is in Cheshire, approximately 25 miles southeast of Liverpool, and is the center of the principal salt-producing district of England. BF and WF apparently visited it in August 1759 on the journey which took them to Scotland; see above, VIII, 430–2.

7. See above, pp. 47–100.

quainted with his subject and possessed of the happy talent of expressing himself with clearness, strength, and precision." Most of the article
consists of summary statements of the arguments advanced in *Remarks
on the Letter Address'd to Two Great Men* against the retention of
Canada, each followed by an extended paraphrase of the rebuttal in
Franklin's Canada Pamphlet.

The *Chronicle* for May 6–8 printed a piece dated "Bath, May 3,
1760," in which the writer vigorously disagreed with the author of *The
Interest of Great Britain Considered.* He had four main criticisms: 1. His
opponent had not properly distinguished between the northern continental colonies (from New England south through Pennsylvania),
which supplied few commodities that Britain needed, and those to the
south (Maryland through Georgia), which furnished such desirable
products as tobacco, rice, and indigo. 2. He had failed to point out that
the provision trade from the northern group to the West Indies was
competitive with the similar trade from Great Britain to the islands. 3.
In describing the "prodigious" increase of the trade of the northern
colonies since 1754 he had not said how much of this was the result of
their clandestine trade with the French islands during wartime. 4. He
had ignored the fact that much of the recent great prosperity of the
northern colonies resulted from the vast expenditures there of British
money in support of the armed forces. In introducing this piece the
publisher of the *Chronicle,* actively supporting Franklin's side of the
controversy, stated "[We have taken the liberty to add a few notes to
prevent a reader from being mislead]" and then inserted at the bottom
of the columns sixteen footnotes defending the Canada Pamphlet from
what he considered unfair or unjustifiable attacks by the critic.

In the *Chronicle* for May 15–17 is a second article by the same writer,
elaborating some of his earlier criticisms and adding new objections to
the arguments in the Canada Pamphlet. The publisher explained in a
headnote that he inserted the piece "not only to show what shifts the
advocates for keeping Guadaloupe, rather than Canada, are reduced to;
but, with their Author, to keep awake the attention of the Publick" to
this important question. He added that he was credibly informed that
the author of the *Remarks on the Letter Address'd to Two Great Men*
(whom he may have thought to be also the writer of these two attacks
on the Canada Pamphlet) "will lose a lucrative place when Guadaloupe
is restored. *Hinc illae lacrimae.*" This was a direct slap at William
Burke, who had been appointed secretary and register of Guadeloupe
in the previous autumn.

Who wrote these two criticisms cannot now be certainly established.
William Franklin told Joseph Galloway a few weeks later that the author

was Josiah Tucker, Dean of Gloucester,[8] and he may have been right, but the present editors have found no evidence for or against this attribution.

In his second article for the *Chronicle* the writer indicated his belief that the footnotes added to the first were written by the author of the Canada Pamphlet. A publisher's footnote to the second piece suggests, without positively saying so, that he was wrong. The present editors have found no evidence that Franklin wrote these notes, or indeed, that he ever completed and published any defense of his pamphlet. That he contemplated doing so, however, is evident both from a statement by his son in the letter to Galloway mentioned above, and from a single page in his handwriting which survives among his papers. This is the draft of the opening of what was evidently intended as a letter to the *Chronicle* replying to the attack in the issue of May 6–8. The reference to that piece as having appeared "in your last Wednesday's Paper" fixes the date of composition as sometime between the appearance of that issue on Thursday, May 8, 1760, and the following Thursday, May 15.[9] How much more Franklin wrote of the draft cannot be determined; the bottom of the page interrupts a quotation from his critic in mid course and no other fragments of this draft have been found among his papers. Search of the *Chronicle* for the next several months reveals nothing which might be even remotely identified as a reply by Franklin to these criticisms of his pamphlet.[1] Probably he concluded on second thought, as he did when Abbé Nollet attacked his electrical theories, that he would let his contribution stand or fall on its own merits, letting other writers pursue the debate if they cared to do so.[2]

Sir   [May 8–15, 1760]

When I think I have receiv'd Information from a new Pamphlet, that I have therefore read with Pleasure, it always mortifies me to find its Positions soon controverted by some Answerer, that seems

8. See below, p. 123.

9. While this issue of *London Chron.* was actually published on Thursday, May 8, the part of the paper in which the article appeared was headed "Wednesday, May 7." The *Chronicle* was regularly divided into dated sections in this way, sometimes with a "Postscript" added to fill out a sheet and to include late news.

1. *London Chron.*, Aug. 19–21, 1760, contains a letter supporting the retention of Canada, but its author makes no reference to the previous pieces in the paper; it uses arguments on the whole rather different from those in the Canada Pamphlet; and its literary style bears little resemblance to BF's.

2. See above, IV, 428, 464; V, 186 n; *Autobiog.* (APS-Yale edit.), pp. 243–4.

equally intelligent, and all the suppos'd Knowledge I had acquir'd reduc'd again to Uncertainty.

This has been my case lately, in reading the *Letter to two Great Men*, the *Remarks* on that Letter, and the *Interest of Great Britain considered with Regard to her Colonies* in Answer to those *Remarks*. The last of these Pamphlets seem'd so full and clear, that I made up my Mind upon it and sat down satisfy'd that I understood something of the Subject. But here comes an apparently sensible Writer from Bath in your last Wednesday's Paper, that perplexes me with an Assurance that the Doctrines of that Piece are *"big with Mischief, tending to entail an eternal War upon us, as long as there remains an Indian Tribe unsubdued or not extirpated from one end of the vast Continent of America to the other,"*[3] that its Reasonings are *fallacious:* That the Author "applies to the *Foibles* and *Passions* of Mankind," that "his Performance is full of Artifice and Chicane, calculated to serve the purpose of the Monopolizers of Jamaica; and is destitute of [*remainder missing*]."[4]

To Alexander Small[5]

MS not found; reprinted from Benjamin Franklin, *Experiments and Observations on Electricity* (London, 1769), pp. 381–3.[6]

Dear Sir,   May 12, 1760.

Agreeable to your request, I send you my reasons for thinking that our North-East storms in North-America begin first, in point

3. Quoted from the second paragraph of the letter from Bath, May 3.

4. The sentence partly quoted here constitutes the seventh paragraph of the first letter attacking the Canada Pamphlet. It reads in full: "Upon the whole, the performance now before me seems to be full of artifice and chicane, calculated to serve the cause of the monopolizers of Jamaica, by putting the people upon a wrong scent, in order that they may prefer the shadow of Quebec to the substance of Guadaloupe;—but destitute of every solid reason and true argument." The reference to "the monopolizers of Jamaica" is a suggestion that the sugar planters of that island preferred the retention of Canada so that the products of Guadeloupe would not come permanently into the British market and so compete with theirs.

5. Alexander Small (1710–1794), a Scots army surgeon, whose home was in London, was a member of the Society of Arts, a correspondent of learned societies in both Europe and America, and a contributor of essays "on agricultural and physiological improvements." He invented the chain plow. He

of time, in the South-West parts:[7] That is to say, the air in Georgia, the farthest of our colonies to the South-West, begins to move South-Westerly before the air of Carolina, which is the next colony North-Eastward; the air of Carolina has the same motion before the air of Virginia, which lies still more North-Eastward; and so on North-Easterly through Pensylvania, New-York, New-England, &c. quite to Newfoundland.

These North-East storms are generally very violent, continue sometimes two or three days, and often do considerable damage in the harbours along the coast. They are attended with thick clouds and rain.

What first gave me this idea, was the following circumstance. About twenty years ago, a few more or less, I cannot from my memory be certain, we were to have an eclipse of the moon at Philadelphia, on a Friday evening, about nine o'clock. I intended to observe it, but was prevented by a North-East storm, which came on about seven, with thick clouds as usual, that quite obscured the whole hemisphere. Yet when the post brought us the Boston news-paper, giving an account of the effects of the same storm in those parts, I found the beginning of the eclipse had been well observed there, though Boston lies N. E. of Philadelphia about 400 miles. This puzzled me, because the storm began with us so soon as to prevent any observation, and being a N. E. storm, I imagined it must have began rather sooner in places farther to the North Eastward, than it did at Philadelphia. I therefore mentioned it in a letter to my brother who lived at Boston; and he informed me the storm did not begin with them till near eleven o'clock, so that they had a good observation of the eclipse: And upon comparing all the other accounts I received from the several

---

and BF were both members of the Committee on Agriculture which the Society set up in 1760. *Gent. Mag.*, LXIV (1794), 864–5; Derek Hudson and Kenneth Luckhurst, *The Royal Society of Arts 1754–1954* (London, 1954), p. 63. BF and Small corresponded on a wide range of topics: grass seed, gout, hospital ventilation, and free trade. BF mentioned him in 1764 as one of the few friends to whom he had given a copy of his "Parable against Persecution." See above, VI, 117.

6. Printed as Letter XXXVI in the 1769 and 1774 editions of *Exper. and Obser.*

7. For earlier discussions of this topic, in the last of which the same facts and analogies were used, see above, III, 149, 392–3 n, 463–5.

colonies, of the time of beginning of the same storm, and since that of other storms of the same kind, I found the beginning to be always later the farther North-Eastward. I have not my notes with me here in England, and cannot, from memory, say the proportion of time to distance, but I think it is about an hour to every hundred miles.

From thence I formed an idea of the cause of these storms, which I would explain by a familiar instance or two. Suppose a long canal of water stopp'd at the end by a gate. The water is quite at rest till the gate is open, then it begins to move out through the gate; the water next the gate is first in motion, and moves towards the gate; the water next to that first water moves next, and so on successively, till the water at the head of the canal is in motion, which is last of all. In this case all the water moves indeed towards the gate, but the successive times of beginning motion are the contrary way, viz. from the gate backwards to the head of the canal. Again, suppose the air in a chamber at rest, no current through the room till you make a fire in the chimney. Immediately the air in the chimney being rarefied by the fire, rises; the air next the chimney flows in to supply its place, moving towards the chimney; and, in consequence, the rest of the air successively, quite back to the door. Thus to produce our North-East storms, I suppose some great heat and rarefaction of the air in or about the Gulph of Mexico; the air thence rising has its place supplied by the next more northern, cooler, and therefore denser and heavier, air; that, being in motion, is followed by the next more northern air, &c. &c. in a successive current, to which current our coast and inland ridge of mountains give the direction of North-East, as they lie N. E. and S.W.

This I offer only as an hypothesis to account for this particular fact; and, perhaps, on farther examination, a better and truer may be found. I do not suppose all storms generated in the same manner. Our North-West thundergusts in America I know are not; but of them I have written my opinion fully in a paper which you have seen.[8] I am, &c.   B. F.

---

8. See BF's letter to John Mitchell, April 29, 1749, above, III, 365–76. On April 13, 1772, Small sent BF a vivid account of a series of thunderstorms he had recently experienced during a voyage from Jamaica to New York.

My Dear friend   Philada: 15. 5 mo. 1760

I am convinced thou thinks it a Duty to pay those Debts, Custom as well as friendship has introduced, in answering Epistle
from thy numerous set of Acquaintance; and tho' thou art bless'd
with a large stock, yet the great demands on thee, must engage a
considerable part of that Time, which thou art endeavouring to
employ in promoting a general Benefit. Then if there should be
any merit in less'ning those demands; I have been entitled to as
great a share as any one of thy real friends, either in Europe or
America.

Some people here enquire do you know what B F is doing, we
hear so little of his proceedings? these are such who are seldom
satisfy'd without a Tumult or a Fray; and put me in mind that
when we receiv'd the important news, that General Forbes by his
prudent advances caused the French to retreat from Fort du
Quisne some of these people appear'd gloomy and shew'd no
marks of rejoycing, because it was a Campaign compleated without the Horrors of a Battle, Ravage and Bloodshed.

Thy friends here really wish to have a sight of thee, and thou
almost stands singular in this, that those who are not so,[1] would be
extreamly pleased at thy return, but since thy presence is indivisi-
ble, we must rest as content as possible, who know thou cannot be
absent from contributing to the real service of mankind, wherever
thou art placed by Providence: yet I have sometimes considered
the station of thy Debby and Sally who ardently wish for thee,
and are in part deprived of so great a blessing; but from all my
observations (and I frequently visit them), they bear thy long
absence with a more resign'd and Christian Spirit than could be
expected; and Sally appears to be a discreat young woman.[2]

The Wafers thou sent have been of great service to the Hospital,[3] which hath lately received some considerable donations;

9. This letter from BF's old friend responds, somewhat belatedly, to one of
Sept. 16, 1758; see above, VIII, 159–61.
1. That is, members of the proprietary party.
2. Sarah Franklin was in her seventeenth year.
3. On June 1, 1758, Roberts, treasurer of the Pa. Hospital, had asked BF
to send him a box of wafers, used for receiving the impression of the Hospital

and altho' it struggles under the want of a sufficient support, yet by the liberality of the people, 2 or £300 a year hath been added, to make up the deficiency; and I wish it was prudent and possible to endeavour to prevail on some of the good people in England to contribute to its Capital. I know thy earnest desire for its promotion, but this I also know, your great Men are not often TENANTS,[4] nor formed for prosecuting the humble employment of begging to advantage.

The fine painting on the Birmingham Tile thou sent, was a great curiosity, and I had it set in a neat frame, but before it came to hand, we red it a File, which may be readily excused, considering my employ, and its coming from an Iron country.[5]

I have endeavoured to gain some knowledge of our Indian affairs, and from all my observations, am of opinion, the only way of treating with success, is by a Manly freedom, ever attended with sincerity of heart, and that using Cunning or Temporizing with them will have no better effect than an European millitary power; and that many Gentlemen who might make a considerable figure at Westmister Hall, would appear but feeble Managers at an Indian Conference.[6]

Pursuant to thy Order, I have 2 or 3 times revisited the ancient Junto (Gentlemen for whom I have a great esteem) and I found some relaxation from the anxiety which attends business,[7] yet I cannot say, that the variety of trivial Chat (to which I am also inclin'd) affords satisfaction when under restraint so that in some

---

seal. He apparently employed them most often in acknowledging contributions. See above, VIII, 82–3. On Sept. 16, 1758, BF had sent the wafers.

4. Apparently a reference to Rev. Gilbert Tennent, who was in Great Britain, 1753–54, raising money for the College of New Jersey; see above, V, 231 n.

5. In his letter of Sept. 16, 1758, BF had written: "I send you a Birmingham Tile. I thought the neatness of the Figures would please you." Apparently Roberts, an ironmonger, had read "Tile" as "File" in BF's letter (BF's T's and F's look somewhat alike) and so had expected this gift from the famous metalworking town of Birmingham would turn out to be a tool for filing iron, not a ceramic tile.

6. As a Quaker, Roberts was probably hinting at his continued criticism of the Pa. administration's Indian policy. Westminster Hall was the site of the higher English law courts.

7. On Sept. 16, 1758, BF had gently chided Roberts for not having attended a meeting of the Junto since BF's departure.

respects there must be an Union of thought and affection to make Company altogether agreable, and the Hours glide with Ease and Pleasure. 'Twas with great anxiety I heard of a late attack against thee, by a malignant Fever,[8] and wish thou would endeavour to purge off the relict of every disorder that might contribute to lessen that chearfulness of heart, with which thou hast been long and happily distinguish'd; and then we shall not be concern'd whatever Dregs remain, if none are worse [in their Conseque]nces[9] than those [that] have appear'd in thee from the early [impressions of] P—btry.[1]

The Politics of our Gentlemen a[llied with "a certain] northern Climate"[2] are now here at a low Ebb, and much [the g]reat[er pa]rt of the people think right (i.e allways as we do) and [al]tho' Sm-th has gained [on] the rapid credulity of some of your Pr-lat-c-l Order,[3] yet with men who do not aim at ingrossing of power, he remains as contemptible as ever, and is shun'd by many of those who formerly appeared some of his greatest advocates; and I believe his vacation from Scribling at present arises from the

8. BF had written DF about this illness in February 1760, and she had probably told Roberts; see above, pp. 25, 27.

9. Here and in the next few lines holes in the MS have obliterated certain words. The letter was printed in *PMHB*, XXXVIII (1914), 290–3, and the words and parts of words inserted here in brackets are given there without indication of any mutilation of the original. While the present editors are not satisfied in every instance that the gaps in the MS are large enough to have included all the indicated writing, and while elsewhere in the letter as previously printed some minor errors in transcription are obvious, it has seemed advisable to give as is done here the earlier reading of these lines on the supposition that the MS was intact in 1914.

1. If the indicated reading is correct, Roberts may have been referring to events as far back as 1735, when BF came to the defense of Rev. Samuel Hemphill, who was under attack by the orthodox leaders of the Synod of Philadelphia. See above, II, 27–33, 37–126.

2. Probably a reference to the Scot William Smith and the Scotch-Irish Presbyterians William Allen and Francis Alison; see above, IV, 467–9 n; III, 296–7 n; IV, 470 n, respectively. The quotation marks may indicate an echo of BF's use of "in the *certain northern latitude*" with reference to Scots in his letter to *London Chron.*, dated May 9, 1759 (above, VIII, 340–56), where he defended the provincials against the slurs of Scottish officers in the British Army. Roberts may well have seen BF's letter in print.

3. Prelatical Order; that is, adherents of the Church of England, of which Smith was an ordained clergyman.

cautious manner of our G——ors conduct, since his last arrival among us.[4]

Dear Friend I hope thou wilt receive the preceeding variety of short notes by the hands of my son George, who as far as a Parent can see, is a Lad of a steady behaviour, and has always been an Obedient Child, his intention is to gain some further knowledge of the Iron Manufactures in England, and I think a few of thy useful hints respecting his conduct and journeyings thro' that Country, might be of particular Service;[5] and if I was to say 'twould lay me under an additional obligation, it must appear too much like a Compliment to a Gentleman whose time seems allotted to the service of the present and succeeding Age; and therefore in some similitude of the freedom of a former Address, in which thou wast concern'd,[6] I am of Opinion, a small share of that time is the right of thy old Friend HUGH ROBERTS

Give my kind respects to Billy

A Copy[7]

Addressed: To / Benjamin Franklin / at London

Endorsed:[8] Copy of a Letter To Benjamin Franklin at London 15 5 mo 1760 per hands of Geo Roberts

4. James Hamilton had arrived and assumed office as governor of Pa., Nov. 17, 1759.

5. While in Great Britain George Roberts (1737–1821) traveled some of the time with his friend Samuel Powel (1739–1793), later mayor of Philadelphia. Roberts was in Birmingham, apparently investigating the iron industry there, as late as December 1761. Some correspondence between the two young men, 1761–65, is printed in *PMHB*, XVII (1894), 35–42; XXX (1906), 244–5.

6. Possibly a reference to the report of an Assembly committee, Sept. 11, 1753, of which both BF and Roberts were members. This report analyzed the Proprietors' answer to an Assembly representation asking the Penns to share in the expenses of Indian treaties. Near the end the committee had commented: "We think the honest free Remarks in this Report, may be more conducive [to the public good and the true interests of the proprietary family] than a Thousand flattering Addresses." Above, v, 56.

7. While the document is an ALS, this was apparently a copy retained by Roberts, not the one his son delivered to BF.

8. In another hand.

To Mary Stevenson

ALS: Feehan Memorial Library, St. Mary of the Lake Seminary; transcript (part MS, part printed): Library of Congress.[9]

Cravenstreet, May 17. 1760.

I send my dear good Girl the Books I mention'd to her last Night.[1] I beg her to accept them as a small Mark of my Esteem and Friendship. They are written in the familiar easy Manner for which the French are so remarkable, and afford a good deal of philosophic and practical Knowledge, unembarras'd with the dry Mathematics us'd by more exact Reasoners, but which is apt to discourage young Beginners. I would advise you to read with a Pen in your Hand, and enter in a little Book short Hints of what you find that is curious or that may be useful; for this will be the best Method of imprinting such Particulars in your Memory, where they will be ready either for Practice on some future Occasion if they are Matters of Utility, or at least to adorn and improve your Conversation if they are rather Points of Curiosity. And, as many of the Terms of Science are such as you cannot have met with in your common Reading, and may therefore be unacquainted with, I think it would be well for you to have a good Dictionary at hand, to consult immediately when you meet with a Word you do not comprehend the precise Meaning of. This may at first seem troublesome and interrupting; but 'tis a Trouble that will daily diminish as you will daily find less and less Occasion for your Dictionary as you become more acquainted with the Terms; and in the meantime you will read with more Satisfaction because with more Understanding. When any Point occurs in which you would be glad to have farther Information than your Book affords you, I beg you would not in the least apprehend that I should think it a Trouble to receive and answer your Questions. It will be a Pleasure, and no Trouble. For tho' I may not be able, out of my own little Stock of Knowledge to afford you what you require, I can easily direct you to the Books where it may most readily be found. Adieu, and believe me ever, my dear Friend, Yours affectionately   B FRANKLIN

9. Printed, with the omission of the postscript, as Letter XLVIII in *Exper. and Obser.* (1769 edit.), pp. 444–5; (1774 edit.), pp. 454–5.

1. For these books, see above, p. 102 n.

My Compliments to Mr. and Mrs. Calender, and Miss Pitt.[2] I hope neither they nor you got any Cold last night.

Miss Stevenson

From the Earl of Bessborough[3]

AL: American Philosophical Society

May the 18 [1760?][4]

Lord Bessborough Complements to Mr. Franklin and desires the favour of his Company at Dinner next Sunday.

From Mary Stevenson Draft: American Philosophical Society

Dear Sir   June 6th. 60

The Happiness I enjoy'd last friday[5] has afforded me pleasing reflections for the week past. I attended with delight to your kind Instructions, and my highest Amusement ever since has been to recollect them. You obligingly condescended to satisfy my Curiosity about the Barometer, and by your explanation I clearly conceived the cause of the rise and fall of the Mercury; but, upon looking at it after you were gone, I was puzzl'd to find out how the Air has access to the end of the Tube which you told me was left open to relieve its pressure, it being cover'd with Wood. You bid me not apprehend you should think it a Trouble to receive

2. In a letter to an unidentified correspondent, Dec. 17, 1761, APS, Mary Stevenson reported that Mr. Callender had gone to Madeira to recover his health, but aside from this reference nothing is known about him and his wife. For Miss Pitt, a young friend of Polly's, see above, VIII, 340 n.

3. William Ponsonby, 2d Earl of Bessborough (c.1704–1793), succeeded to his father's title, July 4, 1758. He was an Irish M.P., 1725–58, and privy councilor, 1741; a British M.P., 1742–54; lord of the Admiralty, 1746–56; and joint postmaster general, July 2, 1759, to November 1762, and July 12, 1765, to November 1766. A Rockingham Whig, he was in "steady opposition" after 1766. *DNB;* Namier and Brooke, *House of Commons,* III, 306–7.

4. This invitation could have been written as early as May 1759 or as late as 1774, but 1760 is probable because, writing to David Hall on June 27 of this year, BF mentioned having dined recently with the postmasters general. See below, p. 179.

5. BF had apparently visited Polly at Wanstead.

and answer my Questions,[6] therefore I take the liberty of desiring you to solve this difficulty when you can afford to bestow a little time upon your grateful Polly.

I have read the first Volume of your Books,[7] which has afforded me great entertainment. I was highly pleas'd with the discription of Insects, which lead me to admire that Wisdom and Power that created them, and assign'd to each their proper use and employment: and taught me to observe there is nothing so trifling but it is necessary and worthy our attention. The Opinion that Corruption produces Insects is very well refuted from the certainty that Chance has no agency, and their always appearing in Putrified Meats is very well accounted for; but I am left in the dark, whether those Insects would ever arrive at the state of their parent. I find moral reflections frequently inserted so that my reading will not be a useless amusement only to satisfy an Idle Curiosity. I am my dear and honourd Friend most gratefully and affectionately yours

M STEVENSON[8]

To Mary Stevenson

ALS: Library of Congress[9]

Dear Polly,   Cravenstreet, June 11. 1760

'Tis a very sensible Question you ask, how the Air can affect the Barometer, when its Opening appears covered with Wood?[1] If indeed it was so closely covered as to admit of no Communication of the outward Air to the Surface of the Mercury, the Change of Weight in the Air could not possibly affect it. But the least Crevice is sufficient for the Purpose; a Pinhole will do the Business. And if you could look behind the Frame to which your Barometer is fixed, you would certainly find some small Opening.

6. BF invited questions from Polly in his letter of May 17, 1760; see above, p. 117.

7. See above, p. 102 n, for BF's gift of Pluche's *Spectacle de la Nature*, the first volume of which has eight dialogues about insects.

8. Written lower on the page and in another hand, probably by one of Mary Stevenson Hewson's sons many years later, appears the notation: "Copies of my mothers letters to Dr Franklin."

9. Printed, except for the postscript, as Letter XLIX in *Exper. and Obser.* (1769 edit.), pp. 445–8; (1774 edit.), pp. 456–8.

1. For many of the matters discussed in this letter, see the document immediately above.

There are indeed some Barometers in which the Body of Mercury at the lower End is contain'd in a close Leather Bag, and so the Air cannot come into immediate Contact with the Mercury: Yet the same Effect is produc'd. For the Leather being flexible, when the Bag is press'd by any additional Weight of Air, it contracts, and the Mercury is forc'd up into the Tube; when the Air becomes lighter, and its Pressure less, the Weight of the Mercury prevails, and it descends again into the Bag.

Your Observation on what you have lately read concerning Insects, is very just and solid. Superficial Minds are apt to despise those who make that Part of Creation their Study, as mere Triflers; but certainly the World has been much oblig'd to them. Under the Care and Management of Man, the Labours of the little Silkworm afford Employment and Subsistence to Thousands of Families, and become an immense Article of Commerce. The Bee, too, yields us its delicious Honey, and its Wax useful to a multitude of Purposes. Another Insect, it is said, produces the Cochineal, from whence we have our rich Scarlet Dye.[2] The Usefulness of the Cantharides, or Spanish Flies, in Medicine, is known to all, and Thousands owe their Lives to that Knowledge.[3] By human Industry and Observation, other Properties of other Insects may possibly be hereafter discovered, and of equal Utility. A thorough Acquaintance with the Nature of these little Creatures, may also enable Mankind to prevent the Increase of such as are noxious or secure us against the Mischiefs they occasion. These Things doubtless your Books make mention of: I can only add a particular late Instance which I had from a Swedish Gentleman of good Credit.[4] In the green Timber intended for Ship-building at the

2. Cochineal is extracted from the dried bodies of females of a species of insect (*Dactylopius coccus*, *Coccus cacti*) native to Mexico and Central America.

3. The *cantharis* or Spanish fly (*Lytta vescatoria*), also known as the blister beetle, is a brilliant green beetle, common in southern and eastern Europe. For medicinal purposes it is dried and powdered; applied externally, it reddens or blisters the skin and serves as a counter-irritant; taken internally, it was formerly used as an irritant or stimulant to the genito-urinary organs and was regarded as an aphrodisiac. It is still sometimes used for the last-named purpose for cattle.

4. Possibly Pehr Bjerchén (1731–1774), a student of Linnaeus and an eminent physician of Stockholm, who became an intimate of Peter Collinson and other scientific friends of BF during a prolonged stay in London, 1758–59.

King's Yards in that Country, a kind of Worms were found, which every Year became more numerous and more pernicious, so that the Ships were greatly damag'd before they came into Use. The King sent Linnaeus,[5] the great Naturalist, from Stockholm, to enquire into the Affair, and see if the Mischief was capable of any Remedy. He found on Examination, that the Worm was produc'd from a small Egg deposited in the little Roughnesses on the Surface of the Wood, by a particular kind of Fly or Beetle; from whence the Worm, as soon as it was hatch'd, began to eat into the Substance of the Wood, and after some time came out again a Fly of the Parent kind, and so the Species increas'd. The Season in which this Fly laid its Eggs, Linnaeus knew to be about a Fortnight (I think) in the Month of May, and at no other time of the Year. He therefore advis'd, that some Days before that Season, all the green Timber should be thrown into the Water, and kept under Water till the Season was over. Which being done by the King's Order, the Flies missing their usual Nests, could not increase; and the Species was either destroy'd or went elsewhere; and the Wood was effectually preserved, for after the first Year, it became too dry and hard for their purpose.

There is, however, a prudent Moderation to be used in Studies of this kind. The Knowledge of Nature may be ornamental, and it may be useful, but if to attain an Eminence in that, we neglect the Knowledge and Practice of essential Duties, we deserve Reprehension. For there is no Rank in Natural Knowledge of equal Dignity and Importance with that of being a good Parent, a good Child, a good Husband, or Wife, a good Neighbour or Friend, a good Subject or Citizen, that is, in short, a good Christian. Nicholas Gimcrack, therefore, who neglected the Care of his Family, to

---

Another source of the Swedish report might have been Linnaeus' "much-loved pupil," Daniel Charles Solander (1736–1782), F.R.S., botanist on Captain Cook's voyages in the *Endeavour* and keeper of the Natural History Department of the British Museum, but Solander does not seem to have arrived in London from Sweden until July 1760. Sir James Edward Smith, ed., *A Selection of the Correspondence of Linnaeus and Other Naturalists* (2 vols., London, 1821), I, 51–2, 97, 125–6, 131–2; Benjamin D. Jackson, *Linnaeus* (London, 1923), p. 382; Norah Gourlie, *The Prince of Botanists Carl Linnaeus* (London, 1953), pp. 245–6; *DNB*.

5. Carl Linnaeus (1707–1778), the great Swedish scientist and father of modern systematic botany.

pursue Butterflies, was a just Object of Ridicule, and we must give him up as fair Game to the Satyrist.[6]

Adieu, my dear Friend, and believe me ever Yours affectionately

B FRANKLIN

Your good Mother is well, and gives her Love and Blessing to you. My Compliments to your Aunts, Miss Pitt, &c.
Miss Stevenson

William Franklin to Joseph Galloway

ALS: Yale University Library

My dear Friend   London June 16. 1760

I wrote you a few Lines on Saturday last to go per the Pacquet,[7] in which I mention'd a Pamphlet wrote by my Father in Answer to the Remarks on the Letter to Two Great Men.[8] I could not send you one by that Opportunity, but as Capt. Monk has inform'd my Father that he is just upon the Point of sailing to America, and will take Charge of any Thing we may have to send, I have troubled him with one of the Pamphlets, and the Remarks, of which I desire your Acceptance. I formerly sent you one of the Letters to Two Great Men, wrote by Lord Bath,[9] so that you will have the whole Merits of the Dispute before you. The Author of the Remarks is thought by some to be Horace Walpole,[1] but 'tis

6. Joseph Addison in *The Tatler*, nos. 216 and 221, created Sir Nicholas Gimcrack, a "virtuoso," who squandered his estate on natural curiosities, died of exhaustion after chasing a butterfly five miles, and bequeathed such things as crocodile eggs, a hummingbird's nest, "English weeds pasted on royal paper," and "rat's testicles" to his friends and family.

7. Not found.

8. The Canada Pamphlet; above, pp. 47–100. WF's categorical statement is further contemporary evidence of BF's authorship.

9. Although WF, in common with many of his contemporaries, attributed *A Letter to Two Great Men, on the Prospect of Peace* to William Pulteney, Earl of Bath (1684–1764), it is now generally accepted that the author was John Douglas (1721–1807), although the earl, his patron, probably instigated the writing. See above, p. 52.

1. Horace Walpole (1717–1797), author and letter writer, son of Sir Robert Walpole. Writing to Henry Zouch, May 3, 1760, he flatly denied authorship of this "answer to my Lord Bath's rhapsody," although it was "true the

generally believ'd to be one Burk who is appointed Secretary of Guadaloupe, and 'tis said was assisted by Mr. Wood Secretary to Mr. Pitt.[2] Something by way of Answer to my Father's Pamphlet has appear'd in the London Chronicle, wrote by one Dr. Tucker a Clergyman,[3] who is an Intimate of Lord Hallifax's and patroniz'd by him, and is one of the bitterest Enemies N. America has in Britain. 'Tis so contemptible a Performance, that my Father could not think it worthy his Notice, were it not that it affords him an Opportunity of saying somethings omitted in his former Publication, and may be a means of silencing the Doctor, or at least of lessening his Influence in American Affairs for the future. On that Account he intends at his first Leisure to take it into Consideration, and publish something by way of Reply. The only Fault I have to find with the Pamphlet is, a Compliment to a certain Person which is by no means merited, but was put in at the Request of a Friend,[4] in hopes it might induce him to look with a more favorable

---

booksellers sold it as mine." Walpole and Bath had long been opponents. Wilmarth S. Lewis et al., eds., *The Yale Edition of Horace Walpole's Correspondence*, XVI (New Haven, 1951), 39.

2. The Board of Trade had recommended the appointment of William Burke to be secretary and register of the recently captured island of Guadeloupe on Aug. 10, 1759, and the Privy Council had approved the appointment, September 12. *Board of Trade Journal, 1759–1763*, pp. 56, 57, 125; *Acts Privy Coun., Col.*, IV, 428. Robert Wood (1717?–1771), traveler, writer, and politician, was undersecretary of state, 1756–63. *DNB*. The *Remarks on a Letter Address'd to Two Great Men* is now generally attributed to Burke. See above, p. 53.

3. Josiah Tucker (1712–1799), clergyman and economist, B.A. Oxon, 1736; M.A., 1739; D.D., 1755. He served successively as curate and rector of churches in Bristol and as a canon of the cathedral there, and in 1758 was appointed dean of Gloucester. His numerous writings on trade began in 1749; they often expressed unpopular views. He was unfriendly to the American colonies; he believed they provided no essential advantages to the mother country, and as the American Revolution approached he recommended that Great Britain let them separate without a struggle. Yet he supported the principle of royal authority in the colonies and was hostile to the political and constitutional views of colonial spokesmen. *DNB*. He and BF disagreed vigorously during later years. Whether he wrote the answers to the Canada Pamphlet which appeared in *London Chron.*, as WF believed, is not now known.

4. The "certain Person" was Lord Halifax; see above, p. 71. The "Friend" was probably Richard Jackson.

Eye on the Colonies. If it has that Effect I shall be glad. But I hate every Thing that has even the Appearance of Flattery.

The Opinion of the Board of Trade on the 11 Pensylvania Acts is not yet known.[5]

My Compliments to all enquiring Friends, and believe me to be with great Sincerity Dear Galloway Yours affectionately

WM: FRANKLIN

P.S. If the Speaker has not seen the *Remarks* please to lend them to him.

From John Sargent[6]   ALS: American Philosophical Society

Dear Sir   Thursday 19 June [1760][7]

I shall be heartily glad to see You at Mayplace on Sunday—or Saturday—and at all Times.

Alas Quebeck! I little thought that We should have to mingle our Sighs for that, when We met.

What a Barbarism in a General threatned with a Siege, to go out to fight Those who found[?] themselves strong enough to undertake forceing Him in his Fastness! There never was such Folly![8]

Adieu—I will not dwell on these unpleasing Subjects. May We meet in Health! Yours most sincerely   J SARGENT

5. See below, p. 126.
6. See above, VII, 322 n.
7. Sargent's anxiety about Quebec dates this letter in 1760. *London Chron.*, June 17–19, 1760, reported that Brig. Gen. James Murray had sallied from Quebec with 3000 men and attacked a French army "supposed to consist of the greatest part of the force of Canada, as they were on their march to make an attempt against the said place." Defeated with heavy losses, Murray retired to the city to prepare to resist a siege.
8. Horace Walpole commented to Sir Horace Mann, June 27, 1760: "Who the deuce was thinking of Quebec? America was like a book one has read and done with but here we are on a sudden reading our book backwards. . . . The year 1760 is not the year 1759." Wilmarth S. Lewis et al., eds., *The Yale Edition of Horace Walpole's Correspondence*, XXI (New Haven, 1960), 414.

From Mary Stevenson

ALS: American Philosophical Society

Dear Sir   Wanstead June 23d. 1760

You who are no Stranger to the Feelings of Humanity will readily conceive the anxiety of my Mind while I thought my Friend[9] in Danger: It is only such a Situation as I was then in that can make me neglect your Favours.

Upon examining the Barometer after I receiv'd your Letter,[1] I found a small Crevice where the piece of hollow wood which covers the Mercury is join'd to the Frame.

You can't imagine how important I felt to find you thought me worthy so much of your time and attention. I thank you my dear Preceptor for your Indulgence in satisfying my Curiosity, and for the pleasing Instruction you give, which I will endeavour shall not be lost. As my greatest Ambition is to render myself amiable in your Eyes I will be careful never to transgress the bounds of Moderation you prescribe. I have so firm a reliance on your sincerity and regard, that I think, if you imagin'd my pursuit of Knowledge would be detrimental, you would not have given me any encouragement, but have check'd my Curiosity, knowing I should have chearfully submitted to your Judgement.

I regard you as one of my best Friends, and to continue you such is the wish nearest my Heart. I am with the highest Esteem and Gratitude Dear Sir your affectionate and obedient humble Servant   M STEVENSON.

Board of Trade: Report on Pennsylvania Laws

Copy: Public Record Office, Colonial Office Papers, 5/1295, pp. 296–413

Franklin's efforts to settle the Assembly's differences with the Proprietors by direct negotiations had ended in November 1758 with their reply to his Heads of Complaint and their refusal to deal further with him personally (above, VIII, 178–83, 193–4). Thereafter it became necessary to transfer the debate to more public platforms and to bring the issues to adjudication by the Privy Council after hearings before the Board of Trade and the Council's Committee for Plantation Affairs.

9. Possibly either Miss Pitt or Mr. Callender (above, p. 118 n).
1. See above, pp. 119–22.

Franklin's petition, early in 1759, in support of Teedyuscung's complaints that the Proprietors had defrauded the Indians of land (above, VIII, 264–76, 379–89, 432–3) may be regarded as a preliminary skirmish in this phase of the struggle. It could settle none of the major issues but it might prove advantageous if it succeeded in drawing attention to the alleged misbehavior of the Penns in the management of their proprietorship.

The major battle took place in 1760, and was the main object of Franklin's attention from February 16, when he first instructed his solicitor, until September 2, when the Privy Council rendered its final orders. At issue was the confirmation or disallowance of nineteen acts passed by the Assembly and approved by Governor Denny between Sept. 20, 1758, and Oct. 19, 1759. The Penns objected to eleven of these measures and sought their disallowance on the grounds that in one way or another these infringed their proprietary rights and privileges or the royal prerogatives entrusted to their exercise by the charter to their father. Franklin and Charles, as agents of the Assembly, sought to have them all confirmed as legally proper and as being necessary for the welfare of the colony and its inhabitants.

The official copies of these acts had all reached England substantially before Dec. 8, 1759, when Thomas Penn wrote Richard Peters that he had ordered Ferdinand Paris to present them to the Privy Council. There were delays, however, because "there have been no [Privy Council] Committees for common Business held yet" and Paris had been seriously ill for about a fortnight.[2] The lawyer died on December 16 and Penn appointed Henry Wilmot to take over his duties, but the Proprietors took no formal action to get the acts considered for nearly three months.

One of the nineteen acts directly concerned Franklin. Approved by Denny on September 29, as one of the last in the series, it authorized Franklin as agent to receive Pennsylvania's share of the £200,000 grant voted by Parliament to be distributed among the colonies in repayment of wartime expenses, and it directed him to deposit the funds received in the Bank of England subject to drafts by the Trustees of the General Loan Office. Unwilling to wait for the Proprietors to act on this bill, Franklin had his solicitor Francis Eyre present it at the Privy Council Office on February 16 in order to get it referred in the usual manner to the Council Committee and the Board of Trade for report.[3] Further to expedite the matter, Eyre went to the Privy Council Office on the 29th,

2. Penn to Peters, Dec. 8, 1759, Penn Papers, Hist. Soc. Pa.
3. *Acts Privy Coun., Col.,* IV, 439; Francis Eyre's bill, above, pp. 22–4. BF's action had a significant effect on the final disposition of this measure.

picked up the order of reference to the Board of Trade dated the 20th, and carried it to the Board's office.[4]

The Proprietors' new solicitor presented the other eighteen acts to the Privy Council on March 13 and its committee referred them to the Board of Trade the same day, together with the Penns' petition against eleven of the acts, including the Agency Act.[5] During March Eyre made "many Attendances at the Board of Trade to try to get the Agency Act considered separately,"[6] but he was unsuccessful. At first, according to Penn, the Board decided that its hearings on all nineteen acts should take place during "Passion Week and Easter" (March 31 to April 6), this being "the only time the Board could hear so long a Cause."[7] But again there were delays: the Board actually put down the hearings for April 18, meanwhile asking its counsel, Sir Matthew Lamb, to report on the acts "in point of law"; then on April 17 it ordered a postponement until May 1 because of the trial for murder of Earl Ferrers, begun the day before in the House of Lords, at which the Penns' counsel, the attorney and solicitor general, were appearing for the Crown; then two further postponements, to May 21, were granted at Thomas Penn's request because of the death of his young son.[8]

At last the hearings took place; they occupied all of the Board of Trade's time on May 21, 22, and 23, and most of it on June 3.[9] Thomas

4. Eyre's bill.

5. *Acts Privy Coun., Col.*, IV, 439.

6. Eyre's bill.

7. Penn to Hamilton, March 8, 1760, Penn Papers, Hist. Soc. Pa.

8. *Board of Trade Journal*, 1759–1763, pp. 98–9, 101, 104, 106–7; Penn to Hamilton, April 10, 1760; to Peters, May 10, 1760, Penn Papers, Hist. Soc. Pa. The trial of Laurence Shirley, 4th Earl Ferrers, for killing his steward, John Johnson, was one of the sensations of the times. Lord Ferrers was convicted and was publicly hanged at Tyburn, May 5. Penn's boy William (July 22, 1756–April 24, 1760), was his third son to die during childhood. *PMHB*, XXI (1897), 346.

9. The account that follows is based on the formal record in *Board of Trade Journal*, 1759–1763, pp. 108–13, and on Thomas Penn's letters: to Hamilton, May 24 and June 6, 1760; to Peters, June 9, 1760, Penn Papers, Hist. Soc. Pa. Most regrettably, none of BF's letters to Norris, Galloway, or any other Pa. Assembly leader during the spring and summer of 1760 has survived. While the final pages of BF's autobiography, written many years later, discuss this contest in general and the later hearing before the Privy Council Committee in some detail, they contain no specific account of the proceedings at the Board of Trade. Thus we have no record of his own reactions, at the time or in later memory, to what took place during these four days when he sat silently in the hearing room and listened to the arguments of counsel for both sides. The Journal as printed gives the third day of the hearings errone-

and Richard Penn were present with their counsel, Charles Pratt, the attorney general, and Charles Yorke, the solicitor general.[1] On the other side, the Assembly agents, Franklin and Charles, and Franklin's son William attended with their solicitor, Francis Eyre, and their counsel, William de Grey and Richard Jackson. In some of his letters Penn expressed satisfaction that none of the London Quakers were present during the hearings, their absence presumably showing their lack of sympathy with the Assembly's position.

Pratt opened for the Proprietors, proposing to take up the laws one by one and to begin with the £100,000 Supply Act of 1759. De Grey objected, pointing out not unreasonably that the Agency Act had come to the Board first, "referred to by a separate order," and that the money was much needed in Pennsylvania "to carry on the public service." But he courteously waived his objection when the attorney general said he had only that morning received notice of this proposed order of procedure and was unprepared to discuss the Agency Act then.[2] Thereupon Pratt began his argument with a general attack on the Assembly's record of encroachment on proprietary rights and the royal prerogative, its "almost rebellious declarations" against royal instructions concerning paper currency, its denial of the Proprietors' right to instruct the governor, and its "other acts of avowed democracy." In a passage reminis-

ously as "Friday, May 24." On Thursday the hearing had been adjourned "till to-morrow eleven of the clock," and Friday was the 23d. Eyre's bill confirms that the correct date was the 23d.

1. Presumably, Henry Wilmot, as solicitor for the Penns, also attended, though he would not have been allowed to speak and is not mentioned in the record. The Penns' engagement of the law officers of the Crown as counsel was something of a *coup*. Penn told Hamilton, March 8, that they had accepted the brief "contrary to their usual practice." He reported to Peters, June 9, that they had stated their resolution at the hearings "while they were in those offices, never to appear against us, as inconsistent with their Duty, but to advocate our Cause as the Cause of the Crown, declaring they now appeared for the Crown as well as for us." The record of the hearings reports that BF's counsel, William de Grey, "opened his argument by observing, in answer to what had been thrown out by the Attorney and Solicitor General, that he was equally bound, though not equally authorized, to support the rights of the Crown." Unquestionably, the official positions of Pratt and Yorke, as well as their personal political connections, were advantageous to the Proprietors.

2. Later de Grey asked permission to postpone until the following day his reply to the attorney and solicitor general's objections to the Supply Act, as he was not fully prepared on them. Lord Halifax, president of the Board of Trade, grudgingly consented.

128

cent of Thomas Penn's interview with Franklin in January 1758,[3] Pratt spoke of "the unreasonable bounty of the first Proprietary, in acquiescing in that law, by which the assembly was made perpetual and indissoluble, [which] in great measure laid the foundation of these usurpations and encroachments," and he added that he hoped to see the day when Parliament would repeal that concession. Pratt then reviewed the Assembly's attempts since 1755 to tax the proprietary estates and the other encroachments on proprietary rights included in the various supply bills presented to the governors. Solicitor General Yorke followed, charging that the Supply Act of 1759 had become law by direct bribery of Governor Denny,[4] pointing out "the arbitrary method of assessment and levy" provided in the measure, and describing its other objectionable features.

Franklin's senior counsel, William de Grey, presented the Assembly's case for the Supply Act on the 22d. He "insisted on the faith and loyalty of his constituents," cited the testimony of British Army officers in America on the "particularly meritorious" conduct of the Assembly, declared that the laws in question had all been passed in complete conformity to the royal charter and the other documents "which together formed the law and constitution of the colony," denied that the proprietors ought to "rely on the Crown for redress" of personal grievances since they bound their deputies financially to obey their instructions, and asserted that there was no proof Denny had been bribed since the sums voted to him "were given in the same way sums given by the Assembly to their Governors for their support were always given." De Grey and Jackson then answered in detail the specific objections of opposing counsel to the Supply Act. The attorney general presented his rebuttal and the session was adjourned. The debate on the Supply

3. This was the interview at which Penn contended that his father had exceeded the authority granted him in the royal charter and, if he had lured prospective settlers with promises he had no right to grant, it was their own fault that they had been "deceived, cheated, and betrayed." BF wrote to Norris that Penn had said this "with a kind of triumphing laughing Insolence, such as a low Jockey might do when a Purchaser complained that He had cheated him in a Horse." When a copy of BF's letter got back to Penn he was enraged and would have nothing more to do with BF. See above, VII, 360–4; VIII, 151, 292–3, 312–13. In reporting the attorney general's argument Thomas Penn seemed to take great satisfaction in Pratt's attack on the Assembly's possession of "such powers of Meeting, as my Father unwarrantably granted to them." To Peters, June 9; see also to Hamilton, June 6, Penn Papers, Hist. Soc. Pa.

4. A reference to the £1000 presented to Denny as a salary grant immediately upon his approving the Supply Act; see above, VIII, 327 n.

Act, clearly the most important of the laws in the minds of all concerned, had required two full days of argument.

On May 23d Solicitor General Yorke and Richard Jackson opened the session by debating the Re-emitting Act of June 20, 1759,[5] and then Pratt and de Grey took up the rest of the day arguing the Act for Recording Warrants and Surveys. No details of these discussions appear in the official record. At the adjourned hearing on June 3, after the Board of Trade had dealt briefly with minor matters concerning two other colonies, they called in the parties to the Pennsylvania dispute and "heard the arguments offered" by both sides on the remaining contested acts. None of them could have required very much time. On June 5 the Board "took into consideration the laws of Pennsylvania" referred to them "and, after some time spent therein, ordered the draught of a report to the Lords of the Committee of Council thereupon to be prepared." The document printed below was bound to be a long one; it required considerable time for the Board's permanent staff to put it in form. On June 24, however, it was laid before the Board and "was agreed to, transcribed and signed."[6] Thus ended the first phase of the great debate.

Penn's letters during the hearings and before the Board released its report show that he was well pleased with the performance of his counsel and confident that it would uphold him on all, or nearly all, the points at issue. Franklin and his son William, he believed, had heard so much said by the attorney and solicitor general in criticism of the Assembly's position, "that we all think he will not dare to attempt such an opposition to Government, when he returns."[7] On June 27 Penn informed Governor Hamilton of the recommendations of the Board, obviously pleased at their general tenor, while he explained the reasons why the Board had recommended approval of four of the eleven acts to which he had objected.[8] He was greatly displeased, however, at the criticism leveled at his brother and himself at the end of the report for their failure to maintain adequately the prerogatives of the Crown entrusted to them.[9]

The disappearance of Franklin's letters to Norris and others in Pennsylvania during this period make it impossible to state just what he felt when he read the Board's report. Certainly he must have been

5. The Journal does not specifically mention the act of September 29, 1759, supplementary to the Re-emitting Act, as having been discussed, but it probably was included in the debate on the main act.

6. *Board of Trade Journal,* 1759–1763, p. 120.

7. Penn to Peters, June 9, 1760, Penn Papers, Hist. Soc. Pa.

8. Penn to Hamilton, June 27, 1760, Penn Papers, Hist. Soc. Pa.

9. See below, pp. 171–3.

greatly disappointed at its tone and at its recommendation of disallowance of some acts Norris had indicated as being most desirable. All was
not yet lost, however, for the Privy Council's Committee still had to
deal with the report and there was at least a chance that it might be
induced to reverse the Board of Trade's recommendations as to one or
more of the important acts, if not as to all. The second phase of the
great debate, therefore, would come in a possible hearing before that
higher authority.[1]

Whitehall June 24th 1760

Report to the Lords of the Committee of Council upon 19 Acts
passed in Pennsylvania in 1758 and 1759.

To the Right Honourable the Lords of the Committee
of His Majesty's most Honourable Privy Council
for Plantation Affairs,

My Lords, Pursuant to your Lordships orders of the 20th of
February and 13th of March last, We have taken into our Consideration 19 Acts passed in the Province of Pennsylvania in 1758.
and 1759, and also a Petition of the Proprietaries of the said
Province, complaining of Eleven of the said Acts: And in Compliance with the Prayer of that Petition, they have been heard by
their Counsel, His Majesty's Attorney and Solicitor General, who
stated themselves as Appearing not only in behalf of the Proprietaries but in virtue likewise of their Office in support of the Rights
and Prerogatives of the Crown. The said eleven Acts have on the
other hand, been supported by the Agent of the Colony on the
part of the House of Representatives, who have likewise been
heard by their Counsel, Mr. De Grey and Mr. Jackson.

And, in order to lay before your Lordships our Opinion in the
most concise and perspicuous manner we are able, and to avoid
that perplexity which must necessarily arise from a long detail of
Verbal Extracts from such a Variety of Laws, containing so many
different Regulations, we shall satisfy ourselves with stating to
your Lordships the General Tendency and principal Provisions of
the several Laws, in the order we shall consider them, referring
to the Laws themselves, to which it will always be more usefull
for your Lordships to recur, if a more particular Satisfaction, and
therefore a more minute and Circumstantial Knowledge of them,
should, in any case, be thought necessary.

1. See below, pp. 196–211.

But before we take the Liberty of Stating to your Lordships our Opinion either upon the General Nature, or upon the particular Provisions of these Laws, we apprehend it will be Necessary for us to remove two Objections which have been oppos'd on the part of the Assembly, to prevent our entring at all into the Merits of those Laws which your Lordships have already, or which, under the same circumstances, you may hereafter think proper to refer to our Consideration.

The first of these Objections is derived from a Construction of that Clause in the Royal Charter by which it is provided that all Laws passed in Pensylvania shall be transmitted to England, and that if they shall be found to contain any thing contrary to the Sovereignty or Prerogative of the Crown, or to the Faith and Allegiance of the Subject, they may within six Months be declared void by His Majesty; if not, that they shall remain in full force. From the Express Mention of those purposes for which the Negative is here declared to be reserv'd, it is contended that the right of annulling the Laws of this Province is confin'd to the preservation of the Prerogative and Sovereignty of the Crown and the meer general Dependance of the Subject.

By the second it is contended, that, however discretionary the Power of exercising that Negative may be in the Crown, the Proprietaries are exclud'd from claiming any Benefit by it, and, that by Consent of their Deputy they are finally tied down, as Parties; without any Title to Complain or any Possibility of Relief.

Upon the first of these Objections, we beg Leave to state the only two Clauses in the Charter relative to the passing Laws in Pensylvania. In the first of these, it is provided, that they shall be consonant to Natural Equity, and, as far as Circumstances will admit, conformable to the laws of England:[2] In the second, that they shall not be contrary to the Sovereignty or Prerogative of the Crown.[3] And we apprehend, my Lords, it would be a Construction

2. Section V of the royal charter to William Penn on judicial powers includes this condition: "PROVIDED nevertheless, That the same Laws [to be enforced] be consonant to Reason, and not repugnant or contrary, but (as near as conveniently may be) agreeable to the Laws and Statutes, and Rights of this Our Kingdom of England." The section then reserves to the King the right of hearing and determining appeals from the judgments of provincial courts.

3. Section VII of the royal charter on the transmission of local laws to England requires that all laws be submitted to the Privy Council within

altogether unreasonable to suppose, that where there are two Reservations, of which the Crown has been equally tender and upon which the Charter is equally Explicit, that the Clause which relates to the Execution, should be confin'd only to one of them, and not extended equally to both; and we are thoroughly perswad'd, that the Crown would and ought to be to the full as jealous, on behalf of the Subject, that Laws shoud not be contrary to Reason or repugnant to the Laws of England, as it would be for the Protection of its own Sovereignty and Prerogative; and it is scarce possible to suppose, that the Crown shoud have reserv'd to itself, by the Appeal, the Judicial Power in its full Extent, which is of less Importance, and inferior Dignity, and at the same time have divested it self of the far Greater part of the legislative, which is essential to its Royalty, and which is always exercised by the King in his own Person.

And that this has been the Construction of these Clauses appears from the uniform Practice of this Board, which has frequently advis'd His Majesty to annull the Laws of this Province not only for being derogatory to His Majesty's Prerogative, not only because they were repugnant to Equity or the Laws of England, but frequently upon a meer consideration of their general Inexpediency. And this Opinion has been so Uniform on the part of the Board that there is no Instance to the contrary, and, on the part of the Province, there has been no Complaint or Remonstrance whatsoever against the Exercise of this Power by the Crown in its utmost Latitude: On the contrary, We beg leave to Observe, that this Power has been ratified in the fullest manner by the Province itself, in an Act of its own. In virtue of the Powers of the Charter, which we have already had Occasion to mention to your Lordships, several Laws had, in the Year 1705, been declared void by order of Her Majesty in Council *only* and not, according

---

five years of enactment, "And if any of the said Laws, within the Space of Six Months after they shall be so transmitted and delivered, be declared by us, Our Heirs and Successors, in Our or Their Privy Council, inconsistent with the Sovereignty or lawful Prerogative of Us, our Heirs or Successors, or contrary to the Faith and Allegiance due to the Legal Government of this Realm," from Penn or his heirs or the inhabitants of the province, and shall be adjudged and declared void by the King under the privy seal, such laws shall be void; otherwise they shall remain in full force.

to the express Words of the Charter, under the Privy Seal.[4] To remove any Doubts which might arise concerning the Repeal of those Acts, and to Supply that Defect of Formality, the Assembly in Pennsylvania passed a Law Confirming the Repeal of all the Acts which before the Year 1734, had been declared void by order in council, amongst which there are Laws of almost every different Description, and but a few of which can be brought under the limited Construction now contended for by the Assembly, as affecting the Sovereignty and Prerogative of the Crown, or the Allegiance of the Subject; And, my Lords it is Material to Observe, that this Law of the Province of Pennsylvania was Passed not to remove any Doubts that had arose from the Power which the Crown had exercised, but merely to Supply the Omission of those Forms which the Crown, in its Charter had prescrib'd.[5]

This, we conceive, my Lords is the Right of the Crown, as it appears upon the Face of the Charter, and this we have stated to your Lordships for no other purpose than to answer those Objections which have been raised against the Power of the Crown, and which have been drawn from the Charter itself, not in anywise Admitting that the Right of the Crown has its Origin or derives any part of its Validity from the Charter, or from any Confirmation of it by the Legislature of Pensylvania; on the contrary we are fully of Opinion, that every British Subject, whilst he remains in any Country under the Allegiance of the Crown, has an indisputable Right to avail Himself of it's just Prerogatives for the Redress of any Grievances which He may suffer; And from this Benifit we apprehend no one Subject can be shut out by any

4. As mentioned in the note immediately above, the Penn charter specified that any disallowance of a law was to be done "under Our or Their Privy Seal." This provision was a departure from the practice operative for the disallowance of laws of all other colonies, which was accomplished and notified by an order in council bearing the seal of the Privy Council and signed by its clerk. The privy seal is next after the great seal in authority among all British seals and ranks substantially higher than the seal of the Privy Council.

5. The special provision for authenticating the disallowance of a Pa. act had apparently been overlooked by officials in England until a lawsuit there involving a disallowance brought the matter to public attention in 1733. At the instigation of the Proprietors Gov. Patrick Gordon proposed an act of Assembly to confirm that all such past disallowed laws were void; it was passed Jan. 19, 1734. *Pa. Col. Recs.*, III, 535, 539, 541–2; *Statutes at Large, Pa.*, IV, 257–60.

Favour or Partiality to another, or by any Grant or Charter what-soever; and that therefore for the exercise of that Protection in it's most essential Part, there is a Reservation of the King's final Negative necessaryly implied, tho' it should not be Actually Expressed, in every Charter by which the King gives Permission to his Subjects to make Laws in America: and it is in consequence alone of this Right of Protection in the Subject and of Superin-tendence, inherent in the Supreme Power and inseparable from it, that His Majesty has frequently abrogated the Laws which have been made in Charter Governments, and particularly in the Colony of Connecticut, where the Power of the Crown is much more limited, where there is no reservation in the Charter of the Royal Negative, nor any Regulation for transmitting their Laws to England, both of which are particularly provided for in the Charter of Pensylvania.[6]

In every Light therefore, My Lords, which we consider it, from the Reason of the thing; from the express words of the Charter; from that Construction of the Regulations which reason requires; from the uninterrupted Course of the Precedents, from the Assem-blies Admission of that Right, and from that inherent Part of Sov-ereignty by which the Crown owes an equal Protection to all its Subjects, we are clearly of Opinion, that His Majesty has an undoubted Right to examine into the Merits of this and every other provincial Law, to give or to withhold his Negative upon any good reasons which may be Suggested to him by the Wis-dom of his Privy Council, or by his own Royal Prudence and Discretion.

We come now to lay before your Lordships, our Opinion upon

6. The leading example of the disallowance of a Connecticut law was the action of the Privy Council, Feb. 15, 1728, repealing the act of 1692 for the distribution of intestate estates. This disallowance was the result of a judicial appeal from the colonial courts in the case of Winthrop *v.* Lechmere. Under the Connecticut law the property of a person dying without a will was to be distributed (after provision for the widow's life interest) in equal shares among all children except the eldest son, who was to receive a double portion. This arrangement was contrary to the English common law whereby the entire estate descended to the eldest son. Charles M. Andrews, "The Con-necticut Intestacy Law," *Yale Review*, Old Series, III (1894), 261–92; revised and printed without notes in 1933 as Pamphlet II of the *Connecticut Tercen-tenary Pamphlet* series.

the second Head of general Objections, that the Proprietaries, having by their Deputy consented to these Laws, are not Entitled to sollicit the Interposition of the Crown, in their behalf. If Your Lordships should approve what we have already stated, as to the Power of the Crown, by the General Reservation of the Charter, we apprehend you will Necessarily be of Opinion, that the Crown should not preclude itself from any Information by whomsoever it may be furnish'd, and by which it may be better qualify'd to direct the exercise of the Power it has reserved; and that the Crown will hear the Proprietaries for that purpose, in common with any other Person in the Province, all of whom must be considered as being, in common with them, Parties to every Law, having by the Nature of the Constitution, given their Assent to it, either actually by themselves, or virtually by their representatives. We apprehend therefore, My Lords, that the Crown will not only permit, but will encourage, the throwing all possible Light upon every Provincial Law that may be passed; that it will dissregard entirely the Person who complains, and attend only to the Justice of the Act, and the Merits of the Complaint. Whatever therefore may be the Situation of the Proprietaries, the Crown will still execise its Negative in such Manner as it thinks proper, and if, by the Strict Letter of the Law, the Proprietaries should be tied down, we apprehend it would be extreamly injurious, that they should in reason and Equity be considered as a Party to those Acts. For, my Lords, in the Course of this hearing it has been made Sufficiently apparent, by the Manner in which the Assembly detained the Salary of the Deputy Governor, till he had given his Assent to those Laws, and by the manner in which they paid it, when He passed them, (A separate sum being received by him upon his Consent to separate Laws) that it was meant by the Assembly and understood by the Governor as a Consideration for his Passing these exceptionable Acts, in Contradiction to his Instructions. And, if it was possible for us to entertain any doubt upon this Head, the Assembly themselves would not permit us: A vote of their House has been produced in which they state, that the Governor had Acted not only against the Proprietary Instructions but against the Remonstrances of the Council appointed to advise him, that they conclude therefore, He will incur the Forfeiture of his Bond, against the Penalties of which by their Vote, they undertake to Indemnify him.[7] And tho' some Instances have been brought in which the Salary of Governors has been permitted to be in Arrear, yet no Instance has been produc'd, that is in any manner parallel to the present. But what peculiarly distinguishes this Case from all others is the Vote of Indemnity, and it would be particularly hard to suffer the Assembly, by taking Advantage of their own wrong, at once by their Vote of Indemnification to declare, that the Assent to these Laws was not the Act of the Proprietaries, and then to Contend that they should be bound by it: For we apprehend, My Lords, that the Position laid down by this Assembly in their Vote that the Deputy Governor is not in any Case bound by the Instruction of his Principal, but is vested, by the Nature of his Office, with discretionary Powers to act as he thinks proper, is not only against the Essential Nature of all deputed Power, which is always qualified by such Limitations as the Principal imposes on it, but, if taken concurrently with their Proceedings in regard to the Salary, would establish an Uniform System of Collusion between the Governor and the Assembly.

We apprehend likewise it would be productive of the greatest Injustice, not only to the Proprietaries but to the Province, if the Assembly should be encouraged in so unwarrantable a Practice, as to apply the Money of the People, first to corrupt the Deputy-Governor, and then to take away the means by which his principals may bind him to his Duty, or punish him for the Violation of it; and that it must also Occasion the most serious Mischief in Government, if, in this Colony, Consisting only of two Branches of Legislature, the one shall be permitted by a Publick Act to corrupt the party entrusted with the Prerogatives of the other: and we are perswaded, that your Lordships will approve our recommending it to His Majesty to discountenance, by every possible method, so Collusive and iniquitous a Practice.

7. "*Resolved, N.C.D.* That in case the Proprietaries shall prosecute or sue the Honourable William Denny, Esq; the present Governor of this Province, for the Breach of any Instruction, in passing any of the said Bills, this House will, as far as in them lies, support the said Governor in the Defence of such Suit, in order to the Determination of the Validity and Legality of such Instructions, in Opposition to the Royal Grant, and the Charters and Laws of this Province, and that they will give Orders to their Agents in London for that Purpose, and also will, and do hereby recommend the same to the next succeeding Assembly." Passed July 7, 1759, *Votes*, 1758–59, pp. 91–2.

137

For these Reasons, my Lords, we are clearly of Opinion, upon the second Head of General Objections, that the Crown will be open to every Information from every Person, That the Proprietaries are in this particular Case not so concluded, by the Act of their Deputy, as to have no Title to Complain; That on the contrary, the Act of their Deputy has given them the Strongest reasons to Complain, and the justest Title to redress; That, as wrong'd Individuals, they have a Right to resort to the Crown for Relief, and, That, as Persons intrusted with some of its most Valuable Prerogatives, they come before His Majesty on the fairest Grounds imaginable: For, my Lords, it has uniformly been the Practice of this Board to preserve to the utmost of their Power the just Prerogatives of the Crown, wherever they may be lodg'd, and even tho' the Trustees should be willing to part with them, much more when, in Pursuance of their Duty, they Come laudably to prevent any Delapidation of them in their Hands.

We have dwelt, My Lords, the longer on these preliminary Points, because it is by the Determination of them, that our Right to a more particular Discussion of these Laws must stand or fall, and because it is upon the latter of these Objections, rather than upon the merits of the particular Regulations, that the Counsel for the Assembly have Supported the whole Body of the Acts Objected to by the Proprietaries; but, above all, because they turn on matters of the Last Importance to his Majesty's Prerogative, and to the Peace, Order and good Government not only of this but of several others of his Majesty's Plantations in America.

These two Points being establish'd, the Right of the Proprietaries to Complain and the Right of the Crown to redress, we come next, my Lords, to Consider how far the several Laws refer'd to us by Your Lordships may deserve his Majesty's Disapprobation or Allowance.

And the first Act upon which we shall take the Liberty of stating our Opinion to Your Lordships is the Act of 1759. for raising one Hundred Thousand Pounds, departing from the order of Your Lordships reference, and pursuing that method in which these several Laws were Objected to by the Counsel for the Proprietaries and Supported in Behalf of the Assembly.

This Act is entituled

138

An Act for granting to His Majesty the sum of one Hundred Thousand Pounds and for striking the same in Bills of Credit, in the manner therein directed, and for providing a Fund for Sinking the said Bills of Credit by a Tax on all Estates, real and personal, and Taxables within this Province.[8]

And the Object of it is, granting a Supply to his Majesty suitable to the Circumstances of the Province and the Exigencies of Government, to be raised by a Tax on all real and personal Property within the Province.

It will be necessary for us to Observe to Your Lordships that before the Year 1755, no Attempt had been made to include the Proprietary Estate in any general Land Tax Bill; the Proprietaries contended Against this Innovation; and, by contributing towards the general Supply by a free Gift of five Thousand Pounds, their Estates were, upon that consideration, not included either in the Land Tax Bill of 1755. or in the Tax Bills of 1757. and 1758. which were considered as Suppliments to it.[9] This Expedient however procur'd but a temporary Suspention of the Dispute, which was reviv'd again and Continued for a long time to Disturb the Tranquility of the Province, and to embarrass the Publick Proceedings. To quiet these Dissensions, the Proprietaries at last consented, that their Estates should be Tax'd, interposing only these very reasonable Conditions, that the Impositions should be laid on Objects properly Taxable, that Equality should be observed in the Quantity and Justice in the mode of Taxation; This gave rise to the Act of 1759, by Your Lordships Reference now under our Consideration, by which the Proprietary Estates were tax'd not only to the Supply then given, but retrospectively towards all the Supplies since 1755 inclusive, allowing them Credit for the sum of five Thousand Pounds received, if it should happen to fall short of their Proportion of the Tax. This Regulation which might appear otherwise unreasonable, was founded on a proposition of the Proprietaries in a Letter to Mr. Franklyin the Agent of the Assembly.[1]

8. Passed April 17, 1759, *Statutes at Large, Pa.*, V, 379–96. For this measure and Norris' comments on it, see above, VIII, 326–7 n, 391–2, 418–20.

9. On these acts see above, VI, 257 n, 273–4, 279–84; VII, 117 n, 131–2, 145–53, 260–1, 370; VIII, 54–5.

1. Ferdinand J. Paris, Answer to Heads of Complaint, Nov. 27, 1758, above, VIII, 179–83.

How far this Act is Consistent with the Royal Prerogative, agreeable to natural Equity and the Laws of England, we shall now take the Liberty of stating to Your Lordships.

In order to make this Matter as clear as its Intricacy will admit, we beg leave to state the Nature and Quality's of the Proprietary Estates in that Country. They Consist, first, of Quit Rents, given on Grants of the Property and Inheritance of Land; secondly, of Rents reserv'd upon Leases for Lives or Years; thirdly, of the waste Lands which are held by them under the Charter and in Virtue of their general proprietary Right; Fourthly, of Located Lands, which are Lands reserv'd by the Proprietaries for their own Use, out of those Tracts which are granted to Private Persons, and which, tho' appropriated as their Demeane, are not cultivated but kept vacant, in order that they may be Occupied, Let or Sold, as they shall judge most Convenient. The two first of these Divisions of their Property, the Quit Rents and reserv'd Rents, the Proprietaries freely Consent should be Taxed; the only dispute therefore is with regard to the third species of Property, the waste Lands, which are not Located, And the Fourth which are the unimprov'd and unsettled demesne Lands, which are Located; and each of these it is Contended (as we apprehend with reason) is a species of Property which is by no means a proper Object of Taxation. For by this means a Tax is annually impos'd upon what yields no annual Produce, or, properly speaking, no produce at all, contrary to reason and contrary to those Rules which in England have been on these Occasions constantly Observ'd. And, my Lords, we Conceive that the Tax imposed by this Act upon Located Lands, tho' unimproved, is not only injurious to the Proprietaries, but to every Individual in the Province who is possess'd of Lands under the same Circumstances. What Adds to the Impropriety of this Tax is, that the annual Imposition on those Lands is limited only from five to fifteen Pounds per Hundred Acres, by which means a great Latitude is left open to Partiality and Injustice in the Assessors.

But with regard to the Proprietaries, there is a peculiar Hardship in that Charge imposed by the first taxing Clause in this Bill on Lands at large, tho they are neither improved or located;[2] a

2. The second section of the act imposed a tax of 18*d.* per pound of the "clear yearly value" of all estates, real and personal, as it "ariseth out of the

Discription which can alone be Applied to the Lands of the Proprietaries. These we apprehend to be rather a more improper Object of Taxation than the former; these are likewise deprived of the Benefit even of those Restrictions used in the former tax as those Restrictions are. The mode and Quantum of the Tax, as far as it relates to this Object, not being limited, as in the other Case, from five Pounds to fifteen Pounds, but Absolutely left open to the Discretion of the Assessors.

It is not, my Lords, in the Object of the Tax alone, that the Proprietaries are Distinguished from every Individual in the Province, but likewise in the Method of Taxation. By this Act, in Cases of Private Property, every Species of Estate is to Support its own proper Burthen, According to its particular Nature and Circumstance; on Nonpayment of the Tax on improved Lands, the Remedy which the Act has Appointed is Distress; For unimproved Lands, because there can be no Remedy by Distress, Recourse is had to sale; and these Remedies are never Displaced, nor is one kind of Land in any Case made Answerable for the Defaults on the other. But this rational and distinguishing Order is Quitted when applied to the Proprietaries; For in their Case there is one only Remedy and that is an Absolute sale of their Lands, whether improved or unimproved, and that for a Default of Payment of the Tax whether on their Quit Rents, their Reserved Rents, their Located demisne, or their Lands at Large. In the ordinary Course likewise of Levying the Tax upon Individuals, they first resort to the Landlord, and, on his Default, to the Tenant, before they proceed ev'n to Distress; In the Case of the Proprietaries, they go only to the Receiver General and on his Refusal or Neglect take no Notice of the Tenant, but have recourse imediately to Sale; giving against the Proprietaries in the first Instance, that Remedy, upon a default of Payment of the Tax for any of their lands or

---

premises, or otherwise to be estimated by the assessors according to their best discretion and judgment, having respect to the quantity and value of the unimproved parts of the same, as also upon all located unimproved tracts of land to be assessed and rated in the manner hereinafter-mentioned, to be paid by the owners or possessors in the manner herein-directed." A careful reading of this section discloses no specific reference to the taxation of unlocated lands, as the Board of Trade report implies here, and on Mar. 14, 1761, the Assembly denied that any "unsurveyed Waste Lands" had been subjected to taxation. *Pa. Col. Recs.*, VIII, 584.

their Rents, which they refuse against the Individual, except in the Last resort, and then for his unimproved Lands alone. And this Regulation, my Lords, is not only partial in its self, but contrary to the Laws of England, which in no Case subject Lands to sale for non Payment of Taxes.

The Proprietaries complain, and, we apprehend, with reason, not only as to the Injustice of the Tax in its Object, as to the Partiality of the Method by which it is inforced, but likewise as to the Inequality which is Observed in the Choice of Assessors for collecting it.

The Inhabitants of this Province, whenever they are tax'd in common with the Proprietaries, may be Considered as their Adversaries, as the former will be exonerated in proportion as the latter are burthened; it would have been but Justice therefore, to have provided indifferently for each. But the Proprietaries, by having no Vote in the Choice of Assessors, nor even a Negative on those who are appointed to dispose of their Property, are not in this respect upon a Footing with the meanest Freeholder in the Province. If they appeal from the Partiality of the Assessors, who are chosen by the People, it is to Commissioners who are elected in the same manner, and are liable therefore to the same Exception.

We ought not, my Lords, to pass over the plea which the Assembly makes in Favour of this Regulation, that the manner of Levying the Tax and of judging an Appeal, as settled by this Law, is the same with that which has been so long in Use by the Act for Levying County Rates, and that no Complaints have been made of any Inconvenience or Oppression. But this Method which was very reasonable when the People only were taxed, becomes altogether unfit, when a new Object is let in, and the Proprietaries are to be Charged: and therefore no Argument can be drawn from the Equality of the former Method, the present Circumstances being, as must be Obvious to Your Lordships, Extreamly different: Added, my Lords to the Appointment of Assessors, and of Commissioners of Appeal, in neither of which the Proprietaries have any share, the Assembly has taken to itself Solely and independent of the Governor a Right of revising and controlling the whole Assessment, which we Apprehend as far as this Object extends, to be no less than Assuming to themselves at once a great Part of the Executive and in effect the whole of the Legislative Power; as, by controlling the Assessment, they may either raise or lower it as they think proper, which is in every respect equivalent to a new Tax. And this extraordinary Power is reserved in words so general and ambiguous, that it is impossible to set any Limits to their Pretentions, especially as they have brought the Interpretation of this Act before no other Tribunal but their own Assembly: In Proportion as they have Departed from Justice; departing from the Constitution and the Laws of England, where the House of Commons have never assumed a power in any manner similar to this. And, my Lords, the Assembly, not content with Levying the money solely by popular Assessors, trying the Appeal before a popular Tribunal, revising and Controlling the whole Taxation by a popular Representative, have Vested in themselves alone, the Application of the money which is thus directed to be raised; usurping by this means one of the most inviolable Prerogatives of the executive Power, not countenanced by any Example of the British Representative, who always consider the Application of the Publick Money subject to Account as one of the most undisputed Powers of the Crown. It is true that the Assembly have in Part of this Act complimented the Governor with a Share in the Application of the Money, but, by the two Clauses immediately subsequent, they have taken Care to render the Concession ineffectual. For, by these, a Majority of the Commissioners are (independent of the Governor) impow'red to Draw upon the Loan Office; not only for the Purposes of this Act, but for the Discharge of Services performed under the Authority of a former Law, and which, through the Deficiency of the Funds set Apart for the Payment of them, had not yet been provided for.[3]

The next exceptional provision, my Lords, is that by which the

3. As in previous supply acts, the Assembly named in the act itself the seven commissioners to expend the funds raised: two councilors and five members of the Assembly. These men, "or the major part of them or of the survivors of them, with the consent and approbation of the governor or commander-in-chief of this province for the time being, shall order and appoint the disposition of the moneys arising by virtue of this act . . .," but two subsequent paragraphs authorizing the commissioners, "or a majority of them," to draw orders upon the trustees of the General Loan Office for payments make no mention of the governor's "consent and approbation" of their orders.

143

Assembly have reserved to themselves the sole and exclusive Nomination of the Officers created by this Act, a Prerogative not only belonging, but absolutely essential to the Executive Power, and on which the Exercise of all the rest Depends: And it will be needless to point out to Your Lordships that in this, as in all other Instances of the same kind, they have far exceeded the largest Claims of the British House of Commons. And this Encroachment, my Lords, they constantly exercise, and in almost every Act, by which a new Officer is appointed, the sole Nomination of the Officer, by an express Provision, is particularly reserved to the Assembly.

In Addition, my Lords, to all these Objections, there is another which we apprehend to be extrem'ly material, arising from that Part of the Act by which it is contended that the Proprietaries should be bound to receive their Rents in Paper Currency; notwithstanding the express Reservation of them, by the Words of their Contracts in Sterling. But, as we shall have Ocasion in the course of our report upon the Subsequent Laws, to state this matter more fully, we shall not now enter into the Discussion of it at large, but satisfy ourselves here with barely pointing it out to your Lordships Observation.

We must not here omit taking notice of one Argument which has been offerd by the Assembly and very strongly insisted on, in order to obtain His Majesty's Approbation of this Act, and that, my Lords, is drawn, not from the Merits of the Act itself, but from the Inconveniencies which they state, must unavoidably attend the Repeal of it. "That the Money being already emitted under the Publick Faith and circulating every where, throughout the Province, if this Act should be annull'd, must of Necessity lose its Credit, and that many therefore would become Sufferers, who were by no means Instrumental in Framing those inequitable Regulations for which the Law was depriv'd of its Validity." We are sensible, My Lords, from the manner in which this Act is framed, that some Inconveniences must follow either the Confirmation or the Disallowance of it; and we have it in our Power; only to Consider which will be Productive of the fewest Mischiefs. This, my Lords, is what we have weighed as deliberately as we are able; and we are clearly of Opinion, that from the Comparative Lightness of the Evil: and from the Comparative Easiness of the

Remedy (as well as for the sake of the Precedent) that the Repeal of this Law is much the least exceptionable Part. If the Act should be confirm'd, a Capital Injustice would be done to the Proprietaries, several Infractions would be made upon the Constitution and several encroachments on the Prerogative; and these, my Lords, during the Subsistance of the Act, could Not Possibly be remedied, and probably would not upon the Expiration of it. For there is not one Provision of the Law which has not been supported by the Assembly on Permanent Principles from which they will not, and from which, if their Opinions were well grounded, they ought not to Depart. The Method of Taxing the Proprietaries is contended for as Consistant with Justice; and the Encroachments on the Prerogative as Agreeable to the Constitution.

If, my Lords, on the other Hand the Act should be Repeal'd, the Bills that have been isued may Possibly be deprived of their Currency: the Odium however of this Inconvenience, we apprehend, must fall upon those who reduced the Crown to this Necessity, not upon the Crown itself; or upon those whose Province it is to Advise it. And this very Inconvenience, it will be in the Power of the Assembly who gave rise to it, instantly to redress, by the Passing an Act to reestablish the Credit of those Bills, simple and unadulterated by those Clauses which gave Ocasion to its being repealed. And we beg leave to Observe, that not one of those Provisions, which we have stated as so exceptionable, are at all essential to the great and Capital Object of the Act, for, my Lords the Sum of one Hundred Thousand Pounds will be raised not only more equitably, but full as effectually, if the Object of the Tax be proper, as if it was an improper one, if the Method of inforcing it was equal, instead of being partial; and if the Proprietaries had a Voice in the Nomination of Assessors, in the Appointment of the Officers, and in the Dispossition of the Money, as if they had not.

In other Governments, my Lords, where Laws have been passed which it has been thought for some reasons not advisable to confirm, and which at the same time, for others, judged not expedient to Repeal, the Crown has for a time suspended it's Decision, still having in itself the Power either of Confirmation or Disallowance at any other more Convenient Opportunity. From this Expedient, in the present Case, even could we recommend it, his Majesty is precluded by the Limitation of the Charter, by the terms of which unless, within 6 Months (part of which is now elapsed,) the Laws are declared Void, they of Course become Valid, and the interposition of the Crown, at any Subsequent Period, will be Totally Ineffectual.[4]

To conclude, my Lords, on the most Attentive Consideration of this bill, from the manifest Injustice of some Parts; from the studied Ambiguity of others; from the Impropriety of some of the Objects of the Tax; from the Injustice which is done to the Proprietaries in their Property as Individuals, and in their Prerogatives, as Governors; from the manner in which the Tax is laid; from the remedies which are prescribed to recover it; from the exclusive Choice of Assessors, Commissioners and Revisers, by which the Tax is Subjected to three Popular Bodies; by the Usurpations and Encroachments in the Choice of Officers and the Application of Money, and by the Compulsary Tender of their Paper Currency notwithstanding the express Reservation in the Contracts of the Proprietaries, in all of which particulars the Act manifestly offends either against Natural Justice and the Laws of England or the Royal Prerogative, we are fully of Opinion that this Act is one of the most proper Objects for the exercise of his Majesty's Power of Repeal, which has been at any time refered to our Consideration, and We Humbly recommend it to be repealed accordingly.

An Act for re-emitting the Bills of Credit of this Province heretofore re-emitted on Loan, and for striking the further Sum of Thirty-Six Thousand Six Hundred and Fiffty Pounds to enable the Trustees to lend Fifty Thousand Pounds to Colonel John Hunter, Agent for the Contractors with the Right Honourable the Lords Commissioners of His Majesty's Treasury, for His Majesty's Service.[5]

4. See above, p. 132 n. 3.

5. Passed June 20, 1759, *Statutes at Large, Pa.*, V, 427–43. The act contained two principal features: 1. The Assembly desired to maintain a supply of currency adequate for the colony's economic needs, in view of the legal requirement for the retirement and destruction at stipulated times of bills of credit authorized by acts of 1739 and 1746. Therefore the trustees of the General Loan Office, named in the act, were to prepare £36,650 in new bills of credit and were to issue £1650 of these bills and reissue all old bills received

A Supplement to the Act, entitled An Act for re-emitting the Bills of Credit of this Province heretofore re-emitted on Loan, and for striking the further Sum of Thirty-Six Thousand Six Hundred and Fifty Pounds to enable the Trustees to lend Fifty Thousand Pounds to Colonel John Hunter Agent for the Contractors with the Right Honourable the Lords Commissioners of His Majesty's Treasury, for His Majesty's Service.[6]

Before we take the Liberty of reporting to Your Lordships the Opinion we have formed upon the Subject of the first of these Bills, we beg leave to premise, that the Paper Currency (which is it's Principal Object) has been issued in this Colony, and in the other Provinces of North America, for two Purposes.

The first, my Lords, is upon Loan, to Supply the Deficiency of Specie and to Serve as a Medium of Circulation within the Province; the Ballance of Trade being so much against them, that Gold or Silver is very difficult to be procured.

The second, tho' it has for its immediate Object only to provide for the Exigencies of Government, becomes in its Operation Subservient to the former Purpose, and Contributes likewise to encrease the Circulation of the Province.

---

but not yet destroyed, and those to be received in repayment of the principal of mortgage loans before Oct. 15, 1769, on new loans secured by real estate mortgages or "good plate." The loans were to run for a term of "sixteen years from the fifteenth day of October in the year of our Lord one thousand seven hundred and fifty-nine" (i.e., until Oct. 15, 1775). The new and old bills were to be current bills of credit "for the payment and discharge of all manner of debts, rents, sum and sums of money whatsoever due, . . . as if the same were tendered or paid in the coins mentioned" in any bond, book account, promise, or contract. 2. In order to assist John Hunter, agent to the contractors for supplying money to the royal forces in America, to meet the demands upon him pending receipt of funds from Great Britain, the trustees of the Loan Office were to lend him a combined total of £50,000 of the new and old bills for twelve months on adequate security, but without interest unless he should default in repayment. In mentioning this act to BF in his letter of July 31, 1759, Norris declared that he had had no part in it. See above, VIII, 420.

6. Passed Sept. 29, 1759, *Statutes at Large, Pa.*, V, 456–60. This act replaced one trustee of the General Loan Office named in the act of June 20, but who had declined to serve; provided for the Assembly to fill any future vacancies among the trustees; and clarified one ambiguous detail in the former act. The Proprietors' objections to this act are printed in *ibid.*, pp. 687–8.

We must observe further to Your Lordships that, when Paper Currency has been struck for the former of these Purposes, to be issued out upon Loan, it has been usual to advance it on proper Security, and at a Legal Interest, the Borrower Stypulating that it should be repaid at a certain Period, and the Legislature providing by their Act that the Bills so issued should, upon the repayment of the Money, be destroyed; But it has frequently happened that, when the Circulation of the Colony seemed in any manner to require it, the Legislature has directed that the Bills, which had been payed in and which were intended to be destroyed, should be again emitted, under the same Security and at the same Interest. By Paper Currency, my Lords, thus issued upon Loans, several Salutary Purposes have at once been answered: The Defect of Circulation from the want of Specie, has been Supplied; by being advanced at a very low Interest, the Cultivation of the Province has been Promoted, and that Interest has been applied to Support the Current Services of Government. Under the Restrictions we have stated to Your Lordships, the Paper Currency of this Province, by various Emissions and reemissions at length amounted to Eighty Thousand Pounds; but, as the final Period of its legal Circulation is distant but a very few Years, and as, by the Laws now Subsisting, the whole would expire in seventeen Hundred and Sixty two, The Assembly propose by this Act to revive the Circulation of these Bills, to re-emit them as they shall be paid in, and to continue their Credit to 1778,[7] by an Additional Term of Sixteen Years. We are far, my Lords, from being of Opinion that the Sum of Eighty thousand Pounds, as stated by the Assembly, may not be necessary for the Circulation of the Colony, considering the great Increase of People, and of Trade more than proportioned to that Increase, in this very thriving and flourishing Province. But we apprehend that the Prolongation of this Paper Currency, for sixteen Years, from 1762, is at present not only absolutely unnecessary but extremely improper. For, first, My Lords, as to it's being unnecessary, we must Observe, that almost the whole sum of eighty Thousand Pounds is still out-Standing in the Province and will

7. The date should be 1775, not 1778; see note 5, next but one above. Apparently, the Board of Trade misread the act and assumed that the 16-year extension would run from 1762 (when the bills were first scheduled to be retired) and not from 1759 as the act clearly specified.

continue in Circulation, by the Laws now Subsisting, till the year 1762, no more than sixteen Hundred and Fifty Pounds having as yet been actually paid in, tho' Twenty seven Thousand Pounds is the sum, which, by the Terms of the several Laws, ought, before this time, to have been discharged. Secondly, my Lords, we apprehend that a want of Circulation cannot possibly be felt in the Province, because great Part of the Bills which have been struck since the Commencement of the War, to Supply the Exigences of Government, and which, as we have Observed to your Lordships, serve the same Purposes of Circulation with the former, are, together with almost the whole of the eighty Thousand Pounds still current in the Province; insomuch, My Lords, that of all the Paper Currency which has been issued in the Years 1755, 57. 58, and 59, the former is alone destroyed. If therefore it is confess'd that the sum of eighty Thousand Pounds is sufficient for the Circulation of the Province, no defect, we apprehend, can be upon that Head reasonably complained of, because from the several Paper Bills which have been passed and which have not been yet destroyed, a much larger sum than that which is stated to be Necessary is now, and will continue to be for some time, out-Standing in the Colony.

As the Emission of Paper Currency in general has never been encouraged, tho' it has in some cases been tolerated by the Crown, the Consideration of this Reemission ought not certainly to have been resumed till as late as possible. But as this Bill was made much earlier than was Necessary, so it was Continued much longer than is Proper.

By the Act for regulating Paper Currency in the New England Governments the Term for the Circulation of Bills issued on Emergencies is extended to five Years only; to those issued for Circulation it is limited to three.[8] And tho', My Lords, this Province is exempted entirely from that Law, yet as that Exemption arose solely from a Perswasion that the Province had, without a Law, come of itself very near the Regulations which the Law would have prescribed. We apprehend to preserve the reasons of

8. The act of 1751, 24 Geo. II, c. 53. Sect. III of the act restricted bills of credit issued in such emergencies as war or invasion to five years. Sect. II restricted such bills "as shall be required for the current Service of the Year" to two years, not three.

this Exemption in all their Validity, it is Necessary still to hold this Province as near as may be, to the Standard of that Act.

Further, My Lords, we must Observe that this Act is liable to that Objection which we only touched upon to Your Lordships in our Report on the Land Tax Act of 1759, and which we shall now take the Liberty of Opening more at Large. And here it will be Necessary to Observe, that the Proprietaries in their Grants had Originally reserved the Payment of their Quit Rents in Stirling Money only, and this Form of Reservation continued till 1732. But since that Period, their Rents have been expressly reserved not only (as before) in Stirling Money, but with the Addition of this new Clause *"or its Value in Currency, regard being had to the rate of Exchange between Philadelphia and London."* In Consequence of several Acts by which Paper Currency was issued in the Province, and by which it was likewise made a legal Tender in the Payment of all Rents &c. a Dispute arose between the Proprietaries and their Tenants, The Tenants insisting on the Tender of Paper Currency under the Authority of the Acts of the Province, and the Proprietaries refusing to receive it, as contrary to the Express reservation of their Grants. To quiet this Dispute, the Assembly agreed to Pay to the Proprietaries a Sum of Twelve Hundred Pounds and a Hundred and Thirty Pounds per Annum till the Year 1749, as a Compensation for the Difference between the Stirling Money which was reserved by the Proprietaries, and the Paper Currency which was tendered by the Tenant; enacting at the same time, that all Quit rents since 1732, should, for the future, be paid according to the Terms of their Covenants: And in this, tho' not amounting to half of the real Difference, the Proprietaries Acquiesced.[9] And tho', My Lords, the Assembly, by this Compensation which they made to the Proprietaries, seem to allow, that they had a Right by such Reservation and a Loss by the Breach of it, yet, notwithstanding their former Sense of this Affair, tho it is not denied that Paper Currency is greatly below Stirling Money in its Value, even at Present, when the large Remittances to North America for the Payment of the Troops and other Services of the War have rendered the Exchange less in their Disfavour than it Otherwise would be; tho' the Tenor of the Grants either before or since 1732 are not questioned, the Paper Currency is by this Act

9. *Pa. Col. Recs.*, IV, 318–36; *Statutes at Large, Pa.*, IV, 322–6.

made a Valid Tender for the Proprietaries Rents as well as for all Payments whatsoever, not excepting even the Contracts that have been made since 1732, as they had before done in the 12th. of the King, nor making in this Case, as they had done in the former, any Compensation, however unequal, for the Loss. And we beg leave upon this Occasion to remind Your Lordships that his Majesty did, in the Course of the last Year, disapprove a Law of North Carolina, by which His Majesty's Quit Rents, being comprized in the general Terms of all Debts and Demands whatsoever, were made payable in Paper Currency; And at the same time His Majesty by Special Instruction directed his Governor to take Care, that in all future Acts for issuing Paper Currency, a Clause be inserted declaring that the Paper Bills of Credit already issued, or thereby to be issued, shall not be a legal Tender in Payment of the said Quit Rents, Nor of any Debt whatsoever that may become due to the Crown.[1]

We have likewise, my Lords, another very material Objection to this Bill as it is now constituted, arising from the Re-emission being connected with the Loan to Colonel Hunter, with which it has not the least necessary relation. By this Method of blending together in the same Bill things which are in their own Nature totally Separate, the Crown is reduced to the Alternative either of Passing what it disaproves, or of rejecting what may be Necessary, for the Publick Service: and this Manner of framing Laws has been always so exceptionable to his Majesty that, in Governments more immediately under the Controul of the Crown, it is a standing

---

1. Once again the Board of Trade seems not to have been entirely accurate in its statements. On April 10, 1759, the Board had reported on North Carolina acts of 1748 and 1754 which it criticized for the reasons set forth in the present report. The Board members had gone on to say that they should have proposed "the immediate Repeal of them did they not consider the infinite Confusion which must arise in the Province" in consequence; instead, they proposed an additional instruction to the governor of North Carolina demanding a new law amending the previous ones to require all debts to British subjects to be payable at the true rate of exchange and declaring that paper currency was not to be legal tender for the payment of quitrents or any debt due the Crown. Such an additional instruction was issued June 8, 1759. Neither act was repealed. *Acts Privy Coun., Col.*, IV, 414–16, 807; William L. Saunders, ed., *The Colonial Records of North Carolina*, VI (1888), 22–4, 43–5; Leonard W. Labaree, *Royal Instructions to British Colonial Governors 1670–1776* (N.Y., 1935), I, 229–31.

Instruction to the Governor, not to give his Assent, whenever it was proposed that matters of a different Nature Should be regulated in the same Law.[2]

But, My Lords, in order to shew, that the Clause relative to the re-imission was inserted only as a Tack to the Loan, it has been alleged by the Counsel for the Proprietaries, that the very same Regulation, being offer'd in a separate Bill, was rejected by the Governor, but obtained his Consent, when connected with the Loan to Colonel Hunter.[3]

2. Granted the empty condition of the Pa. Treasury, this charge of "tacking" one matter to another in a single act is only partially valid. If the Assembly was to authorize a loan to Hunter of all or any significant part of the £100,000 he asked for, the money had to be provided either by a new issue of bills of credit, by the re-emission of old bills, or by a combination of the two. The proceeds of the recently passed £100,000 Supply Act were earmarked for other purposes. The Assembly chose the last of these possibilities and, quite reasonably, combined in one measure the provisions for the bills of credit and the authorization of the loan. Valid criticism for "tacking" could be directed only at those sections of the act which authorized the re-emission of all bills of credit to be received in the future in repayment of principal on loans before Oct. 15, 1769, and declared that the bills were to be legal tender.

3. This allegation by the Proprietors' counsel, repeated without investigation by the Board of Trade, is not clearly supported by the record. There is no evidence in the journals of the House or the minutes of the governor's Council that this Assembly even considered a re-emitting bill between its first sitting on Oct. 14, 1758, and May 31, 1759, or that Denny rejected such a bill, as alleged. On May 29 a memorial from John Hunter asking for a loan of £100,000 and a supporting letter from General Stanwix were read in the Assembly, and the next day the members voted "by a great Majority" against bringing in a bill to strike £100,000 in bills of credit to lend to Hunter. *Votes,* 1758–59, pp. 71–3. Then on May 31 the House, for the first time, took "into Consideration the Expediency of preparing and offering" a measure to re-emit old bills of credit and ordered such a bill prepared. *Ibid.,* p. 74. When the bill was debated at its second reading, June 6, the House voted to recommit it for certain amendments and again "by a great Majority" ordered the inclusion of a clause to authorize the loan to Hunter of an unspecified sum. *Ibid.,* pp. 76, 77. What political pressures or tactical considerations led to this vote are not recorded. The bill as amended and with the provision of a loan of £50,000 to Hunter (half what he had asked for) went to Denny on June 9. *Ibid.,* p. 78. The bill was shown to Hunter and Stanwix and Hunter appeared before the Council asking that the time stipulated for repayment be extended from six to twelve months and that the loan be increased to £75,000. The councilors favored the loan but, without suggesting where the money was to come from, took strong exception to the other features of the bill on much

None of those Inconveniences which may possibly attend the repeal of the Land Tax Act are in this Case to be apprehended. For the Money having been advanced by Colonel Hunter to the Contractors with his Majesty's Treasury, has been already repaid, and will probably be received in Pensylvania before the repeal of this Act can Possibly arrive there: And thus, My Lords, Publick Justice will be done without Injury to any Individual.

We must, in Addition to these Objections, also Mention to Your Lordships, that the Assembly have in this Instance likewise, taken to themselves the sole Disposition of the Interest arising from the eighty Thousand Pounds which at four Thousand Pounds per annum for sixteen Years, would amount to Sixty four Thousand Pounds. But we shall not repeat what we have Already taken the Liberty of Offering to Your Lordships upon the Application of all Money being Assumed by the Assembly in the former Act, especially as we imagine we have already given Sufficient reasons for the Support of our Advice to His Majesty, that this Act may be repealed.

The Act, my Lords, intitled A suplement to this Act is liable to the same Objections with the Act itself. If Your Lordships should approve what we have stated, upon the Act, this Suplement will meet of Course with His Majesty's Disallowance.

There is however one Additional Objection to this Suplemental Act, that the Nomination of Officers, which by the Act itself was to be exercised by the Assembly with the Concurrence of the Governor, is here to be exercised by the Assembly only.

> An Act for recording of Warrants and Surveys and for rendering the real Estates and Property within this Province more secure.[4]

In order to comprehend the Object and to judge of the Equity of this Law, it will be necessary for Us to state to Your Lordships

---

the same grounds as are found here in the Board of Trade report. Denny, however, reminded them of his obligation "to promote the King's Business," and after the Assembly had rejected all of his proposed amendments except the extention of the time for repayment, approved the bill, June 20, in spite of a formal protest from the councilors. *Pa. Col. Recs.*, VIII, 342–3, 350–2, 353–4, 357–60, 362; *Votes*, 1758–59, pp. 80, 81, 83, 87.

4. Passed July 7, 1759; *Statutes at Large, Pa.*, V, 448–55. Various documents relating to this measure are in *ibid.*, pp. 670–87. Norris called it "a

the Method which is now pursued in granting Lands in Pensylvania: Upon Application being made to the Proprietaries a Warrant is directed to the Surveyor General to Survey the Lands, that have been appli'd for. That Survey, when made, is returned into the Secretaries Office, and upon the entire Payment of the Purchase Money, a Patent is made out. By this Bill it is proposed that a new Office shall be erected for the registration of those Warrants and Surveys; there being no Office in the Province which by Law is bound to record them, as they are at present kept only in the Office of the Proprietaries, at their Discretion, under the Direction of an Officer of their Appointment, receiving a Salary from their Bounty, and liable to be removed at their Displeasure.

We cannot possibly, My Lords, Object to any Regulations which seem to carry with them a probable Tendency of establishing the Evidences of Property, and of Preventing Litigation in the Province. But we are of Opinion, that the Scope and Drift of this Act, which, tho' it is expressed somewhat ambiguously in a Clause of the Act itself, is yet very clearly explaind by a Message of the Assembly, is extremely exceptionable. By the Act it is implied only, but not explicitly avowed, that a Warrant and Survey are in Law a Compleat Title to an Estate of Inheritance in Lands; for it declares, that Estates are claimed and held under Warrants and Surveys and *other Writings;* specifying in clear and express Words the Warrants and Surveys, as if they were the only or most material Part of the Title, and Passing by the Patent or involving it only in the general Term of *other Writings,* as a matter of little or no importance, tho we apprehend it is in reality the only Legal Conveyance of an Estate. But, My Lords, as we have already Observed, the Ambiguity of their Act is taken away by the Clearness of their Message, for the Assembly being pressed on the Part of the Governor to explain themselves on this Point, they expressly Affirm that the true Right of Property is vested from the Moment that the Warrant is delivered.[5]

Just and equitable Law between the Proprietaries and the People" and advised that "no reasonable Expence should be spared" to get it confirmed. He believed that "it guards us against the Iniquity of the Land Office which has Tyranized over this poor Colony so many Years without Countroul, in my Opinion without Mercy and without Justice." See above, VIII, 419–20, 428–9.

5. On July 4, 1759, during the controversy over the bill, the Assembly

And this Regulation of the Bill we apprehend, My Lords, to be highly exceptionable, as it establishes a Title to an Estate, different from that which prevails by the Common Law; we apprehend it is likewise extremely unequitable to the Proprietaries. For, from the Terms upon which Lands are usually granted in Pensylvania, it seldom happens, that, upon the issuing a Warrant and Survey, the whole of the Purchase Money is paid down: Part only, and that commonly a very small Part, is advanced at first; and the Payment of the Remainder, according to the Circumstances of the Case, is to be compleated at some other, and often at a very distant, Period: And this, my Lords, by a Policy very rational in itself, and highly conducive to the Settlement of the Province; for by this means the Purchaser, instead of being totally exhausted by the Purchase, has Money left to be expended in the Cultivation of his Land.

As the Laws now Stand, independent of this Bill, the Proprietaries and the Grantee have a Mutual, and, as near as the Nature of the thing will admit, an equal Remedy against each other. But if the Bill proposed should pass into a Law, and the meer Warrant and Survey, which now only gave a Conditional Right to an Estate, upon the Performance of the Terms of the Contract, should confer a Right, Absolutely and of course, the Proprietaries would be deprived of their Proper and only certain Remedy Against the Grantee, The regaining Possession of their Land by an Ejectment; for the Personal Remedy against the Settler, might in any Case be rendred ineffectuall by the Settler himself, who having, by the Principles of this Act, a Compleat Title to his Estate by the meer Warrant and Survey, might, in Virtue of that Title convey and alien it to another, and the Person claiming under that Conveyance would be confirmed in the Possession of the Estate, and the Proprietaries Personal Remedy must cease of course,

---

sent to Denny a paper of remarks on the governor's criticisms of the bill. It was written by Joseph Galloway, described as "a Gentleman of the Law, a Member of our House." In it he declared unequivocally: "A Warrant and Survey returned into the Surveyor General's Office, without more has ever been adjudged by all our Courts of Justice, to give a good Title as well against the Proprietaries as all Subsequent Purchasers, and this is founded on an Original Covenant on Record with the People." *Pa. Col. Recs.*, VIII, 363–9; *Statutes at Large, Pa.*, V, 678–85.

upon the Absence of the Person to whom the Grant was originally made.

Nor, my Lords, as we conceive would the Establishment of
such a Title, be more injurious to the Proprietaries than to the
real Interest of the Province itself. For, if the Proprietaries should
be discouraged from making out any Warrants till the whole of
the Purchase Money is discharged, the Method of Paying by
installments, which has hitherto been followed, not only with so
much Benefit to the Proprietaries, but with so much Advantage to
Individuals, and to the General Advancement and Cultivation of
the Province would be entirely taken away.

There are likewise other Objections to which the said Act in
our Opinion is liable, which it will be Necessary for us only just
to Mention, and for which together with those already stated to
Your Lordships, we beg Leave to offer it as our Opinion that this
Bill should not, by receiving his Majesty's Approbation, be permitted to pass into a Law.

We are of Opinion, my Lords, that the time in which the Surveyor is limitted to execute every Warrant and Survey that may
be sent him, being only forty Days, is unreasonably short; That
his Compliance with this Provision in the Act may in some Cases
be impossible, and in others extreamly difficult, and we see no
Inconvenience that would possibly have arisen from an Extension
of that Term.

We conceive that the Directions under which, by this Act, the
Surveyor is to execute his Office, are equally injurious to the
Proprietaries Rights and to the common good of the Province.
With respect to the Proprietary, by the Surveyors being Obliged
to survey to the Claimant whatsoever Spots or Parcels of Lands
He shall think most eligible for his Purpose, the Proprietaries are
deprived of that Preoption which they always had and to which
they are undoubtedly intitled, in the Reservation of such Parcels
of Lands as they may prefer to be set apart for their own Demesne.
With regard to the Province, as the Lands of Pensylvania are
various in their Nature and Advantages, with respect to Wood,
Water and Fertility of Soil, by inabling the first Grantee to select out those Particular Parts which are in every Spot the most
Advantageous for a Settler, the Refuse of the Land will be
left only for those who succeed him, to the great discourage-

ment of new Purchasers and to the manifest Disadvantage of Settlement.

We apprehend likewise, that the Penalty of five hundred Pounds to be levied upon the Officer on his neglect to register any Paper or Minute of Property whatsoever, by which any Person may be affected, is much too heavy; and that where the Duty is so very extensive, and the Directions of the Act are so very minute, the Penalty should not be so extremely considerable.

But tho', My Lords we cannot possibly approve, for the reasons we have stated, the Particular Regulations that are Proposed by the Assembly in this Act, we are far from being of Opinion that no Regulation is Necessary; on the Contrary, we think it highly expedient, that the Office constituted by the Proprietaries and now solely under their Direction, should be converted into a Publick Office, not only for the Registration of Patents, but of Warrants and Surveys and of any other transactions which may be thought advisable, and which relate to the Purchase of Lands: That while the Proprietaries may not be Invaded in their Rights, every Individual in the Province may be satisfied as to the Fidelity of the Record, and the Integrity of the Officer: That Security should be given for the good Behaviour of the Officer, and that he should be liable to Penalties for Mal-administration. Such Regulations, we are of Opinion, will answer the Purposes of removing effectually all the real Inconveniences that are complained of, and all the Jealousies of the Assembly, as far as they are well grounded, without Oppression or Injustice to the Proprietaries. And we are, my Lords, the more inclined to Approve of the Plan we have suggested to your Lordships; Because, in the Government of Virginia, where the Patents of Grantees were registered in an Office under the immediate Controul of the Crown, similar to that which is now Subsisting in Pensylvania under the Authority of the Proprietaries, His Majesty did, of his own Motion, recommend it to the Assembly of that Province, to Pass a Law, by which that Office, which had till then been more immediately under the Direction of the Crown, should be converted into a Publick Office, under the several Circumstances which we have already pointed out to Your Lordships, his Majesty however reserving to Himself, in Maintenance of his just Prerogative the exclusive Nomination of the Officer.

An Act for the more Effectual Suppressing and Preventing Lotteries and plays.[6]

This Act, My Lords, has two Objects in it's View, as the Title of the Bill imports, the one for the more effectual Suppression of Lotteries, the other for Prohibiting, under a very severe Penalty, the Exibition of Stage Plays or any Theatrical Representation whatsoever. With respect to the first, the Suppression of Lotteries, there is a Law now in being for that Purpose, which is stated to be ineffectual, and of which it is proposed, by this Bill, to inforce the Execution, by adding to the Penalty.[7] On the one hand, it has not been denied that, not-withstanding the Law now in force, several Lotteries have been set up; and, on the other, it has been confessed that the Money arising from them has been constantly Applied, to the Support of a very laudable Institution, the Academy in Pensylvania. If the Suppression of Lotteries, My Lords, had been the single Object of the Law, tho' we think the Penaltys imposed by it extremely heavy; and tho we are not without some Susspicion, by those Penalties being transfered by this Law to the Hospital at Philadelphia, which is Particularly Patronized by the Assembly, from the Academy, which has been largely contributed

6. Passed June 20, 1759, *Statutes at Large, Pa.,* v, 445–8. When the bill was first presented the Council told the governor they believed it "was principally intended to destroy the College, Academy, and Charity School," and that "of Late the Academy had drawn its principal Support" from lotteries. *Pa. Col. Recs.,* VIII, 339–41. The bill was introduced, however, only after the Assembly had received addresses, May 22–26, from the Society of Friends, the Presbyterian Synod, and the Lutheran and Baptist Congregations, who were aroused by the building of a theater, then in progress, for the permanent use of the Hallam (or "American") Company, at this time under the direction of David Douglass. *Votes,* 1758–59, pp. 69–71. The Council, dominated by the more "worldly" Anglicans, objected to the ban on plays as well as to that on lotteries. On the beginnings and early growth of the theatre in Philadelphia, see Carl and Jessica Bridenbaugh, *Rebels and Gentlemen Philadelphia in the Age of Franklin* (N.Y., 1942), 137–46. That BF put much heart into the defense of this act is difficult to believe. For his instigation of two lotteries in Philadelphia in 1747–48 and his connection with others, see above, III, 220–4, 229–31, 288–99, 470; v, 435–7, 505–11; VI, 361, 403–4, 424. There is considerable scattered evidence in his own correspondence and that of friends showing his attendance at the theatre while in London.

7. For the method by which the former lottery law was regularly evaded, see above, v, 436 n.

to by the Proprietaries, that together with the Desire of Suppressing of Lotteries, there has mixed some Dissatisfaction at the Preference which has been shewn to the Academy.[8] We should nevertheless, had the Act been confined to the Single Object of Suppressing Lotteries, have recommended it to his Majesty's Approbation. Because, My Lords, we are clearly of Opinion, that the raising Money contrary to Law, tho it may in some degree be Palliated, can not possibly be justifyed by the unexceptionable Application of it.

Tho' my Lords, the two Objects of Suppressing Lotteries and Plays, have been in this Act connected together by the Assembly, tho' they have been considered as equally deserving of Discouragement, and therefore are to be attended with exactly the same Penalty, yet we beg leave to Observe that the Crown has Perpetually distinguished and considered them in a very different Light. To Laws for the Suppression of Lotteries it has in many of it's Governments consented, and there is as we have already stated to your Lordships, a Law now subsissting in Pensylvania for that Purpose. To the total Prohibition of Theatrical Representations, we do not recollect the Consent of the Crown has in any of it's Governments been given or even asked, and we know that to Propositions of this sort from the Assembly in Pensylvania, it has frequently been refused.[9] The Argument, my Lords, upon which this Part of the Act has been Principally supported, is drawn from a Clause in an Act of the Present King, by which it is declared that stage plays shall be allowed only in Places of Royal Residence.[1] We apprehend, My Lords, that it is an Acknowledged

8. Although BF had been instrumental in founding the Academy, its head was William Smith, vigorous critic of the Assembly recently tried by it for libel, and Richard Peters, the proprietary secretary, had replaced BF as president of the Academy Board of Trustees in 1756. BF's connection with the Hospital, and that of many political friends, continued close.

9. An Act against Riots, Rioters and Riotous Sports, Plays and Games, passed Nov. 27, 1700, and An Act against riotous Sports, Plays and Games, passed Jan. 4, 1706, were disallowed, Feb. 7, 1706, and Oct. 24, 1709, respectively. *Statutes at Large, Pa.,* II, 4–5, 186–7, 449–56, 489–90, 526–9.

1. Sec. v of the so-called Licensing Act of 1737, 10 Geo. II, c. 28, forbids any form of play or entertainment of the stage except in the city of Westminster and any place where the King may reside, and then only during his residence there.

Method of Construction, that no Statute Law whatsoever can be supposed to extend either to Ireland or the Plantations by mere General words, and by Implication only, and unless they are specifically mentioned: and we Apprehend that Theatrical Representations continue to be not only permitted but encouraged in Ireland, exactly in the manner that they were before the Passing the said Act, without any real or supposed Violation of it. But tho we don't see any sufficient reason for an absolute Prohibition of all Theatrical Representations in Pensylvania, and therefore shall beg leave to propose, that this Act may not receive His Majesty's Allowance, Yet we do not mean, My Lords, to encourage the unbounded and irregular use of them. We are throughly sensible of the Mischiefs which might ensue from the Establishment of any thing, that had even a probable Tendency to introduce Idleness and Prodigality, in a Colony which seems so peculiarly indebted for it's Prosperity to Frugality and Industry. To prevent these Inconveniencies we should therefore wish to see some Law, which if properly framed, we doubt not would meet with his Majesty's Approbation, that might at once admit the moderate regulated Use of such Amusements and at the same time by proper Limitations prevent the Inconveniences that may attend their Excess.

A Supplement to the Act entitled An Act for establishing Courts of Judicature in this Province.[2]

The first Object of this Act is to regulate the jurisdictions of the several Courts in Pensylvania and, in particular, to transfer the decision of the Estates of Orphans and Intestates from the Orphans Court to the County Court. As far, my Lords, as relates to this Part of the Act, no Objection has been made on the Part of the Proprietaries, and the regulations upon this head, as far as we are capable of judging, appear altogether unexceptionable. The second Object of the Law is to change the tenure by which the judges now hold their Offices not only in the Province of Pensylvania but in every other Colony in North America and the West Indies, from *durante bene placito* to *Quamdiu se bene gesserint*. With respect to this latter point, it will be necessary for us only to remind Your Lordships of the decision of the Crown upon this Question when the same Principle was adopted by the Assembly

2. Passed Sept. 29, 1759, *Statutes at Large, Pa.*, v, 462–5.

of Jamaica, and a Law passed to the same Purpose, which the Crown thought proper to repeal upon an Opinion given by his Majesty's Attorney and Solicitor General, "that it was not expedient for the Interest of either the Mother Country or the Colonies, that Judges in the Plantations should hold their places Quam diu se bene gesserint"[3] And as your Lordships probably retain the same Opinion upon the same point, we apprehend that this Act will not be permitted by the Crown to pass into a Law. And we shall beg leave to assign some reasons why we think that the Principle adopted by your Lordships in the case of Jamaica, ought, for still stronger reasons, to be adhered to in this Colony. In the original Charter granted by Charles the second to Mr. Pen, the Crown has delegated, not merely by Virtue of their general Proprietary Powers, but by the most express and positive Terms, a Right to the establishment of Courts of Judicature and to the Nomination of Judges, under no limittation whatsoever; and we apprehend it would not be conformable to the justice and lenity of the Crown, to permit a Law (obtained against their Consent and by undue means) by which the Proprietaries should be limitted in the exertion of those Privileges to which they are intitled by the Charter, when nothing has been urged that can Induce the Crown to believe, that the Proprietaries have, by an improper exercise of those Privileges, committed any thing which could

3. The Jamaica act of 1751 was repealed Feb. 28, 1754. *Acts Privy Coun., Col.*, IV, 215–17. The question of whether colonial judges should have tenure during pleasure (*durante bene placito*), as the officers of the Crown insisted, or during good behavior (*quamdiu se bene gesserint*), as had been the practice in England since the Revolution of 1688 and as many Americans demanded, became a critical issue in several royal provinces at just about this time. It involved the central question of the independence of the judiciary. It is a matter of special interest here because BF's old political antagonist Robert Hunter Morris, now chief justice of New Jersey, insisted that when Governor Josiah Hardy renewed his commission following the accession of George III it should continue his former tenure "during good behavior." The New Jersey Assembly supported this demand and, in spite of strict instructions to the contrary, Hardy weakly gave way. When word of his disobedience reached England in the spring of 1762, the King promptly dismissed Hardy from office and to the governorship thereby vacated soon appointed none other than BF's son William. The widespread and protracted controversies over tenure of the judiciary are discussed in Leonard W. Labaree, *Royal Government in America* (New Haven, 1930), pp. 388–401.

Induce or justify the Resumption or limittation of them; and, particularly, as no complaint whatsoever has been made, or any inconvenience stated to have arisen, from the want of justice in the Province being properly and Regularly administred. On the contrary it has been confess'd that Men of the greatest Property and characters have been from time to time appointed to the station of chief justice, and that the rest of the Judicial Offices were filled by Persons as well qualified as the Colony could supply or a Salary, so small as the present, could engage. And we cannot think that it would be Advisable to depart from what experience has shown to be attended with no Ill effects in this Colony, and under which it is confest, on all hands, Justice has been hitherto so very unexceptionably administred.

Tho the Arguments in favour of this Bill are supported by analogy to the Practice of the Mother Country, we must Observe that the change which the tenure of judges underwent at the Revolution proceeded upon the most conclusive and repeated Proofs of the most arbitrary Interposition upon Points of the greatest Importance to the constitution and of the Highest moment to the subject. In this Colony the case is directly reversed; and therefore there cannot, we apprehend, be the same necessity for extending that Principle to Pensylvania. And as we are convinced that this Act can convey no real benefit to the inhabitants of this Province, so neither can we, by recommending it to His Majesty's Allowance, give countenance to an Opinion of its being beneficial, least we should excite a just jealousy in the other Colonys, by seeming to extend Advantages to this Proprietary Government, which have been denied to those under his Majesty's more immediate care. My Lords, independant of the General merits of this Act, we are humbly of Opinion, that it would not be prudent to establish it in the manner that is proposed; for by leaving no Power in the Proprietaries of appointing new judges, it perpetuates in the seat of Justice, for the lives of the Present Possessors, men (excepting the Chief justice only) of Inferior Knowledge and of secondary capacity; tho' by the Growing wealth of the Province a Salary may be advanced more adequate to the employment, and the Proprietaries be thus enabled to procure others more suitable to that station, and better qualified for the Discharge of a trust, in which every individual of the Province is so Materially interested.

An Act for the Relief of the Heirs, Devisees and Assigns of Persons born out of the Kings Liegeance, who have been Owners of Lands within this Province and died unnaturalized.[4]

The professed intention of the Act, my Lords, which is now before us, is to relieve the Heirs and devisees of foreigners, settled and possessing Lands in the Province of Pensylvania, who have died unnaturalized, by which their Estates have in Law escheated to the Proprietaries. The Act proposes to take away from the Proprietaries this Benefit of escheat, and to vest the Lands escheated in the Heirs and Devisees of such foreigners Dying unnaturalized, exactly in the same manner as if they had Descended from Natural born Subjects. We apprehend that, tho' this Bill professes a tenderness to Suffering Heirs and Devisees, its real Object is to take away another of the Proprietaries rights; for tho it is set forth, in the Preamble of this Act, that Inconveniences have happened from the want of such a Law, no Evidence has been produced, nor has there been a Suggestion offerd at our Board of any Grievance, or complaint whatsoever: But on the contrary the Custom has uniformly been, on proper application to make out a new Grant to such Heirs or Devisees Conformable to the Nature of the Inheritance or the Purport of the Devise, without imposing any fine, or any new Terms, or drawing any Lucrative advantage whatsoever from the escheat. We see therefore no reason for recommending to his Majesty's Approbation an Act, by which it is intended to take away from the Proprietaries a Right to which they are indisputably intitled by their Prerogative, and which they seem constantly to have exercised in so Disinterested a Manner. And we conceive that this Act, with regard to its present and avowed Object, seems alltogether unnecessary; for, as it is now Circumstanced, its Opperation will be only retrospective, and by that means it will provide only for those who have, by the Confession of all Parties, already been provided for by the Proprietaries Indulgence; and, with respect to the Proprietaries, it would only confirm to the Heirs and Devisees the Possession of those Lands in which they had before voluntarily invested them

4. Passed June 20, 1759, *Statutes at Large, Pa.*, v, 443–5. The Proprietors' objections are printed in *ibid.*, pp. 669–70. Norris called it "a Righteous and valuable Law." For his comment and a summary of the act, see above, VIII, 420 and n.

by their Grants. But, under this ineffective Appearance, the real design of the Act we apprehend to be this; that, the General Principle of such a Bill being once admitted as proper, and the Bill itself being now established as necessary, a Necessity of the same *kind* must in a short time again occur, and, what is now only to opperate retrospectively, would be extended as a permanent regulation, to opperate in future. Nor indeed do we perceive any reason why the Law should be limitted in its Operation, if the Principle, upon which the Law is founded, could be approved.

We beg leave further to observe To your Lordships that the Benefits, purposed to be conferr'd by this Act, are extended equally, and without Distinction, to Strangers of every sort, and it is not our sense that any further Privileges than those extensive ones, already allowed by the Charter, should be granted to any other foreigners than Protestants, conformably to the Act of the thirteenth Year of his present Majesty *for naturalizing foreign Protestants in America;*[5] and it may not be improper to Inform your Lordships that an Act of this Province passed in 1700, was repealed by the Crown in 1705, on the Advice of His Majesty's Attorney General, chiefly, because, it contained a Provision similar to that which is the Object of this Law.[6]

> An act for appointing an agent to apply for and receive the distributive share and Proportion which shall be assigned to this province of the sum of money granted by Parliament to his Majesty's colonyes in America.[7]

The Object of this Act is the Appointment of an Agent for the Particular Purpose of receiving the Proportion of the money which shall be allotted to this Province out of the sum of two Hundred Thousand Pounds granted by Parliament in the Year 1759, to be distributed to the several Colonies in North America. The Act Directs that the money should be received by Mr. Franklin, the Agent Nominated for that Purpose, and should be by Him

5. 13 Geo. II, c. 7, 1740.

6. An Act for the Effectual Establishment and Confirmation of the Freeholds of This Province and Territories, Their Heirs and Assigns, in Their Lands and Tenements (sect. x), passed Nov. 27, 1700; disallowed Feb. 7, 1706, *Statutes at Large, Pa.,* II, 118–23, 449–56, 495–6.

7. Passed Sept. 29, 1759, *Statutes at Large, Pa.,* V, 460–2. On the parliamentary grant, see above, VIII, 292–3 n, 333, and below, this volume, p. 186 n.

deposited in the Bank of England, liable to the Draught of the Trustees of the Loan Office in Pensylvania. The Principal Objection made to the Act, my Lords, is this; that it cannot possibly be complyed with in the manner there prescribed; for that the money being deposited in the Bank by Mr. Franklin, the Governors will not enter into any correspondence with the Trustees of the Loan Office aforesaid, or with any person but Mr. Franklin Concerning that sum; and that they cannot issue money paid in by one Person at the Draught of another, tho the money should be paid in expressly for their Use, tho we are inclineable to believe, that the practice of the Bank is as it has been stated, Yet we are not satisfied that this can be applyed as a Conclusive Objection to this Act, nor even if it could should we think it a sufficient reason, under the Present Circumstances of the Province to advise his Majesty to anull it; for, my Lords, by the manner in which the Act is worded, it is far from being perfectly clear whether, when the Money was once Deposited in the Bank as a Place of Security it was not the Intention of the Assembly that the Trustees of the Loan Office should draw upon Mr. Franklin and not upon the Bank; and this construction has been contended for by the councel on the part of the Assembly. If Your Lordships should be of Opinion that this was their Intention, the Act stands free from the Objection which has been made; but, my Lords, whether that was, or was not the Case, we Apprehend that the Intention of the Assembly was clearly this; to receive their Proportion of the Money with as much expedition and security as possible. With respect to the first Object, the expedition; their Intention in that will be totally defeated, If the Act now before Your Lordships is to be repealed. No Money will be issued from the Treasury till his Majesty's Disallowance of this Act is known in Pensylvania, till a new Act is passed in Consequence of it, and that again transmitted to England. With respect to security, we apprehend, it will stand nearly upon the same footing. Mr. Franklin will be equally responsible for the money he receives, and will be equally bound under the Terms of the Act to deposit it in the Bank; And we beg leave to Observe to Your Lordships that the money Distributed in the other Colonies, in consequence of the votes of Parliament, has frequently been received by the Agents of those Colonies under their General Powers of Agency only, or by Virtue of a particular Appointment, subject to no other Restriction than meerly the General Direction of remitting it to the Colony which appointed them. As therefore no personal Objection has been made to Mr. Franklin, and as the Opposition to this Act is founded principally upon a supposition that, from the manner of wording the Act, the Intention of the Assembly cannot be strictly complyed with, we shall beg leave to recommend it to his Majesty's Approbation; because we are clearly of Opinion that the Intention of the Assembly, and, what is more material, of the British House of Commons will be better Answered, that the Interest, not only of the Province, but the Publick in General will be more effectually promoted by letting this Act be carried into execution, than by suffering the Money intended for the Encouragement of this Colony to lie useless in the Treasurey, whereby the Publick Service very possibly may be retarded; and therefore the very Intention of Parliament in giving this Money by that means be frustrated, mearly because the Assembly did not know, with sufficient accuracy, or did not attend, with sufficient care, in the Directions of the Act, to that precise manner, in which money is received and issued at the Bank. And, my Lords, we are the more Inclinable to recommend this Act to his Majesty's Approbation, because when we look back upon the Conduct of this Province, when we consider how offten and how Ineffectually they were solicited at the commencement of the war to contribute to the Publick Service, we are extremely Disinclined to furnish not only any real discouragement, but even any colourable Pretext for withholding that Assistance in which the welfare of the Publick and of the Province may be so essentially interested.

With regard to the Disposition of the money which is in this Act reserved solely to the Assembly, independant of the Proprietaries,[8] we have had often Occasion to state our Opinion to Your Lordships, in the Course of this report; and we admit this Act to be in that respect very exceptionable; Yet, my Lords, still adhering to our Principle of uniformly disapproving such incroachment,

8. The act provided that when the trustees of the Loan Office finally received the proceeds of the grant they were to purchase Pa. bills of credit and turn these over to the committees of the Assembly annually appointed, who were thereupon to "burn, sink and destroy" the bills "unless the same shall be otherwise disposed of by act of assembly."

our respect to the sense of the British Legislature, which Intended that this remittance should meet with as few delays as possible, and, our regard to his Majesty's service have Induced us, in this one Instance to suffer, tho Nothing can Induce us to Approve or for the future to advise his Majesty to permit, such a deviation from the Constitution.

An Act for the Continuance of an Act of Assembly of this Province intitled A Supplementary Act to the Act intitled An Act for Preventing the exportation of Bread and Flour not merchantable, and for the new Appointment of Officers to put the same in Execution.[9]

An Act for the further Continuance of an Act of Assembly of this Province, intitled An Act for the Continuance of An Act of Assembly of this Province intitled A Supplementary Act to the Act, intitled an Act for preventing the Exportation of Bread and Flour not Merchantable and for the new Appointment of Officers to put the said Law into Execution.[1]

An Act to prevent the Exportation of bad or Unmerchantable Staves, Heading Boards and Timber.[2]

In delivering our Opinion upon the Subject of these three Bills, in Order, to avoid giving any unnecessary trouble to Your Lordships, we shall beg leave to consider them together, as their Objects are nearly of the same Nature; as they are liable only to one Objection, and as that Objection is common to them all.

The purpose my Lords, of these Bills is to prevent the Commission of those frauds which frequently have been practiced in this Province in three of the most material Articles of their Trade, Bread, Flour, and Staves, and to take care that they shall be exported for the future in a Merchantable Condition, suitable to the Regulations which are therein prescribed.

To these Regulations no exception has been made, as they are manifestly Calculated for the publick good, as they tend only to

9. Passed Sept. 27, 1758, *Statutes at Large, Pa.*, v, 374–6. For the Proprietors' objections, see *ibid.*, pp. 663–5.

1. Passed Oct. 19, 1758, *Statutes at Large, Pa.*, vi, 5–6. For the Proprietors' objections, see *ibid.*, v, 688–9.

2. Passed April 21, 1759, *Statutes at Large, Pa.*, v, 400–5. For the Proprietors' objections, see *ibid.*, pp. 666–9.

Discourage fraud, and to Support the Credit of the Province and are not Detrimental to any Individual.

The only Objection which has been made to these Acts is that the Appointment of the Officers, for carrying them into execution, is taken from the Proprietaries, to whom by their Charter it properly belongs. This, my Lords, is a just and Valid Objection to almost all the Acts Against which the Proprietaries Complain; and though in these Acts this Objection has its weight, Yet, as the Privelidge here Assumed is not like the cases we had before the Honour of Stating to Your Lordships, a total change of constitutional powers and a deviation from the whole Course of Proceeding in England, but merely the Appointment of a Ministerial Officer to put in execution a particular and temporary regulation of police. We do not think the Objection considerable enough to out weigh the usefull Provisions of these Bills, and therefore we humbly recommend that they may be suffer'd to pass into Laws.

With respect to the several other Acts referr'd to Us by Your Lordships said Order, and to which no Objection has been made, we beg leave to observe that the three following are expired, viz.

An Act in Addition to an Act intitled An Act for regulating the hire of Carriages to be employ'd in his Majesty's Service.[3]

An Act for extending several Sections of an Act of Parliament passed in the thirty second Year of the present Reign, Intitled An Act for punishing Mutiny and Desertion and for the better payment of the Army and their Quarters.[4]

An Act for regulating the Officers and Soldiers in the pay of this Province.[5]

And that the remaining five, as far as we are capable of judging, are extremely unexceptionable, the Objects of them being confined to the internal Government of the Province, to mere regulations of Police and matters of domestic Oeconomy; they are intitled,

A Supplement to the Act entitled An Act for regulating the hire of Carriages to be employed in his Majesty's Service.[6]

3. Passed Sept. 29, 1758, *Statutes at Large, Pa.*, v, 376–7.
4. Passed April 21, 1759, *Statutes at Large, Pa.*, v, 409–20.
5. Passed April 21, 1759, *Statutes at Large, Pa.*, v, 424–7.
6. Passed Sept. 20, 1758, *Statutes at Large, Pa.*, v, 372–4.

A Supplement to an Act Intitled An Act for preventing Abuses in the Indian Trade for supplying the Indians, Friends and Allies of Great Britain, with Goods at more easy Rates and for securing and Strengthening the peace and Friendship lately concluded with the Indians Inhabiting the northern and Western Frontiers of this Province.[7]

A Supplement to an Act Intitled An Act for granting to his Majesty a Duty of Tonnage upon ships and Vessells, And also certain Duties upon Wine, Rum, Brandy, and other Spirits, and a Duty upon sugar for Supporting and maintaining the Provincial Ship of War, for protecting the Trade of this Province and other purposes for his Majesty's service.[8]

An Act for regulating the hire of Carriages to be employed in his Majesty's Service.[9]

An Act to continue an Act Intitled An Act for directing the Choice of Inspectors in the Counties of Chester, Lancaster, York, Cumberland, Berks and Northampton.[1]

Having, in Obedience to Your Lordships orders, stated our Opinion upon the several Acts distinctly which have been referr'd to our Consideration, and having assign'd our reasons why we think they may deserve his Majesty's disapprobation or Allowance, we beg leave, after having shown how (Separate and Independant of each other) they are repugnant to Justice in a private View, to state, by considering them collectively and together, how fatal they would be to the Constitution, in a publick one. That Your Lordships may be satisfyed how entirely the Prerogatives of the Crown, which it has reserved either for its own Exercise, or which it has deligated to the Proprietaries, must of Necessity be destroy'd, if the Laws, as they have been passed, should be approved by his Majesty; or the more dangerous Claims, which have been set up to support them, should once be Admitted. For, amongst all the laws, referr'd to us by Your Lordships and Objected to by the Proprietaries, there is not a single Act, not only amongst those which we have Advised his Majesty to annull, but

7. Passed April 17, 1759, *Statutes at Large, Pa.,* v, 396–400.
8. Passed April 21, 1759, *Statutes at Large, Pa.,* v, 406–9.
9. Passed April 21, 1759, *Statutes at Large, Pa.,* v, 420–24.
1. Passed Sept. 29, 1759, *Statutes at Large, Pa.,* v, 465–6.

even which we have, from peculiar Circumstances, thought ourselves bound to recommend to his Majesty's Approbation, that does not contain either some Encroachment on the Prerogative of the Proprietaries, as they are Trustees for the Crown, or on their Property as Land holders in the Province, and in several of the Laws Your Lordships will have perceiv'd that both these Purposes are united. By the Land Tax Act, their Property is charged with the utmost Partiality and Injustice, and thereby, in a degree taken away. By the Act for recording Warrants and Surveys they are deprived of all legal Remedy for the Recovery of their Lands, by the Establishment of a Title unreasonable and inconclusive in itself, and unknown to the Common Law. By the Act for the Relief of Devisees their Right of Escheats, which is inseparable from Sovereignty, is cut off. By the Supplemental Bill for Courts of Judicature, their clearest Power in the Appointment of Judicial Officers, tho not absolutely taken away, is considerably abridg'd. By the Substitution of Paper Money for Sterling, in the Reemission Act, their Rents are unequitably reduc'd, and thereby their express Contracts virtually annull'd; and in all the Acts which relate either to the Nomination of Officers, or to the Disposition of the Publick money, the most sacred and inviolable Parts of the Executive Power are transferr'd from the Proprietaries and drawn into the hands of a popular Assembly. To stop these Encroachments and to restrain such Irregularities, there are but two Checks, of which the Constitution, in its Nature, admits. The one is in the Hold which the Proprietaries have over the Governor, the other is in his Majesty's Prerogative of Repeal. And Abridgement of that Prerogative has been contended for by the Assembly, the Right of the Proprietaries to instruct their Deputy they have denied; and the Justice of indemnifying him against his Principal has been supported, agreeable to what we have stated to Your Lordships at the Opening of our Report.[2]

2. This paragraph was intended, of course, as a strong defense of the Proprietors and a scathing criticism of the Assembly. It would certainly be read as such by members of the Privy Council Committee to whom it was addressed. To readers of a later century, however, the paragraph may suggest some of the features of the proprietary system of colonial control which many Pennsylvanians found most obnoxious. Joining in the hands of one or two private individuals in far-off England, as the system did, both inherited powers of government and the overlordship of the soil of the province,

And tho my Lords we think it incumbent upon us to declare that no Instance has been produced of any improper Exercise of their Prerogatives, on the part of the Proprietaries; Yet we cannot help lamenting that they have not been more consistent and uniform in the Support of them: for it is Observable, that even to the Nomination of Officers, which is so much insisted on by the Assembly, they do not pretend a Right from the Constitution itself, but derive it meerly from the Concessions of the Proprietaries; and tho they profess to be very sensibly affected at any Encroachment on the Prerogative of the Crown, and state themselves very properly as intrusted with its Preservations, yet we cannot help Observing that instead of supporting the Constitution of the Colony and their own Dignity, as a very material Part of the Legislature, they seem to have Consider'd themselves only in the narrow and Contracted View of Landholders in the Province, and to have been regardless of their Prerogatives as long as their Property remained secure, and never to have felt for their Privileges, as Proprietaries, till, by the Diminution of those Privileges their Interests were affected, as Individuals.[3]

But, my Lords, we Apprehend it is our Duty to hear, and, if they are just, to recommend to redress the Complaints of the Proprietaries, from whatever Motives they may proceed; to bring back, as far as shall be thought advisable by your Lordships, the Consti-

---

feudal in origin, it seemed to promote inefficiency of administration and an almost classic example of conflict of interest. Though such men as BF and Norris might recognize that direct royal government was not likely to be any more liberal, they could well believe that its substitution for proprietary government would remove the special handicaps under which only Pennsylvania, the lower counties on Delaware, and Maryland, among all British colonies in the New World, still suffered.

3. This and the following paragraphs greatly vexed Thomas Penn. In a letter to Governor Hamilton, June 27, 1760, he wrote: "They [the Board of Trade] have been pleased in a manner I do not so well like, to censure us for not attending so closely to the proceedings of the Assembly as to prevent their incroachments on the prerogative, and say we look upon our selves as Landholders only, which I think is not to be accounted for when they know we have been disputing with the Assembly for twenty years past in support of the prerogative of the Crown. However as they have reported against these Laws we must put up with that and the more readily for that it shews their disapprobation of the encroachments and claims of the Assembly." Hist. Soc. Pa.

tution of the Colony to its proper principles; to put the Government in a regular Course of Administration; to give to every branch of it the Exercise of its proper powers; to restore to the Crown, in the Persons of the Proprietaries, its just Prerogatives; to check the growing Influence of the Assembly, and to Distinguish what they are perpetually confounding, the Executive from the Legislative Parts of Government.

We are satisfied that there is nothing so likely to preserve the Tranquility of the Province itself or its Dependance upon the Mother Country as the maintaining, with a strict and steddy Hand, the necessary Powers and just Prerogatives of the Crown, and the Preferring an uniform and settled Principle of Government to an occasional Departure from it, for temporary Convenience. Every days' Experience Convinces Us that it is in vain to negotiate away His Majesty's Prerogative; every new Concession becomes the foundation of some new demand, and that, my Lords, of some new dispute.

This, which is true in general, Your Lordships will perceive has been particularly so in the Province of Pensylvania. For, tho no Principle of the Constitution is more known or better establish'd than the Right of the Crown, and therefore, in this case of the Proprietaries, to the sole Nomination of Officers and the exclusive Application of money, it is now contended, that the Proprietaries should not even partake in the Exercise of either of those Powers. The Proprietaries consent to share their Prerogatives with the Assembly; the Assembly insists upon ingrossing them. And even should it be apprehended that, after so much Supineness on the part of the Proprietaries and such long Usage on the Part of the Assembly, the Constitution could not, without difficulty, in every Circumstance be reestablished; We conclude Your Lordships cannot therefore be of Opinion that it ought in every Circumstance to be departed from.

If, my Lords, it could be necessary to support the Propriety of maintaining the Constitution of the Colony, by any other Reasons than those which we have already offer'd to Your Lordships, we apprehend that there are Circumstances peculiar to this Province, which make the Restrictions we have mention'd particularly Necessary. This Colony, tho in its Form of Government nominally indeed the same with those which are under the immediate

Controul of the Crown, consisting like them of a Governor Council and Assembly, is in reality extremely different: The Governor
and the Assembly being the only branches of the Legislature, and
the only Purpose of the Council being to assist the Governor with
their Advice; not that their consent is in any manner necessary,
and their Advice, he may adopt or reject, as he thinks proper. By
which means there is not in this Colony, as in other Governments
or as in the Mother Country, any intermediate Power that may
interpose between the Encroachments of the Assembly, on the
one hand, or the Oppression of the Proprietaries on the other. The
Assembly, My Lords, claims likewise to be intitled, from its Institution, to the Possession of very extraordinary Powers, to be a
Body perpetually subsisting subject neither to Prorogation nor
Dissolution, by the Authority of the Governor. It seems therefore
particularly necessary, by the constitutional Interposition of the
Crown, to restrain the Powers of the Assembly, sufficiently great
by it's Institution, from becoming exorbitant beyond measure, by
its Encroachments; And to protect likewise the Rights of His
Majesty, which have been gradually departed from by the Proprietaries, and which must always be invaded, while the Prerogatives of Royalty are placed in the feeble hands of Individuals, and
the Authority of the Crown is to be exercised, without the Powers
of the Crown to support it. We are, My Lords, Your Lordships'
Most obedient Humble Servants,   DUNK HALIFAX.
                                                  SOAME JENYNS.
                                                  W G. HAMILTON.
                                                  WM. SLOPER.
                                                  ED. ELIOT.

To Deborah Franklin   Duplicate:[4] American Philosophical Society

Copy—Original per Budden   London, June 27, 1760
My dear Child
    I wrote a Line to you by the Pacquet, to let you know we were
well, and I promis'd to write you fully per Capt. Budden, and
answer all your Letters, which I accordingly now set down to do.[5]

4. In WF's hand, signed by BF.
5. Not one letter written by DF during 1760 has been found. *Pa. Gaz.,*

I am concern'd that so much Trouble should be given you by idle Reports concerning me.[6] Be satisfied, my dear, that while I have my Senses, and God vouchsafes me his Protection, I shall do nothing unworthy the Character of an honest Man, and one that loves his Family.

I have not yet seen Mr. Beatty,[7] nor do I know where to write to him. He forwarded your Letter to me from Ireland.

The Paragraph of your Letter inserted in the Papers, related to the Negro School.[8] I gave it to the Gentlemen concern'd, as it was a Testimony in favour of their pious Design: But did not expect they would have printed it with your Name. They have since chosen [me] one of the Society, and I am at present Chairman for the current year. I enclose you an Account of their Proceedings.

I did not receive the Prospect of Quebec which you mention that you sent me.[9]

Peter[1] continues with me, and behaves as well as I can expect, in a Country where there are many Occasions of spoiling Servants, if they are ever so good. He has as few Faults as most of them, and I see with only one Eye, and hear only with one Ear; so we rub on pretty comfortably. King, that you enquire after, is not with us. He ran away from our House, near two Years ago, while we were absent in the Country; But was soon found in Suffolk, where he had been taken in the Service of a Lady that was very fond of the Merit of making him a Christian, and contributing to his Educa-

---

Sept. 18, 1760, reported the entry of the *Philadelphia Packet*, Capt. Richard Budden.

6. It is not known what these "idle Reports" alleged.

7. For the Rev. Charles Beatty, who was in the British Isles trying to raise money for indigent Presbyterian ministers, see above, p. 30 n.

8. See above, VIII, 425, for the extract which BF gave to the Bray Associates. For their plans to establish Negro schools in America and for BF's assistance therein, see above, pp. 12–13, 20–1.

9. Among the contents of *Father Abraham's Almanack* for 1761, advertised in *Pa. Gaz.*, Oct. 9, 1760, were "Plans of the three illustrious Gems which now sparkle with resplendent Beauty in the British Crown, viz. Of Fort Du Quesne, Quebec and Montreal . . . ." It may be that the publisher of this almanac, William Dunlap (above, V, 199 n), DF's relative through marriage, supplied her an advance copy of the plan of Quebec which she sent to BF.

1. For BF's "Negro Man" Peter, see above, VI, 425 n. King, mentioned below, was WF's.

tion and Improvement. As he was of little Use, and often in Mischief, Billy consented to her keeping him while we stay in England. So the Lady sent him to School, has him taught to read and write, to play on the Violin and French Horn, with some other Accomplishments more useful in a Servant. Whether she will finally be willing to part with him, or persuade Billy to sell him to her, I know not. In the meantime he is no Expence to us.

The dried Venison was very acceptable, and I thank you for it. We have had it constantly shav'd to eat with our Bread and Butter for Breakfast, and this Week saw the last of it. The Bacon still holds out; for we are choice of it. Some Rashers of it, yesterday relish'd a Dish of Green Pease. Mrs. Stevenson thinks there was never any in England so good. The smok'd Beef was also excellent.

The Accounts you give me of the Marriages of our Friends are very agreeable. I love to hear of every thing that tends to increase the Number of good People. You cannot conceive how shamefully the Mode here is a single Life. One can scarce be in the Company of a Dozen Men of Circumstance and Fortune, but what it is odds that you find on Enquiry eleven of them are single. The great Complaint is the excessive Expensiveness of English Wives.

I am extreamly concern'd with you at the Misfortune of our Friend Mr. Griffitts.[2] How could it possibly happen?

'Twas a terrible Fire that of Boston.[3] I shall contribute here

2. The Philadelphia merchant, William Griffitts (above, VIII, 328 n), went bankrupt in the spring of 1760. Threatened with imprisonment by a few creditors who were dissatisfied with the arrangements he had made to pay them, Griffitts and several of his other creditors petitioned the Pa. Assembly, Sept. 11, 1761, for relief. That body passed a bill, Sept. 23, 1761, approving his financial plans and exempting and discharging him "from confinement on account of any debts heretofore contracted." Governor Hamilton signed the bill three days later. 8 *Pa. Arch.*, VI, 5257–8, 5265, 5268–9; *Statutes at Large, Pa.*, VI, 118–23.

3. *Boston Post-Boy,* March 24, 1760, *Pa. Gaz.* April 3, 1760, and *London Chron.,* May 17–20, 1760, carried reports of a fire, "supposed to be greater than any that has been known in these American Colonies," which raged in Boston on March 20, 1760; although it took no lives, the fire destroyed 400 dwellings valued at around £300,000. Gov. Thomas Pownall solicited donations for the sufferers, and Pa. Assembly on April 12, 1760, voted a free gift of £1500 to be disposed of by the Boston selectmen or the overseers of the poor. 8 *Pa. Arch.*, VI, 5132; *Pa. Gaz.*, May 8, 1760.

towards the Relief of the Sufferers. Our Relation[s] have escap'd I believe generally, but some of my particular Friends must have suffer'd greatly.

I think you will not complain this Year as you did the last, of being so long without a Letter. I have wrote to you very frequently;[4] and shall not be so much out of the Way of writing this Summer as I was the last.[5]

I hope our Friend Batram is safely return'd to his Family;[6] remember me to him in the kindest Manner.

Poor David Edwards[7] died this Day Week of a Consumption. I had a Letter from a Friend of his, acquainting me, that he had been long ill and incapable of doing his Business, and was at Board in the Country. I fear'd he might be in Straits, as he never was prudent enough to lay up any thing. So I wrote to him immediately that if he had occasion he might draw on me for Five Guineas. But he died before my Letter got to hand. I hear the Woman at whose House he long lodg'd and boarded, has buried him and taken all he left, which could not be much, and there are some small Debts unpaid. He maintained a good Character at Bury where he lived some Years, and was well respected, to my Knowledge by some Persons of Note there. I wrote to you before, that we saw him at Bury, when we went thro' Suffolk into Norfolk, the Year before last.[8] I hope his good Father, my old Friend, continues well.

Give my Duty to Mother and Love to my dear Sally. Remember me affectionately to all Enquiring Friends; and believe me ever, my dearest Debby, Your loving Husband   B FRANKLIN

P.S. June 29. Since I have finish'd my Letter I have found another of yours, by which I perceive I had forgot to purchase the Eider Down and Corn Plaster you wrote for. I beg you would excuse

4. See above, pp. 25, 27, 32–3, 35–6, 37–9.
5. In the summer and fall of 1759, BF toured northern England and Scotland; see above, VIII, 430–2.
6. During the first part of 1760 John Bartram (above, II, 378–9 n), the famous Quaker botanist, was doing field work in Va. and the Carolinas. William Darlington, *Memorials of John Bartram and Humphrey Marshall* (Phila., 1849), pp. 223–4, 225, 394.
7. See above, VII, 275 n; VIII, 277. The correspondence referred to in the next sentences has not been found.
8. For this trip, see above, VIII, 132 n.

this seeming Neglect. I cannot now get it to send by this Ship, but you may depend on having it sent by the next.[9] In Capt. Budden is a Box mark'd S.F. No. 1. which I mention'd in mine of March 29.[1] as being sent by another Ship; but we fail'd of getting it on board that Ship. It contains a Bundle of Books for Mr. Sturgeon,[2] and 4 Setts of Husbandry Books that are my own. They cost me £4 16s. Desire Mr. Hall or Mr. Delap[3] to sell them for me.

I shall take care to do what I can for the Ransomer at Bourdeaux.[4] A Merchant has promis'd me to write to Bourdeaux and enquire into the Affair; the Account you sent me [*remainder missing*].

Endorsed: Copy of Letter per Capt Budden

To David Hall

ALS: Edward Laurence Doheny Memorial Library, St. John's Seminary[5]

Dear Mr. Hall, London, June 27. 1760

By the last Pacquet I sent you the Protests of two of your Bills, one for £200 the other for £100 drawn by Scot and McMichael on Messrs. Portis.[6] My Banker informs me, that they now offer to

9. For the shipment of these articles, see below, p. 183.

1. Not found.

2. For Rev. William Sturgeon, whom BF recommended to supervise the Bray Associates School at Philadelphia, see above, VII, 252 n. The books sent him were probably John Berriman, ed., *Christian Doctrines and Duties Explained and Recommended; in forty sermons preached . . . by W[illiam] Berriman* (2 vols., (London, 1751) and Thomas Bray's edition of *Erasmi Ecclesiastes* (London, 1730). Richard I. Shelling, "Benjamin Franklin and the Dr. Bray Associates," *PMHB*, LXIII (1939), 287.

3. That is, William Dunlap.

4. *Pa. Gaz.*, Oct. 18, 1759, published a letter from Barton and Delap, merchants at Bordeaux, soliciting assistance for two American seamen who were languishing there in a "loathsome Goal." One of the prisoners, Thomas Eastwick, whose ship was being detained for £200 ransom, was identified as having been married in Philadelphia, and it may be that his friends requested DF to ask BF to help him.

5. From the Estelle Doheny Collection of the Edward Laurence Doheny Memorial Library, St. John's Seminary, Camarillo, Calif.

6. For BF and Hall's subsequent actions in regard to these bills, see above, p. 34 n.

pay the Money; and tho' the Protests intitle us to 20 per Cent. from the Drawers, yet as I conceive from some Circumstances I have heard, that they have been hardly us'd by their Correspondent, I think it a neighbourly Act to accept the Money now 'tis offer'd here, and forego that Advantage. I shall therefore direct my Banker to receive it; not doubting but you will approve my acting the generous and friendly Part towards them, and not insist on the Damages, nor on being paid the principal Money there, till you hear from me whether it is or is not paid here.

I hope the Fount of Brevier, which went from hence last Winter in Capt. Gibbon, is long since in your Hands, tho' I have not yet heard of his Arrival.[7] I suppose he was long detain'd in the Channel, with the other Ships waiting for a Convoy.

I am very sensible that we do, as you say, suffer a great deal of Loss in our Debts, for want of getting them regularly in. I wish therefore you would endeavour to find a proper Person to be entrusted and employ'd in the Collection. I shall willingly bear my Proportion of the Expence.

I was in great Hopes of seeing you and my other Friends this Summer; but I now find it impracticable.[8] I hope however to be with you early in the Spring.

As yet we know nothing of Certainty concerning a Peace. It is only in general conjectur'd that the Want of Money with all the Powers at War, must compel a Peace in the ensuing Winter.[9] But even this Reason is perhaps not solid. For my own Part, I think that for $\frac{1}{2}$ per Cent. more, the Money wanted here may be raised as readily for next Year, as it was for this.[1] And perhaps the same may hold good with our Enemies.[2]

7. For the shipment and receipt of the brevier type, see above, p. 34 n.

8. The delay was due to the prolonged hearings before the Board of Trade and the Privy Council on the confirmation of the acts passed by the Pa. Assembly, 1758–59.

9. The British and French governments conducted conversations directed towards a peace settlement in the spring and summer of 1761, but these proved abortive and the preliminaries of peace were not concluded until November 1762.

1. For one of BF's earlier schemes for increasing British revenues, see above, VIII, 214–15.

2. Hall printed this paragraph in Pa. Gaz., Sept. 11, 1760, as an extract from a letter from London.

I order'd you some Copies of a Pamphlet[3] that went by way of New York. I suppose Mr. Strahan who sent them wrote to you with them. Please to sell them for my Account. It sold here extreamly well, and your Friend has gain'd some Reputation by it: But has more Pleasure in the Hopes of its doing some Service to the Colonies.

Mr. Potts, now Secretary of the Post Office,[4] show'd me a Letter of yours lately, (when I met him at Dinner with the Postmasters-General,[5] relating to the Chronicle[6] to be sent you per Pacquet; and I agreed to be answerable to him for the Expence.

If in any thing I can serve you before I leave London, let me know in your next, and I shall do it with Pleasure; being with sincere Esteem, Dear David, Yours affectionately   B FRANKLIN

Addressed: To | Mr David Hall | Printer | Philadelphia
Endorsed: B. Franklin June 27. 1760

From David Hall   Letterbook copy: American Philosophical Society

Sir,   Philada. July 2. 1760.
Yours, of the 28th of March,[7] I received, owning the Receipt of a Bill for £200 Sterling, drawn by William Plumsted.

The Brevier came safe to hand by Gibbon, looks very well, but sticks, when distributed, most intolerably. Believe it will turn out pretty perfect.[8]

By the Captains Falconer and Killner to London, I sent you the

3. *The Interest of Great Britain Considered;* see above, pp. 47–100. It was reprinted in Philadelphia by William Bradford, who advertised it as "Just published" in *Pa. Gaz.*, Dec. 4, 1760.

4. Henry Potts (d. 1768), sorter in the Post Office, 1723; controller of the Inland Office, 1744; secretary, 1760–62, 1765–68. Kenneth Ellis, *The Post Office in the Eighteenth Century* (London, 1958), pp. 83–4, 87–90, 94.

5. The joint postmasters general, 1759–65, were Lord Bessborough (above, p. 118 n) and the Honorable Robert Hampden-Trevor (1706–1783; born Robert Trevor; succeeded as Baron Trevor, 1764).

6. *The London Chronicle.*

7. See above, pp. 39–40.

8. For BF's purchase and shipment of a font of Brevier type, see above, p. 34 n.

first and second Copies of a Bill of Exchange for £100 Sterling.[9] Inclosed you have now the third Copy of same Bill, in case of Miscarriages, I shall soon remit you more, tho' at present it does not suit me to do it. I am, Sir, Yours. &c.   DAVID HALL

To Mr. Franklin

By the Myrtilla, Captain Bolitho, to London[1]

From Isaac Norris[2]

Letterbook copy: Historical Society of Pennsylvania

Dear Friend B Franklin   July 28 1760
It is some time since I wrote—my last being of the 15th April[3] since which I have recd yours 9th January 19. 21. 29 Feb and 11 March with several Copies.[4] The Proprietors endeavouring to repeal our late Laws is what we might expect from their Conduct towards us for some Years past.[5] But the Confusion the dissallowance of our Mony Act,[6] and especially those granting Supplies to the Crown[7] would throw the Province into and the Necessity as well as reasonableness of the Acts themselves I trust will protect us from so great a Calamity notwithstanding the known Inclinations of some who perhaps will sit as Judge upon them. The Care of them is now intrusted with our Agents and

9. For this bill, drawn by Scott & McMichael of Philadelphia on George and James Portis of London, see above, pp. 34 n, 100.

1. *Pa. Gaz.*, July 17, 1760, records the clearance of the *Myrtilla*, Capt. John Bolitho. *London Chron.*, Aug. 9–12, 1760, reports its arrival in the Downs after a passage of twenty-five days.

2. This letter is canceled in the letterbook and apparently was never sent, being superceded, as the memorandum at the end shows, by the one dated August 24.

3. See above, pp. 43–7.

4. None of these letters have been found.

5. See above, pp. 125–31, for the proprietary opposition to the laws passed by the Pa. Assembly, 1758–59.

6. The Re-emitting Act, passed June 9, 1759; see above, VIII, 419 n, and this vol., pp. 145–53.

7. Primarily the Supply Act of April 1759 (above, VIII, 326–7 n, but Norris may also have been thinking of the Supply Act of April 1760 (above, p. 43 n), which because of its similarities to the former act, would probably be similarly dealt with.

we must wait the Event: You are too exactly acquainted with their consequence and importance to need any further Advice on that Head.

Governor Hamiltons passing our last Grant to the Crown,[8] must I apprehend make this Opposition more Difficult to the Proprietors. And I trust it will not be in their Power to succeed in ruining their Province for the paultry Advantage they propose to themselves of being exempted from Taxes, which I am informed are amaizingly small in proportion to the rest of the Inhabitants and their great Estate amongst us.[9] As it has ever been my Opinion that we have been contending for a Matter of Right rather than Mony I am well pleased the Commissioners and Assessors have acted with so much moderation. To the Acts already past we are using our utmost Endeavours in settling a Quota Bill for the several Counties which I have great Hopes may be brot to some perfection at our next meeting;[1] But as it requires the best Notices we can procure we were under a Necessity of postponing it at our last Sitting, for want of the Returns from many of the Counties which had not finished their Assessments according to the Directions of the last Act passed by Governor Denny tho' I think they are all returned sometime since to the Committee appointed by the House to receive and examine them in Order to lay them before the Assembly in September next. In pursuance of those Acts we have already obtained and the Quota Bill the Province in all probability will in a little Time come to as near a proportion of the Share of each Particular as the Nature of publick Taxes will admit at least as near as any of the other Colonies—Or our Mother Country.

8. See above, p. 43 n. In letters of May 24 and June 6, 1760, Thomas Penn told Hamilton that he approved the governor's passing this bill under the circumstances. Penn Papers, Hist. Soc. Pa.

9. A committee of the Pa. Assembly reported, March 12, 1761, that while the inhabitants of Pa. in one year had paid £27,103 12s. 8d. under the Supply Act of April 1759, the proprietary taxes had amounted to only £566 4s. 10d. Thomas Penn himself admitted that "the tax does not seem great, and we by no means think it hard that we should supply such a one for the public service." 8 *Pa. Arch.*, VI, 5216; to Richard Peters, March 10, May 8, 1760, quoted in William R. Shepherd, *History of Proprietary Government in Pennsylvania* (N. Y., 1896), p. 465 n.

1. See above, p. 29 n.

Our American Military Affairs have a fair Appearance.[2] May they succeed, and may that Success never—never be thrown away.

I have inclosed a First Bill of Exchange N 1876 drawn by J. Hunter on Messrs. Thomlinson &c. for One Hundred Pounds Sterling which please to receive.[3] Col. Hunter[4] came to Town a few Days ago with his Family a sharp, short Indisposition has prevented my seeing them tho' they are in our Neighbourhood, at a New House built by Dr. Moore near your Plantation,[5] but as I am finely recovered I do propose to wait upon them in a Day or Two. I suppose they will spend the Summer with us at least and I am pleased we are so near together.

When you see my Friend R. Charles[6] pray make my Complements to himself and Family. I have not heard from him a long while.

There are, I hear, Dissentions in the Church.[7] Several Persons

2. *Pa. Gaz.* in July 1760 carried numerous accounts of the French failure to recapture Quebec, of their subsequent retreat to Montreal, and of the flourishing condition of the British armies under Amherst and Murray which were expected to attack them.

3. BF recorded the receipt of this bill on Oct. 27, 1760. "Account of Expences," p. 56; *PMHB,* LV (1931), 128.

4. For Col. John Hunter, agent for Thomlinson & Hanbury, money suppliers of the British forces in North America, see above, VI, 223 n.

5. Possibly Samuel Preston Moore (above, IV, 295 n) and a pasture BF owned in the Northern Liberties of Philadelphia; see above, II, 310.

6. For BF's fellow agent, Robert Charles, see above, VI, 230 n.

7. In 1759–60 the Anglican Church in Philadelphia, Christ Church, was rent by controversies caused by the Rev. William McClanachan (1714–1765?). First a Presbyterian and then a Congregational minister, McClanachan conformed to the Church of England at Boston in 1754. Dissatisfied with his position as an Anglican missionary in Maine, he went to Virginia in 1759 to seek a more remunerative parish and visited Philadelphia in the spring of that year. Permitted to preach in Christ Church, McClanachan, an "avowed Methodist," immediately attracted a considerable following by imitating George Whitefield's "wild incoherent rhapsodies," as William Smith called them. Supporters in the vestry appointed him assistant minister, but opponents interceded with the Bishop of London, who refused to license him to preach, whereupon McClanachan and his followers left Christ Church (June 1760), met for a while in the State House, and then founded St. Paul's Church. See Horace W. Smith, *Life and Correspondence of the Rev. William Smith, D. D.* (Phila., 1880), I, 215–60; Frederick L. Weis, "The Colonial Clergy of the Middle Colonies," Amer. Antiq. Soc. *Proc.,* n.s., LXVI (1956), 266.

of Rank and Note amongst us are lately Dead. And others are born. I hear your Family is well.

Pray accept Yourself and tender to Billy (by the Time he returns home it must be William) my kindest good Wishes.   I N

This Letter lay in Town for want of an Opportunity of sending it till the Date of the succeeding Letter of the 24 August when CN returnd it and I wrote what follows page 112—which went by Captain Friend.[8]

To Deborah Franklin   ALS: American Philosophical Society

My dear Child,   London Augt. 23. 1760.

I receiv'd your Letters by Mr. Keene,[9] and some others, which I shall answer fully by Capt. Faulkner, who sails in a few Days.[1]

By him I send the Eider Down Cover lid, and Bag for the Feet, which cost 12 Guineas;[2] also the Camlet a second time for Sister Peter, to supply what was lost in Capt. House:[3] with some other little things that I shall mention hereafter. They are in a Box mark'd SF.

This serves to let you know we are well, and to cover a Pacquet for the Speaker which you will carefully deliver.[4]

8. For Norris' letter of August 24, entered at p. 112 of his letterbook, see below, pp. 184–6. "CN" was his brother Charles. *Pa. Gaz.*, Aug. 28, 1760, reported the clearance of the *James and Mary*, Capt. James Friend.

9. Samuel Keene (1734–1810), A.B., College of Philadelphia, 1759, had come to London to take orders in the Church of England, Sept. 29, 1760. He spent the remainder of his life ministering to various parishes in Maryland. Horace W. Smith, *Life and Correspondence of the Rev. William Smith, D. D.* (Phila., 1880), I, 242–6; Frederick L. Weis, *The Colonial Clergy of Maryland, Delaware, and Georgia* (Lancaster, Mass., 1950), p. 51. None of DF's letters written during 1760 have been found.

1. Capt. Nathaniel Falconer in the *Friendship* reached Deal, September 3, *London Chron.*, Sept. 2–4, 1760. He had arrived at Philadelphia, according to *Pa. Gaz.*, Nov. 13, 1760.

2. See above, pp. 176–7.

3. BF's sister-in-law, Mary Harman Franklin (C. 9). The *Juliana*, Capt. House, was captured by a French privateer in the spring of 1760; see above, p. 15 n.

4. Isaac Norris acknowledged the receipt of BF's letter of Aug. 22, with "inclosed Papers" (not found) on Oct. 22, 1760; see below, p. 236.

My Duty to Mother, Love to Sally and all Friends. I am concern'd you should be so perplex'd about a House, and hope you
are settled before this time.[5]

Your ever [loving husb]and   B FRANKLIN

In the Box are sundry Parcels for Mrs. Gambier.[6]

Mrs. Franklin

From Isaac Norris

Letterbook copy: Historical Society of Pennsylvania

Dear Friend B. Franklin   24th Augt, 1760

It is some Time since I wrote last, which I perceive by Your
last, was come to hand, being Dated on the 15th April past, Your
Several Dates of 9th January, 19th, 21st 29th february and 11th
March With Several Copies, got to me in Due Time, and a few
Days Ago the 14th June by the Packet,[7] it will be Needless to
Say, That all the Letters by Capt. House Miscarried,[8] but I have
been inform'd That Several of them were Infamously Picked up,
opend and forwarded to Philadelphia. Several Stories are Propa-
gated Concerning Them, to which I give little Credit being long
used to the reports of the Gentleman in whose Custody they Are
said to be,[9] I have enclos'd a first Bill of exchange No. 1876
Drawn by Col. J. Hunter on Messrs. Thomlinson &c. for £100

5. Since 1756 the Franklins had been renting a house in Market Street from
John Wister for £42 a year. In April 1761, however, DF and Sally moved to
a house which Adam Eckert, a joiner, had recently bought at what is now
326 Market Street, and the family lived there until early in 1765. Then DF
and Sally moved to their new house at 318 Market Street, which had been
under construction since 1763. Hannah B. Roach, "Benjamin Franklin
Slept Here," *PMHB*, LXXIV (1960), 164–74; see also map, above, II, following 456.

6. Probably the wife of either John or Samuel Gambier, public officials in
the Bahamas; see above, VII, 325 n, VIII, 424 n.

7. For Norris' letter of April 15, see above, pp. 43–7. None of BF's
letters here acknowledged have been found.

8. The *Juliana*, Capt. House, was taken by a French privateer early in
1760. See above, p. 15 n.

9. Nicholas Scull; see below, pp. 221–2.

Sterl. which pray receive,[1] as it becomes Due. The Proprietarys endeavouring to repeal our late Laws, is Consistent With their Conduct towards us for many Years past,[2] but the Confusion and Ruinous Consequences, the Disallowance of our Mony Bills, especialy Those granting aids to the Crown, Would throw the Province into, I Trust will Protect Them, as well as the reasonableness of the Acts themselves, especialy as they will be strengthen'd, by Governor Hamilton's Passing our last Supply Bill, of which I advised You in my Last of 15th April. It is Surprising how little the Proprietarys Taxes amounted to, for the Estate they hold, Compard with the Taxes the Inhabitants and other Owners of Lands here are rated. So That I have been inform'd some of the Proprietarys Officers have said the Proprietarys themselves Will Scarcly beleive it, Till Their Accounts are bro't in, by what I have heard of them they are too Low, but as it was ever my Opinion, we have been Contending for a Matter of Right, rather than Mony, I am pleas'd, the Comissioners and Assessors have err'd on that Side, all our Laws, by exempting the Unlocated Lands, Can never Tax their estate in full Propotion to the other Inhabitants and land holders, but as we are useing our utmost endeavours to Settle A Quota Bill Against our Next Seting, I do not Doubt, we Shall in a little while, Come to as near a Proportion, of the Share of each Particular, as the Nature of Publick Taxes will Admit, at least, as near, as any of the Other Colonies, and Much nearer Than our Mother Country,[3] I need not enlarge on Any General Heads which Concern this Province, because they are so well known to You and we have no doubt of your Care and Abilities to defend us Against those who have an evil eye over us, and yet Unfortunatly, Must have too great a share in Judging our Cause. At our Next Seting, We shall Consider your proposals for the Disposal of Parliamentry Grants, and be Then enabled to provide a remedy and give Orders less Subject to the Objections Made in England, Some of which I apprehend Would have Come into my mind had

1. BF received this bill on Oct. 27, 1760. "Account of Expences," p. 56; *PMHB*, LV (1931), 128.

2. For Thomas Penn's opposition to eleven of the nineteen acts passed by the Pa. Assembly in 1758–59, see above, pp. 125–31.

3. Many of the phrases used in this discussion of proprietary taxes and a quota bill appear in Norris' letter to BF of July 28, 1760; see above, pp. 180–1.

I been Able to Attend the House in their last Session,When That Law was Pass'd by Governor Denny.[4] That Gent[leman] is going Passenger with Capt. Hamet[5] a few days hence, he has Promisd to Call Upon me before his Departure, and if any thing further occurs worth Notice, I shall add and Commit it to his Care, Governor Hamilton's Behaviour has been very Civil hitherto, he Declares That he has the greatest Inclination to live on good Terms with the People, Acts of Justice Towards them, will soon have all the Good Effects, he, or his Constituents Can Wish or Desire; I am my Good friend, Your Affectionate Assured friend

Original by Captn. Friend[6]   I NORRIS
Duplicate by Capt. Hamet

First Bill of Exchange N 1876 £100. 0. 0

4. In response to Parliament's appropriation of £200,000 to reimburse the colonies for their expenditures in the campaign of 1758 (see above, VIII, 333), the Pa. Assembly passed the so-called Agency Act, Sept. 29, 1759 (*Statutes at Large, Pa.*, V, 460–2), which appointed BF agent to receive the colony's share of the money, directed him to deposit it in the Bank of England, and added somewhat ambiguously that it was to remain there "subject to the drafts and bills of exchange of the trustees of the general loan office." After the money was received in Pa. it was to be used to sink outstanding bills of credit "unless the same shall be otherwise disposed of by act of assembly." Penn opposed the act initially on the score that the money ought to be paid "to Persons appointed by the whole Legislature [i.e., the governor and Assembly] and not to the Agent." Later he also pointed out that the grant to Pa. and the Delaware counties was made jointly, "so that I think we shall keep it out of Franklin's hands," and that it was contrary to the Bank's policy to allow a deposit made by one person to be drawn on by others, as the Agency Act seemed to provide. Thomas Penn to Richard Peters, Aug. 3, Dec. 8, 1759, Penn Papers, Hist. Soc. Pa. In its report on this act the Board of Trade considered the first and third of these objections but did not find them of sufficient force to warrant disallowance, especially since prompt payment was most desirable. The Board agreed, however, that the Assembly ought not to have excluded the Proprietors from the disposition of the money. See above, pp. 164–7. By the time the Privy Council got around to dealing with the matter the six-months' time limit for consideration of the act had expired anyway, so it could not have disallowed the measure in any case. See below, p. 209.

5. *Pa. Gaz.*, Sept. 4, 1760, recorded the clearance of the *Dragon*, Capt. Francis Hammett.

6. *Pa. Gaz.*, Aug. 28, 1760, recorded the clearance of the *James and Mary*, Capt. James Friend.

From David Hall ^{Letterbook copy: American Philosophical Society}

Sir,   Philada. August 26. 1760.

I received yours, of the 14th of June, with two Protests inclosed for £300 Bills of Exchange,[7] which I immediately presented to the Gentlemen they were drawn by, who seemed a good Deal surprised that they should have come back protested, and shewed me a Letter from the Portis's telling them they had paid all their Draughts that had been presented to them, amounting to between Eight and Nine Thousand Pounds Sterling; however, they made no Objection to the renewing them, with the Damages, as they were returned; only they observed, that the Bill for £100 was protested for Non-acceptance, and that very often it happens, tho' a Bill is refused to be accepted, yet when it becomes due, is paid; but they very readily renewed it likewise, upon my promising to refund them, in case their first Draught should be paid.

Inclosed you have now a fresh Draught from them for £360 Sterling, which is your full Damages, and which I thought myself obliged to send you by the very first Opportunity, as what Bills I remit you, are at your own Risque, and of Course the Damages on any that may be protested, are likewise most justly yours.[8] There is a small Matter for the Protests, which is not included, but that can be settled with them at any Time. They are reckoned very honest Men, and most generous Dealers, consequently meet with a good Deal of Sympathy and Compassion from every Body here, as their Business, no Doubt, must have been interrupted, in some Measure, by their Connections with that House; but it is hoped that every Thing will soon be set to Rights, and that they, in the End, will be no great Sufferers by the Portis's, which will give great Pleasure to every Body, as they have the general good Wishes of the Place.

I should have made you a fresh Remittance now, but on speaking to Mrs. Franklin a few Days before the Packet arrived, she advised me not to do it, as she certainly expected you here this Fall; but as it has happened otherwise (which I am sorry for on

7. BF's letter of June 14 has not been found; on the protested bills see above, pp. 34 n, 177–8, and below, p. 235.

8. BF recorded receipt of this bill, Nov. 27, 1760, but with the note that, since the £300 originally due had since been paid, he would return the new bill to Hall. "Account of Expences," p. 56; *PMHB*, LV, (1931), 128–9.

several Accounts) I shall soon send you another Remittance. I shall be glad to hear from you by Budden,[9] and every other opportunity, while you remain in England; and, during your Stay, shall continue, as I have hitherto done, to do my best for your Interest, as well as my own, which, in our present Situation, I think are inseparable. I am, Sir, Yours, &c.   D. HALL

NB. You will please observe the Bill is drawn on Messieurs Allen and Marder, likewise, in case of being refused by the Portis's.

To Benjamin Franklin Esqr

Sent by the James and Mary, Captain Friend.[1]
Aug. 31. 1760. A Copy sent by the Dragon, Captain Hammit, with the second Copy of the above mentioned Bill inclosed.[2]

William Franklin to Joseph Galloway

ALS: Yale University Library

My Dear Friend,   London, Tuesday, Augst. 26. 1760
    The Mail was made up and sent for Falmouth on Saturday last, so that whether this may reach you by that Conveyance is uncertain. But as I imagine you must all be extremely anxious about the Fate of your very important Acts, and glad to know of every Thing relative to them from time to time,[3] I have scribbled over as fast as possibly I could, two Papers which have occur'd since my Father's last Dispatches,[4] in hopes of getting them to Falmouth

9. The *Philadelphia Packet*, Capt. Richard Budden, was reported as having arrived at Philadelphia in *Pa. Gaz.*, Sept. 18, 1760. It carried BF's letter to Hall of June 27; see below, p. 235.

1. *Pa. Gaz.*, Aug. 28, 1760, reported the clearance of the snow *James and Mary*, Capt. James Friend, for London; *London Chron.*, Oct. 11–14, 1760, reported its arrival at Plymouth.

2. *Pa. Gaz.*, Sept. 4, 1760, reported the clearance of the ship *Dragon*, Capt. Francis Hammett, for London; *London Chron.*, Oct. 4–7, reported its arrival at Portsmouth. Thus it had a substantially faster Atlantic crossing than the *James and Mary*.

3. For the Board of Trade and Privy Council Committee hearings and reports on nineteen Pa. acts of 1758–59, see above, pp. 125–73, and below, pp. 196–211.

4. Probably BF's letters and postscripts to Norris of June 27, July 12, 15, and 17, 1760, which have not been found but which Norris acknowledged September 20 and 26.

by the Post (which is just upon the Point of setting off) before the sailing of the Pacquet. The first is a Copy of the Attorney and Sollicitor Generals Report on the Question (which I some time ago sent to the Speaker) about His Majesty's Right of repealing particular Clauses in Acts;[5] the other is a Copy of a Letter from my Father to Mr. Pitt, imploring his Protection for the Province.[6] What Intention the Lords of the Committee could have in proposing so strange a Question, it is difficult to say; but some are inclin'd to suspect that it covers a Design that may not be altogether to our Advantage.[7] It's being referr'd to our Adversaries Council has all along been look'd upon here by some disinterested People as an extreme partial Procedure. They go so far as to say, that as the Attorney and Sollicitor General are the only proper Persons for His Majesty to consult on such Matters, that they ought by no means to be concern'd as Advocates for either Side, as they must in all Probability become so bias'd thereby as not to be able to give His Majesty that impartial Advice the Occasion may require.[8] [Between you and I, it is said, that we may look upon them all to be a Pack of d—d R—ls; and that unless we bribe them all higher than our Adversaries can do, and condescend to do every Piece of dirty Work they require, we shall never be able to attain common Justice at their Hands.][9] You'll see that they have acknowledg'd (and it would have been strange indeed if they had not) that His Majesty must exercise his Right of Repeal in the *entire,* where all

5. The "Question" was one the Privy Council Committee sent, July 15, 1760, to the law officers of the Crown (Pratt and Yorke, who were also counsel to the Penns in the hearings on the Pa. laws) as to whether under the Pa. charter the King might disallow clauses in an act of Assembly without disallowing the rest of the act. The Committee's question and the law officers' opinion, dated August 19, are printed in full in *Statutes at Large, Pa.,* v, 660–1, 735–7. For an account of this incident and a summary of the opinion, see below, pp. 196–7. WF probably sent a copy of the Committee's question to Norris with his letter of July 15 (not found). See below, p. 223.

6. Not found.

7. Thomas Penn was as displeased as were the Franklins at the Privy Council Committee's raising the question of a partial disallowance. See below, p. 197 n.

8. See above, p. 128 n.

9. In the MS this sentence is enclosed in brackets and canceled by zig-zag lines, but the words are left fully legible. WF explains this cancellation later in the paragraph.

the Parts of the Act are relative to the same Subject. But then they go on to make some Distinctions, and to establish some Doctrines, which tho' somewhat specious, are liable I think to many Objections, and if admitted may be productive of dangerous Consequences. I mean what they say with regard to Laws being void *ab Initio,* and Laws consisting of different Parts on different Subjects. I have not Time to give you my Sentiments in that respect, but I dare say they and many more will occur to you upon reading the Report. Those 2 Paragraphs, however, tho' express'd in general Terms, seem to be levell'd against some of our particular Acts now before them, and intended to fix a Precedent for some future Occasion.Whether we may promise ourselves any Advantage by the Application to Mr. Pitt is uncertain; but methinks it can do no Harm.[1] The Words which have a Line drawn thro' them[2] were sent exactly in the same Manner to Mr. P. that he might see what was in the Writer's Thoughts to say, if the Occasion had been proper. This is a new Species of Rhetoric, which (as there is no hanging a Man for his Thoughts) would be of considerable Service to those who write and publish Libels, if they could get them printed in that Manner. Many of the Merchants of London who trade to Pensylvania have sign'd a Petition in favour of the Paper money Acts,[3] which will be presented tomorrow. This Matter would have been much more forward had it not been for the cold Water thrown on it by D[avi]d Barclay and Company[4] and I hope

1. In his Journal of Negotiations in London, begun at sea, March 22, 1775, BF recalled that during his first mission he had made "several Attempts," all unsuccessful, to meet the then William Pitt (later Lord Chatham), but the first minister "was then too great a Man, or too much occupy'd in Affairs of greater Moment. I was therefore oblig'd to content my self with a kind of non-apparent and un-acknowledg'd Communication thro' Mr. Potter and Mr. Wood his Secretaries." Lib. Cong.
2. As indicated in a footnote above. If, as WF goes on to say here, BF had similarly written, and then canceled, the same sentence in a letter to Pitt, it seems most unlikely that he had begun it with the words "Between you and I."
3. Not found, and there is no record of such a petition at this time in the appropriate volumes of *Board of Trade Journal* and *Acts Privy Coun., Col.*
4. David Barclay (1682–1769), the son of Robert Barclay (1648–1690) who wrote the celebrated *Apology for the ... Quakers* (1678), was a wealthy London merchant engaged primarily in the North American trade. His sons John (1728–1787) and David (1729–1809) expanded the family business and invested in brewing and banking, founding what is now Barclays Bank. The

the Friends of the Province will remember them accordingly. The Report of the Board of Trade, My Father's Notes thereon,[5] and the Paper drawn up to induce the Merchants to petition in our Behalf have been all sent you. If after Consideration of them, you and the Speaker, and any other of the Members of Assembly would send us such Observations on them as occur, they may possibly come Time enough to be of Service to my Father, in drawing up what he may find necessary to publish to the World on the Occasion.[6] For that the Plan of Attack must be chang'd from the Proprietors to the Board of Trade seems to me highly probable. Till the iniquitous System of Government which they would establish in the Colonies, for their own selfish Purposes, is fully expos'd, I think we can hope for no good from that Quarter. I write my Sentiments freely to you as I know no undue Use will be made of them.

The Books of Husbandry which were lost in House, I shall send other Copies of by either Faulkener or McDougal, who sail in a few Days.[7] By the first I have sent you *Venus,* and I hope her Ladyship will prove acceptable.[8]

firm subscribed generously to the Academy of Philadelphia in its early years; above, IV, 35. The younger David acted as intermediary in the informal peace negotiations between BF and certain highly placed Englishmen during the winter of 1774–75. The Barclays were connected by marriage with the Penns, handled mercantile commissions for Thomas Penn, and were sureties for Gov. James Hamilton and later for Gov. John Penn. Hubert F. Barclay and Alice Wilson-Fox, *A History of the Barclay Family* (3 vols., London, 1934); Arthur Raistrick, *Quakers in Science and Industry* (N.Y., 1950), pp. 69, 286, 322–3. On June 6, 1760, Thomas Penn wrote Hamilton that he had persuaded "Mr. Barclay and his Sons" to talk with other merchants about the danger from "an encrease of paper money" in the colony. Penn Papers, Hist. Soc. Pa. Apparently this maneuver met with some success.

5. Not found.

6. BF does not seem to have published anything to the world on this occasion.

7. The *Juliana,* Captain House, was taken by a French privateer early in 1760; see above, p. 15 n. The *Friendship,* Captain Falconer, reached Deal, outward bound, September 3, and had arrived at Philadelphia by November 13. *London Chron.,* Sept. 2–4, 1760; *Pa. Gaz.,* Nov. 6, 1760. The *Boreas,* Capt. Henry Allan McDougall, reached Deal September 20, made two ineffectual sorties, but was unable to get away for more than seven weeks, spent more time at Falmouth, and arrived at Philadelphia only in mid-February. *London Chron.,* Sept. 20–23, Oct. 23–5, Nov. 8–11, 11–13, 1760; *Pa. Gaz.,* Jan. 15, Feb. 19, 1761.

8. Probably Robert Strange's engraving of Guido Reni's "Venus Attired

I have not Time to wonder or I should most prodigiously, at not having heard from you this Twelve-month; in which Time I have wrote you 5 or 6 Letters;[9] so that you have repaid all my former Negligences, with Interest.

There is News this Day come to Town of the K. of Prussia's having by forc'd Marches from Saxony got before M. Daun into Silesia, and there attack'd General Laudoun and totally defeated Him, having kill'd 7, of 8,000, and taken 4,000 Prisoners, 90 Pieces of Cannon, and all their Baggage.[1] That the Battle to be fought Tomorrow, which is *the great and important Day big with the Fate of Pensylvania*,[2] may be as successful on our Side, is the sincere and fervent Prayer of, Dear Galloway, Your very affectionate humble Servant   WM: FRANKLIN

P.S. We have received no Minutes of your Proceedings since Governor Hamilton's Arrival,[3] except a Copy of his propos'd Amendments, and a few Messages relative to the last £100,000 Act inclos'd in a Letter from the Speaker.[4] But the Act itself (which would now be of use) nor any other public Paper has been sent, which I am much surpriz'd at. The Proprietor says he has authentic Accounts of great Injustice done him in the Assessments. Of this we know nothing particular. If he means in Cumberland County I should be inclin'd to suspect it was a concerted Thing in order to throw an Odium on the Assembly, as he and his Party have such Influence there as to be able to procure whatever they Please.[5]

To Mr. Galloway

---

by the Graces." R.T.H. Halsey, "Benjamin Franklin: His Interest in the Arts," *Benjamin Franklin and His Circle* (N.Y., 1936), p. 5.

9. Only WF's letters to Galloway of Dec. 28, 1759 (Yale Univ. Lib.) and June 16, 1760 have been found.

1. Frederick II defeated the Austrian Field Marshal Baron Gideon Ernst von Laudon near Liegnitz on Aug. 15, 1760, and then fought a bloody but inconclusive battle with Field Marshal Count Leopold Joseph Maria Daun at Torgau on November 3. Gipson, *British Empire*, VIII, 59–60.

2. The hearing before the Privy Council Committee on the Pa. laws, which began on August 27.

3. James Hamilton arrived in Philadelphia Nov. 17, 1759. *Pa. Gaz.*, Nov. 22, 1759.

4. See above, p. 43.

5. On April 2, 1760, Hamilton laid before the Pa. Assembly a representation signed by Richard Hockley, the Penns' receiver general, and by Secretary

From Isaac Norris

Letterbook copy: Historical Society of Pennsylvania

B Franklin   Augt. 27th. 1760

Above is Copy of my Last[6] by Captain Friend. This incloses a second Bill of Exchange for £100—Sterl N 1876 drawn by Colonel J. Hunter on Messrs. Thomlinson &c. as it is uncertain whether our late Governor Denny will call and I do not certainly know when Capt. Hamet (by whom I purpose to send this) will sail) I shall send it to Town to be forwarded by My Brother. Captain (late Governor) Denny has repeatedly promised me to do us all the Services in his Power. His Connections and even intimacies with some considerable Persons in the Ministry he tells me are such that he hopes they may be of some use to the Province.[7] I wish it may prove so on Tryal; his private Oeconomy may possibly have done him some disservice with regard to this Government at least we are told so. It has certainly been very odd and uncommon.

General Stanwix who is probably in England before now likewise promised me to serve us especially in regard to the Re Emitting Bill upon which I had several Conferences with him before it was enacted into a Law.[8] It is rumoured here by the Proprietary

---

Richard Peters, purporting to show that in Cumberland Co. the Proprietors had been taxed for income they had not received. Hockley and Peters contended that the local assessors had assumed that every person who occupied land in the county paid the Proprietors a quitrent, on which a tax was then levied, when in fact many of the landholders were squatters and many more held land by warrant only and were not therefore legally obliged to pay rent. This paper was almost certainly one of the "authentic Accounts of great Injustice" which Penn said he had. *Pa. Col. Recs.*, VIII, 472–7; 8 *Pa. Arch.*, VI, 5123–5. Penn wrote Peters, June 9, 1760, approving of his representation, which would be very useful in the hearings against the Supply Act. Penn Papers, Hist. Soc. Pa.

6. See above, pp. 184–6.

7. Far from countenancing Denny when he returned to England, the ministry seriously considered prosecuting him for his scandalous sale of flags of truce to the merchants of Pa. See above, VI, 490 n.

8. On this act see above, pp. 146–53. Gen. John Stanwix (above, VII, 45 n; VIII, 419 n) appears to have been less than candid with Norris, because on June 17, 1759, Peters reported that the general had promised to expose "to the King's Ministers in its true Light" the conduct of the Pa. Assembly in regard to this measure, so that such "Acts of Injustice . . . might not be confirmed." *Pa. Col. Recs.*, VIII, 356.

Party that the Lottery Act the Court and the Land Office Laws will be repealed.[9] I am ut Supra   I N.

by Capt. Hamet

From Mary Stevenson   Draft: American Philosophical Society

Dear Sir   [Bristol, August? 1760][1]

Since you are pleas'd to say you shall be glad of a Line from me I will find Leisure.

In my Letter to my Mother, I mention'd I had a Question to ask you. It is this, What is the reason the Water at this place becomes warm by pumping tho it is not so at the spring?[2] Pardon my Impertinence. Goodnatur'd persons have always more impos'd on them than others; yet I believe the satisfaction which they receive from their Actions counterballances their fatigue in performing them. There is my encouragement and my excuse.

9. These rumors were well founded; all three acts were repealed by the King in Council, Sept. 2, 1760. See below. pp. 205, 210.

1. BF's reply, September 13, indicates that this "agreable Letter from Bristol," had reached him some time before and that since then he had been "much engag'd in Business." See below, p. 212. The draft of a note from Polly to another person, written on the same sheet as this letter, shows that she was at Bristol with Mrs. Tickell and Miss Pitt.

2. Warm springs, called the Hotwells, in the parish of Clifton on the west side of Bristol, became famous for medicinal purposes in the seventeenth century. The lower reaches of the nearby Avon River are affected by tidal flow and, to protect the spring water from contamination, pumps were installed in 1695, raising it through pipes thirty feet to the "Hotwell-house." An eighteenth-century guide book reports that "in the common spring water of the neighbouring rockhouse, Farenheit's thermometer stood at 50 degrees, the water of the Hotwell taken immediately from the pump raised it to 76." The water was esteemed for a variety of uses: "to temper an *hot acrimonious blood,* to palliate or cure *consumptions, weakness of the lungs, hectic fevers and heats,*" and a host of other ailments ranging from loss of appetite to diabetes and cancer. "Large and elegant public rooms" in Clifton provided "public breakfasts during the season" (May to September or October), cotillions, country dances, and balls for the entertainment of "the company at the Hotwells." *The New History, Survey and Description Of the City and Suburbs of Bristol, or Complete Guide, And informing and useful Companion for the Residents and Visitants of this ancient, extensive and increasing City, the Hotwells and Clifton* (Bristol, 1794), pp. 98–105.

I remember you told me in your last obliging Conversation that the rising of Tides in Rivers was not owing to a greater quantity of Water in them but to the Moon's attraction. Now my dear Sir it appears to me that the Rivers are augmented by the water flowing into them from the Sea, because they begin to rise first at the part nearest it whether there Course is contrary or the same with the Moon, and are reckon'd saltest at high Water. Whether my last assertion may not be a false one I will not presume to determine, but it is the common opinion, tho I don't comprehend why there should not retire an equal quantity of fresh as salt Water. I offer my sentiments to you without reserve, trusting to your Candour, and hoping to have my Errors corrected. I hope you know my Heart well enough to believe I do it with becoming Diffidence.

We purpose leaving Bristol next Thursday. I cannot say I have been entertain'd with the Publick Diversions of the Place tho I have attended the Rooms mo[st nigh]ts and danc'd at the Balls, but I have few Acquaintance. Miss Pitt and I generally quit the Rooms as soon as my Aunt is engag'd at Cards, and spend the remainder of the evening with two Young Ladies who lodge in the same House with us, one of them being in too ill a state of Health to permit her to go out much. We have a sensible agreeable Man of our select party. The Country is delightfully pleasant, as I suppose you will take an opportunity of seeing before you leave England. I was one day at Redcliff Church which is allow'd to be a fine piece of Architecture.[3] There is something very Noble when you enter it, but it stands so disadvantageously that the outside is quite lost. There are some Paintings at the Altar, but I own they did not please me, and I had the satisfaction of hearing them disapprov'd by one who has more Judgment.

From hence we go to Sir Robert Longs[4] where I intend to write to my Mother but at present this Letter must suffice for both. Therefore my rever'd Preceptor, and honour'd Mother, I hope will together accept the duty and good wishes of their affectionate Pupil and Daughter   M STEVENSON

3. St. Redcliff in Bristol was built for the most part in the fourteenth century. Queen Elizabeth I has been quoted as calling it "the fairest, the goodliest, and most famous parish church in England."

4. Sir Robert Long, 6th Baronet, of Draycot Cerne, Wilts (1705?–1767). His seat lay near Chippenham, about twenty miles east of Bristol. He was

Order in Council

DS (two) and copy: Pennsylvania Historical and Museum Commission[5]

On July 4, 1760, Francis Eyre, Robert Charles and Franklin's solicitor, drew up and presented on behalf of his clients a petition to the King in Council asking to be heard in opposition to the Board of Trade report on the nineteen Pennsylvania acts.[6] Then Eyre prepared "long Observations on the Report being 8 close Brief Sheets, in Answer to the several Charges in the Report, to serve by way of Brief," and during the following weeks held several late evening conferences with the barristers de Grey and Jackson on how to present the Assembly's case at the forthcoming hearing.[7]

Meanwhile the Privy Council Committee for Plantation Affairs had begun consideration of the Board's report. On July 15 the Committee referred the report to the attorney and solicitor general for an opinion on the following question: In case any of these acts contained clauses "not consonant to reason," or repugnant or contrary to the laws of England, or inconsistent with the King's sovereignty or prerogative, or contrary to the allegiance due from the Proprietors or inhabitants, or not warranted by the powers granted by the charter for making laws, might the King repeal or annul such clauses without disallowing "other unexceptionable parts" of these acts; and if so, would such repeal be effective immediately?[8] The Committee did not tell the law officers

---

M.P., 1734–67; often reckoned a Tory in politics, he was generally independent like most Wiltshire members, and voted for the repeal of the Stamp Act in 1766. Namier and Brooke, *House of Commons*. III, 53.

5. There are in the Pa. Archives two sealed and signed texts of this order in council: Records of the Provincial Council, Crown Correspondence, 1726–75, nos. 59 and 60. There is also a contemporary copy in Records of the Provincial Council, Provincial Record, 1682–1775 (Minutes of the Provincial Council), Vol. S, pp. 74–8. The version printed here is the original order, Crown Correspondence, no. 60, because no. 59 is slightly mutilated and contains a demonstrable clerical error.

6. Eyre's bill, under date of July 4; see above, p. 24. A careful search among the Unbound Papers in the Privy Council Office has not produced the petition. No copy is known to have survived. For the Board of Trade report, June 24, 1760, see above, pp. 125–73.

7. Eyre's bill, under date of July 4, 12, 14, August 22, 26. Like the petition, the "long Observations" have not been found.

8. *Acts Privy Coun., Col.,* IV, 440; also *Statutes at Large, Pa.,* V, 660–1, where the order of reference is printed in full. Thomas Penn told Governor Hamilton, Aug. 22, 1760, that the referral was moved in the Committee by Lord Mansfield. Penn Papers, Hist. Soc. Pa.

which acts they had specifically in mind, but one, at least, must have been the Re-emitting Act of June 20, 1759, which the Board of Trade had so severely criticized on the score of "tacking."[9]

The attorney and solicitor general reported back, August 19, that in general under the Pennsylvania charter the Crown must either accept or reject the whole of an act, although there might be cases in which particular provisions of an act "may be void *ab initio*," as when an act of Parliament was contravened or the "legal right of a private subject bound without his consent." Furthermore, the law officers seemed to believe, though they did not fully commit themselves on the point, that if matters "totally foreign and as much unconnected with one another as any two of the nineteen acts now under consideration" were joined in one act, the King might disallow that part of the act relating to one of the matters it contained.[1] Neither the Proprietors nor the Assembly agents were pleased that the Council Committee had raised this question of a partial disallowance,[2] but the opinion of Pratt and Yorke did not lead to any such action by the Council in the pending controversy.

The hearing before the Privy Council Committee took place at the Council Office in the Cockpit on August 27 (from noon to five o'clock, according to Eyre) and on the 28th. As at the Board of Trade sessions, Attorney General Pratt and Solicitor General Yorke appeared for the Proprietors and William de Grey and Richard Jackson for the agents, Franklin and Charles. In addition, Eyre engaged a Mr. Cooke to take shorthand notes of the proceedings, but unfortunately neither these notes nor any other detailed records of the hearing have been found.[3] Writing in his autobiography nearly thirty years later Franklin repeated "the purport of what I remember as urg'd by both Sides" regarding the £100,000 Supply Act, and described his private conference with Lord Mansfield (quoted in a footnote below) which led to a sort of com-

9. See above, pp. 146–53.

1. The opinion is printed in full, *Statutes at Large, Pa.,* v, 735–7.

2. The Proprietors conceived that the exercise of such a power "would be very injurious to the Province, as it would enable the Crown to take any money that should be granted, and not apply it for the purpose it was intended, and tho it was very probably intended to secure us, we did not wish to see it brought into practice, unless it was a manifest tack foreign to the design of the Bill." Penn to Hamilton, Aug. 22, 1760, Penn Papers, Hist. Soc. Pa. Penn had not yet seen the law officers' opinion when he wrote this. For WF's comments, which probably reflected the views of his father after getting a copy of the opinion from Eyre, see above, pp. 189–90.

3. Undated entry in Eyre's bill. Cooke received ten guineas for his services. The Assembly had a copy of the pleadings in 1764, taken from the shorthand notes, as a message informed the governor. *Votes,* 1763–64, p. 90.

promise on this act.[4] For the rest, the report of the Committee to the plenary session of the King in Council which is contained in the document printed here provides the best indication of what transpired during those two days of debate in the Cockpit.

Later writers have disagreed as to the extent to which the final determination of the Privy Council was a great victory or a resounding defeat for Franklin.[5] Impartially considered, the truth seems to lie, as usual, somewhere between these extremes. Of the eleven acts opposed by the Proprietors, six were disallowed; one (the Supply Act), also opposed by the Board of Trade, was allowed to stand on a compromise basis, and so was indirectly confirmed when September 13 arrived, six months after its first presentation to the Privy Council; one (the Agency Act), recommended for approval by the Board of Trade, had already been indirectly confirmed on August 16 by the lapse of time; and the remaining three were confirmed by the Privy Council on the recommendation of the Board of Trade. Thus on a strictly numerical basis the Proprietors won the disallowances they sought for six of the eleven laws and Franklin won acceptance for the other five.

A scorecard, however, is not the most useful device for recording the results of this sort of contest. The acts under dispute were not all of equal importance. By any reasonable scale of values it would be difficult to conclude, for example, that the disallowance of the Act Suppressing Lotteries and Plays was a major political defeat for Franklin and the Assembly, or that the confirmation of the Act to Prevent the Exportation of Bad Staves was a glorious victory.[6] If we may judge by the sub-

4. *Autobiog.* (APS-Yale edit.), pp. 265–6.

5. For example, Bernard Faÿ, whose account of the whole affair is factually somewhat inaccurate, directs his attention almost entirely to the £100,000 Supply Act and remarks in summary: "Franklin's promise [of modifications in the law] remained a scrap of paper, and the meeting of the Privy Council on September 2, 1760, was transformed by his care and skill into a complete victory for the Pennsylvania Assembly. The estates of the Penns were no longer immune from taxation and both the Penns and the King admitted it." *Franklin, The Apostle of Modern Times* (Boston, 1929), p. 290. The most recent writer on the subject, William S. Hanna, who displays some anti-Franklin bias in his discussion of the politics of these years, takes the opposite view of the outcome: "On all the major issues Franklin and the Assembly suffered an overwhelming defeat." *Benjamin Franklin and Pennsylvania Politics* (Stanford, Calif., 1964), p. 138.

6. Penn was displeased, however, at the confirmation of the acts regarding the export of flour and staves, which placed the appointment of inspectors in the hands of the Assembly. He told Benjamin Chew, Oct. 17, 1760, that although the Board of Trade said they did not intend to approve such acts for

stance of the acts themselves, the known attitudes of the contending parties towards them, and the relative attention given each at the hearings and in the Board of Trade report, the most important of the measures, in a political and constitutional sense, should be ranked in something like this order: the £100,000 Supply Act, the Re-emitting Act, the Agency Act, the Act for Recording Warrants and Surveys, and the Supplementary Act for Establishing Courts of Judicature. The Penns succeeded in getting disallowed the Re-emitting Act and those concerning warrants and surveys and the judicial system; Franklin got what he and the Assembly wanted with regard to the Agency Act; the Supply Act, certainly the most important of all, resulted in a compromise which requires further comment.

The issue of the taxation of proprietary estates, repeatedly in dispute since the summer of 1755, was the central point of contention in the Supply Act of 1759, just as it had been by far the most important issue that had sent Franklin to England in 1757. In the course of the struggle the Proprietors had at first stood firmly against any sort of concession to the Assembly view that they or their American estates ought to share in the costs of provincial defense. In the autumn of 1755, after news of Braddock's disastrous defeat reached England, they yielded to pressure at home to the extent of making a voluntary contribution of £5000 to be paid from the arrears of quitrents as these should be collected in Pennsylvania.[7] Although Thomas Penn privately admitted to his supporters in the colony during the summer of 1756 that the Proprietors might permit a very limited taxation of their personal estates, the instructions to Governor Denny, shown to the Assembly in September 1756, made no such concession. In fact, they went so far as to express intense displeasure that the Assembly should "pretend, by any Act of theirs, to charge the Proprietary Estate in the Province with the Burden of any Taxes."[8] Then in November 1758, in answer to Franklin's representations in his "Heads of Complaint" and on the advice of the attorney and solicitor general, they stated in somewhat vague terms that they were willing "to have the annual Income of their Estate enquired into" and were "ready to contribute whatever the said Sum [of £5000] shall fall short of what has been laid on the Inhabitants in general, for every

the future, "I do not see how they can avoid it, after suffering these to pass when so strenuously opposed." Penn Papers, Hist. Soc. Pa.

7. See above, VI, 257 n. At the time of the passage of the Supply Act of 1759, here under consideration, £600 of the £5000 contribution was still unpaid. See above, VIII, 304.

8. See above, VI, 515–31, esp. p. 522, and Penn to Peters, July 12, 1756, printed in William R. Shepherd, *History of Proprietary Government in Pennsylvania* (N.Y., 1896), p. 452 n.

Part of their Estate, that is in its Nature taxable."[9] When Franklin asked for an explicit statement as to how they proposed the inquiry to be conducted, whether they would consent to a law for the purpose, what parts of their estate they considered taxable, and what other arrangements they had in mind, they refused to give him a direct reply.[1] They had, however, withdrawn some distance from their original position of a total refusal to be taxed.

The Supply Act of 1759 was the first measure involving a land tax to be passed after the Assembly received word of this concession. While the Board of Trade hearings were in progress Penn learned that Governor Hamilton has passed the £100,000 Supply Act of April 12, 1760, which contained essentially the same provisions as that of 1759 then under consideration. By this time the Proprietors had come to realize that they must submit to having their estates taxed, whether they were willing or not, and Penn's chief concern had become that it should be done fairly. Writing to the governor, June 6, he declared: "I desire nothing more than to have such parts of the estates of my Family taxed, as are to be taxed, on the same calculation with the estates of other people. It would be knight errantry to desire a more exact calculation, in order to pay more in proportion, and to pay less I should think extreamly scandalous."[2] Such a statement represents a major retreat from the instructions to Denny four years earlier and even from the answer to the "Heads of Complaint" in November 1758.

The Proprietors considered, as their supporters in the colony had done when the Supply Act of 1759 was passed, that this law was improper because, among other reasons, it was vague as to whether their unlocated as well as their located estates were to be taxed, because the assessments on their properties were to be determined entirely by officials in the appointment of whom they had no share, and because their governor was in effect excluded from a voice in the expenditure of the money raised by the act. First the Board of Trade and now the Privy Council Committee agreed that these objections were valid. In order to avoid a disallowance Franklin and Charles, therefore, pledged that the Assembly would pass an amending act to remove these criticisms. On this basis the Privy Council allowed the law to stand.

The primary issue that had taken Franklin to England was now settled by the highest authority in his and the Assembly's favor: It was proper that the proprietary estates in Pennsylvania should be taxed, as the Assembly had been insisting for several years. Two questions, however,

9. See above, VIII, 182.
1. See above, VIII, 186–8, 193–4.
2. Penn to Hamilton, June 6, 1760, Penn Papers, Hist. Soc. Pa.

remained for the future to decide: Would the Assembly honor the pledge Franklin and Charles had given and pass an act amending the law of 1759 in accordance with the six points laid down by the Privy Council? And would the Assembly include these provisions in all future bills imposing taxes on the proprietary estates? Immediately after the Privy Council hearing and before the order in council was issued, Thomas Penn wrote Hamilton that the Assembly agents had been told "of the Solemnity of the Engagement, that no Bill shal ever pass for raising any money that shal not be appropriated in this manner, that if the conditions are not complied with the £100,000 Bill [of April 12, 1760] passed by you shal be immediately repealed, without any reference to the Board of Trade, and Parliament applyed to, to do it and to abolish all their encroachments, on the Constitution they are by Charter intitled to."[3] Penn seemed confident that this was no idle threat. His letters to Pennsylvania during the fall reflect, on the whole, considerable satisfaction with the decision of the Privy Council. Again, unfortunately, Franklin's letters to Norris about the order in council have disappeared.[4]

Repeatedly during the next four years Governor Hamilton and his successor John Penn pressed the Assembly for a bill to amend the Supply Act of 1759; the House never categorically refused, but responded each time by saying that, as their examinations of the assessors' proceedings showed, full justice had been done to the Proprietors in the levying of the tax. Strong complaints about the assessments in Cumberland County during the first year had appeared even before the decision of the Privy Council in 1760,[5] but adjustments seem to have been made and such complaints died away. So long as proprietary government remained in Pennsylvania no Assembly consented to a formal amendment of the act of 1759 or its successor of the next year.[6] The first question remaining in 1760 was answered in the negative.

3. Penn to Hamilton, Aug. 30, 1760, Penn Papers, Hist. Soc. Pa.

4. Bernard Faÿ makes the following wholly undocumented statement: "As soon as Franklin knew that the law had been approved, he wrote to his political friends in Pennsylvania to let them know that the promise was neither regular nor legal and could not bind them. He advised them to be moderate in their taxation of the Penn grounds and then kept quiet." *Franklin, The Apostle of Modern Times,* p. 290. The editors have been unable to find any letter either by or to BF or any other contemporary document to suggest that he ever wrote about the Council's action in this vein.

5. See above, pp. 192–3 n.

6. What actually happened to the Supply Act of 1760 remains unclear. On June 6, 1760, Penn had told Hamilton that "We do not purpose to present the Law you have passed 'til the fall so as to have it finished before Christmas, as we would not have it repealed 'till the Campaign is over, and the publick

In time, however, the representatives gave way on the six points stipulated in the order in council. Bills for a land tax in April 1761 and in March 1762 failed of acceptance by the governor because they did not observe all of these requirements. In March 1762, after the British declaration of war on Spain, and in October 1763, after the outbreak of the Indian uprising called Pontiac's Conspiracy, the Assembly voted supplies which Hamilton accepted because they used other means than a land tax to fund the bills of credit. Then from January to May 1764, with John Penn, son of Richard and nephew of Thomas, in office as governor, and with Franklin back in his seat in the Assembly, occurred one of the most acrimonious disputes of the whole long series. In view of the grave dangers to the colony from the Indians and the state of domestic turmoil created by the Paxton Boys, the Assembly yielded fully, as a majority of its members believed, to the requirements of the Privy Council's six points. But the new governor, who had attended the hearings of 1760 as an interested spectator, insisted on what the assemblymen considered a wholly unwarranted and unjust interpretation of one of them. Finally, after Isaac Norris had resigned the speakership on the plea of illness and Franklin had been elected to take his place, the Assembly gave way and amended the bill to incorporate Penn's interpretation. On May 30, 1764, for the first time, a Pennsylvania governor was able to accept an act which complied fully with the terms laid down by the Privy Council in 1760.[7]

Early in 1765 Governor Penn had the mortifying experience of reporting to the Assembly that his father and uncle were willing to accept the Assembly's interpretation of the disputed point after all, and of asking the House to amend the act accordingly.[8] The protracted dispute of

---

has the benefit of it." But he did not present the act to the Privy Council in the fall, and on May 9, 1761, he told Richard Peters that he had determined to postpone the matter further on the advice of Hamilton and William Allen that the Assembly was becoming "somewhat better disposed and that this Disposition may increase so as to incline them in time to comply." He added: "I have not the Least objection to pay the Sum we are Taxed at, but we are until the Act stipulated for shall be passed at the Mercy of the Assessors." Penn Papers, Hist. Soc. Pa. The editors have been unable to discover any record that Penn presented this act to the Privy Council at any time before April 12, 1765, when the five-year limit stipulated by the charter expired, or that the Privy Council ever took any action upon it.

7. A footnote at the appropriate place in the text of the order in council below, explains the difference in interpretation. In a later volume will appear several documents relating to this dispute of 1764.

8. Henry Wilmot to John Penn, May 30, 1764, *Statutes at Large, Pa.*, VI, 585–8; *Pa. Col. Recs.*, IX, 237, 240–1, 244, 245.

1764, however, had inevitably added to the bitterness against the Proprietors which had been building up within the opposition party; two months before the governor's recantation Franklin had sailed for England to seek the end of proprietary government. Thus the Proprietors finally got the Assembly to obey, literally as well as in general intent, the terms of the order in council, and the second question still open in 1760 was answered in the affirmative, although at the cost of increased antagonism between the Assembly and the Proprietors.

In the final analysis, then, the Assembly gained full recognition of the right to tax the proprietary estates, and the Penns won legislative safeguards of the principle that they should not be discriminated against in future taxation. Neither side can be said to have achieved a complete victory on this major point of dispute. The colony as a whole, however, benefited most of all because the matter of taxing the proprietary estates, a barrier to effective government since 1755, was never again a central issue of Pennsylvania politics.

[Privy
Council
Seal]

At the Court at Kensington
the 2d: day of September 1760.

PRESENT
The Kings most Excellent Majesty

Arch Bishop of Canterbury	Viscount Falmouth
Lord President	Viscount Barrington
Duke of Newcastle	Lord Berkeley of Stratton
Earl of Cholmondeley	Lord Mansfield
Earl of Halifax	

WHEREAS there was this day read at the Board, a Report from the Right Honourable the Lords of the Committee of His Majestys most Honourable Privy Council for Plantation Affairs, upon considering Nineteen Acts passed in the Province of Pensilvania in the years 1758 and 1759, Which Report is dated the 28th: of last month, and is in the words following Vizt:

"Your Majesty having been pleased, by Your Orders in Council of the 16th: of February, and the 13th: of March last, to referr unto this Committee, Nineteen Acts passed in the Province of Pensilvania in the years 1758 and 1759, as likewise a Petition of the Proprietaries of the said Province, complaining of Eleven of the said Acts, and praying to be heard thereupon before they received Your Majestys Royal Confirmation. The Lords of the Committee thought it proper to transmit the said Acts, together with the said Petition, to the Lords Commissioners for Trade and Plantations, to examine into all the said Nineteen Acts, and to hear the Petitioners upon each of the said Acts, against which they had made their Complaint; And the said Lords Commissioners having accordingly examined into the said Acts, and heard Counsel upon the Petition of the said Proprietaries against Eleven of them, as likewise Counsel on behalf of the House of Representatives of the said Province in Support of the said Eleven Acts, the said Lords Commissioners have made their Report upon all the said Acts to this Committee; And it appearing by the said Report, that the said Lords Commissioners were of Opinion, that Seven out of the said Eleven Acts complained of by the said Proprietaries, were proper to be Repealed by Your Majesty, the Agents for the House of Representatives made Application to this Committee, praying to be heard in Support of the said Seven Acts, and having entered into the usual Security, according to the Rules of the Council Board, to be answerable for Costs, in Case it should be judged necessary to require them to pay the same, the Lords of the Committee thought proper to comply with their request, and accordingly on the 27th: of this Instant, and likewise on this day, took the said Nineteen Acts and Report into Consideration, and heard Counsel on behalf of the said Agents in Support of the said Seven Acts, as likewise Counsel on behalf of the said Proprietaries against the same, and do agree humbly to Report to Your Majesty,

"That as to the Six following Acts[9] Intituled,

"'An Act for Re-emitting the Bills of Credit of this Province heretofore Re-emitted on Loan, and for striking the further sum of thirty Six thousand Six hundred and fifty pounds to enable the Trustees to lend Fifty thousand pounds to Colonel John Hunter Agent for the Contractors with the Right Honourable the Lords Commissioners of His Majestys Treasury, for His Majestys Service. (Passed 20: June 1759)'

"'A Supplement to the Act intituled An Act for Re-emitting the Bills of Credit of this Province heretofore Re-emitted on Loan, and for striking the further sum of thirty Six thousand Six

9. For the Board of Trade's adverse comments on these acts, in which the Council Committee concurred, see above, pp. 147–64.

hundred and fifty pounds to enable the Trustees to lend fifty thousand pounds to Colonel John Hunter Agent for the Contractors with the Right Honourable the Lords Commissioners of His Majestys Treasury for His Majestys Service. Passed 29: Septr. 1759)'

" 'An Act for Recording Warrants and Surveys, and for rendering the Real Estates and Property within this Province more Secure. (Passed 7: July 1759)'

" 'An Act for the more effectual Suppressing and preventing Lotteries and Plays. (Passed 20: June 1759).'

" 'A Supplement to the Act intituled An Act for establishing Courts of Judicature in this Province. (Passed 29: Septr. 1759).'

" 'An Act for the Relief of the Heirs, Devisees and Assigns of Persons born out of the Kings Liegeance, who have been Owners of Lands within this Province, and have died unnaturalized. (Passed 20: June 1759)'

"The Lords of the Committee are of Opinion, that it may be adviseable for Your Majesty to adjudge and declare, under Your Privy Seal, all the said Six Acts to be Void.

"That as to the Act Intituled

" 'An Act for granting to His Majesty the Sum of One hundred thousand pounds, and for striking the same in Bills of Credit in the manner hereinafter directed, and for Providing a Fund for sinking the said Bills of Credit, by a tax on all Estates, Real and personal, and taxables within this Province. (Passed 17: April 1759)'

"The Lords of the Committee were of Opinion that the said Act is fundamentally wrong and unjust, and ought to be Repealed, unless the following Alterations and Amendments could be made therein. Vizt:

"1. That the Real Estates to be taxed, be defined with Precision, so as not to include the unsurveyed waste Land belonging to the Proprietaries.[1]

1. In reference to this condition the Assembly told Governor Hamilton, March 14, 1761, "that no part of the unsurveyed Waste Lands belonging to the proprietaries, have in any instance been included in the Estates taxed." *Pa. Col. Recs.*, VIII, 584; see also, above, pp. 140–1 n.

"2. That the Located uncultivated Lands belonging to the Proprietaries shall not be assessed higher than the lowest Rate at which any located uncultivated Lands belonging to the Inhabitants shall be assessed.[2]

"3. That all Lands not granted by the Proprietaries within Boroughs and Towns, be deemed located uncultivated Lands and rated accordingly and not as Lots.[3]

"4. That the Governors Consent and Approbation be made necessary to every issue and Application of the money to be raised by Virtue of such Act.

"5. That Provincial Commissioners be named to hear and determine Appeals brought on the part of the Inhabitants as well as of the Proprietaries.

"6. That the Payments by the Tenants to the Proprietaries of their Rents, shall be according to the terms of their respective Grants, as if such Act had never been passed.

"The Proprietaries Thomas Penn and Richard Penn, and Benjamin Franklin and Robert Charles, Agents for the Province, being acquainted with the Opinion of this Committee, the Proprietaries

2. This is the stipulation which caused such bitter conflict in 1764. The bills presented that year provided that located but unimproved lands should be assessed at from £5 to £15 per hundred acres, depending on quality, and specified that such lands belonging to the Proprietors should not "be assessed higher than the lowest Rate at which any located uncultivated Lands belonging to the Inhabitants thereof, *under the same Circumstances of Situation, Kind and Quality* [italics added], shall be assessed." When Governor Penn objected, the Assembly asked him if he thought the Privy Council stipulation meant that "the *best* and *most valuable*" of the proprietary lands "should be Taxed no higher than the worst and least valuable of the Lands belonging to the People." He replied that, whatever was the lowest assessment on any such lands of the inhabitants, "none of the located, uncultivated Lands of the Proprietaries shall be assessed higher." The Assembly considered this interpretation highly unjust and reminded Penn that his predecessor Hamilton had assured a former Assembly that "nothing was further from his Thoughts, than to desire the Proprietaries Estate should be exempted from paying a proportionable part of the Supplies for the current Service." In the end, however, the Assembly resolved that the necessity of raising money for provincial defense was "so great and pressing" that it would waive its parliamentary rights and amend the bill to conform to the governor's interpretation. *Votes,* 1763–64, pp. 64, 69, 71, 88.

3. Because of its phraseology, this stipulation became involved in the controversy over the one immediately above.

declared, that for the sake of Peace, and to avoid further Contest, they would instruct their Governor to Assent to an Act for discharging the said Debt of One hundred thousand pounds in the form of the said Act now under Consideration, so altered and amended.

"And the said Agents for the Province, proposed, that in Case this present Act should not be Repealed, they would undertake, that the Assembly will prepare, pass the Assembly, and offer to the Governor, An Act to amend this Act in such manner, as if it had originally been penned according to the Amendments and Alterations above proposed, and will indemnify the Proprietaries from any damage they may sustain by such Act not being so prepared, passed by the Assembly, and offered to the Governor, and have signed such undertaking in the Books of the Council Office in the following words—Vizt.[4]

"WE the undersigned Benjamin Franklin and Robert Charles, Agents for the Province of Pensilvania, do hereby consent, that in Case An Act passed in the said Province in April 1759, Intituled 'An Act for granting to His Majesty the sum of One hundred

4. Writing the last pages of his autobiography about 1789, BF summarized the arguments of opposing counsel on the Supply Act and then continued: "On this Lord Mansfield, one of the Council rose, and beckoning to me, took me into the Clerks' Chamber, while the Lawyers were pleading, and ask'd me if I was really of Opinion that no Injury would be done the Proprietary Estate in the Execution of the Act. I said, Certainly. Then says he, you can have little Objection to enter into an Engagement to assure that Point. I answer'd None at all. He then call'd in Paris [BF's error of memory for Wilmot; Paris was dead] and after some Discourse his Lordship's Proposition was accepted on both Sides; a Paper to the purpose was drawn up by the Clerk of the Council, which I sign'd with Mr. Charles, who was also an Agent of the Province for their ordinary Affairs; when Lord Mansfield return'd to the Council Chamber where finally the Law was allowed to pass. Some changes were however recommended and we also engag'd they should be made by a subsequent Law; but the Assembly, did not think them necessary. For one Year's Tax having been levied by the Act, before the Order of Council arrived, they appointed a Committee to examine the Proceedings of the Assessors, and On this Committee they put several particular Friends of the Proprietaries. After a full Enquiry they unanimously sign'd a Report that they found the Tax had been assess'd with perfect Equity." *Autobiog.* (APS-Yale edit.), pp. 265–6. Careful comparison of this account with the order in council shows some discrepancies, doubtless caused by BF's loss of exact memory after nearly thirty years, but there seems to be no reason to question the credit he assigned to Lord Mansfield for suggesting the compromise.

thousand pounds, and for striking the same in Bills of Credit in the manner hereinafter directed, and for providing a fund for sinking the said Bills of Credit by a Tax on all Estates, Real and Personal, and Taxable within this Province,' shall not be Repealed by His Majesty in Council, We the said Agents do undertake that the Assembly of Pensilvania will prepare and pass, and offer to the Governor of the said Province of Pensilvania, An Act to amend the aforementioned Act, according to the Amendments proposed in the Report made by the Lords of the Committee of Council this day (upon the said One hundred thousand pound Act, and other Pensilvania Acts) and We will indemnify the Proprietaries from any damage that they may sustain by such Act not being so prepared and passed by the Assembly, and offered to the Governor. WITNESS Our Hands this 28th: day of August 1760.

"Lest some inconveniencies should arise from the Repeal of the said Act in respect of the good purposes thereof, the Lords of the Committee are humbly of Opinion, that your Majesty may rely upon the undertaking for the Assembly of Pensilvania by their Agents, and permit this Act to stand unrepealed, because the Objections upon which this Committee should have founded their Advice for the Repeal, will certainly be removed in a Way more agreable and convenient to the Province.

"That as to the Eight following Acts, Intituled

"'An Act for the continuance of an Act of Assembly of this Province, intituled, A Supplementary Act to the Act intituled An Act for preventing the exportation of Bread and flour not Merchantable, and for the new Appointment of Officers to put the said Law in Execution (passed 27: Septr: 1758).'

"'An Act for the further continuance of An Act of Assembly of this Province intituled A Supplementary Act to the Act for preventing the Exportation of Bread and flour not Merchantable, and for the New Appointment of Officers to put the said Law in Execution (passed 19: Octr. 1759)'

"'An Act to prevent the Exportation of bad or Unmerchantable Staves, Heading Boards, and Timber (passed 21st: April 1759)'

"'A Supplement to the Act intituled An Act for regulating the Hire of Carriages to be employed in His Majestys Service (passed 20th: Septr. 1758)'

" 'A Supplement to An Act intituled An Act for preventing Abuses in the Indian Trade, for supplying the Indians, friends and Allies of Great Britain, with Goods at more easy Rates, and for securing and strengthening the Peace and friendship lately concluded with the Indians inhabiting the Northern and Western frontiers of this Province (passed 17: April 1759)'

" 'A Supplement to the Act intituled An Act for granting to His Majesty a Duty of Tonnage upon Ships and Vessels, and also certain duties upon Wine, Rum, Brandy, and other Spirits, and a Duty upon Sugar, for supporting and maintaining the Provincial Ship of War for protecting the Trade of this Province, and other purposes for His Majestys Service (passed 21st: April 1759.)'

" 'An Act for regulating the Hire of Carriages to be employed in His Majestys Service (passed 21: April 1759.)'

" 'An Act to continue An Act intituled An Act for directing the Choice of Inspectors in the Counties of Chester, Lancaster, York, Cumberland, Berks and Northampton (passed 29: September 1759.).'

"The Lords of the Committee do humbly Report to Your Majesty that they have no Objection thereto.

"And the Lords of the Committee do further humbly Report to Your Majesty that as to the Act Intituled,

" 'An Act for appointing an Agent to apply for and receive the Distributive share and proportion which shall be assigned to this Province of the sum of money granted by Parliament to His Majestys Colonies in America (passed 29th: September 1759.).'

"The Lords Commissioners for Trade and Plantations not having Offered any Objection to this Act, it has been permitted to run out Six months since it was first laid before Your Majesty, and by that means it stands confirmed by Virtue of the Proprietaries Charter.[5]

5. Since Eyre, acting for Franklin, had presented the Agency Act to the Privy Council on February 16, the six months allowed by the Pa. charter for its consideration, had expired on August 16, and it could not have been disallowed thereafter in any case. The time limit on the other eighteen acts, all presented by Penn on March 13, was to expire on September 13, so this order in council beat that deadline by a matter of eleven days.

"And that with regard to the three following Acts intituled

" 'An Act in Addition to an Act intituled An Act for regulating the Hire of Carriages to be employed in His Majestys Service (passed 29: September 1759.)'

" 'An Act for extending several Sections of An Act of Parliament passed in the thirty Second Year of the present Reign, intituled An Act for punishing Mutiny and desertion, and for the better Payment of the Army and their Quarters (passed 21: April 1759)'

" 'An Act for regulating the Officers and Soldiers in the Pay of this Province (Passed 21: April 1759)'

"The Lords of the Committee do humbly Report to Your Majesty, that the said three Acts are expired, and that it will therefore be unnecessary for Your Majesty to give any Orders thereupon."

HIS Majesty this day took the said Report into His Royal Consideration, and was pleased, with the advice of His Privy Council, to approve of all that is therein proposed to be done with respect to the said Laws, and having adjudged and declared void the Six Acts first mentioned in the said Report, His Majesty hath thought proper to direct the Lord Privy Seal to prepare and pass under the Privy Seal a proper Instrument, signifying such His Majestys adjudication and declaration of all the said Six Acts to be void.[6] And His Majesty doth hereby further Declare, and Order that with respect to the Act for granting to His Majesty the sum of One hundred thousand pounds and for striking the same in Bills of Credit &ca. the same do stand unrepealed; And as to the Eight following Acts, to which the Lords of the Committee have offered no Objection, His Majesty is hereby pleased to signify His Royal Approbation thereof. And the Proprietaries of Pensilvania, their

6. As stated above, p. 134 n, the Pa. charter required that the disallowance of any act of that colony should be signified by an instrument under the privy seal, not, as was the case in other colonies, merely by an order in council. Penn wrote Hamilton, Sept. 5, 1760, that he was sending the order in council, but that he was keeping the privy seal there. It should, of course, be among the Penn Papers, but some of these were destroyed in the nineteenth century and others scattered. Although the Historical Society of Pennsylvania had made strenuous efforts to reassemble the collection as completely as possible, members of the Society's staff, who have conducted a careful search for this document for the present editors, report they have been unable to find it.

Lieutenant or Deputy Governor, and the Assembly of the said Province, and likewise all others whom it may concern, are to take Notice and Govern themselves accordingly.   W: BLAIR.[7]

Thomas Collinson to His Uncle[8]

ALS: American Philosophical Society

Dear Uncle   London Sept 12th 1760

As I am no Stranger to the frequency of Petitions that sometimes interrupt your Retirement; I have been ever very cautious not to encrease the Number, by a too liberal Use of the Priveledge you favoured me with; of Recommending my Friends and Acquaintances.

But as the worthy Gentleman Mr. Benjn Franklin of Philadelphia—the Bearer of this; is a Person every way deserving of a more consequential Esteem than mine; I flatter myself the introducing him to your Acquaintance will be mutually agreeable:[9] as you will find him a very sensible knowing Gentleman of an original Turn and Genius; of great Modesty; and rather delibirate in communicating the Treasures of his Mind, than forward in displaying his Ability.

He may be esteemed as a second Prometheus who has stolen the Ærial fire, by his invention of extracting the Thunder from the Clouds by the electrical Apparatus of an Iron Bar &c. You know (I fancy) that he is Agent here for the Assembly in opposition to the Proprietors.

By one Means or another I have been able to collect great

7. One of the clerks of the Privy Council.
8. Thomas Collinson (c. 1726–1803), nephew of BF's friend Peter Collinson and son of James (d. 1762) and Jane Barclay Collinson. Since Peter and James were their parents' only surviving children, and Thomas was as yet unmarried, he was probably writing to one of his maternal relatives, but the identification is elusive: his mother had two brothers, two sisters, two half-brothers, and six half-sisters. Bevan, Barclay, Gurney, and Stedman are among the most important surnames in the Collinson connection. The mention of Warmley in the postscript suggests that the uncle lived in or near Bristol.
9. BF and WF were about to start on a journey which would take them to various places in the west of England and through part of Wales.

Quantities of Goods, without paying you a Visit so early as I first thought would be necessary: But whilst our Family is at Bath, which I believe will be in about a Fortnight, intend running down and accepting of your kind Offer for a few Nights.

A Letter lately received from Bramshot[1] inform'd us all Friends were well there.

With all our sincere Loves to you and all yours—remain affectionately Your obliged Kinsman   THO. COLLINSON

P.S. Warmley[2] will be a very entertaining Sight to Mr. Franklin and Son, who accompanies him and is a very agreeable accomplished Gentleman.

To Mary Stevenson   ALS: Library of Congress[3]

My dear Friend,   London, Sept. 13. 1760

I have your agreable Letter from Bristol,[4] which I take this first Leisure Hour to answer, having for some time been much engag'd in Business.

Your first Question, *What is the Reason the Water at this Place, tho' cold at the Spring, becomes warm by Pumping?* it will be most prudent in me to forbear attempting to answer, till, by a more circumstantial Account, you assure me of the Fact. I own I should expect that Operation to warm, not so much the Water pump'd as the Person pumping. The Rubbing of dry Solids together, has been long observ'd to produce Heat; but the like Effect has never yet, that I have heard, been produc'd by the mere Agitation of Fluids, or Friction of Fluids with Solids. Water in a Bottle shook for Hours by a Mill Hopper, it is said, discover'd no sensible Addition of Heat. The Production of Animal Heat by Exercise, is therefore to be accounted for in another manner, which I may hereafter endeavour to make you acquainted with.

This Prudence of not attempting to give Reasons before one is

1. Bramshot is in eastern Hampshire, eight miles from Petersfield. The "Friends" there have not been identified.
2. Warmley lies four and a half miles from Bristol.
3. Printed as Letter L in *Exper. and Obser.* (1769 edit.), pp. 449–56; (1774 edit.), pp. 459–66.
4. See above, pp. 194–5.

sure of Facts, I learnt from one of your Sex, who, as Selden tells us,[5] being in company with some Gentlemen that were viewing and considering something which they call'd a Chinese Shoe, and disputing earnestly about the manner of wearing it, and how it could possibly be put on; put in her Word, and said modestly, *Gentlemen, are you sure it is a Shoe? Should not that be settled first?*

But I shall now endeavour to explain what I said to you about the Tide in Rivers, and to that End shall make a Figure, which tho' not very like a River, may serve to convey my Meaning. Suppose a Canal 140 Miles long communicating at one End with the Sea, and fill'd therefore with Sea Water. I chuse a Canal at first, rather than a River, to throw out of Consideration the Effects produc'd by the Streams of Fresh Water from the Land,

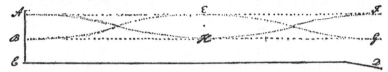

the Inequality in Breadth, and the Crookedness of Courses. Let A, C, be the Head of the Canal, C D the Bottom of it; D F the open Mouth of it next the Sea. Let the strait prick'd Line B G represent Low Water Mark the whole Length of the Canal, A F High Water Mark: Now if a Person standing at E, and observing at the time of High water there that the Canal is quite full at that Place up to the Line E, should conclude that the Canal is equally full to the same Height from End to End, and therefore there was as much more Water come into the Canal since it was down at Low Water Mark, as could be included in the oblong Space A. B. G. F. he would be greatly mistaken. For the Tide is *a Wave,* and the Top of the Wave, which makes High Water, as well as every

5. BF recounted the anecdote somewhat differently from the form in the original: "The Reason of a Thing is not to be enquired after, till you are sure the Thing it self be so. We commonly are at [*What's the Reason of it?*] before we are sure of the Thing. 'Twas an excellent Question of my Lady Cotten, when Sir Robert Cotten was magnifying of a Shooe, which was Moses's or Noah's, and wondring at the strange Shape and Fashion of it: But Mr. Cotten, says she, *are you sure it is a Shooe.*" Brackets in the original. *Table Talk; Being the Discourses of John Selden Esq; or his Sence of Various Matters of Weight and High Consequence Relating especially to Religion and State* (London, 1689), p. 50.

other lower Part, is progressive; and it is High Water successively, but not at the same time, in all the several Points between G, F. and A, B.—and in such a Length as I have mention'd it is Low Water at F G and also at A B, at or near the same time with its being High Water at E; so that the Surface of the Water in the Canal, during that Situation, is properly represented by the Curve prick'd Line B E G. And on the other hand, when it is Low Water at E H, it is High Water both at F G and at A B at or near the same time; and the Surface would then be describ'd by the inverted Curve Line A H F.

In this View of the Case, you will easily see, that there must be very little more Water in the Canal at what we call High Water than there is at Low Water, those Terms not relating to the whole Canal at the same time, but successively to its Parts. And if you suppose the Canal six times as long, the Case would not vary as to the Quantity of Water at different times of the Tide; there would only be six Waves in the Canal at the same time, instead of one, and the Hollows in the Water would be equal to the Hills.

That this is not mere Theory, but conformable to Fact, we know by our long Rivers in America. The Delaware, on which Phila-delphia stands, is in this particular similar to the Canal I have supposed of one Wave: For when it is High Water at the Capes or Mouth of the River, it is also High Water at Philadelphia, which stands about 140 Miles from the Sea; and there is at the same time a Low Water in the Middle between the two High Waters; where, when it comes to be High Water, it is at the same time Low Water at the Capes and at Philadelphia. And the longer Rivers have, some a Wave and Half, some two, three, or four Waves, according to their Length. In the shorter Rivers of this Island, one may see the same thing in Part: for Instance; it is High Water at Gravesend an Hour before it is High Water at London Bridge; and 20 Miles below Gravesend an Hour before it is High Water at Gravesend. Therefore at the Time of High Water at Gravesend the Top of the Wave is there, and the Water is then not so high by some feet where the Top of the Wave was an Hour before, or where it will be an Hour after, as it is just then at Gravesend.

Now we are not to suppose, that because the Swell or Top of the Wave runs at the Rate of 20 Miles an Hour, that therefore the

Current or Water itself of which the Wave is compos'd, runs at that rate. Far from it. To conceive this Motion of a Wave, make a small Experiment or two. Fasten one End of a Cord in a Window near the Top of a House, and let the other End come down to the Ground; take this End in your Hand, and you may, by a sudden Motion occasion a Wave in the Cord that will run quite up to the Window; but tho' the Wave is progressive from your Hand to the Window, the Parts of the Rope do not proceed with the Wave, but remain where they were, except only that kind of Motion that produces the Wave. So if you throw a Stone into a Pond of Water when the Surface is still and smooth, you will see a circular Wave proceed from the Stone as its Center, quite to the Sides of the Pond; but the Water does not proceed with the Wave, it only rises and falls to form it in the different Parts of its Course; and the Waves that follow the first, all make use of the same Water with their Predecessors.

But a Wave in Water is not indeed in all Circumstances exactly like that in a Cord; for Water being a Fluid, and gravitating to the Earth, it naturally runs from a higher Place to a lower; therefore the Parts of the Wave in Water do actually run a little both ways from its Top towards its lower Sides, which the Parts of the Wave in the Cord cannot do. Thus when it is high and standing Water at Gravesend, the Water 20 Miles below has been running Ebb, or towards the Sea for an Hour, or ever since it was High Water there; but the Water at London Bridge will run Flood, or from the Sea yet another Hour, till it is High Water or the Top of the Wave arrives at that Bridge, and then it will have run Ebb an Hour at Gravesend, &c. &c. Now this Motion of the Water, occasion'd only by its Gravity, or Tendency to run from a higher Place to a lower, is by no means so swift as the Motion of the Wave. It scarce exceeds perhaps two Miles in an Hour. If it went as the Wave does 20 Miles an Hour, no Ships could ride at Anchor in such a Stream, nor Boats row against it.

In common Speech, indeed, this Current of the Water both Ways from the Top of the Wave is call'd *the Tide;* thus we say, *the Tide runs strong, the Tide runs at the rate of 1, 2, or 3 Miles an hour,* &c. and when we are at a Part of the River behind the Top of the Wave, and find the Water lower than High-water Mark, and running towards the Sea, we say, *the Tide runs Ebb;* and when we are before the Top of the Wave, and find the Water higher than Low-water Mark, and running from the Sea, we say, the *Tide runs Flood:* But these Expressions are only locally proper; for a Tide strictly speaking is *one whole Wave,* including all its Parts higher and lower, and these Waves succeed one another about twice in twenty four Hours.

This Motion of the Water, occasion'd by its Gravity, will explain to you why the Water near the Mouths of Rivers may be salter at Highwater than at Low. Some of the Salt Water, as the Tide Wave enters the River, runs from its Top and fore Side, and mixes with the fresh, and also pushes it back up the River.

Supposing that the Water commonly runs during the Flood at the Rate of two Miles in an Hour, and that the Flood runs 5 Hours, you see that it can bring at most into our Canal only a Quantity of Water equal to the Space included in the Breadth of the Canal, ten Miles of its Length, and the Depth between Low and Highwater Mark. Which is but a fourteenth Part of what would be necessary to fill all the Space between Low and High-water Mark, for 140 Miles, the whole Length of the Canal.

And indeed such a Quantity of Water as would fill that whole Space, to run in and out every Tide, must create so outrageous a Current, as would do infinite Damage to the Shores, Shipping, &c. and make the Navigation of a River almost impracticable.

I have made this Letter longer than I intended, and therefore reserve for another what I have farther to say on the Subject of Tides and Rivers. I shall now only add, that I have not been exact in the Numbers, because I would avoid perplexing you with minute Calculations, my Design at present being chiefly to give you distinct and clear Ideas of the first Principles.

After writing 6 Folio Pages of Philosophy to a young Girl, is it necessary to finish such a Letter with a Compliment? Is not such a Letter of itself a Compliment? Does it not say, she has a Mind thirsty after Knowledge, and capable of receiving it; and that the most agreable Things one can write to her are those that tend to the Improvement of her Understanding? It does indeed say all this, but then it is still no Compliment; it is no more than plain honest Truth, which is not the Character of a Compliment. So if I would finish my Letter in the Mode, I should yet add something that means nothing, and is *merely* civil and polite. But being naturally awkward at every Circumstance of Ceremony, I shall not attempt it. I had rather conclude abruptly with what pleases me more than any Compliment can please you, that I am allow'd to subscribe my self Your affectionate Friend   B FRANKLIN

Miss Stevenson

From Mary Stevenson ALS and draft: American Philosophical Society

My dear Sir   Draycot[6] Sep. 16. 1760

Such a Letter is indeed the highest Compliment.[7] What you conclude it with I should think too far strain'd to be sincere if I did not flatter myself it proceeded from the warmth of your Affection, which makes you see Merit in me that I do not possess. It would be too great Vanity to think I deserve the Encomiums you give me, and it would be Ingratitude to doubt your Sincerity. Continue, my indulgent Friend, your favourable opinion of me, and I will endeavour to be what you imagine me.

I implore your pardon, Dear Sir, for asking you the Reason before I could assure you of the Fact.[8] I promise never again to abuse the liberty you grant me in such a manner. For, tho my chief aim is attain'd when I can procure a Letter from you, I will be careful to avoid Impertinence, lest you should at last be wearied with it and no longer regard me. I confess it was not from my own observation I told you the Water at Bristol, though cold at the Spring, became warm by pumping, I had only heard that it was so. If it is a Fact, that the Water is warmer after they have pump'd for some time, I should account for it in this manner. The Water I imagine springs warm, but being kept long in the Well grows cold; after they have pump'd some time the Water which was in the Well is exhausted, and what they then pump is fresh from the Spring. This I apprehend may be the cause of the Water being

6. Draycot Cerne, Wiltshire, where Polly, her aunt Mrs. Tickell, and her friend Miss Pitt were visiting Sir Robert Long. See above, p. 195.

7. See immediately above.

8. In her last letter Polly had asked why the water at Hotwell, Bristol, should be warmer after pumping than it was at the spring, and in his reply BF had gently chided her for asking the question before determining that it was so. For this and other matters mentioned here, see the letters cited in the two notes immediately above.

warmer after they have drawn a great Quantity. It is I own great Assurance in me to say so much but I hope it will not offend my dear and honour'd Friend. The familiar agreable manner in which you deliver Instruction renders it easy and pleasant; but you must bear patiently with me if I do not always comprehend things as clearly as might be expected. I still conceive that the rising of the Tides in Rivers is not owing to the immediate Influences of the Moon on them, but produc'd from the Effect it has upon the Sea, which is communicated to them in a weaker degree. But I hope soon to have the pleasure of seeing you, or if I cannot have that happiness I shall take an opportunity of writing to you again, therefore I will not add to the length of this Letter. I could not forbear returning my earliest Thanks for the charming Letter I receiv'd yesterday; and am always ready to lay hold of the Privilege you give me of subscribing myself (though I acknowledge it is too presumptuous) Your sincerely affectionate Friend

M STEVENSON

Dr. Franklin

Henton Brown to Goldney, Smith and Co.[9]

LS: American Philosophical Society

Gentlemen   London 16 Sept. 1760

My particular friend Benjamin Franklin Esqr. and his Son of Philadelphia intending in a tour they are going to take to call at Bristol I take the liberty to recommend them to your notice, whose personal merit is so well known that I need add nothing farther, but that I am with great esteem your obliged Friend—if they should have occasion for any money please to supply them and place it to our Account.

I am for Self and Son Your Obliged Friend   HENTON BROWN

To Goldney Smith & Com: Bristol

Addressed: To / Goldney Smith & Co: / Bristol

9. Henton Brown (*c.* 1698–1775), a London Quaker, and his son James, associated in business as Henton Brown & Son, were BF's bankers. "Account of Expences," pp. 24, 43, 44, 48, 56, 59; *PMHB*, LV (1931), 115, 116, 125, 130; see also above, VII, 379. Peter Collinson probably introduced them. His

Peter Collinson to Capel Hanbury[1]

ALS: American Philosophical Society

Sep: 16: 1760

I recommend to my Dear Friend Capple Hanbury my Worthy Ingenious Friends the Bearers Mr. Franklin and his Son—pray Oblige them with a Sight of all your Curious Operations In Iron and Tinn.

I need not say more your Hospitality I know and your Good Ladys to whom I Devote my Friends—and am yours Affectionatly

P COLLINSON

Addressed: To | Capel Hanbury Esqr | at | Pont Pool

To William Cullen[2]

LS: American Philosophical Society

Dear Sir   London, Sept. 17, 1760

I beg leave to recommend to your Notice the Bearer Mr. Shippen,[3] who intends to reside some Time in Edinburgh for his

---

nephew Thomas Collinson later married Henton Brown's daughter and in 1770 became a member of the firm. Thomas Goldney, William Smith, and others, opened a bank in Bristol in 1752. John Latimer, *The Annals of Bristol in the Eighteenth Century* (n.p., 1893), p. 297.

1. Capel Hanbury (1707–1765) of Pontypool, Monmouthshire; M.P., 1741–65; member of a family one branch of which developed and operated important ironworks in Monmouthshire and South Wales and another branch, moving to London, became leaders in the colonial tobacco trade (e.g., John Hanbury, above, VIII 249 n). The family ironworks were notable for their production of tin plate and rolled sheet iron. Namier and Brooke, *House of Commons*, II, 576–7; Arthur Raistrick, *Quakers in Science and Industry* (N.Y., 1950), pp. 146–8.

2. On William Cullen, professor of chemistry at Edinburgh, see above, VII, 184 n.

3. William Shippen, Jr. (1736–1817), son of Dr. William Shippen (above, III, 428 n), and nephew of Edward Shippen "of Lancaster" (above, V, 195 n). He graduated from the College of New Jersey, 1754, studied medicine in London, then in Edinburgh, where he took his M.D. in 1761, presenting a copy of his thesis, *De Placentae cum Utero Nexu*, to BF. Later he became chief of the medical department of the Continental Army and a founder of the College of Physicians of Philadelphia. *DAB;* Betsy C. Corner, *William Shippen, Jr. Pioneer in American Medical Education A Biographical Essay* (Phila., 1951).

Improvement in Physick and Surgery. He is the Son of a particular Friend of mine in Philadelphia, and bears himself the Character of an ingenious sober and discreet young Man, which persuades me that any Countenance you may show him will not be misplac'd. I suppose he would gladly obtain a Degree with you, if the Time of Residence requir'd will not make that impracticable. If after some Time you find him otherwise worthy that Honour, I beg for him your friendly Advice and Assistance in furthering his Desires.

With the greatest Esteem, I am, Dear Sir, Your most obedient, and most humble Servant,   B FRANKLIN

Dr. Cullen.

To Sir Alexander Dick   ALS: Western Reserve Historical Society

Dear Sir Alexander   London, Sept. 17. 1760

It gave me great Pleasure to learn from Dr. Robertson,[4] that you and Lady Dick and your lovely Bairns,[5] were all well and happy. Now that the long Litigation between our Province and the Proprietaries, which I had the Care of, is finished,[6] I hope to be a better and more punctual Correspondent. My Time will be more my own. I am in debt to my Friends in Scotland for their kind Letters, which I shall endeavour to discharge as soon as I return from a Journey I am just going.[7] Will, too, intends to grow good; and as an Earnest of it, remembers his Promise to Lady Dick and sends the Chapter.[8]

4. William Robertson (1721–1793), famous Scottish historian, published by Strahan; principal of Edinburgh University, 1762; moderator of the General Assembly, 1763. He was a robust Presbyterian, but defended John Home in the controversy over the play *Douglas* (above, p. 4 n.). He was a close friend of Hume and Gibbon, and Walpole called his *History of Scotland* "the best modern history." See above, VI, 94 n, on his interest in American Indian language. *DNB*. Direct correspondence between BF and Robertson will appear in later volumes.

5. On the Dicks and their children, see above, VIII, 440 n. Lady Dick died about three months after this letter was written.

6. See above, pp. 196–211.

7. On this journey see below, p. 231 n.

8. BF's "Parable against Persecution," above, VI, 114–24. The copy sent is in WF's hand.

Sir Alexander Dick, Bart.

The Bearer, Mr. Shippen, I beg Leave to recommend to your Countenance and Protection, as an ingenious worthy young Man, and the Son of my Friend.[9] He goes to Edinburgh to improve himself in Physic and Surgery, and hopes to obtain there the Sanction of a Degree, if found to merit it. Your friendly Advice with regard to his Studies, and kind Influence and Interest in facilitating his Affair, will, I am persuaded, be a Favour conferr'd not improperly. With the sincerest Wishes of Health and Happiness to you and yours, I am, Dear Sir, Your most obedient and most humble Servant   B FRANKLIN

Sir Alexr. Dick

From Isaac Norris[1]

Letterbook copy: Historical Society of Pennsylvania

Dear Friend BF   Fairhill Septr. 20 1760
    Since my Last 24 and 27 August which acknowledged your Several Letters to the 14 of June last I have received the 27th and PS. 29 June and Copy with addition of the 12th July.[2] These acknowledgments of Dates may be satisfactory to know what Letters have fal'n [fallen] into right Hands for it is certain some of those wrote by Captain House got to Philadelphia[3] and there sent open to the Persons to whom they were directed, at least I know it to be so in my own Case for a few Days ago I received Robt. Charles' Letter directed to me dated the 1st of November 1759 with the Report of the Lords of Trade and Order to Sir Wm. Johnson upon Our Indian Affairs[4] under Cover and a few Lines

9. On Shippen, see the document immediately above.
1. Not sent; see Norris' memoranda at the end of the letter.
2. For Norris' letters of August 24 and 27, see above, pp. 184–6, 193–4. None of BF's letters mentioned here have been found.
3. For Captain House, whose ship, the *Juliana*, was taken early in 1760 by a French privateer commanded by Capt. Sebière du Chateleau, see above, p. 15 n.
4. For the Board of Trade report and the order in council on the petition concerning Teedyuscung, see above, VIII, 379–89, 432–3. Writing to Charles, Oct. 22, 1760, Norris said that these documents and Charles's covering letter of Nov. 1, 1759, had apparently been among those captured by Chateleau but sent on to Philadelphia. They reached Norris with the following note:

from N. Scull[5] and it is as certain that to this Day I have not received your Original Letter by Captain House.[6] It is said that Mr. Chatelleau neglected the Letters after tiring or diverting himself with some of them and that a Son of Ralph Asheton[7] took the Opportunity of securing the rest to divert the People here, but I do not warrant the Story nor do I so much as know the young man.

It is difficult to assign any Reasons the Chief Justice could have to enquire of my Brother in the Street "whether the Letters which were in Mr. Scull's Hands belonging to me were ever sent and whether he [my Brother][8] had seen or heard of any such being sent." They were not at that Time but came about, a Week after opened as I have said above without any Account or Apology for that Letter's comming to me in that Manner nor any Information how he came by it, Only barely telling me these Papers had been some Time with him and he was prevented by Sickness from sending them sooner. I have not seen Nicholas Scull since to make further Enquiry, but how he came by those Papers may very easily be guest at, as the Gentlemen could not keep their own Secrets.[9]

"Sir. The inclosed Papers came to my Hands about a Month ago, my severe Illness has been the Reason you have not had them sooner, however as I think they were intended for you I have now sent them. I am your sincere and obliged friend NICHO SCULL." Norris Letterbook, Hist. Soc. Pa.

5. Nicholas Scull (1687–1761), surveyor, cartographer, and early member of the Junto, has been mentioned several times in earlier volumes of this edition; see indexes. He was a partisan of the Penns, to whom he was indebted for his position as provincial surveyor general, 1748–61.

6. Probably BF's letter of Jan. 9, 1760 (not found.)

7. This son of Ralph Assheton (1695–1746), lawyer and provincial councilor, was probably Ralph Assheton, Jr. (1736–1773), who received a medical degree at St. Andrews, Aug. 1, 1759, and was in London in the fall of that year. He could therefore have sailed with Captain House, who apparently cleared for Philadelphia early in January 1760. Charles P. Keith, *Provincial Councillors of Pennsylvania* (Phila., 1883), pp. 281–307; Betsy C. Corner, *William Shippen, Jr.,* (Phila., 1951), pp. 22–4, 42.

8. Brackets in the original.

9. The chief justice was William Allen, one of the principal leaders of the proprietary party; "my Brother" was Charles Norris. The editors can offer no explanation as to how these papers came into Scull's hands. It may be pointed out, however, that they would have interested him since they dealt with the inquiry into the Walking Purchase of 1737, and Scull, who had been

I received besides the Letters I have mentioned above a long encouraging Letter by your Son dated the 15th of July.[1] I have it not by me as I thought it necessary to forward it to Town to stop the Uneasinesses which began to appear in the People under the Fears of having £200,000 of Blank Paper scattered among them instead of Mony.[2] I hope it will have a good Effect, tho' I had tollerably digested in my own Mind a pretty good Security for sinking most or all those Bills out of the Mony allowed by Parliament with what we have Reason [to] expect the next Year[3] and had drawn a Bill at the Desire of the Committee for that Purpose which is now in the Hands of the Committee and the Mode assented to unanimously by the House by which you will, if they approve of the Bill, have Power to purchase Stocks bearing an Interest till drawn out for the Use of the Publick by Bills of Exchange free from the Objections made by the Bank, who no Doubt are best acquainted with their own Modes, and thought they had sufficient for refusing to take our Mony on the terms of the last Law.[4]

I am now fully engaged on the short Adjournment the House have made now near the Expiration of the Assembly Year[5] and

---

present at that affair, testified at the Provincial Council twenty years later that no charges of fraud had been made at the time. See above, VII, 111.

1. Not found, but probably the one in which WF informed Norris of the Privy Council Committee's query about the power of the Crown to disallow parts of an act passed by a colonial legislature; see above, p. 189. Apparently WF had expressed hope that the Privy Council would allow the Supply Act of 1759 to stand, in spite of the Board of Trade's adverse recommendation.

2. This would have been the consequence of the disallowance of the Supply Acts of April 17, 1759, and April 12, 1760.

3. Pa.'s share of the £200,000 voted by Parliament to reimburse the colonies for their war expenditures in 1758 was £26,902 8s. (see below, p. 241). On March 31, 1760, the House of Commons resolved to grant another £200,000 to reimburse the colonies for their expenditures in the campaign of 1759 and of this sum Pa. eventually received £26,611 1s. 9d. See *Votes of the House of Commons in the Seventh Session of the Eleventh Parliament* (1759–1760), p. 379; Sargent, Aufrere & Co. to Charles Norris, July 8, 1762, Hist. Soc. Pa.

4. For the conflict between the terms of the Agency Act of 1759 regarding the handling of the parliamentary grant and the Bank of England's policy on deposits, see above, p. 186 n; and for Norris' draft bill to remedy the situation, see the document immediately below.

5. On Sept. 13, 1760, the Pa. Assembly adjourned until September 22. 8 *Pa. Arch.*, VI, 5138.

shall close this Letter, to go by a Vessel via Bristol,[6] especially as the Business of the Assembly is not finished.

Pray make my Complements to your Son for the seasonable Care he has taken to forward Intelligence of so much importance to us.

I send inclosed a third Bill of Exchange J. Hunter on Thomlinson &c. No. 1876 for £100. Sterling.[7] I have forborn the purchase of another in Hopes the Exchange might lower a little but I see no signs of it tho' I think they will not rise. I am &c.

NB[8] did not send the above but instead thereof wrote the following Letter by a Snow of John Taylors to Bristol vizt.

NB I sent this Letter to Town hearing the Vessel would sail—but going to Town to the Assembly on the 22d I found it was not [delivered] by CN.[9] so that I took the Letter back and opend it—but did not send it. Instead of which I wrote the Letter that follows this. Via Bristol dated 26. September.

did not send this Letter

From Isaac Norris

ALS: American Philosophical Society; letterbook copy: Historical Society of Pennsylvania

Dear Friend Benjamin Franklin   Philada. Septr. 26th. 1760
Since my last of the 24th and PS of the 29th of June last I have received the 27 and P S 29 June and Duplicate with Addition of the 12th of July—with a long Letter from your Son of the 15th[1] and Duplicate from yourself of the 12th and Addition of the 17th of July[2] with the Report of the Board[3] partial and Vissibly tending

6. Probably the snow *Gordon,* Capt. Ferdinando Bowd, which cleared for Bristol about the beginning of October. *Pa. Gaz.,* Oct. 2, 1760.

7. See above, p. 182.

8. The first of these memoranda is written at the end of the text in Norris' letterbook, the second in the margin at the beginning of the text and the third in the margin at the top of its second page. The substitute letter mentioned in the second memorandum is the one printed immediately following.

9. Norris' brother Charles.

1. For these letters, see the document immediately above.

2. Not found.

3. See above, pp. 125–73.

224

to encrease the Power of that Board, but as it appears by that Report that the Acts were presented by the Proprietaries on or before the 20th of February[4] their confirmation or disallowance must by the Limited time be over before now.

We have sent up to the Governor a Bill to enable the Agents to receive the Monies which have been or may be allotted to this Province upon the Parliamentary Grants[5] and if I can keep this Letter till we know the Governors Resolution upon that Bill it shall be added. The Bill gives the Agents Power to receive the Monies and Purchase Stock in their own Names for the Use of the Province subject to the Bills of Exchange to be drawn upon Robert Charles and Your Self by the Trustees when thereto required by the Assembly. and Notice given to you under the

4. BF had presented to the Privy Council the Agency Act, concerning the parliamentary grant, on Feb. 16, 1760, but the proprietary agent, Henry Wilmot, had not presented the other eighteen laws of 1758–59 until the following March 13. See above, pp. 126–7.

5. The Agency Act of 1759 had authorized BF to receive the colony's share of the parliamentary grant for military expenses of 1758 and directed him to deposit the money in the Bank of England subject to drafts and bills of exchange by the trustees of the General Loan Office. By September 1760 the Assembly had learned both that the rules of the Bank would not permit such a procedure and that Parliament had made a further grant of £200,000 to be distributed among the colonies in reimbursement of their expenses during the campaign of 1759. Consequently Norris drafted a bill authorizing BF and Robert Charles to receive this money and invest it in interest-bearing public stocks until drawn out by bills of exchange. See the document immediately above. The Assembly passed this measure, Sept. 24, 1760, and sent it to Governor Hamilton. 8 *Pa. Arch.*, VI, 5137–8, 5140. While it met the difficulties posed by the Bank's rules, it by no means satisfied the governor, because it failed to allow him any voice in choosing the persons to receive the money in England or in determining when and for what purposes it was to be transferred to Pa. and expended there. *Ibid.*, p. 5248. Consequently Hamilton returned the bill on September 25 "with a Paper of Amendments thereon." These included substitution of David Barclay, Jr., and John Barclay for Robert Charles to act with BF. The House considered the amendments on the morning of the 26th (the day Norris wrote this letter), accepted "Two triffling ones," but rejected the others, and sent the bill back to Hamilton, as the speaker told BF in the letter immediately below. 8 *Pa. Arch.*, VI, 5141, 5144; *Pa. Col. Recs.*, VIII, 501–3. Hamilton remained dissatisfied, the bill was dropped, and the Assembly of 1759–60 ended its last session, September 27, without further action on the matter. For proceedings early in the next Assembly, see below, pp. 234–5, 236–7.

Great Seal of this Province of such Drafts to be made by their Order upon which you will have a Power to sell and transfer the said Stocks for the Purpose.

We are at present among Rocks and Sands in a Stormy Season and it depends on you to do every Thing in your Power in the present Crisis for it is too late for us to give you any Assistance. Had it been in my Power you should not have had so many Difficulties to struggle with, but the House were of another Mind as well in the Tack and other Parts of our Re-Emitting Act,[6] as the Bargain and Engagements with Governor Denny for which there was no Necessity[7] but possibly all may, under Providence, end better than Expectation and[8] for if the Time should be suffered to elapse or the principal Acts be confirmed we shall be made more easy in our Controversies with the Proprietaries for the Future, especially as the War in Canada is at an End and the French entirely subdued in that Quarter.[9]

The Two Pamphlets, sent I suppose, by Captain House,[1] never came to my Hands but I procured and read them as well as your Judicious Answer to One of them upon which pray receive my

6. The Re-emitting Act (above, pp. 146–7 n), signed by Governor Denny on June 20, 1759, combined two disparate matters: a loan of £50,000 to John Hunter, agent for the money contractors of the British forces in America, and the re-emission of the provincial bills of credit. In its report of June 24, 1760, the Board of Trade attacked the latter clause because it was "a tack to the loan." *Statutes at Large, Pa.,* V, 716.

7. Thrice during 1759 the Pa. Assembly paid Governor Denny £1,000— on April 17 after he signed the £100,000 Supply Act, on June 20 after he signed the Re-emitting Act, and on July 7 after he signed the "Act for Recording Warrants and Surveys"; see above, VIII, 419–20 n. In addition to these payments, in effect bribes, the Assembly resolved, July 7, 1759, that in case the Proprietors sued Denny "for the Breach of any Instruction, in passing any of the said Bills," it would "as far as in them lies, support the said Governor in Defence of such Suit." 8 *Pa. Arch.,* VI, 5028.

8. The "and" was obviously a slip of the pen; it does not appear in the letterbook copy.

9. On Sept. 8, 1760, Montreal, at which all of the French troops in Canada had collected, capitulated to Gen. Jeffery Amherst, the commander of the largest of the three British armies which had converged upon the city. *Pa. Gaz.,* Sept. 25, 1760, carried news of the French surrender. See Gipson, *British Empire,* VII, 444–67.

1. Capt. House's ship, *Juliana,* was taken by a French privateer early in 1760.

Complements among the others, for I approve and value it much.[2] The Chief Justice[3] told me he was of the same Sentiments and by what I can learn it gives general Satisfaction here.

I send inclosed a third Bill of Exchange N 1876. drawn by J. Hunter on Messrs. Thomlinson &c. for One Hundred Pounds Sterling and a First bill of Exchange No. 1770 Drawn by Col. Hunter on the same Gentlemen for One Hundred Pounds Sterling which please to receive.[4]

The House have received the Governors Amendment to our Bill for appointing Your Self and R Charles to negotiate our Part of the Parliamentary Grant. I shall enclose a Copy of the Bill and Amendments which need no Comment.[5]

I am informed the Vessel is just going[6] and am obliged to close. Your Affectionate Friend   ISAAC NORRIS

To David Hume[7]   ALS: Royal Society of Edinburgh

Dear Sir,   Coventry, Sept. 27. 1760

I have too long postpon'd answering your obliging Letter,[8] a Fault I will not attempt to excuse, but rather rely on your Goodness to forgive it if I am more punctual for the future.

2. For these pamphlets on Canada vs. Guadeloupe, see above, pp. 52–3. BF's "judicious Answer" was, of course, the Canada Pamphlet.

3. William Allen.

4. For the first of these two bills, see above, p. 182. BF recorded the receipt of the second one on Nov. 20, 1760. "Account of Expences," p. 56; *PMHB*, LV (1931), 129.

5. The bill mentioned in the second paragraph of this letter. No copy of it has been found.

6. The letterbook copy bears the following notations not found on the ALS: "Via Bristol by a Snow belonging to Jno Taylor." "First Bill of Exchange £100. 0. 0. N 1770." "Sent Copy of the Bill and Governors Amendments Copied by the Clerk." The snow was the *Gordon,* Capt. Ferdinando Bowd; see the document immediately above.

7. David Hume (1711–1776), philosopher and historian, was born in Edinburgh, the son of a Scottish advocate with an estate in Berwickshire. He matriculated at the University of Edinburgh before his twelfth birthday but never took his degree, spending some years instead in private reading and in travel and study in France. His published writings before 1752 were chiefly on philosophical subjects. In 1746 he served as secretary and later as judge advocate to Lieut. Gen. James St. Clair, commander of a projected expedition

[*The rest of note 7, and note 8, on next page.*]

I am oblig'd to you for the favourable Sentiments you express of the Pieces sent you;[9] tho' the Volume relating to our Pensilvania Affairs, was not written by me, nor any Part of it, except the Remarks on the Proprietor's Estimate of his Estate, and some of the inserted Messages and Reports of the Assembly which I wrote when at home, as a Member of Committees appointed by the House for that Service; the rest was by another Hand. But tho' I am satisfy'd by what you say, that the Duke of Bedford was hearty in the Scheme of the Expedition, I am not so clear that others in the Administration were equally in earnest in that matter.[1] It is certain that after the Duke of Newcastle's first

---

against Canada which, after much vacillation by the Duke of Newcastle, secretary of state, was diverted to what proved to be an abortive attack on the coast of Brittany. In 1752 he was appointed keeper of the Advocates' Library in Edinburgh, a post which he held until 1757 and which gave him access to the books necessary to the preparation of his *History of England*. This work was published in six volumes between 1754 and 1761; unsuccessful at first it became in time the standard history of the period from Julius Caesar to the Revolution of 1688 and brought Hume a large income, to which his later writings on various subjects added substantially. He was secretary to the British ambassador in France, 1763–65, serving part of the time as chargé d'affaires, and was under secretary of state, 1767–68. *DNB;* Ernest C. Mossner, *The Life of David Hume* (Austin, Texas, 1954). BF probably met him through William Strahan when Hume was in London during the winter of 1758–59; he was Hume's house guest in Edinburgh during an extended visit in 1771.

8. Not found.

9. Just what "Pieces" BF had sent Hume is not fully known. Certainly the list included Jackson's *Historical Review of the Constitution and Government of Pensylvania,* which contained texts or extracts from some of the Assembly documents BF had composed and his remarks on Penn's estimate of the proprietary estate (above, VIII, 360–79). From the discussion below on BF's use of unusual words it is almost equally certain that he had sent a copy of the Canada Pamphlet (above, pp. 47–100), with which was reprinted BF's "Observations concerning the Increase of Mankind" (above, IV, 225–34). He may also have sent his long letter printed in *London Chron.,* May 10–12, defending the provincials against the criticisms of Scottish military officers (above, VIII, 340–56), although this paper might seem too hard on the Scots to offer to a friend in Edinburgh. What other "Pieces," if any, BF had sent is a matter of pure speculation.

1. Probably a reference to the proposed expedition against Canada in 1746, for which WF had served as a subaltern in a Pa. volunteer unit and Hume had been secretary to the intended British commander-in-chief, Lieut. Gen. James St. Clair. The mismanagement in Great Britain is described in Mossner, *David Hume,* pp. 188–93; see also above, III, 89 n, 142 n.

Orders to raise Troops in the Colonies, and Promise to send over Commissions to the Officers, with Arms, Clothing, &c. for the Men, we never had another Syllable from him for 18 Months; during all which time the Army lay idle at Albany for want of Orders and Necessaries; and it began to be thought at least that if an Expedition had ever been intended, the first Design and the Orders given, must, thro' the Multiplicity of Business here at home, have been quite forgotten.

I am not a little pleas'd to hear of your Change of Sentiments in some particulars relating to America; because I think it of Importance to our general Welfare that the People of this Nation should have right Notions of us, and I know no one that has it more in his Power to rectify their Notions, than Mr. Hume. I have lately read with great Pleasure, as I do every thing of yours, the excellent Essay on the *Jealousy of Commerce:*[2] I think it cannot but have a good Effect in promoting a certain Interest too little thought of by selfish Man, and scarce ever mention'd, so that we hardly have a Name for it; I mean the *Interest of Humanity,* or common Good of Mankind: But I hope particularly from that Essay, an Abatement of the Jealousy that reigns here of the Commerce of the Colonies, at least so far as such Abatement may be reasonable.

I thank you for your friendly Admonition relating to some un-usual Words in the Pamphlet. It will be of Service to me.[3] The *pejorate,* and the *colonize,* since they are not in common use here, I give up as bad; for certainly in Writings intended for Persuasion and for general Information, one cannot be too clear, and every Expression in the least obscure is a Fault. The *unshakeable* too, tho' clear, I give up as rather low. The introducing new Words where we are already possess'd of old ones sufficiently expressive, I confess must be generally wrong, as it tends to change the

2. "Of the Jealousy of Trade," an additional essay, printed at the front of David Hume, *Essays and Treatises on Several Subjects. A New Edition* (London, 1758), but paged as 187–9.

3. "Pejorate" occurs in "Observations concerning the Increase of Mankind" (above, IV, 231, line 12); "colonize" in the Canada Pamphlet (above, p. 95, line 18); "unshakeable" also in the Canada Pamphlet (above, p. 93, line 8). Hume's criticism of BF's Americanisms may perhaps be explained by his sensitivity about the possible appearance of Scotticisms in his own writings and those of his Scottish friends. Mossner, *David Hume,* pp. 89, 266, 298, 373, 395–6, 606.

Language; yet at the same time I cannot but wish the Usage of our Tongue permitted making new Words when we want them, by Composition of old ones who Meanings are already well understood. The German allows of it, and it is a common Practice with their Writers. Many of our present English Words were originally so made; and many of the Latin Words. In point of Clearness such compound Words would have the Advantage of any we can borrow from the ancient or from foreign Languages. For instance, the Word *inaccessible*, tho' long in use among us, is not yet, I dare say, so universally understood by our People as the Word *uncomeatable* would immediately be, which we are not allow'd to write. But I hope with you, that we shall always in America make the best English of this Island our Standard, and I believe it will be so.[4] I assure you, it often gives me Pleasure to reflect how greatly the *Audience* (if I may so term it) of a good English Writer will in another Century or two be encreas'd, by the Increase of English People in our Colonies.

My Son presents his Respects with mine to you and Dr. Monro.[5] We receiv'd your printed circular Letter to the Members of the Society, and purpose some time next Winter to send each of us a little Philosophical Essay.[6] With the greatest Esteem I am, Dear Sir, Your most obedient and most humble Servant   B FRANKLIN

[*Added in another hand:*] Dated Coventry. Sepr. 27. 1760.

[*Endorsed:*] 27 Septr. 1760 Dr. Franklin

4. For BF's defense of American English, especially when criticized by a Scot, see above, VIII, 342.

5. Alexander Monro the Younger (1733–1817), anatomist; M.D. University of Edinburgh, 1755; appointed in the same year professor of anatomy and surgery, coadjutor with his father. He studied further in London and on the Continent and became a fellow of the Edinburgh College of Physicians in 1759. He and Hume were joint secretaries of the Philosophical Society of Edinburgh. *DNB.*

6. So far as is known neither BF nor WF sent a "little Philosophical Essay" to the Philosophical Society of Edinburgh in response to this printed circular during the winter of 1760–61. On Oct. 2, 1761, BF apologized to Lord Kames for being "so useless a member of your philosophical society" since his election and hoped to contribute soon. Under date of Jan. 24, 1771, however, the Society's *Essays and Observations, Physical and Literary,* III (1771), 129–40, printed a letter from BF to Hume on how to secure houses from the effects of lightning.

To Lord Kames

ALS: Scottish Record Office

My dear Lord, Coventry, Sept. 27. 1760

We are here upon a Journey which when first proposed was to have extended farther than the Season will now permit;[7] we design'd going over to Ireland, and, having made the Tour of that Country, we were to have cross'd from its Northern Part to Dumfries, or some other Port on your Coast, which would have given us the pleasing Opportunity of seeing once more our Friends in Scotland.[8] This, if we could have left London early in the Summer: But the Litigation between our Province and its Proprietor, in which we were engag'd, confin'd us in London till the middle of this Month.[9] That Cause is indeed at length ended, and in a great degree to our Satisfaction; but by its continuing so long, we are disappointed in our Hopes of spending some more happy Days at Kaims, with you and your amiable Family.

I do not pretend to charge this to your Account as a Letter. It is rather to acknowledge myself in your Debt, and to promise Payment. It is some time since I receiv'd your obliging Favour of June last.[1] When I return to London, which we intend after seeing Cheshire, Wales, Bristol, and spending some time at Bath, I hope

7. Very little is known about the journey that BF and WF took in the autumn of 1760. This letter and the one immediately above to David Hume are the only ones BF is known to have written on the trip, and surviving letters after his return mention few details. But from what is said here and from a few other references it appears that they left London soon after September 17, visiting Coventry, Worcester (below, pp. 243–4), and Birmingham. There they saw the type founder John Baskerville (below, pp. 258 n, 259) and BF performed an electrical experiment with Matthew Boulton (BF to Ebenezer Kinnersley, Feb. 20, 1762), to whom he had carried a letter of introduction on his 1758 trip. Robert E. Schofield, *The Lunar Society of Birmingham* (Oxford, 1963), p. 24; published too late for inclusion at its proper place in this edition. They then planned to travel up to Cheshire and back down through parts of Wales to Pontypool in Monmouthshire (above, p. 219), to Bristol and nearby Warmley (above, pp. 218, 212), and then to Bath, where, according to this letter, they hoped to spend "some time." Probably the journey occupied about six weeks. No document has been found placing BF back in London before November 4.

8. BF did not make the projected journey to Ireland and Scotland until 1771.

9. The business concerned the approval or disallowance of the Assembly acts of 1758–59; see above, pp. 196–211.

1. Not found.

to be a more punctual Correspondent. My Son joins in the sincerest Wishes of Happiness to you and yours, with, My dear Lord, Your Lordship's most obedient and most humble Servant   B FRANKLIN

Our Thanks to Lady Kaims for the Receipt. Inclos'd we send the Chapter.[2]

Lord Kaims

[*Addressed:*] To / The honourable Lord Kaims / Edinburgh / Per favour of / Mr Shippen[3]

From Isaac Norris

Letterbook copy: Historical Society of Pennsylvania

Dear Friend B Franklin   Philada. Septr. 27th. 1760

I wrote Yesterday[4] but Joshua Howell[5] calling to let me know he was just going to N York to take his leave of our Friend Christopher Kilby,[6] I shall enclose this and request my old Friend C. Kilby to take the trouble of delivering it and wish him a good Voyage. I sent by way of Bristol in my above mentiond Letter a

2. BF's "Parable against Persecution." See above, VI, 114–24, for its text and history and especially pp. 116–17, 118, for the use Lord Kames made of the copy sent him.

3. These words suggest that young William Shippen (above, p. 219 n) accompanied BF and WF as far as Coventry before heading north to Edinburgh to pursue his medical studies there.

4. See above, pp. 224–7.

5. Joshua Howell was a Quaker merchant and, at least until the end of 1758, a sub-contractor for the London firm of Baker, Kilby, & Baker, provision contractors for the British forces in North America. According to a contemporary, he was an able man, but "was frequently under the greatest difficulties, and could have never have carried on the business, but for the assistance the whole body of Quakers from time to time afforded him." Alfred E. James, ed., *Writings of General John Forbes* (Menasha, Wis., 1938), pp. 108, 111, 183–4, 213. Thomas Balch, ed., *Letters and Papers Relating Chiefly to the Provincial History of Pennsylvania* (Phila., 1855), p. 176.

6. Christopher Kilby (1705–1771), a wealthy New England merchant who settled in London, was agent for Massachusetts Bay (1741–48), and provision contractor for the British forces in America during both the War of the Austrian Succession and the Seven Years' War. *DAB*, Supplement One; Charles W. Tuttle, "Christopher Kilby, of Boston," *New-Eng. Hist. and Gen. Reg.*, XXVI (Jan. 1872), 43–8; above, III, 213 n; VI, 492 n.

Copy of our Bill for appointing Agents to receive the Mony granted to this Province by Parliament and the Governors Amendments. We have returned the Bill with our Dissent to all his Amendments except Two triffling Ones and do not expect the Bill to pass, so that the House will probably rise this Day. I will endeavour to get the Commissioners and Assessors Vindication against the Receiver General and Secretary's Charge in relation to their taxing the Proprietary Estate in Cumberland County.[7] I send herewith a Second Bill of Exchange No. 1770 for £100. sterling (the First in mine Yesterday) Col. Hunter on Messrs. Thomlinson &c.

I have been to the House since writing the above and the Governor adhering to his Amendments as to the Principal Intention, and the House adhering to their Bill, the Bill is droped, And the House propose before they rise to give you all the Powers they can to receive and dispose of the Share already allotted to this Province by a Resolve of Assembly.[8] I am obliged to Close Your Affectionate Friend   I N

From Isaac Norris

Letterbook copy: Historical Society of Pennsylvania

Dear Friend BF   Fairhill 8br. 5. 1760
     I wrote on the 26 and 27 of 7 br. last[9] the First via Bristol and the other intended by our Friend C Kelby who is taking shipping at NY. in the 1st I sent our Agent Bill and the Governors proposed Amendments copied by the Clerk and in the other the Vindication

7. For Richard Hockley's and Richard Peters' allegations that the proprietors had been unfairly taxed in Cumberland Co., see above, pp. 192–3 n. An address from the commissioners and assessors defending their conduct, was read before the Pa. Assembly on Sept. 23, 1760. 8 *Pa. Arch.,* VI, 5140. Writing to Peters, June 9, 1760, Penn expressed his high approval of Hockley and Peters' remonstrance, which he expected to be very useful. Penn Papers, Hist. Soc. Pa.
     8. For the next Assembly's actions on this matter at its first session in October 1760, see below, pp. 236–7 n.
     9. See above, pp. 224–7, 232–3, for these letters and for the matters mentioned in this paragraph.

of the Commissioner and Assessors of Cumberland County against the Representation of RH. and RP[1] the Proprietary Rec. General and Secretary in relation to their taxing the Proprietary Estate in that Co. I have not the Opportunity or Time to send Copies—I hope the Original will get to your Hands.

Our Elections are over[2] and the Old Members, that were alive, generally chosen as far as I have heard the Ch. Justice told me at the last sitting that he should not be in the House this Year—I have not heard from that County.[3] I send inclosed a 3d. Bill of Exchange N 1770 for £100 Sterl. drawn by Col. Hunter on Messrs. Thomlinson &c.[4] and like wise a 1st Bill No. 1798 drawn by the same on the same Gentleman for £100 sterling which I have endorsed payable to your Self[5]—please to receive them.

The Bill for appointing Agents to receive our Part of the Mony granted by Parliament drop'd upon the Governors proposed Amendments.[6] The Design of those Amendments is too obvious to need any Remarks upon them. The Members of the last Assembly were Unanimous in rejecting them except the C.J. who thought they were reasonable and accordingly reasoned and Voted by himself on that Occasion. It would have been a Noble Fund for paying the present Governor the Salary of his former Administration and the Proprietary Expences in soliciting the repeal of our late Acts &c. &c. It is probable the Assembly at their next Setting may make some Order upon it in the best manner they can.[7] It was not pro-

1. Richard Hockley and Richard Peters.

2. Elections for the Pa. Assembly were held on Oct. 1, 1760. *Pa. Gaz.*, Oct. 2, 1760.

3. Chief Justice William Allen was returned to the Assembly from Cumberland Co., but did not take his seat until Jan. 27, 1761. On Oct. 20, 1760, he wrote an English correspondent that he was contemplating a trip to London, if peace were concluded during the winter and this intention may account for his statement to Norris. 8 *Pa. Arch.*, VI, 5157, 5175. Lewis B. Walker, ed., *The Burd Papers. Extracts from Chief Justice William Allen's Letter Book* (1897), p. 43.

4. For this bill, see above, p. 227.

5. BF recorded the receipt of this bill on Nov. 20, 1760. "Account of Expences," p. 56; *PMHB*, LV (1931), 129.

6. For this bill and for the governor's amendments, see above, pp. 225 n, 232–3.

7. The "next Setting" commenced on Oct. 14, 1760. For the actions of the Assembly and governor during this session, see below, pp. 236–8.

posed at our last Sessions for some prudential Reasons. I am Your Affectionate Friend   I N

By the Ship American Captn. Stiles[8] BF recd this—See Letter datd Novr. 22. 1760

First Bill Excha No 1798 £100.0.0

From David Hall   Letterbook copy: American Philosophical Society

Sir,   Philada. October 6. 1760.
   Yours I received by the Philadelphia Packet, Captain Budden, relating to the two protested Bills of Scott and McMichael's;[9] but I had got them renewed, with the Damages, and sent them off, before yours came to hand; however, that does not signify much, as the last Sett, of Course, will not be presented for Payment. I am glad to find, as you will see by my Letter, that we were both of a Mind with respect to these Gentlemen, as they are reckoned very honest Men, and most genteel Dealers.
   I am at a Loss what to do as to remitting you, Exchange rises so fast: it is now 70. and it is thought, in a Week or two will be 80. however I will send some more before the Winter sets in, and hope to see you early in the Spring; and am, Yours, &c.   D. HALL

To Benjamin Franklin Esq:

Sent by the American Captain Stiles. to London[1]

---

8. *Pa. Gaz.*, Oct. 9, 1760, reported the clearance of the ship *America*, Capt. Henry Stiles, for London. *London Chron.*, Nov. 18–20, 1760, reported its arrival at Portsmouth, but it passed Gravesend on its way up the Thames only on December 28, according to the same paper's issue of December 27–30.
   9. For BF's letter of June 27, 1760, see above, pp. 177–9. *Pa. Gaz.*, Sept. 18, 1760, reported the arrival of the *Philadelphia Packet*, Capt. Richard Budden. On the protested bills, see above, pp. 34 n, 177–8, 187.
   1. See the last footnote to the document immediately above.

From Isaac Norris

Letterbook copy: Historical Society of Pennsylvania

October 22d 1760.

Since the above, Duplicate of my Last,[2] I have received yours by the Packet of the 22d and PS 23d of August [3] with the inclosed Papers which bring us down to a preparation for a Hearing upon our Acts on the 27th.[4] where, on this Side the Water, we must leave the Issue under Providence to your Care of which we have no Doubt; I am, however, pleased that the Attorney and Solicitor General have given their Opinion that our Acts cannot be repealed in part;[5] The Contrary of which must have been attended with fatal Consequences and palpable Absurdities.

Our last sitting produced an Order of the House to receive the Distributive Share of the Parliamentary Grant.[6] The proceedings upon it and the Governor's refusing to affix the Great Seal to the appointment of our Agents this Year is referr'd to the Committee of Correspondence who will transmit to you, no doubt a full Account of that Transaction.[7]

2. See above, pp. 233–5.

3. Not found.

4. The hearings before the Privy Council Committee, Aug. 27–8, 1760, on the disposition of the 19 acts passed by the Pa. Assembly, 1758–59; see above, p. 198.

5. For the law officers' opinion, Aug. 19, 1760, on the question of whether some parts of a colonial statute might be disallowed, other parts confirmed, see above, p. 197.

6. On the deadlock over this matter, see above, p. 225 n.

7. On Oct. 15, 1760, the day after the new Assembly convened, it adopted resolutions reappointing BF agent to transact the colony's business "in Pursuance of the Powers and Instructions given to him by the last Assembly, and of such further Instructions as may be hereafter given him by this House," and reappointing Robert Charles as agent to assist BF during the latter's stay in Great Britain, and thereafter as sole agent. The House then ordered its clerk to prepare and send to England copies of these resolutions under the great seal (which was always in the governor's custody). 8 *Pa. Arch.*, VI, 5159. Hamilton refused to affix the seal, explaining to the Assembly, October 18, that he did not know what instructions had been given the agents, but that he suspected these instructions might have empowered them "under these general Powers of Agency" to receive the province's share of the parliamentary grants, thereby by-passing the governor and his right to a voice in the matter. He offered to certify the appointments only if the Assembly would amend

The Governor's Apprehensions seem to arise from the Report of the Board of Trade "that the Mony distributed in the other Colonies in consequence of the Votes of Parliament has frequently been received by the Agents of those Colonies under their general Powers of Agency only."[8] Tho' I presume even that has been with the concurrence of the Governors of the respective Colonies; will you take the trouble of explaining this minutely for our future Conduct with respect to the further Parliamentary Grants.

I am sorry my very ill State of Health prevented my attendance at the House on Governor Denny's passing that Act,[9] it would have been, had the Act been properly drawn and well considered, a fine provision against the Confusion the repeal of our Mony Grants to the Crown must introduce should we be so extreamly unfortunate as to have those Acts disallowed—which God forbid.[1] I hope the Order of the House which you will receive by this Vessel will be effectual for the Mony already allotted to this Province, and if so

---

the resolutions to include "an express Prohibition" against the agents' receiving any money from the parliamentary grants without a specific law for the purpose and the governor's consent in writing. *Ibid.,* pp. 5164–6. Immediately upon receiving this message the Assembly ordered its clerk to have the original resolutions certified by a notary public and to prepare an affidavit of the governor's refusal of the great seal. Then the House adopted resolutions indignantly denouncing the Hamilton's refusal of the seal, contrary to precedent, and ordered that BF receive the money due under the 1759 grant, as empowered under the act of that year, and deposit it in the Bank of England under the names of himself, Charles, and four designated London merchants, the survivors among them, their heirs, and assigns. The order empowered the trustees of the General Loan Office to draw upon these men personally (not directly on the Bank) for transhipments to America. *Ibid.,* pp. 5165–7. No letter to BF from the Committee of Correspondence with "a full Account of that Transaction" has been found. On Sept. 19, 1761, the Assembly noted that no word had yet arrived indicating that BF had ever received these resolves of Oct. 18, 1760, "though transmitted by different Opportunities." *Ibid.,* p. 5263.

8. A quotation from the Board of Trade report, June 24, 1760; see above, p. 165.

9. The act signed by Governor Denny on Sept. 29, 1759, empowering BF to manage Pa.'s share of the parliamentary grant for 1758; see above, VIII, 442 n. For Norris' illness at that time, see above, VIII, 436–7.

1. Norris had not yet heard that the Privy Council had allowed the Supply Act of 1759 to stand under the conditions BF and Charles had agreed to. See above, pp. 205–8.

I think it might be convenient to get Copper Plate Bills of Exchange struck and sent over for the Use of the Trustees.[2]

The Commissioners and Assessors of Cumberland County assert, and it is known to be the constant Decission in our Courts of Justice, that a Warrant to survey a Tract of Land from the Proprietarys who at the Time of granting Their Warrant receive above One third Part of the Purchase Mony, and a regular Return of that Survey into the Surveyor General's Office, does give a just Title to that Land and the Land it Self, whatever Transfers are made from Hand to Hand remains (in the nature of a Mortgage) and Security for the remaining Purchase Mony.[3] This was the Opinion of T. Francis when Attorney General under the Proprietor[4] and all the Justices Judges and Lawyers here generally regulate their Decisions accordingly.

I perceive the Lords of Trade pretty openly conclude their Report with recommending to the Crown a resumption of the Proprietary Grant, when they assert "that the Rights of his Majesty have been gradually departed from by the Proprietarys and which must always be invaded while the Prerogatives of Royalty are placed in the feeble Hands of Individuals and the Authority of the Crown is to be exercised without the Powers of the Crown to support it."[5] This Resumption, to me, appears at no great distance; when a sufficient part of the Odium is taken off by the intermediate Powers, which are to be supported for that Purpose. "Then Aaron shall lay both his Hands upon the Head of the live Goat and confess over him all the Iniquities of the Children of

2. For BF's endorsement of this suggestion, see below, p. 254.

3. In a representation to the governor and council, April 3, 1760 (above, pp. 192–3 n), Richard Hockley and Richard Peters had contended that, among other reasons, the proprietary tax in Cumberland Co. was unfair because the assessors and commissioners there had levied it on quitrents which they assumed the proprietors received from persons holding land by warrant of survey, when in fact these warrants vested no legal title in the occupants, who were not therefore obliged to pay rent and seldom did. The address of the assessors and commissioners, in which they defended themselves against Hockley and Peters' charges, was read before the Assembly on Sept. 23, 1760. 8 *Pa. Arch.*, VI, 5140.

4. Tench Francis (d. 1758) was provincial attorney general from 1741 to 1755.

5. See above, p. 173.

Israel and all their Transgressions and all their Sins, putting them upon the Head of the Goat and shall send him away by the Hand of a fit Man into the Wilderness"[6] where, if I judge right, he[7] will never be able to leave his Posterity such Marks of skill in peopling and cultivating it, as his Father has left to him and his Family, at least in so Short a Time. I now inclose a 2d Bill of Exchange for £100 Sterl N 1798 drawn by Colonel Hunter on Messrs. Thomlinson &c. which please to receive.[8] I sent a Power of Attorney by Chas. Beatty[9] as I apprehended you requested it but I can see no use of that Power as I am perfectly satisfied that my Stock continue in your Name,[1] 'till your Return, or other Accident may Make it necessary to transfer it, in which Case, after returning my Complements to Sampson Lloyd junior[2] and his Brother Osgood Hanbury for their kind offer be pleased to transfer it to them in my Behalf. I am Your Affectionate Friend   I N

B. Franklin

To BF. by Captn Budden[3]

By T. Lloyd[4] to whom I gave a Separate Letter to B.F.[5] with a Credit for about £100—if he (TLl) should have Occasion for it. The order dated 8 br. 22. 1760

6. Leviticus 16:21.
7. Thomas Penn.
8. For this bill, see above, p. 234 n.
9. See above, pp. 31–2.
1. For BF's investments on Norris' behalf, see above, VIII, 147–8.
2. Sampson Lloyd III (1728–1807), customarily called junior, managed the family iron business and with his brother-in-law, Osgood Hanbury (1731–1784), founded the banking firm of Taylor, Lloyd, Hanbury & Bowman (1770). Samuel Lloyd, *The Lloyds of Birmingham* (3d edit., London, 1909), pp. 55–6. Arthur Raistrick, *Quakers in Science and Industry* (N. Y., 1950), p. 120.
3. *Pa. Gaz.*, Oct. 30, 1760, reported the clearance of the *Philadelphia Packet*, Capt. Richard Budden.
4. See above, p. 27 n, and VI, 380 n.
5. Not found.

From John Canton[6]

ALS: The Royal Society[7]

Dear Sir   Spital Square, 31 Octr. 1760

Having procur'd some thin Glass Balls of about an Inch and a half in Diameter, with Stems, or Tubes of eight or nine Inches in length, I electrified them, some positively on the inside, and others negatively, after the manner of charging the Leyden Bottle, and sealed them hermetically. Soon after, I applied the naked Balls to my Electrometer, and could not discover the least Sign of their being electrical; but holding them before the Fire at the distance of six or eight Inches, they became strongly electrical in a very short time, and more so, when they were cooling.[8] These Balls will, every time they are heated, give the electrical Fluid to, or take it from other Bodies, according to the plus or minus State of it within them. Heating them frequently, I find, will sensibly diminish their Power; but keeping one of them under Water a Week, did not appear in the least degree to impair it. That which I kept under Water was charged on the 22d of September last, was several times heated before it was kept in Water and has been heated frequently since, and yet it still retains its Virtue to a very considerable degree. The breaking two of my Balls accidentally, gave me an Opportunity of measuring their Thickness, which I found to be between seven and eight parts in a Thousand, of an Inch.

A down Feather in a thin Glass Ball hermetically sealed, will not be affected by the Application of an excited Tube, or the Wire of a charged Vial, unless the Ball be considerably heated. And if a Glass Pane be heated till it begins to grow soft, and in that State be held between the Wire of a Charged Vial, and the discharging Wire, the Course of the electrical Fluid will not be through the Glass, but on the Surface, round by the Edge of it. I am, with the greatest Respect, Dear Sir Your most Obedient humble Servant

To Benjn. Franklin Esqr.   J:C.

6. On John Canton, electrical experimenter, see above, IV, 390 n.

7. The MS, surviving among the Canton Papers, appears to be a retained copy. Franklin quoted the letter in full (omitting only the address, salutation, and complimentary close) in a letter to Ebenezer Kinnersley, Feb. 20, 1762, printed in the 1769 edition of *Exper. and Obser.*, where the quotation appears on pp. 401–2.

8. The effect of heat on the permeability of glass by electricity was at this time attracting the attention of several experimenters.

State of the Transaction at the Exchequer[9]

I. N.   London, Nov. 4. 1760
   State of the Transaction at the Exchequer, relating to the
          Parliamentary Grant for the Year 1758[10]

The Sum given to Pennsylvania and the Lower Counties jointly, for their 2727 Men, is	£29,993	o	o

By General Abercrombie's Report,[11]
   there were of these effective Men in
   the Field,

From Pennsylvania	2446	
From Lower Counties	281	
	2727	

Therefore the Proportion

to Pensilvania was	£26,902	8	o
to the Lower Counties	3,090	12	o
	29,993	o	o

Paid Fees and Gratuities at the Exchequer, viz.

To the Tellers	£73	19	8
Auditor	35	o	o
Do. Extra. a Gratuity	5	5	o
Mr. Wilford, Sign Manual and Gratuity	2	12	6
Mr. Lucas	15	19	6
Mr. Willis		10	6
	133	7	2

Remains to be divided between the two Governments	£29,859	12	10

9. This statement, in BF's hand but bearing Isaac Norris' initials in the upper left-hand corner, is almost identical, down to the notation above the signature, with the first part of an entry in "Account of Expences," pp. 54–5; *PMHB*, LV (1931), 127–8. Conceivably BF wrote an accompanying letter to Norris on November 4, but no such letter has been found and he probably sent this statement somewhat later. For other similar accounts of this transaction, see below, pp. 244–6.   [*Notes 10 and 11 on next page*]

Of which the Share of
Pensilvania is   £26,782 14 10
Paid to Mr. Barclay[12] that
  of Lower Counties   3,076 18   0

                               £29,859 12 10[1]

Fees at the Treasury still to be paid
of which Mr. Barclay is to repay
me the Proportion of Lower Counties.

                                              B FRANKLIN

Endorsed: State of the Transaction at the Exchequer, London,
Nov. 4. 1760 No. 1

---

10. See above, VIII, 333, for the £200,000 voted by Parliament to reimburse
the colonies for their expenditures in the campaign of 1758. See this volume,
pp. 164–7, for the Board of Trade's discussion of the Pa. act of Sept. 29,
1759, authorizing BF to receive the money. That act acquired indirect confirmation by lapse of time; see above, p. 209.

11. Maj. Gen. James Abercromby was commander-in-chief of the British
forces in North America during the spring and early summer of 1758.

12. Either David Barclay, Jr., or John Barclay, whom Hamilton wished to
have substituted for Robert Charles in the Assembly's agency bill of September 1760. See above, pp. 190–1 n, 225 n.

1. In "Account of Expences" (see the first note to this document) BF
omitted the remainder of this statement but entered the following memoranda:
"I receiv'd the whole, Mr. Barclay Agent for the Lower Counties being present. I paid to him the above £3,076 18s. 0d. I immediately went to the Bank,
and lodg'd there the Sum remaining in
my hands viz.—   £26,800 0 0
"Without deducting what I had advanc'd
in Fees &c. at the Exchequer, viz.   £17 5 6
"Or my Commission on 26,902 8s. 0d.
at ½ per Cent.   134 10 0   151 15 6

"So that the neat Sum in the Bank, belonging to the Prov-⎫ £26,648 4 6
ince, after I have drawn out the above Articles will be ⎭
Excepting the Treasury Fees, of which I have not yet
an Account, but they must be deducted when paid.

                                           B. FRANKLIN

"Paid for Treasury Fees and Gratuity charg'd me by the
Soll[icito]r   13 13 0
"Memo. Mr. Barclay is to pay me his Proportion of the
above £13 13s. 0d."
A detailed check of these figures shows a discrepancy of 4d. at one point;
this is offset, however, by an equal and opposite discrepancy at another.

To John Canton

ALS: The Royal Society

Dear Sir   Wednesday Nov. 12 [1760]
What pass'd at the Society last Thursday night, was chiefly, a Motion for an Address to the King, which was agreed to, and a Committee appointed to make a Draft.[2] The Society adjourn'd to Monday night, to hear the Address and agree upon it, which was also done. On Thursday next at the Meeting we are to be inform'd when it is to be presented. I hope I shall have the Pleasure of seeing you there at that time; and am Sir, Your most obedient Servant   B FRANKLIN

P.S. I doubt I shall not be ready with the Paper, but have other Reasons for desiring you not to be absent.[3]

From William Thomson[4]

ALS: American Philosophical Society

Sir   Worcester 18th Novr. 1760
I take this Opportunity to return you my sincere thanks not only for the pleasure your Company afforded me during your short stay

2. Following the death of George II, Oct. 25, 1760, and the accession of George III, the Royal Society, like many other organizations, presented a "humble Address" to the new monarch. Following its preparation and acceptance by the membership as described in this letter, Secretary of State William Pitt, F.R.S., arranged for the presentation, which took place on November 17. The text of the address and a brief account of the ceremony are in Charles R. Weld, *A History of the Royal Society* (London, 1848), II, 20–1.

3. What "Paper" BF had in mind is not clear; perhaps he wished to study more carefully Canton's letter of October 31 (above, p. 240) in order to discuss it when they met. The "other Reasons" for wanting Canton's presence at that particular meeting are unknown. It may be noted, however, that at the Society meeting on Thursday, November 13, there was read a paper of Benjamin Wilson's dealing with the permeability of glass, as Canton's letter of October 31 had done. *Phil. Trans.*, LI, Part II (1760), 896–906.

4. William Thomson (d. 1802), originally a dissenting minister and tutor to young gentlemen, studied medicine at Leyden, and practised, first at Ludlow, then at Worcester. He was physician to the Worcester Infirmary, 1757–92. He died "aged upwards of 80, much esteemed as a humane and good man." John Nichols, *Illustrations of the Literary History of the Eighteenth Century*, IV (London, 1822), 725–6 n.

in Worcester,[5] but also for the Entertainment I am confident I owe to you after your Departure—*The Interest of Great Britain with Respect to her Colonies*[6] gave me a more distinct view than I ever had before of our Connexions with our fellow Subjects in distant parts of the Globe; And I hope the methods proposed there, for our mutual Advantage, will be properly attended to by those, whose Duty it is to listen to every Hint or Scheme laid down [for] promoting the Interest of those who intrust them with their [Property,] Liberty, and Life.

I thought to have commissioned our friend Mr. Small[7] to return thanks to you in my Name, but, for my own Sake, I take the liberty to do it in this manner, as I am glad to embrace every Opportunity of improving the Acquaintance I thought myself so happy in beginning, and of assuring you and Mr. Franklin that I am, with great Esteem, your faithfull and obedient Servant

WILLM THOMSON

Addressed: To / Doctor Franklin

Endorsed: Dr Thomson Worcester

To Isaac Norris

Copy:[8] American Philosophical Society

Dear Sir   London, Novr. 19. 1760

This is just to acknowledge the Receipt of your Favours of August 24 and 27. with the Bill for £100 on Messrs. Thomlinson &c. No. 1876,[9] and to acquaint you, that I have at length receiv'd the Money from the Exchequer and lodg'd it in the Bank as nearly agreeable to the Directions of the Act as I possibly could;[1] for

5. This is the only known evidence that BF and WF visited Worcester in their autumn journey of 1760.

6. BF apparently sent Thomson anonymously a copy of the Canada Pamphlet after his Worcester visit.

7. Probably Alexander Small; see above, p. 110 n.

8. In WF's hand.

9. See above, pp. 184–6, 193–4; for the bill on "Messrs. Thomlinson," see p. 184 n.

1. For BF's account of his transaction at the Exchequer, see above, pp. 241–2; the act to which he was trying to conform was that passed by the Pa. Assembly on Sept. 29, 1759 (above, VIII, 442 n), appointing him agent to receive Pa.'s share of the parliamentary grant for the year 1758 and directing him to deposit

they would not, as I acquainted you before, receive it subject to the Drafts of the Trustees in Pensylvania, it being contrary to their Rules. The House will consider what is to be done with it, and send me the necessary Directions.[2] If I were to advise, it should be to lay it out in the Stocks, which will certainly at a Peace produce a Profit of near 20 per Cent. besides the intermediate Interest. I am applying for the Grant of 1759, but nothing is yet done in it.[3] I shall write more fully per Bolitho.[4] With the greatest Esteem, I am &c.   B.F.

P.S. The Sum lodg'd in the Bank belonging to the Province is £26,648 4s. 6d. out of which I have some Fees to pay, of which I have not had the Account.

To Isaac Norris, Esqr. Speaker (Copy)

To Isaac Norris

Extract: American Philosophical Society; copy: Historical Society of Pennsylvania[5]

[November 22, 1760]
The Share allotted by the Lords of the Treasury to Pensylvania and the Lower Counties, of the Parliamentary Grant for 1758, was

---

it in the Bank of England, subject to the drafts of the trustees of the General Loan Office. For the Bank's objections to this act, see above, p. 186 n.

2. On Oct. 18, 1760, the Pa. Assembly ordered BF to deposit its share of the parliamentary grant in the Bank of England in the names of himself, Robert Charles, and four London merchants, and directed the trustees of the Loan Office to draw on these men personally. Apparently, however, BF never received these instructions. See above, pp. 236–7 n.

3. On March 31, 1760, Parliament resolved to grant the American colonies a second £200,000 to reimburse them for their expenditures in the campaign of 1759; see above, p. 223 n.

4. The *Myrtilla*, Capt. John Bolitho, reached Deal by November 27 and remained there with other outward-bound vessels, held back by adverse winds, until January 6. It reached Spithead under convoy on the 8th and, apparently a part of the West Indian convoy, sailed a few days later. It reached Philadelphia by March 5. *London Chron.*, Nov. 27–29, Dec. 16–18, 1760; Jan. 6–8, 8–10; *Pa. Gaz.*, Feb. 26, March 5, 1761.

5. The extract, in WF's hand, is headed "Extract of B.F.'s Letter to Mr. Norris, Novr. 22, 1760." The copy, in a clerk's hand, has the initials "I.N." in the upper left-hand corner and has no heading but begins by repeating the

£29,993. The Rule their Lordships follow'd in the Division of the £200,000 was, to proportion the Sums for each Colony according to the Number of effective Men each had in the Field. These Numbers they took from Gen. Abercromby's Report. By that Report it appear'd that Pensylvania had 2446 and the Lower Counties 281 in all 2727 Men; for which the Allowance was £29,993, as above. This Sum divided by the same Rule between Pensylvania and the Lower Counties, was

For Pensylvania	£26,902	8	0
For the Lower Counties	3,090	12	0
	29,993	0	0

Out of this was paid sundry Fees and Customary Gratuities at the Exchequer,

viz To the Tellers	£73:	19:	8			
To the Auditor	35.	0:	0			
To Do Extra, a Gratuity	5:	5:	0			
To Mr. Wilford, Sign Man. ⎫ and Gratuity ⎭	2.	12:	6			
To Mr. Lucas	15.	19.	6			
To Mr. Willis	—:	10:	6	133:	7:	2
				29,859.	12.	10

Of which the Share						
of Pensylvania is	£26,782.	14.	10			
of Lower Counties	3,076.	18.	0	29,859.	12.	10

The above Share of Pensylvania after deducting the Commissions allow'd me by the Act, is lodg'd in the Bank. When the Trustees draw for it, the Drafts must be upon me; for the Bank, as I wrote you before, will have no Account with them.[6]

---

postscript of the letter of November 19 printed immediately above, citing that date. It begins the text below with the dating notation "22d." The copy omits the two sentences at the end of the extract, following the tabulation. Since no ALS survives, it is impossible to say with certainty whether this document represented a separate letter from that of November 19, or was originally a second postscript to it written three days later. The document is largely a repetition of that of November 4, above, pp. 241–2.

6. The extract bears no endorsement, but the copy is endorsed: "Novr 19. 1760 Parliamentary Allotment, Lodged in the Bank &c."

To John Canton

AL: The Royal Society

Monday morning, Nov. 24. [1760][7]
Mr. Franklin's Compliments to Mr. Canton, and is sorry to find
that he cannot have the Pleasure of waiting on him this Evening,
being oblig'd to attend a Committee at the Society of Arts;[8] but
as he expects to see Mr. Canton on Thursday at the Royal Society;
some other Evening convenient to Mr. Canton may then be
agreed on.

To Mary Stevenson

ALS: Library of Congress[9]

My dear Friend   [November? 1760][1]
    It is, as you observed in our late Conversation, a very general
Opinion, that *all Rivers run into the Sea,* or deposite their Waters

7. The Minute Book of the Society of Arts shows that, as indicated in this
letter, BF attended a committee meeting on Nov. 24, 1760.

8. On the Society for the Encouragement of Arts, Manufactures and Commerce (sometimes called the Premium Society and now the Royal Society of
Arts), and on BF's election as a corresponding member in 1756, see above, VI,
186–9, 275–7, 458, 599–600. The Society's records show that during 1760 BF
attended twenty-three committee meetings and on December 3 accepted the
co-chairmanship of the Committee of Colonies and Trade.

9. Printed as Letter LVI in *Exper. and Obser.* (1769 edit.), pp. 469–72,
465–6; some pages numbers are repeated and the sheets are variously bound
in surviving copies; (1774 edit.), pp. 479–83.

1. The ALS (which may have been the copy sent to the printer in 1769) is
undated, but in *Exper. and Obser.* the date is given as "September 20, 1761."
This seems most improbable. At that time BF, WF, and Richard Jackson were
returning from a journey through Flanders and Holland and, after a stormy
crossing in a leaky sloop, just "made shift to get [to London] time enough
for the Coronation" of George III, which took place on September 22. BF to
DF, Utrecht, Sept. 14, 1761; WF to Sarah Franklin, London, Oct. 10, 1761,
below, p. 368. The contents of the present letter show that it followed up the
exchanges between BF and Polly Stevenson on tides and rivers begun in their
letters of August and Sept. 13 and 16, 1760 (above, pp. 194–5, 212–17,
217–18), and probably preceded his letter of March 30, 1761, on the same
subject (below, pp. 296–7). When the MS was put up for auction in 1920 the
sales catalogue dated it Oct. 1, 1760, but without saying why (Stan V. Henkels
Catalogue No. 1262, July 1, 1920, p. 9). This date too seems unlikely. Polly
was still in Wiltshire as late as September 16, and BF and WF left London soon
after the middle of the month for a trip to Cheshire, Wales, and Bristol, and

there. 'Tis a kind of Audacity to call such general Opinions in question, and may subject one to Censure: But we must hazard something in what we think the Cause of Truth: And if we propose our Objections modestly, we shall, tho' mistaken, deserve a Censure less severe, than when we are both mistaken and insolent.

That some Rivers run into the Sea is beyond a doubt: Such, for Instance, are the Amazones, and I think the Oranoko and the Missisipi. The Proof is, that their Waters are fresh quite to the Sea, and out to some Distance from the Land. Our Question is, whether the fresh Waters of those Rivers whose Beds are filled with Salt Water to a considerable Distance up from the Sea (as the Thames, the Delaware, and the Rivers that communicate with Chesapeak Bay in Virginia) do ever arrive at the Sea? and as I suspect they do not, I am now to acquaint you with my Reasons; or, if they are not allow'd to be Reasons, my Conceptions, at least of this Matter.

The common Supply of Rivers is from Springs, which draw their Origin from Rain that has soak'd into the Earth. The Union of a Number of Springs forms a River. The Waters as they run, expos'd to the Sun, Air and Wind, are continually evaporating. Hence in Travelling one may often see where a River runs, by a long blueish Mist over it, tho' we are at such a Distance as not to see the River itself. The Quantity of this Evaporation is greater or less in proportion to the Surface exposed by the same Quantity of Water to those Causes of Evaporation. While the River runs in a narrow confined Channel in the upper hilly Country, only a small Surface is exposed; a greater as the River widens. Now if a River ends in a Lake, as some do, whereby its Waters are spread so wide as that the Evaporation is equal to the Sum of all its Springs, that Lake will never overflow: And if instead of ending in a Lake, it was drawn into greater Length as a River, so as to expose a Surface equal, in the whole to that Lake, the Evaporation would be equal, and

---

with the intention of spending "some time at Bath" (above, p. 231), so there hardly seems time or opportunity for the "late Conversation" with Polly mentioned in his opening sentence, until after his return to London. Probably he was gone most if not all of October, since the first document that places him back in the city is dated November 4 (above, p. 241). November 1760 seems therefore the earliest that he could have written this letter, so it is placed here, but the correct date could have been a month or two later.

such River would end as a Canal; when the Ignorant might suppose, as they actually do in such cases, that the River loses itself by running under ground, whereas in truth it has run up into the Air.

Now many Rivers that are open to the Sea, widen much before they arrive at it, not merely by the additional Waters they receive, but by having their Course stopt by the opposing Flood Tide; by being turned back twice in twenty-four Hours, and by finding broader Beds in the low flat Countries to dilate themselves in; hence the Evaporation of the fresh Water is proportionably increas'd, so that in some Rivers it may equal the Springs of Supply. In such cases, the Salt Water comes up the River, and meets the fresh in that part where, if there were a Wall or Bank of Earth across from Side to Side, the River would form a Lake, fuller indeed at some times than at others according to the Seasons, but whose Evaporation would, one time with another, be equal to its Supply.

When the Communication between the two kinds of Water is open, this supposed Wall of Separation may be conceived as a moveable one, which is not only pushed some Miles higher up the River by every Flood Tide from the Sea, and carried down again as far by every Tide of Ebb, but which has even this Space of Vibration removed nearer to the Sea in wet Seasons, when the Springs and Brooks in the upper Country are augmented by the falling Rains so as to swell the River, and farther from the Sea in dry Seasons.

Within a few Miles above and below this moveable Line of Separation, the different Waters mix a little, partly by their Motion to and fro, and partly from the greater specific Gravity of the Salt Water, which inclines it to run under the Fresh, while the fresh Water being lighter runs over the Salt.

Cast your Eye on the Map of North America, and observe the Bay of Chesapeak in Virginia, mentioned above; you will see, communicating with it by their Mouths, the great Rivers Sasquehanah, Potowmack, Rappahanock, York and James, besides a Number of smaller Streams each as big as the Thames. It has been propos'd by philosophical Writers, that to compute how much Water any River discharges into the Sea, in a given time, we should measure its Depth and Swiftness at any Part above the Tide, as, for the Thames, at Kingston or Windsor. But can one imagine, that if all the Water of those vast Rivers went to the Sea, it would not first have pushed the Salt Water out of that narrow-mouthed Bay, and filled it with fresh? The Sasquehanah alone would seem to be sufficient for this, if it were not for the Loss by Evaporation. And yet that Bay is salt quite up to Annapolis.

As to our other Subject, the different Degrees of Heat imbibed from the Sun's Rays by Cloths of different Colours, since I cannot find the Notes of my Experiment to send you, I must give it as well as I can from Memory.[2]

But first let me mention an Experiment you may easily make your self. Walk but a quarter of an Hour in your Garden when the Sun shines, with a Part of your Dress white, and a Part black; then apply your Hand to them alternately, and you will find a very great Difference in their Warmth. The Black will be quite hot to the Touch, the White still cool.

Another. Try to fire Paper with a burning Glass. If it is White, you will not easily burn it; but if you bring the Focus to a black Spot or upon Letters written or printed, the Paper will immediately be on fire under the Letters.

2. BF probably performed this experiment, described in detail further on in this letter, in 1732 or a little later, after he had read the discussion of the general subject in Hermann Boerhaave, *Elementa chemiae, quae anniversario labore docuit, in publicis, privatisque, scholis* (2 vols., Leyden, 1732), or the English translation by Timothy Dallowe, *Elements of Chemistry* (2 vols., London, 1735). BF evidently devised the experiment he told Polly about, made it himself, and also called it to the attention of his friend Joseph Breintnall (above, I, 114 n), for under date of Aug. 3, 1737, Breintnall wrote an account of a very similar experiment he had performed the preceding January 25, which, he said, he "was induced to make about seven years ago, and lately to repeat, from some Hints given me by Benjamin Franklin." Logan Papers, Hist. Soc. Pa. A copy of the central part of this memorandum is in Franklin Papers, APS, dated Jan. 25, 1736–7. Both are printed in I. Bernard Cohen, "Franklin's Experiments on Heat Absorption as a Function of Color," *Isis*, XXXIV (1942–43), 404–7. Breintnall undoubtedly erred in remembering that BF had given him the "Hints" as much as seven years earlier, for the underlying principle was first published only in 1732 in Boerhaave's work mentioned above. In his discussion the Dutch chemist had also cited, as BF does in this letter, the different speeds at which black and white cloths dry in the sun and the greater rapidity with which a "burning glass" can ignite blackened paper than white. BF's contribution was in contriving the simple but effective experiment by which he could ascertain precisely the relative order in which the various colors absorb the solar heat. For an extended discussion, see I. Bernard Cohen, *Franklin and Newton* (Phila., 1956), pp. 215–22.

Thus Fullers and Dyers find black Cloths, of equal Thickness with white ones, and hung out equally wet, dry in the Sun much sooner than the white, being more readily heated by the Sun's Rays. It is the same before a Fire; the Heat of which sooner penetrates black Stockings than white ones, and so is apt sooner to burn a Man's Shins. Also Beer much sooner warms in a black Mug set before the Fire, than in a white one, or in a bright Silver Tankard.

My Experiment was this. I took a number of little Square Pieces of Broad Cloth from a Taylor's Pattern Card, of various Colours. There were Black, deep Blue, lighter Blue, Green, Purple, Red, Yellow, White, and other Colours or Shades of Colours. I laid them all out upon the Snow in a bright Sunshiny Morning. In a few Hours (I cannot now be exact as to the Time) the Black being warm'd most by the Sun was sunk so low as to be below the Stroke of the Sun's Rays; the dark Blue almost as low, the lighter Blue not quite so much as the dark, the other Colours less as they were lighter; and the quite White remain'd on the Surface of the Snow, not having entred it at all. What signifies Philosophy that does not apply to some Use?[3] May we not learn from hence, that black Cloaths are not so fit to wear in a hot Sunny Climate or Season as white ones; because in such Cloaths the Body is more heated by the Sun when we walk abroad and are at the same time heated by the Exercise, which double Heat is apt to bring on putrid dangerous Fevers? That Soldiers and Seamen who must march and labour in the Sun, should in the East or West Indies have an Uniform of white? That Summer Hats for Men or Women, should be white, as repelling that Heat which gives the Headachs to many, and to some the fatal Stroke that the French call the *Coup de Soleil?* That the Ladies Summer Hats, however should be lined with Black, as not reverberating on their Faces those Rays which are reflected upwards from the Earth or Water? That the putting a white Cap of Paper or Linnen *within* the Crown of a black Hat, as some do, will not keep out the Heat, tho' it would if plac'd *without*[?] That Fruit Walls being black'd may receive so much Heat from the Sun in the Daytime, as to continue warm in some degree thro' the Night, and thereby preserve the Fruit from Frosts, or forward its Growth?—

3. This sentence is often quoted to illustrate BF's interest in the application of scientific knowledge to human welfare.

with sundry other particulars of less or greater Importance, that will occur from time to time to attentive Minds? I am, Yours affectionately,   B. FRANKLIN

Miss Stevenson

To Cadwallader Colden[4]   ALS: New-York Historical Society

Dear Sir,   London, Dec. 5. 1760[5]

I take this first Opportunity of congratulating you most sincerely on your Accession to the Government of your Province, which I am the more pleas'd with, as I learn that the Ministry are well satisfy'd the Administration has fallen into so good Hands, and therefore that you are not like to be soon superseded by the Appointment of a new Governor.[6]

The Abbé Nollet has lately published another Volume of Letters on Electricity, in which he undertakes to support his Principles against the Attacks they have met with from all Quarters.[7] He has sent me a Copy, and another for your Son Mr. David Colden. I

4. On this N. Y. political leader and scientific correspondent of BF, see above, II, 386 n.

5. The day of the month is overwritten and could be read as either "3" or "5." It is printed here as "3" since Colden's endorsement shows that he accepted that date as correct.

6. James DeLancey, lieutenant governor of N. Y., who had been acting governor since the departure of Sir Charles Hardy in 1757, died suddenly on July 30, 1760. Colden, his senior councilor, automatically succeeded to the administration with the title of president and commander-in-chief. Through friends in England he sought a commission as lieutenant governor, and Lord Halifax told Peter Collinson that he thought well of Colden but he had some reservations because of the New Yorker's age—almost 73. On April 14, 1761, some months after the accession of George III, the commission was issued, and at the same time Gen. Robert Monckton (1726–1782) was appointed governor. Three times more before his death in 1776 at the age of eighty-eight, the administration of the colony devolved on Colden. *Colden Paps.*, V, 346–7, 370–1; VI, 26–7; Alice M. Keys, *Cadwallader Colden A Representative Eighteenth Century Official* (N.Y., 1906), pp. 260–74.

7. On Jean-Antoine Nollet and his attack on BF's electrical theories, see above, IV, 423–8. In 1760 he issued a new edition with a second volume: *Lettres sur L'Electricité. Dans lesquelles on soutient le principe des Effluences et Affluences simultanées contre la doctrine de M. Franklin et contre les nouvelles prétentions de ses partisans, Seconde Partie.*

take the Freedom of forwarding it under your Cover, with my best Respects to that very ingenious young Gentleman, whose valuable Work on the same Subject I am sorry has not yet been made publick.[8]

With the greatest Esteem and Regard I have the Honour to be Dear Sir, Your most obedient and most humble Servant

B FRANKLIN

Honble. Cadr. Colden Esqr.

Endorsed: Franklin Decr 3 1760

To Isaac Norris

Copy:[9] American Philosophical Society

Dear Sir   London, December [16, 1760][1]

Agreeable to what I wrote in mine of the 13th.[2] I [have] ventur'd to agree by my Broker for the following [*torn*] Stocks, on Account of the Province, to be deliver'd [*torn*] Week from this Day, viz.

£1000 of the 4 per Cent. Annuities 1760, at 92 per Cent.		£[920:	0: 0]³
£1500	Do.	at 91⅞	137[8: 2: 6]
3000	Do.	91⅞	2756: 5:[0]⁴
2000	Do.	92	1840: 0: 0
1,000	Do.	92	920: 0: 0
3,000	Do.	91⅞	2756: 5: 0
3,500	Do.	91¾	3211: 5: 0
£15,000			£13781: 17: 6⁵

8. On David Colden and his defense of BF against Nollet, see above, V, 135–44, 435; on his paper sent to BF in England but never published, see above, VII, 263–4; VIII, 170–2.

9. In WF's hand.

1. Norris' letter of May 1, 1761 (below, p. 310), acknowledges the receipt of BF's letter of the 16th of December last, dealing with the "purchase of stocks."

2. Presumably December 13 (not found).

3. Because of a tear in the MS this amount and part of that immediately below are missing; the figures have been supplied from BF's record in "Account of Expences," p. 58. That record is headed "Paid for the Stock bought for the Province, viz" and is dated "Dec. 18." The fifth item (for £1000) is dated, however, "Dec. 19," and the final item (for £3500) is dated "23." It would appear, therefore, that BF made actual payment on these separate dates.

4. In "Account of Expences," p. 58, this amount is given as "2757: 10: 0,"
[*The rest of note 4, and note 5, on next page.*]

I was advis'd to buy rather the Annuities of 1760 than those of 1758 and 1759 which I formerly bought for you and myself,[6] they being but 3 per Cents and cost 78 and ½ while these 4 per. Cents were but about 92 and consequently cheaper. However, finding the Stocks still falling, tho' they had been thought at the lowest, I have held my Hand, not knowing whether I had best venture any farther at present or wait for the new Loan of 1761, which it is suppos'd will be still cheaper, especially near the Time of the first Payment. On a Peace, 'tis thought by those who know most of these Things, that the Three per Cents will be at par, if not higher, and the four per Cents at about 124.

I believe I shall have the Bills you advis'd to be printed, with proper Checks, to be made use of by the Trustees in their Drafts, ready so as to send per next Ship;[7] but hope they will not think of drawing till a Peace; which now cannot be far off. However that is as the House may think proper.

With the greatest Esteem, I am, &c. B.F.

P.S. The Reason of the present Lowness of the Stocks is that the Subscribers to the new Loan for 1761 are selling out to enable themselves to comply with their Engagements to the Government.

I write this to send after the Mail, hoping [to] reach the Pacquet at Falmouth.

To Isaac Norris, Esqr (Copy)

---

but at the end of the list is a minus entry, "Recd. of the Broker Cash overpaid in the third Article 1: 5: 0," thereby reducing the total to the same figure as appears here below.

5. In "Account of Expences," p. 58, BF noted at the end: "Memo. Broker's Commission not yet paid."

6. For BF's additional stock purchases, May 5 and July 5, 1761, see below, pp. 313, 335. In the interim he loaned to Jared Ingersoll, agent for Conn., Jan. 23, 1761, £2000 in cash, repayable on demand with 4 percent interest and secured by £2500 of 4 percent annuities. Ingersoll repaid the loan, March 27, 1761, with £14 accrued interest. "Account of Expences," pp. 58, 59; *PMHB*, LV (1931), 130.

7. Norris had advised BF, Oct. 22, 1760 (above, p. 238) "to get Copper Plate Bills of Exchange struck" for the use of the trustees of the Provincial Loan Office, who had been empowered to draw upon BF, Charles, and four other men for the parliamentary grant. Apparently, however, BF did not follow up the suggestion, for in the following September the trustees had bills of exchange printed in Pa.; see below, pp. 362 n, 372–3.

From William Strahan   AL: American Philosophical Society

Saturday Evening Decr. 27. [1760?][8]
Mr. Strahan's respectful Compliments to Dr. Franklin—called to
know how he does, and to reproach him (gently) for not calling in
New Street to see his Wife,[9] who he told him last Monday Sev-
enight was to be in Town the following Thursday—Is afraid he
will, at least, do himself no good by feasting every Day, as he is
informed he hath done for some time past, and therefore wishes
him to come soon and have one meagre Day in New Street.
Addressed: To / Dr. Franklin

From Managers of the Pennsylvania Hospital

MS not found; abstract reprinted from Thomas G. Morton and Frank
Woodbury, *The History of the Pennsylvania Hospital 1751–1895* (Philadelphia, 1895), p. 43.

"On December 29, 1760, a letter was written to Franklin for some
necessary drugs and medicines,[1] and he was also asked 'to join with
some others of our fellow citizens, now in London, in soliciting contributions on behalf of the Hospital from several merchants who, we
apprehend, may be induced to encourage the progress thereof.'"[2]

8. December 27 fell on Saturday in 1760 and again in 1766. There is no
evidence showing to which year this note belongs; it is printed here in accordance with the general principle of placing a document at the earliest of all
possible dates.
9. Strahan had moved his family in 1748 to a house in New Street, between
Shoe Lane and Fetter Lane, north of, and roughly parallel to Fleet Street.
Later he erected a large printing house nearby. [Richard A. Austen-Leigh],
*The Story of a Printing House Being a Short Account of the Strahans and
Spottiswoodes* (London, 1912), pp. 2–4, 11–14.
1. There is no record in "Account of Expences" of such purchases for the
Hospital, but the omission is of little significance since during the final year
or two of BF's first mission there are very few entries which do not deal with
public funds and his investments for Isaac Norris.
2. On previous hopes that BF would be able to get contributions in England
for the Pa. Hospital and on efforts to raise additional funds in the province,
see above, VIII, 82 n.

From Thomas Taunton

ALS: American Philosophical Society

Few documents could be more exasperating to editors trying conscientiously to do their duty by future readers. Nothing has been found to identify the writer beyond what he himself says here or in the three other letters printed below, pp. 267–9. This letter gives a month and day of writing but no year and the other three bear no dates at all. The sheet on which this is written is badly torn, as is one other, and in most instances imagination fails when one attempts to supply missing words befitting the writer's inimitable style. Three of these missives carry on their address pages, seemingly as contemporary endorsements, surnames of unknown persons in unidentified handwriting. Perhaps these are the names of friends of Taunton who carried the letters to the post-office. Lastly, Franklin's surviving account books record no payments made to or on behalf of Thomas Taunton during either of his English missions.

Under these regrettable circumstances the editors have decided to print all these letters from Taunton close together, purely for convenience, though they may not in fact all belong to the same year. We have chosen 1760 as probably the earliest year in which any of them may have been written. Admittedly, we can show no adequate basis for this assignment beyond the fact that, apparently in equally deplorable uncertainty, I. Minis Hays suggested this year for most of these letters in his *Calendar of the Papers of Benjamin Franklin*, I, 21.

Honored Sir   Decem: 29 [1760?–1775]

The favour of yourn I received on Christmas day with my Penshon, for which I Return you many thanks for it, and I pray god make you amens, for it, I wish [my] hard would gieve my tong the Liberty to Express [my-]self in a moer agreabell maner for so great [*one or two words missing*] it would be moear agreabell to me, but [I am in ill?] stat of helth. and pain and thinging of my m [*missing*] Burdonsom to my frinds, Renders me [*missing*] of Expressing my self to such [*missing*] but parden me, But I [*missing*] HARTY prayer for you [*missing*] From your Dutifull hum[ble Servant]   THO: TAUNTON

Addressed: To / [*torn*] Franklin / at Mrs. Stevenson / in Craven Streat / in the Strand.

Endorsed: Bennet

To John Baskerville[3]

MS not found; reprinted from *The General Evening Post.* (*London*), Aug. 9–11, 1763; *The London Chronicle: or, Universal Evening Post*, Aug. 11–13, 1763; *The St. James's Chronicle; or, The British Evening-Post*, Aug. 13, 1763.

In the spring of 1758 Franklin had subscribed through Dr. Fothergill for six copies of Baskerville's new edition of Vergil and had ordered all six bound in vellum and another copy in calf.[4] He sent one as a gift to Harvard College and several to Philadelphia for Isaac Norris and other

---

3. John Baskerville (1706–1775), designer of type, printer, manufacturer, was born at Sion Hill, Wolverley, Worcestershire. An expert penman, he moved to Birmingham as a young man and earned his living there by teaching writing and bookkeeping and by cutting inscriptions on tombstones. About 1740 he turned to the business of making painted and japanned articles such as salvers, tea trays, waiters, and breadbaskets. He continued this enterprise throughout life but his love of fine lettering led him in about 1750 to the designing of a new printing type as a substitute for that made by William Caslon (above, V, 82 n), who held a virtual monopoly of the English production. During the next seven years Baskerville worked to produce his new type face, to improve his press, his paper, and his ink, to devise a new method of operation which would result in the finest possible over-all result, and to bring out his first book, an edition of Vergil (above, VIII, 53 n). It appeared in 1757. He published his editions of Milton's *Paradise Lost* and *Paradise Regain'd* the next year. His *magnum opus*, a folio edition of the Bible, appeared in 1763. During his career he also published handsome editions of the *Book of Common Prayer* and of the works of other classical and British writers. Baskerville's type face, thicker in the heavy strokes, finer in the light ones, and sharper at the angles than Caslon's, produced mixed responses. Most of the English printers, whose offices were well stocked with the conventional fonts, criticized it severely, but more objective persons, such as Franklin, found it both highly legible and thoroughly attractive. Over the years it won increasing acceptance and in time came to be one of the most popular of all British-designed type faces. Baskerville's printing methods produced brilliant results, but they were costly and he made small profits from the many works he published. Several times he considered selling out, but he never completely withdrew from the business. *DNB;* Ralph Straus and Robert K. Dent, *John Baskerville A Memoir* (Cambridge, 1907); Joseph H. Benton, *John Baskerville Type Founder and Printer 1706–1775* (Boston, 1914); William Bennett, *John Baskerville, The Birmingham Printer and His Press, Relations, and Friends* (2 vols., Birmingham, 1939); Talbot B. Reed, *A History of the Old English Letter Foundries,* new edit., revised and enlarged by A. F. Johnson (London, [1952]), pp. 267–88.

4. "Account of Expences," pp. 13, 33; *PMHB,* LV (1931), 109, 112.

friends there.[5] Apparently when he was in Birmingham during that summer looking up Deborah's relatives, he went to Baskerville's place of business and made several purchases, for his accounts show that on Nov. 2, 1758, he "Paid Baskerville's Bill" of £7 9s., of which £2 4s. were "for Teaboard and Waiters etc."[6]—japanned ware which for many years had been the principal source of the Englishman's income. This was probably the occasion of Franklin's first meeting with Baskerville; the senior partner of the Philadelphia printing firm would hardly have failed to take the opportunity of making the acquaintance of the man who had recently created such a sensation in the printing world and for whose initial work he had shown so much enthusiasm.

If Franklin passed through Birmingham on his journey to Scotland in August 1759, as seems probable, he may have called on Baskerville again. In any case, it is certain that he and William were in Birmingham in late September 1760, after their stop-over in Coventry and before their journey through Wales to Bristol and Bath.[7] By that time four editions of Baskerville's Milton had appeared and at least two of the *Book of Common Prayer,* and the printer had begun work on a collection of *Select Fables of Esop And other Fabulists* for the bookseller Robert Dodsley, and had prepared specimen pages for his great folio Bible to be printed at Cambridge for the University. Franklin could not have allowed himself to miss this chance to visit Baskerville while in Birmingham and to see and discuss the work in progress. The friendship of the two men continued through their lives.

When Baskerville was at last ready to issue his Cambridge Bible, August 1763, he placed identical advertisements in several London newspapers. The announcement read: "This Day was published, BASKERVILLE'S FOLIO BIBLE. The subscribers to him are desired to apply for their Volumes at his Printing-Office at Mr. Paterson's, in Essex-House in the Strand. Where may be had, His Long-Line and Column Octavo and Twelves Common-Prayer-Books; Milton's Poetical Works, in two Volumes, Octavo, Royal large Paper; Juvenal and Persius, in Quarto Royal; and a Pocket Horace, by John Livie, A.M. The above may be had also of the following Booksellers [here follow twenty-three names]." Then comes a heading: "Extract of a Letter from

5. See above, VIII, 53 n, 79, 80.
6. See above, VIII, 133–46; "Account of Expences," p. 36; *PMHB*, LV (1931), 115.
7. See above, p. 231 n. In a letter to Ebenezer Kinnersley, Feb. 20, 1762, BF mentioned "Being at Birmingham, in September 1760," and performing electrical experiments there with Matthew Boulton, engineer and scientist. *Exper. and Obser.* (1769 edit.), p. 400.

B. Franklin Esq; to J. Baskerville." and the text of the letter printed below. Franklin was back in Philadelphia when the advertisement appeared and it seems doubtful that he knew Baskerville would use his private letter in this way. Its printing stands, however, as an early example of the use of a personal letter as a testimonial in advertising, and whatever Franklin would have thought about it, we may be grateful to the Birmingham printer for preserving thus one of Franklin's most delightful hoaxes.

As Baskerville printed it, the letter is undated. When Temple Franklin reprinted it in 1817,[8] he added "1760" to the address line, and this year has been used by all later editors. Franklin mentions in the second sentence that the incident he describes took place "Soon after I returned," and Temple's assumption that these words refer to the Birmingham visit of 1760 seems reasonable. The present editors believe that Franklin must have written the letter near the end of 1760 or very soon thereafter; hence it is reprinted at this point.

Dear Sir,   Craven-Street, London. [1760?]
Let me give you a pleasant Instance of the Prejudice some have entertained against your Work. Soon after I returned, discoursing with a Gentleman concerning the Artists of Birmingham, he said you would be a Means of blinding all the Readers in the Nation, for the Strokes of your Letters being too thin and narrow, hurt the Eye, and he could never read a Line of them without Pain. I thought, said I, you were going to complain of the Gloss on the Paper, some object to:[9] No, no, says he, I have heard that mentioned, but it is not that; 'tis in the Form and Cut of the Letters themselves; they have not that natural and easy Proportion between the Height and Thickness of the Stroke, which makes the common Printing so much more comfortable to the Eye.[1] You see this Gentleman was a Connoisseur. In vain I endeavoured to support your *Character* against the Charge; he knew what he felt, he

8. WTF, *Memoirs*, II, 4.

9. One of the characteristics of Baskerville's books was the high gloss on the paper, especially in his later publications.

1. One of the most distinguished of twentieth-century authorities on typography, Daniel B. Updike, upholds the criticism that Baskerville's type does try the eye, and that the difficulty comes from the type, not the gloss on the paper or the dense black ink he used. *Printing Types Their History, Forms, and Use A Study in Survivals* (Cambridge, Mass., 1922), II, 115.

could see the Reason of it, and several other Gentlemen among his Friends had made the same Observation, &c. Yesterday he called to visit me, when, mischievously bent to try his Judgment, I stept into my Closet, tore off the Top of Mr. Caslon's Specimen, and produced it to him as yours brought with me from Birmingham, saying, I had been examining it since he spoke to me, and could not for my Life perceive the Disproportion he mentioned, desiring him to point it out to me. He readily undertook it, and went over the several Founts, shewing me every-where what he thought Instances of that Disproportion; and declared, that he could not then read the Specimen without feeling very strongly the Pain he had mentioned to me. I spared him that Time the Confusion of being told, that these were the Types he had been reading all his Life with so much Ease to his Eyes; the Types his adored Newton is printed with, on which he has pored not a little; nay, the very Types his own Book is printed with, for he is himself an Author; and yet never discovered this painful Disproportion in them, till he thought they were yours.

I am, &c.

To [Ann Penn?] ALS: University of Chicago Library

If the proposed identification of the addressee is correct, this letter is the first of several among Franklin's papers relating to a complicated situation in the Penn family.[2] William Penn 3d (1703–1747) had become by 1731 the sole surviving grandson of the founder of Pennsylvania in the senior line, that is, through William Penn's first marriage, to Gulielma Maria Springett (1644–1694). In accordance with the founder's rather loosely drawn will, William 3d in time inherited certain specific lands in Pennsylvania and Ireland, but all other lands and the proprietorship of the province passed, after extended litigation and negotiation, to the founder's three sons by his second marriage to Hannah Callowhill

2. The relationship of the persons concerned and the details of the dispute are set forth in various passages of Howard M. Jenkins, "The Family of William Penn," an extended account printed in eleven installments in *PMHB*, xx–xxii (1896–98); see especially, xxi, 151–3, 324–6; xxii, 171–87. See also *ibid.*, xxxix (1915), 240–1, 247–8; William R. Shepherd, *History of Proprietary Government in Pennsylvania* (N.Y., 1896), pp. 198–204; and BF's correspondence with Edward Penington and Ann Penn later in this volume and those that will follow.

(1664–1726): John (1700–1746), Thomas (1702–1775), and Richard (1706–1771).

William 3d was twice married; his first wife, who died in childbirth, bore him one daughter Christiana Gulielma (1733–1803), who married Peter Gaskell in 1761; his second wife Ann Vaux (d.1767) bore him one son Springett (1739–1766). Within a few years William 3d and his wife Ann became estranged; he sued for divorce but either withdrew his charge against her or failed to prove it in court. Under the terms of his will his half-uncle Thomas Penn became guardian of Christiana and Springett upon their father's death in 1747 and until the boy should attain his majority, when Springett was to become executor of the estate. Thomas arranged for Springett's schooling, then, according to Franklin (below, p. 316), first proposed to send him off to the East Indies, then to Russia, and finally articled him to a lawyer in Sussex. This arrangement did not work out well and Springett rejoined his mother, Mrs. Ann Penn.

Thomas seems to have delayed turning the estate over to Springett when the young man attained his majority, March 1, 1760, for on April 25 of that year Springett wrote his uncle demanding all his "papers without exception, that there may be no more troubles, delays, or mistakes whatsoever."[3] Thomas, whose own son had died the day before, as Springett knew, replied with indignation at such "ingratitude," and the matter was finally turned over to the lawyers of both parties for adjustment. Later Thomas offered to buy Springett's lands in Pennsylvania, and both Franklin and Edward Penington, a Philadelphia relative of the youth, thought that Thomas Penn was less than fair and honorable in his proposals.

How Franklin became involved in the affair is not known; probably Springett and his mother appealed to him for advice and help, turning over to him their papers for examination. Franklin, for his part, was certainly far from averse to assisting any relative to expose possible chicanery on Thomas Penn's part. Writing to Richard Jackson, March 31, 1764, Franklin suggested that Springett might be able to prove his right to the proprietorship and, if so, would be willing to surrender it to the Crown for a reasonable sum.[4] Surviving correspondence shows that Franklin took a continuing interest in the dispute until Springett died unmarried in 1766 and his mother, now married to one Alexander Durdin of Dublin, died the next year.[5]

3. *PMHB*, XXII (1898), 181.
4. Carl Van Doren, ed., *Letters and Papers of Benjamin Franklin and Richard Jackson 1753–1785* (Phila., 1947), p. 154.
5. Upon Springett's death his rights passed to his mother, the former Ann

Thursday Evening [1760?][6]

Dear Madam.

I return the Box of Papers, and believe you will find none of them missing. I am glad to learn by the Bearer that you are well; and hope your intended Journey into the Country will contribute to keep you so, and prove otherwise agreable. I am, with the utmost Esteem and Respect, Dear Madam, Your most obedient humble Servant   B FRANKLIN

To Mary Stevenson   ALS: American Philosophical Society

Among the surviving letters between Franklin and Mary Stevenson are two from him and two from her bearing incomplete dates or none at all, which cannot be even approximately placed by other evidence, although they seem to belong to the general period from May 1, 1760, when Franklin and Polly agreed to correspond on subjects of moral and natural philosophy, to August 1762, when he sailed back to Philadelphia. In accordance with editorial practice in this edition they are printed together at this point.

Dear Polly   Friday morning. [1760–1762]
    You have obliged me very much by so readily fulfilling your Promise, and by adding the very pretty Letter to Mrs. Franklin.[7]
    I have just received one from her, and another from Sally, who both desire to be affectionately remembered to you.
    Your good Mother is about House as usual, but complaining a little. She seems however to be rather better to day than for some days past.
    I was out of Town till yesterday Afternoon, and till then had not your Letter, or should sooner have answered it.
    My Respects to Mrs. Tickel.[8] I am, my Dear Friend, with great Truth, Yours affectionately   B FRANKLIN

Penn, and through her to Durdin. Subsequently Springett's half-sister, Christiana Gulielma Gaskell, and Durdin became involved in extended litigation over her claims, which was not concluded until 1800. *PMHB*, XXII (1898), 184–5.

6. So dated on the assumption that the papers referred to in this letter were those that Springett finally secured from Thomas Penn during this year.

7. No letter from Mary Stevenson to DF is known to have survived.

8. The aunt with whom she lived at Wanstead.

To Mary Stevenson

ALS: American Philosophical Society

Friday 2. PM [1760–1762]

Here is a Coach from your House, and no Line to me from you. I will never forgive you, if you do not immediately write me a long Letter in the room of that you stole from me yesterday. You know the Penalty of the old Law was four fold.[9] See that you punish yourself fully, and thereby disarm the Resentment of Your injured Friend

B F

To ——

Draft (fragment): Library of Congress

This fragment in Franklin's hand is written on what appears to be the top segment of a page of letter paper; a caret in the margin of the first line seems to indicate that it was intended, according to his usual method, as an insertion in the body of what he had drafted on the opposite page. Neither the addressee nor the date is known. The wording suggests that Franklin may have been writing from England to some friend in the Pennsylvania Assembly, possibly Norris or Galloway. What petition he is referring to is not certain; on the other hand, "the difficult Business of a general Valuation" may relate to a proposal which occupied some of the Assembly's attention between March and September 1760 "for ascertaining the proportional Sum to be yearly paid by the several Counties" towards sinking the outstanding bills of credit. 8 *Pa. Arch.*, VI, 5114, 5118, 5119, 5133–4, 5141. On the basis of this slender clue the paper is printed here at the end of 1760 in the hope that it may be useful to some future student of Pennsylvania history.

[1760?]

that you had mention'd to me the Probability that the House would have remonstrated on all their other Grievances; had not their Time been taken up with[1] the difficult Business of a general Valuation; and since the Complaint of this Petition was likely alone to give Offence, it might perhaps [be] judg'd adviseable to give the Offence of all our Complaints at once, rather than in Parts and after a Reprimand received; I say, upon the whole I thought it best *[remainder missing]*

9. "If a man shall steal an ox, or a sheep, and kill it, or sell it; he shall restore five oxen for an ox, and four sheep for a sheep." Exod. 22:1.

1. Here BF first wrote "preparing for a Tax Bill by," then struck out these words and substituted "the difficult Business of."

From Mary Stevenson

Draft: American Philosophical Society

Dear Sir   [1760–1762]

You find I endeavoured to maintain an opinion which I imperfectly understood but I hope I shall be pardon'd when it is consider'd that the desire of obtaining intelligence and conviction was my motive. I believe I told you before that nothing had fallen under my observation to justify the opinion that men are carried to excellence in the exertion of their faculties in one direction rather than another, and I must now acknowledge that you have driven me out of every conjecture I had formed to support it.

I hope I said nothing to deny the Equivoque of referring the expression of strength and agility to Mind when I understood that strength denotes ability; yet give me leave to observe that those who suppose men are carried to excellence by this inherent occult cause do not suppose that genius is incompatible with weakness of mind.

Pardon me, dear Sir, for saying you would allow a distinction which you have prov'd to be erroneous. I could not have suppos'd that works of Fancy and of Judgment require such similar operations of the mind as by a discreminate view you have shewn they do.

I knew you never contended for the sameness of intellectual power as any other than a natural endowment, for I remember you said he who exerts all his strength in one direction will move farther in that direction than if he had exerted it in several but then he will be less able to move in any other.

I am entirely of your opinion that those who have multiplied the duties of Christianity have been its most effective Enemies, and allow me to say that I thought Ditton wrongs his cause in saying Christianity requires more than the strict discharge of moral obligation.[2] It indeed enhances and gives us motives for the per-

2. Humphrey Ditton (mathematician, clergyman), *A Discourse Concerning the Resurrection of Jesus Christ* (London, 1714), pp. 399–414. In this passage Ditton argues at length against the Deists in support of the duty and necessity for a Christian to believe in the resurrection of the body with its prospect of future rewards in Heaven. Such a belief is essential according to Ditton, as "the most effectual Encouragement to the Exercise of all Grace and Vertue, and the Discharge of every Duty on us, in our Christian Course."

formance of moral obligation, but I know no more that it requires of us; and I believe the Gospel precepts are equally calculated to make us happy Here as Hereafter. The Yoke of Christianity is easy and it's Burthen light; but there are those who will submit to no yoke and bear no burthen.

I am pleased to find that you lov'd me even when you thought me abominably idle, such indulgence will make me industrious to shew my Gratitude, [*two lines struck out*] prove myself Dear Sir Your faithful and affectionate Servant   M STEVENSON.

From Mary Stevenson

Draft (incomplete): American Philosophical Society

Dear Sir   [1760–1762]
Your last Letter[3] gave me great pleasure though the thoughts of having laid you under a necessity of writing it fill me with Confusion, for it was so unreasonable to draw you in to write a third Letter after you had condescendingly written two, that you ought to have punish'd me for it; but you have us'd the most effectual method to make me sensible of my fault by obliging me more than I wish to be oblig'd. While we think the Pleasure of the Benefactor in bestowing is equal to ours in receiving, our pride is not hurt by obligations, but when we begin to fear he acts by constraint we wish not to be oblig'd. These sentiments arise from reading the first sentence in your Letter, what the second excites I am unable to express, and I can answer it only by telling you I will endeavour to deserve your compliments. I am afraid the generality of people will be apt to think my giving up my opinion to Dr. Hawkesworth[4]

3. No letter from BF has been found to which this one seems in general to be a response, although the last sentence of the first paragraph recalls BF's undated letter, above, VIII, 455–7, in which he thinks she had the best of a dispute even if she did give up the argument "in Compliance to the Company."
4. John Hawkesworth (1715?-1773), LL.D., essayist, editor, and playwright, lived at this time at Bromley, Kent, where he was in charge of his wife's school for young ladies. With Samuel Johnson and others he produced and wrote essays for *The Adventurer*, 1752–54. He was a contributor to *Gent. Mag.*, and in 1765 became its reviewer of new books. In 1754–55 he edited and published a twelve-volume edition of the works of Jonathan Swift and added other volumes during the next eleven years. In 1773 he published a

is rather the effect of vanity than humility, for they will imagine I am not able to defend my argument, therefore chuse to come off with the appearance of having sense enough to be convinc'd.

You start a supposition that our Saviours fasting and temptation in the Wilderness was visionary, a supposition my mind is very ready to receive, for I have been always at a loss what to think of those transactions. The power of God I should not question, but there the power is Satan's, who performs miracles upon the Son of God. Jesus consider'd as an omnipresent God had no need of being carried up into on high to see all the kingdoms of the earth, and as man he could not see really them from the summit of the highest mountain, therefore I think the fact appears to be visionary. Besides the shewing him all the Kingdoms of the earth and the glory of them must be visionary, for it is not possible to be real. St. Luke says Jesus, being full of the Holy Ghost, returned from Jordan, and was led by the Spirit into the wilderness.[5] I know the general acceptation of this expression is that he was guided by the Holy Ghost; but will it not bear interpretation of his being carried thither in a vision? Those who have read the Gospel in the original Language can determine that better than I can. I remember one day while I was at Bromley Mrs. Hawkeworth and I enter'd upon the subject of our Saviour's temptation in the wilderness, but something prevented our discussing at that time, and we never resum'd it. Our dear little Friend you know is cautious of enquiring into subjects she holds sacred; we know and admire the piety of her sentiments, but I cannot help wishing she had not imbib'd some superstitions, that are prejudicial to that Religion she so warmly professes, and the duties of which she so devoutly practices. I have [*remainder missing*].

---

three-volume collection of accounts of voyages to the South Seas, which was seriously criticized. In the same year he was appointed a director of the East India Co., but took little part in its affairs during the last months of his life. *DNB*. There are many references to Dr. and Mrs. Hawkesworth in Polly Stevenson's letters to BF; she appears to have been on intimate terms with them and visited them frequently at Bromley.

5. Luke 4:1.

From Thomas Taunton[6]   ALS: American Philosophical Society

[1760?–1775]

I [hope you] will not be angrey at my writing b [*missing*] me, I know you ar Intament with mr. St[rahan] [*missing*] god will kepe me in my troubell but k [*missing*] e to help myself the least thing Cant dres now [*missing*] [*with*]out help, If mr. troauen will be so Cind as to [*missing*] for to Ogment my salery I am told it is great [ly?] in his pour, and have know frind in all the world but you, the Compeny gieves me Fiftean shillings a Qarter my por daughter is now indent to pay for my soport and when I Recd: my moity my frinds gieve me I have but a Leven shillings to soport me till the next Quarter Com round, but what the Compney gieves me and then must put my trust in god, had I amongest all my aqaintains, that would but gieve me but won shilling a weak it would be an Estates to me, but amongst all never Lit of so much humanity as In you and mr. strawon. Litell did I think wons I should lit with such a frind or I Even should want, God Reward you and mr. Strawon. I hop he will Repay it, I should be glad whe[n] you ar in your Charot, would strain a pint to see me, my duty to mr. strawn god bless you doe let me see you wons moer it Cant be long from your dutifull servant   THO: TAUNTON

I Log at mr. Turners At no. 5 In the Vinard walk near the smallpox Ospatell[7] Clarkenwell

Addressed: For / Doctr. Franklen / at Mrs. Stevenson's / in Craven Streat / In the Stran

Endorsed: Watson

From Thomas Taunton   ALS: American Philosophical Society

Honred Sir   [1760?–1775]
I hop you will pardin my fredom in writin to you, should be glad to have waited on you but never shall see you moer so bad with the stoan not abell to goe to the hall for my penshon but the

6. On this and the two following letters by Taunton, see above, p. 256.
7. For the London Smallpox and Inoculation Hospital, located in Cold Bath Fields, on the west side of Clerkenwell, see above, VIII, 285 n.

treasourer is so Cind as to send it god reward him for it, I had a long winter never been out tell march with my breth nor abell to go to bed know mor then a child, and sins I have been abell to goe a litell way to Church which is a miell it is a ouer and halfs work for me, and coming hom I have a frind gieves me a diner Every sunday if abell to goe for it, I had a sudon shake going a long which I believe lowsen the Stoan it was on a Thursday it set me abliding thrwo the penis tell monday the Shurgon never had such a troubell in his lief to stop befour to my great pain and troubell he did it greatis Elis [else?] I mus been lost but weak still Louizing so much blod, it was stopt by won mr. Renells at Higgat, I Log still at mr. Houes neare the Cock at holay Ieslington⁸ I would have wroat to mr. Strwon but am a fraid I doe not drict [direct?] properly to him from your dutifull humbell Servant   T. TAUNTON

N.B. know frind to goe with a leter know or any thing Eles without mony the caes is oltred know, the Treasourer sent a man yesterday to hear how I was god I hop will reward him for his goodnes.

Addressed: For | Doctr. Franklin | at Mrs. Stevenson's | in Craven Streat | in the Strand

Endorsed: Jones

From Thomas Taunton   ALS: American Philosophical Society

most worthey Sir   [1760?–1775]
    I hop you will pardon the fredom I have takeen, I have been to the bishop's palies at lamboth to see for the old Cook that did Lieve with the late bishop,⁹ but to my mortifycasion am Desieved

8. Perhaps Taunton meant the hamlet of Holloway in what was then the almost rural parish of Islington, which extended north from Clerkenwell to Highgate and Hornsey.

9. Lambeth Palace is the London residence of the Archbishop of Canterbury. The "late bishop" may have been Thomas Herring (1693–1757), who became Archbishop of Canterbury in 1747 but did not live in Lambeth Palace after 1753; or his successor Matthew Hutton (1693–1758), who held the see less than a year and never lived at Lambeth at all. If the editors have badly misdated these Taunton letters, the reference might be to Thomas Secker (1693–1768), who succeeded Archbishop Hutton in 1758.

she is gon, I went to see If I Could have got my daughter to been under for som tiem to had som Experence in the Chiken bisnes it would have been of great servies to her and that would been of greter help to me for I have knothing but what Coem from her and my frinds and aqaintence tsill [still] bad with the gout, Stoan, and asma, and woer out being upords of 78 years old should be glad if you Could think of any pleas I was abell to doe, I lodg at mr. Slaters neare the hair at hogsdon,[1] I beg Leave to Conclud with my best Respects to you from your Dutyfull humbell Seruant

TH0: TAUNTON

Addressed: For | Mr. Franklen | Thease

From Mary Stevenson   Draft: American Philosophical Society

Dear Sir   Wanstead, Janr. 13th. 1761

It is long since I troubled you with a Letter, which I am afraid you will impute to Indolence rather than Modesty. The Subject you are so condescending to enter upon with me would afford frequent matter of inquiry for me and give you too much trouble did I not suppress my inclination.

The continual Engagements I am in prevent my spending as much time as I should chuse in the pursuit of Knowledge. I would not be thought to speak from an Affectation of Wisdom, or a Discontent at my Situation; but I cannot help wishing I might employ some of that time in reading, which is devoted to the Card Table.

When I have had opportunity for Study I have attended chiefly to the Discourse on the Nature and Properties of Air.[2] Nothing ever more excited my Wonder and Admiration than the Effects of this Invisible Body [*torn*][3] useful to us. I did not think I should [*torn*] comprehended the Evaporation of Water; [*torn*] observes, it

1. Hoxton, formerly sometimes spelled Hogsdon or Hogsden, is northeast of Clerkenwell and southeast of Islington.

2. Polly had been reading Pluche's *Spectacle de la Nature*, a set of which, in the eighth edition of Samuel Humphreys' edition, BF had started giving her in May 1760; see above, p. 102 n. In this edition the passage she quoted here is in the third volume, p. 169, but because that volume was not published until 1762, she must have been using an earlier edition of it.

3. There are several tears in the MS, including one at this point by which two or three words are lost from each of three lines.

appears at first View impossible and contrary to Reason, as Water is of much greater specifick Gravity than Air; but the means by which it is render'd lighter, are very fully explain'd. He[4] says, "The burning Matter which the Sun darts upon the Earth, as it finds easy Admittance through the Surface of all fluid Bodies, insinuates itself into the Folds and Interstices of the Air, which gives Fluidity to the Water, thereby rarefying the Air, and consequently those Globules of Water in which it is inclos'd. These fiery Particles being reflected back from the surface of the Earth and Water carry with them those little watery Bubbles into which they insinuate themselves, and together with them several Corpuscles of a different Nature that happen to be intermix'd with them. The Fire and rarefied Air occupy the Inside of the Bubbles while the Water and other gross Particles, which are repell'd on every side from the Centre go to form the Shell. These little Globules thus form'd, being lighter than so many equal Bulks of compress'd Air at the Bottom of the Atmosphere, must necessarily ascend into those Regions where the Air is of the same specifick Gravity with themselves." This is a very clear Account; but take away the Fire, and the whole Hypothesis is destroy'd. How then does Water evaporate where there is no Fire? My Author is silent here, and there[for I refer?] to my indulgent Preceptor, whose Instructions [torn], and pleasing.

My Mind is not always idle when I have not a Book before me. The Book of Nature is ever open, and I frequently observe Things that excite my Curiosity, and employ my Thoughts to discover their Causes. I have often remark'd as I sat at the Tea Table, that when a Cup has been turn'd down, and there has been some Tea in the Saucer, the Cup would be lifted up, and Bubbles would rise in the Tea. I think I can discover the Cause of this to be the Heat rarefying the Air within the Cup, which endeavouring to expand itself lifts up the Cup, and forces its way out at the Bottom where the Tea rises in Bubbles. To confirm the Truth of this Suggestion I try'd the Experiment with cold Water, and then the Effect ceas'd.

How happy am I in a Friend who has Judgment to correct my Errors, and Candour to excuse them. To [him] therefore I dare deliver my Thoughts without reserve, and confess I am ambitious

4. Pluche.

he should approve them, tho ready at all times to submit to his Reproofs. As you love me Sir endeavour to make me worthy of that Love; and believe me I am ever Dear Sir Your most grateful and devot[ed *remainder and signature missing*].

Endorsed:[5] Copies of my mothers letters to Dr Franklin

From William Heberden[6]   AL: Historical Society of Pennsylvania

Jan. 17. 1761.
Dr. Heberden sends his Compliments to Dr. and Mr. Franklin and hopes they are well, and that it was no accident of a bad nature,[7] which hinder'd him from having the pleasure of their company at dinner yesterday.

Addressed: To | Dr. Franklin

Endorsed: Given me by Mr. Sparks in Oct [?] 37. R. G.[8]

From Francis Eyre[9]   AL: Library Company of Philadelphia

Tuesday 20th Jan 1761
Surry Street, Strand
Mr. Eyre's Compliments to Mr. Franklin, and Mr. Moore's Act[1] was this Day referred by the Committee of the Privy Council to the Lords of Trade.

5. Probably by Mary Stevenson's daughter, Elizabeth Hewson Caldwell, to whom she bequeathed this group of letters.

6. For Dr. William Heberden, physician, see above, VIII, 281 n.

7. The nature of the "accident" is not known.

8. "Mr. Sparks" was presumably Jared Sparks (1789–1866), one of BF's early editors and later president of Harvard. "R.G.," as the signature initials appear to be, may have been Robert Gilmer, a nineteenth-century Baltimore autograph collector.

9. For Francis Eyre, BF's attorney since the beginning of 1760, see above, p. 22 n.

1. On Sept. 27, 1757, Gov. William Denny signed a bill empowering Samuel Preston Moore (above, IV, 295 n), his wife Hannah Hill Moore, and his father-in-law Dr. Richard Hill (1698–1762) "to comply with, establish, ratify and confirm" land sales which Moore and his brother-in-law, Richard Hill, Jr. (1722–1754), had previously made. Hill, Jr., sometimes acting singly

Mr. Bunce[2] brot it in only the 15th. as he had promised Mr. Eyre sometime before.

Addressed: To / Benj. / Franklyn Esq

From the Earl of Morton[3]   AL: American Philosophical Society

Brook Street friday 23d Janry [1761?][4]
Lord Morton's Compliments to Dr: Franklin, and desires the favor of his Company to Dinner on Sunday next, between 3 and 4 o'Clock.

---

and sometimes in conjunction with Moore, had sold land in and around Philadelphia on the condition that a purchaser would receive a "good and sufficient title" only after agreeing to pay a yearly ground-rent in perpetuity and erecting a certain number of buildings within a specified time. Young Hill died in 1754, devising his property to Moore, to his sister Hannah Moore, and to his father to act as trustees for his younger brothers and sisters, some of whom were living in Madeira, others of whom were quite young. Since these children were either physically or legally incapable of conveying land titles to purchasers who had fulfilled the terms of their contracts with Richard Hill, Jr., the Pa. Assembly, in its act of Sept. 27, 1757, empowered the trustees to grant titles in their stead. This act was presented to the King in Council on Jan. 15, 1761, and was referred to the Council's Committee for Plantation Affairs the next day. *Statutes at Large, Pa.,* V, 315–19, 647–8. For the Hill family, see John Jay Smith, ed., *Letters of Dr. Richard Hill and his Children* (Phila., 1854). Although this was a private act and should have contained a suspending clause, it did not; nevertheless it was confirmed, June 25, 1761. For further correspondence on this matter, see below, pp. 278, 279, 333, 340–1. The Market Street lot BF had bought from Samuel Preston Moore and his wife Hannah in 1752 (above, IV, 295–6) had at one time been involved in the tangled Hill-Moore real-estate transactions but does not appear to have been one of those with which this act was concerned.

2. Probably an employee of Thomas Penn's agent Henry Wilmot.

3. James Douglas, 14th Earl of Morton (1702–1768), F.R.S., 1733, physicist and writer on astronomy, was first president of the Edinburgh Society for Improving Arts and Sciences, 1739; lord clerk register of Scotland, 1760; and the successor to the Earl of Macclesfield as president of the Royal Society, 1764. *DNB.*

4. January 23 fell on Friday in both 1761 and 1767. Following editorial practice, this note is placed at the earlier date.

From David Hall Letterbook copy: American Philosophical Society

Sir, Philada. Feb. 9. 1761.

I received a few Lines from you, dated September 6. by the Boreas Captain McDougall, acknowledging Payment of the Bills drawn by Scott and McMichael on the Portis's.[5] The Letters inclosed were delivered.

The Brevier seems pretty perfect; only the Lower Case r's run short; therefore wish you would send about a Couple of Pounds of them by the first Ship.[6]

Inclosed I have now sent you the first Copy of a Bill of Exchange for £200 Sterling, drawn by Charles Ward Apthorp, and Company, of Boston, on Messieurs Trecothick, Apthorp, and Thomlinson, Merchants in London; the Receipt of which you will please advise me of, and give me Credit for, when paid;[7] Exchange Seventy; and should have sent you more before this Time, had I not flattered myself with the Hopes of seeing you before the Spring.

I forgot to own the Receipt of Mr. Strahan's Letter by Captain McDougall[8]; please to let him know it came safe to Hand; and desire him to acquaint Messieurs Johnson and Unwin I likewise received theirs by the same opportunity, but know nothing of the

5. BF's letter referred to here has not been found. The *Boreas,* Capt. Henry Allan McDougall, reached Deal, outward bound, Sept. 20, 1760 (*London Chron.,* Sept. 20–23, 1760); it was long delayed by adverse winds in the English Channel and by ice in Delaware Bay, and *Pa. Gaz.* reported its arrival at Philadelphia only on Feb. 19, 1761. Obviously its mail must have been brought up to the city from the Delaware Capes by land. For the Scott & McMichael bills, see above, p. 34 n.

6. On July 2, 1760, Hall acknowledged the receipt of a font of brevier type which BF had shipped him in the spring of 1760. There is no record of BF shipping him more type, although in a letter of Dec. 10, 1761 (below, p. 398), he told Hall that he had "some Time since bespoke the Brevier you last desired, and hope it will now soon be ready."

7. BF acknowledged the receipt of this bill in a letter to Hall of April 9, 1761. Charles Ward Apthorp (d.1797), the son of the opulent Boston merchant, Charles Apthorp (1698–1758), was agent for the London firm of John Thomlinson and Barlow Trecothick, money contractors for the British forces in America. The son was also a provision contractor for the army. Wendell D. Garrett, *Apthorp House 1760–1960* (Cambridge, 1960).

8. Neither this letter nor that of Johnson and Unwin has been found.

Condition of the Goods, as the Ship has been above a Month at the Capes, occasioned by the severe Winter we have had;[9] but as there is now a Prospect of the River's opening, hope to see the Ship in a few Days. I am, Sir, Yours, &c.   D. HALL

To Mr. Franklin

Sent by the Edward, Capt. Davis, Via New York[1]

To Joseph Morris[2]   Copy: Library Company of Philadelphia[3]

Dear Friend   London Feby: 20th. 1761

I received your's of Oct: 21 and Nov: 11 relating to the Library Affairs,[4] which I have endeavoured to comply with by engaging a very honest and diligent Book-seller[5] to provide and send the Books ordered by the Directors. Enclosed is the Invoice and Bill of Lading. I hope they will come safe to Hand and give Satisfaction. He has by my Direction added some late Books not in your List, but which I imagine the Company would like to have. My best Respects to the Directors my old Friends, whom I long once more to see. I have acquainted Mr. Collinson[6] with the Mistake

9. *Pa. Gaz.*, Jan. 8, 1761, reported that "Our Navigation has been stopt by the Ice since Thursday" (Jan. 1). Not until Feb. 12, did the paper report entry of a ship at the port of Philadelphia.

1. *N.-Y. Mercury*, Feb. 9, 1761, reported the clearance of the *Edward*, Capt. William Davis, *London Chron.*, March 28–31, 1761, reported that the *New Edward*, Captain Davis, from N. Y., had passed Gravesend for London on March 29.

2. Joseph Morris (1715–1785) was a member of the Board of Managers of the Pa. Hospital (above, v, 290), 1751–57, 1769–81, and a member of the first Board of Directors of the Philadelphia Contributionship (above, IV, 290). At this time he was treasurer of the Library Co. Robert C. Moon, *The Morris Family of Philadelphia* (Phila., 1898), I, 274–6.

3. In the minutes of the Board of Directors.

4. Neither of these letters has been found.

5. Thomas Becket of Tully's Head in the Strand, the publisher of BF's *The Interest of Great Britain Considered*. Laurence Sterne also found Becket "a man of probity." H. R. Plomer, G. H. Bushnell, E. R. McC. Dix, *A Dictionary of the Printers and Booksellers . . . in England Scotland and Ireland from 1726 to 1775* (Oxford, 1932), pp. 20–1.

6. Peter Collinson had been a purchasing agent for and benefactor of the Library Co. since its inception. See above, I, 248–9; III, 49.

of the £30. Bill and shall settle the Company's Account with him as you desire. I believe he has put some Books into the Box which he had bought for the Company before your letter to me came to hand.   B: FRANKLIN

To Mr. Jos: Morris

London 1761 Benjamin Franklin Esq. Dr. to Thos. Becket (for the Library Company Philadelphia) shipt on Board the Dragon Capt. Hammet[7]

Jany. 24th [?] Philada.

Linnaeus on Botany. by Lee 8vo.[8]	£- 5: -
Hill's British Herbal. Folio	1: 10: -
Magen's on Insurances. 2 Vol: Quarto	1: 8: -
Rowning's Nat: Philos: 2 Vol: 8vo	- 14. -
Sherlocks Sermons. 4 Vols. do	1: 0: -
Macquere's Chymistry. 2 Vol. do[9]	- 10: -
D'a Costa's Nat: Hist: of Fossils Vol: 1 4to.	- 13: -
Davilla's Hist: of France. 2 Vol. 4to	1: 15: -
Cantillon's Analysis of Trade &c.	- 5: -
Du Hammel's Husbandry 4to.	- 15: -

7. The *Dragon*, Capt. Francis Hammett, sailed from Portsmouth, March 31, 1760, and arrived in Philadelphia, May 24, 1761. *Pa. Gaz.*, May 28, 1761.

8. The first five works in this list may be identified as follows: James Lee, tr., *An Introduction to the Science of Botany . . . Extracted from the Works of Linnaeus* (London, 1760); Sir John Hill, *The British Herbal; An History of Plants and Trees Natives of Britain* (London, 1756); Nicholas Magens, *An Essay on Insurances* (2 vols., London, 1755); John Rowning, *A Compendious System of Natural Philosophy* (3d edit., reprinted, 2 vols., London, 1759); Thomas Sherlock, *Several Discourses Preached at the Temple Church* (4 vols., London, 1759). Here and in the following notes the editions sent at this time have sometimes been determined by reference to *The Charter, Laws, and Catalogue of Books, of the Library Company of Philadelphia* (Phila., 1764). In some instances of very long titles only the essential first parts are given here, and the remainder silently omitted.

9. The five works beginning with this one are: Pierre-Joseph Macquer, *Elements of the Theory and Practice of Chymistry. Translated* (2 vols., London, 1758); Emanuel Mendes da Costa, *A Natural History of Fossils*, I, pt. 1 (London, 1757); Enrico Caterino Davila, *The History of the Civil Wars of France . . . A New Translation . . .* by Ellis Farneworth (2 vols., London, 1758); Philip Cantillon, *The Analysis of Trade, Commerce, Coin, Bullion, Banks, and Foreign Exchanges* (London, 1759); Duhamel du Monceau, *A Practical Treatise of Husbandry* (London, 1759).

Memoirs of a Protestant condemn'd to the Gallies[1]	£-	6: -
Coopers Art of Distilling	-	4: -
Clarendon's PosthumousWorks 3 Vol:	-	18: -
Newton on Prophecy 3 Vols.	-	15: -
Dalrymple on Feudal Property	-	5: -
Harris's Justinian[2]	-	15: -
Crit: Enq: into Opinions ant[ient] Philosophers	-	4: 6
Abbe La Pluche's Evangelical Hist: 2 Vol.	-	10: -
The figure of the Earth demonstrated	-	5: -
Warner's Life of Sir Thos. Moore	-	5: -
Basnages Continuation of Josephus[3]	-	18: -
Edward's Cannons of Criticism	-	5: -
Chapman's Cyder Maker	-	2: -
Handmaid to the Arts 2 Vol.	-	12: -
Smallet's Hist: of England 4 Vol: 4to.	3:	10: -
Jewish Letters 5 Vols.[4]	-	15: -

1. The five works beginning with this one are: [Jean Marteilhé], *Memoirs of a Protestant Condemned to the Galleys of France for His Religion* (London, 1758); Ambrose Cooper, *The Complete Distiller* (London, 1757); Edward Hyde, Earl of Clarendon, *The Life of Edward Earl of Clarendon . . . Written by Himself. Printed from His Original Manuscripts* (3 vols., London, 1759); Thomas Newton, *Dissertations on the Prophecies* (3 vols., London, 1759); Sir John Dalrymple, *An Essay towards a General History of Feudal Property in Great Britain* (3d edit., London, 1758).

2. The five works beginning with this one are: George Harris, *D. Justiniani Institutionum Libri quatori . . . translated into English with Notes* (2d edit., London, 1761); John Towne, *A Critical Inquiry into the Opinions and Practice of the Ancient Philosophers* (2d edit., London, 1758); Noël Antoine Pluche, *The Truth of the Gospel Demonstrated* (2 vols., London, 1751); Pierre-Louis Moreau de Maupertuis, *The Figure of the Earth Determined* (London, 1738); Ferdinando Warner, *Memoirs of the Life of Sir Thomas More* (London, 1758).

3. The five works beginning with this one are: Jacques Basnage de Beauval, *The History of the Jews, from Jesus Christ to the Present Time . . . Being a Supplement and Continuation of the History of Josephus* (London, 1708); Thomas Edwards, *The Canons of Criticism and Glossary; the Trial of the Letter Y, and Sonnets* (London, 1758); Thomas Chapman, *The Cyder-Maker's Instructor* (Cirencester, [1757]); [Robert Dossie], *The Handmaid to the Arts* (2 vols., London, 1758); Tobias Smollett, *A Complete History of England* (4 vols., London, 1757-58).

4. The five works beginning with this one are: Jean-Baptiste de Boyer, Marquis d'Argens, *The Jewish Spy. Being a Philosophical, Historical and Critical Correspondence* (5 vols., London, 1744); *Memoirs of the Bashaw Count Bonneval* (London, 1750); George, 1st Baron Lyttelton, *Dialogues of the*

Memoirs of the Bashaw Count Bonneval	£- 6: –	
Lord Lyttleton's Dialogues	– 5: –	
Yorick's Sermons 2 Vol.	– 6: –	
Walker's Voyages	– 6: –	
Birche's Life of P. Henry[5]	– 6: –	
Mountagu on Republic's	– 5: –	
Webb on Painting	– 3: –	
Hooke's Negotiations	– 4: 6	
Ferguson's Lectures	– 7: 6	
Hurde's Dialogues[6]	– 5: –	
Fragments of antient Poetry	– 1: –	
Historical Law Tracts	– 6: –	
Principles of Equity	– 16: –	
Law of Coroners	– 10: 6	
Fabricius's Letters[7]	– 5: –	
Considerations on the German War	– 2: –	
Vindication of the Ministry	– 0: 6	
Revolutions in Bengal	– 2: –	
Box, Cordage, Custom House Entry's Bills of Lading &c.	– 15: –	
Freight and Primage	– 12: 6	
Insurance on £24 at 12 Guineas per Cent.	3: 0: 6	
	£28: 9: 6	

Dead (London, 1760); Laurence Sterne, *The Sermons of Mr. Yorick* (vols. I and II, London, 1760); *Voyages and Cruises of Commodore* [George] *Walker during the Last Spanish and French Wars* (2 vols., London, 1760).

5. The five works beginning with this one are: Thomas Birch, *The Life of Henry, Prince of Wales* (Dublin, 1760); Edward Wortley Montagu, Jr., *Reflections on the Rise and Fall of the Antient Republics* (London, 1759); Daniel Webb, *An Inquiry into the Beauties of Painting* (London, 1760); Nathaniel Hooke, *The Secret History of Colonel Hooke's Negociations in Scotland, in Favour of the Pretender, in 1707* (London, 1760); James Ferguson, *Lectures on Select Subjects in Mechanics, Hydrostatics, Pneumatics, and Optics* (London, 1760).

6. The five works beginning with this one are: Richard Hurd, *Moral and Political Dialogues* (London, 1759; 2d edit., 1760); James Macpherson, *Fragments of Ancient Poetry, Collected in the Highlands of Scotland* (Edinburgh, 1760); Henry Home, Lord Kames, *Historical Law-Tracts* (Edinburgh, 1761); Henry Home, Lord Kames, *Principles of Equity* (London, 1760); Edward Umphreville, *Lex coronatoria; or the Office and Duty of Coroners* (2 vols., London, 1761).

7. This and the remaining works listed are: Ernst Friedrich von Fabrice, *The Genuine Letters of Baron Fabricius . . . to Charles XII of Sweden* (London, 1761); [Israel Mauduit], *Considerations on the Present German War* (London,

277

To Samuel Preston Moore

ALS: Library Company of Philadelphia

Dear Sir   London, Feb. 21, 1761

I wrote to you per Capt. Calef, via New-York, that I had receiv'd yours[8] with a Copy of the Act that I had put it into the Hands of our Solicitor Mr. Eyre, and would do what I could to forward it.[9] But the Copy you sent me not being under Seal, we could not present it; and were oblig'd to wait Mr. Penn's Leisure, who had the regular Copy in his Hands. By the enclos'd Notes you will see what Progress has been made.[1] I shall defray all necessary Expences as you desire;[2] being with great Regard, Dear Sir, Your most obedient humble Servant   B Franklin

To S. P. Moore, Esqr

Endorsed: From Benjn. Franklin Esqr. Feb. 21. 1761

From David Hall

Letterbook copy: American Philosophical Society

Sir,   Philada. February 21. 1761.

This serves to confirm the above,[3] and to inclose the second Copy of the above mentioned Bill for Two Hundred Pounds Sterling, from Yours, &c.   D. Hall

To Mr. Franklin Sent by the General Wall Packet Boat Captain Lutwyche.[4]

1760); possibly [anonymous] *A Vindication of the Conduct of the Present War* (London, 1760); John Campbell, *Memoirs of the Revolution in Bengal, anno. Dom. 1757* (London, 1760).

8. Neither BF's nor Moore's letter mentioned here has been found.

9. For an explanation of the private act in favor of Moore and Richard Hill, see above, pp. 271–2 n.

1. Penn presented this act with others to the Privy Council, Jan. 15, 1761; they were referred to the Privy Council Committee the next day, and by the Committee to the Board of Trade on the 20th. The Board of Trade in turn referred them to its counsel, Sir Matthew Lamb, on February 5. *Statutes at Large, Pa.*, V, 646–8. BF's "Notes" have not been found.

2. Eyre's itemized and receipted bill of Aug. 10, 1761, indicates that the expences totaled £36 15s., which BF paid. Lib. Co. Phila. See also "Account of Expences," p. 61; *PMHB*, LV (1931), 131.

3. Hall's letter of Feb. 9, 1761; see above, pp. 273–4.

4. The *General Wall*, Capt. Walter Lutwidge, sailed from N.Y. on March 3. *N.-Y. Mercury*, March 9, 1761.

From Francis Eyre

ALS: Library Company of Philadelphia

Sir   Surry Street 24. Feb. 1761.

I wrote you an Account on the 20th. of January of Mr. Moore's Act being that Day referred to the Board of Trade.[5] Since which the Board of Trade have referred it with several other Pensilvania Acts to their Counsell Sir Mathew Lambe, And as this is a private Act he makes a seperate Report thereon, for which I have already payd him his Fee of five Guineas, And as he is satisfyed that the Proprietor dos not oppose it (for he brought it in himself with other Acts) he on *Wednesday last* promised me his Report thereon in a few Days, which I hope will be the Middle of next Week;[6] And if he finds no Difficulty in Point of Law, the Bill will afterwards pass easily; if he has any Difficulty, which he dos not seem to have, I must attend him in a more solemn Manner to remove it, but the lighter I make of it, the less Reason I have to suppose he will starte any such. I shall give it all the Dispatch I possibly can, when it comes from him, and I shall quicken him also, if he keeps it long. I am Sir Your most obedient humble Servant   FRAS. EYRE

Addressed: To / Benjn. Franklyn Esqr.

To Hugh Roberts

LS:[7] Historical Society of Pennsylvania

Dear Friend,   London, Feb. 26, 1761.

I think I have before acknowledg'd the Receipt of your Favour of the 15th. of the 5th. Month 1760.[8] (I use your own Notation because I cannot tell what Month it was, without Reckoning.)[9] I

---

5. See above, pp. 271–2, for Eyre's letter and an explanation of the act in favor of Moore and Richard Hill.

6. Lamb delayed his report to the Board of Trade until May 19, and then reported on this act and four others together. He raised no objections to any of them "in point of law," even though this one, as a private act, failed to contain a clause, required in such cases by royal instructions, suspending its effect until the King's approbation had been secured. *Statutes at Large, Pa.*, V, 648–9.

7. In WF's hand.

8. See above, pp. 113–16.

9. BF would never have teased a Quaker in this way except a very close friend.

thank you for it, however, once more; I receiv'd it by the hand of your Son,[1] and had the Pleasure withal of seeing him grown up a solid sensible young Man. You will have, I see, a great deal of Satisfaction in him, and I congratulate you cordially on that head.

I was glad to hear that the Hospital is still supported. I write to the Managers by this Ship.[2] In my Journeys thro' England and Scotland, I have visited several of the same kind, which I think are all in a good Way.[3] I send you by this Ship sundry of their Accounts and Rules, which were given me; possibly you may find a useful Hint or two in some of them. I believe we shall be able to make a small Collection here; but I cannot promise it will be very considerable.[4]

You tell me you sometimes visit the ancient Junto. I wish you would do it oftner. I know they all love and respect you, and regret your absenting yourself so much. People are apt to grow strange and not understand one another so well, when they meet but seldom. Since we have held that Club till we are grown grey together, let us hold it out to the End. For my own Part, I find I love Company, Chat, a Laugh, a Glass, and even a Song, as well as ever; and at the same Time relish better than I us'd to do, the grave Observations and wise Sentences of old Men's Conversation: So that I am sure the Junto will be still as agreeable to me as it ever has been: I therefore hope it will not be discontinu'd as long as we are able to crawl together.

I thank you for the frequent kind Visits you are so good as to make my little Family. I now hope in a little Time to have the Pleasure of seeing them, and thanking my Friends in Person.

1. George Roberts was in England to investigate the iron industry; see above, p. 116.

2. The letter to the managers of the Pa. Hospital has not been found. It was apparently in answer to theirs of Dec. 29, 1760; see above, p. 255.

3. BF probably visited the Edinburgh Infirmary during his Scottish trip in 1759 with Sir Alexander Dick, president of the College of Physicians of that city. He may also have visited the Infirmary at Worcester, with the physician of which, Dr. William Thomson (above, p. 243 n), he became friendly during a short stay in that city in September 1760.

4. On the eve of his departure for England in 1757 and again in December 1760, the managers of the Pa. Hospital had asked BF to help in soliciting contributions in London for the Hospital. The editors have found no evidence that BF succeeded in this endeavor.

With the sincerest Esteem and Regard, I am, Dear Friend, Yours affectionately   B FRANKLIN

Billy presents his Respects.

To Mr. H. Roberts.

Addressed: To / Mr Hugh Roberts / Philadelphia / Per the Dragon / Capt. Hammet

Endorsed: Letter from Benja. Franklin London 26 Febry 1761 recd per the Dragon Hammet

To Deborah Franklin   ALS: American Philosophical Society

My dear Child   London, March 3. 1761
  I have wrote to you and [to][5] my Friends per Capt. Hammet.[6] [My] Letters are in a little Box directed for you. There are also in the Box two Books to be delivered to Mr. Coleman.[7] Hearing that another Vessel is [to] sail about the Same time,[8] I write [this] by her, just to let you know [that we] are well, and have wrote fully as above. My Love to all. I am, Your affectionate Husband
                                           B FRANKLIN

Addressed: To / Mrs Franklin / Philadelphia / per / Capt. Lane

  5. A large blot on the MS has obliterated some words; they have been supplied conjecturally.
  6. No letter to DF by the *Dragon*, Capt. Francis Hammett, has been found.
  7. William Coleman, an original member of the Junto, a trustee of the College of Philadelphia, and a justice of the Supreme Court of Pa. See above, II, 406 n. One of the books BF sent him was almost certainly Lord Kames's *Principles of Equity* (Edinburgh, 1760). Writing to Kames, Oct. 21, 1761, BF said he had sent a copy to "a particular friend" who was on the Pa. Supreme Court and that BF had since received two letters from him commenting on it.
  8. The *Fanny,* Capt. R. Lane, left London March 3 and arrived at Philadelphia April 29, according to *Pa. Gaz.,* April 30, 1761. The vagaries of ocean crossings in this period are illustrated by the fact that the *Dragon,* Capt. Hammett, which sailed from London "about the same Time," left Portsmouth only on March 31, and did not reach Philadelphia until May 24, or 25 days behind the *Fanny. Pa. Gaz.,* May 28, 1761.

From Charles Hargrave[9] als: Historical Society of Pennsylvania

My Good frend Mr. Frankling   Greenich March 6th 1761

   I am very Sorry that I have been Guilty of So much Ill manners in not acquainting you of my receiving your present[1] which I give you many thanks for all favours I Should have done my Self the pleasur of Seing you to return you thanks, had I not been taken with a very bad fitt the gout in both my feett and hands that I have not been out off the Infermiry this Six weeks but have been fead by the Nurse for I Could not help my Self, But I thank God I have gott a little Use of my hands again and hope to gett out of the Infermiry Next Week then please God the first Oppertunity I will do my Self the Pleasure to Wait on you I hope so [sic] you will Excuse this Scrible pray Give my love to your Son and hope that he and yourself is both in good health. I received yours the 3d Instant[2] and am Sir your unfortunate humble Servat to Command   Charles Hargrave

From Ebenezer Kinnersley[3] als: The Royal Society[4]

Sir,   Philada. March 12. 1761.

   Having lately made the following Experiments, I very chearfully communicate them in Hopes of giving you some Degree of

9. The "Infermiry" at Greenwich from which Hargrave wrote this letter can be no other than the famous seamen's hospital there. The author must then have been a seafaring man. A Charles Hargrave, or Hargrove, is listed as master of a vessel built in Baltimore Co., Md., in 1750, and of others registered in Philadelphia, 1729–52. He is probably the captain who carried David Hall to Philadelphia in 1744 in the *Mercury* and the one whose ship, sailing from Md., took a letter from BF to Strahan in 1745. "Commission Book, 82," *Md. Hist. Mag.*, xxvi (1931), 346; *PMHB*, x (1886), 87; xxiii (1899), 264, 385, 512; xxv (1901), 278; and above, iii, 50.

1. No information about this gift has come to light.

2. Not found.

3. For Kinnersley, the most important of BF's electrical collaborators in Philadelphia, see above, ii, 259 n.

4. Printed in *Exper. and Obser.*, 1769 edit., pp. 284–97, as Letter xxxvii. On Dec. 9, 1761, BF sent a copy of the last part to France to Thomas-François Dalibard, the first man to carry out BF's proposed experiment proving the identity of lightning and electricity (above, iv, 302–10). Dalibard translated

Pleasure, and exciting you to further explore your favourite, but not quite exhausted, Subject ELECTRICITY.[5]

Exp. 1. I placed myself on an Electric Stand, and, being well electrised, threw my Hat to an unelectrised Person, at a considerable Distance, on another Stand, and found that the Hat carried some of the Electricity with it; for, upon going immediately to the Person who received it, and holding a flaxen Thread near him, I perceived he was electrised sufficiently to attract the Thread.

Exp. 2. I then suspended, by Silk, a broad Plate of Metal, and electrised some boiling Water under it, at about four Feet Distance, expecting that the Vapour, which ascended plentifully to the Plate, would, upon the Principle of the foregoing Experiment, carry up some of the Electricity with it; but was at length fully convinced, by several repeated Trials, that it left all its Share thereof behind. This I know not how to account for; but does it not seem to corroborate your Hypothesis, That the Vapours, of which the Clouds are formed, [leave][6] their Share of Electricity behind in the Common Stock, and ascend in a negative State?[7]

Exp. 3. I put boiling Water into a coated Florence Flask, and found that the Heat so enlarged the Pores of the Glass that it could not be charged. The Electricity passed thro' as readily, to all Appearance, as thro' Metal; The Charge of a three-pint Bottle went freely thro' without injuring the Flask in the least. When it

---

it and, after first proposing to publish it himself, gave it to Jacques Barbeu Dubourg (above, V, 254 n), who printed in his *Gazette d'Epidaure, ou Recueil de Nouvelles de Médecine*, III (1762), no. XI, 82–6. See below, p. 396. It was also printed in *Phil. Trans.*, LIII (1763), 84–97.

5. On Feb. 20, 1762, BF replied that electricity "still affords me pleasure, though of late I have not much attended to it." *Exper. and Obser.*, 1769 edit., p. 397. According to Thomas Penn, however, after the conclusion of the hearings on the Pa. laws in the summer of 1760, BF "spent most of his time in philosophical, and especially in electrical matters, having general company in a morning to see those experiments." Penn to James Hamilton, April 13, 1761, Hist. Soc. Pa.

6. Illegible in the MS; this and other words in brackets are supplied from *Exper. and Obser.*, 1769 edit.

7. Kinnersley seems to be referring to the thesis BF developed in a letter to Collinson, September 1753 (above, V, 68–79), but he may also have had in mind an experiment described in a letter to John Lining, March 18, 1755 (above, V, 524–5), although that letter had not yet been published when Kinnersley wrote.

became almost cold, I could charge it as usual. Would not this Experiment convince the Abbé Nolet of his egregious Mistake?[8] For, while the Electricity went fairly thro' the Glass, as he contends it always does, the Glass could not be charged at all.

Exp. 4. I took a slender Piece of Cedar, about eighteen Inches long, fixed a brass Cap in the Middle, thrust a Pin, horizontally and at Right Angles, thro' each End, (the points in contrary Directions) and hung it, nicely balanced like the Needle of a Compass, on a Pin, about six Inches long, fixed in the Center of an Electric Stand. Then, electrising the Stand, I had the Pleasure of seeing what I expected; the wooden Needle turn'd round, carrying the Pins with their Heads foremost. I then electrised the Stand negatively, expecting the Needle to turn the contrary Way, but was extremely disappointed, for it went still the same Way as before.

When the Stand was electrised positively, I suppose that, the Natural Quantity of Electricity in the Air being increased on one Side, by what issued from the Points, the Needle was attracted by the lesser Quantity on the other Side. When electrised negatively, I suppose that the Natural Quantity of Electricity in the Air was diminished near the Points; in Consequence whereof the Equilibrium being destroyed, the Needle was attracted by the greater Quantity on the opposite Side.

The Doctrine of Repulsion in electrised Bodies, I begin to be somewhat doubtful of. I think all the Phaenomina on which it is founded may be well enough accounted for without it. Will not Cork Balls electrised negatively, separate as far as when electrised positively? And may not their Separation, in both Cases, be accounted for upon the same Principle; namely, the mutual Attraction of the Natural Quantity in the Air, and that which is denser, or rarer in the Cork Ball? It being one of the established Laws of this Fluid, that Quantities of different Densities shall mutually attract each other, in order to restore the Equilibrium.

I can see no Reason to conclude that the Air has not its Share of the Common Stock of Electricity as well as Glass, and, perhaps, all other Electrics per se. For tho' the Air will admit Bodies to be electrised in it either positively or negatively, and will not

8. Apparently a reference to Nollet's contention that glass is permeable by electricity. See above, IV, 426.

readily carry off the Redundancy in the one Case, or supply the Deficiency in the other; Exp. 5. yet let a Person in the negative State, out of Doors in the Dark, when the Air is dry, hold, with his Arm extended, a long sharp Needle, pointing upwards, and he will soon be convinced that Electricity may be drawn out of the Air; not very plentifully, for, being a bad Conductor, it seems loath to part with it; but yet some will evidently be collected. The Air near the Person's Body, having less than its natural Quantity, will have none to spare; but, his Arm being extended as above, some will be collected from the remoter Air and will appear luminous as it converges to the Point of the Needle.

Let a Person electrised negatively present the Point of a Needle, horizontally, to a Cork Ball suspended by Silk, and the Ball will be attracted towards the Point, till it has parted with so much of its natural Quantity of Electricity as to be in the negative State, in the same Degree with the Person who holds the Needle; then it will recede from the Point; being, as I suppose, attracted the contrary Way by the Electricity, of greater Density in the Air behind it. But, as this Opinion seems to deviate from Electrical Orthodoxy, I should be glad to see these Phaenomina better accounted for by your superiour and more penetrating Genius.

Whether the Electricity in the Air, in clear dry Weather, be of the same Density at the Height of two or three hundred Yards, as near the Surface of the Earth, may be satisfactorily determined by your old Experi[ment] of the Kite. Exp. 6. The Twine should have, through-out, a very small Wire in it; and the Ends of the Wire, where the several Lengths are united, ought to be tied down with a waxed Thread to prevent their acting in the Manner of Points. I have tried the Experiment twice, when the Air was as dry as we ever have it, and so clear that not a Cloud could be seen; and found the Twine, each Time, in a small Degree electrised positively. The Kite had three metaline Points fixed to it; one on the Top, and one on each Side. That the Twine was electrised, appeared by the separating of two small Cork Balls suspended on the Twine by fine flaxen Threads, just above where the Silk was tied to it, and sheltered from the Wind. That the Twine was electrised positively, was proved by applying to it the Wire of a charged Bottle; which caused the Balls to separate further, without first coming nearer together. This Experiment shewed that the

Electricity in the Air, at those Times, was denser above than below. But that cannot be always the Case; for you know we have frequently found the Thunder Clouds in the negative State, attracting Electricity from the Earth. Which State it is probable they are always in when first formed, and till they have received a sufficient Supply. How they come afterwards, towards the latter End of the Gust, to be in the positive State, which is sometimes the Case, is a Subject for further Enquiry.

After the above Experiments with the wooden Needle, I formed a Cross of two Pieces of Wood, of equal Length, intersecting each other at Right Angles in the Middle; hung it, horizontally, on a central Pin, and set a Light Horse, with his Rider, upon each Extremity; whereupon, the whole being nicely balanced, and each Courser urged on by an electrised Point, instead of a Pair of Spurs, I was entertained with an Electrical Horse-race.

I have contrived an Electrical Air-thermometer, and made several Experiments with it that have afforded me much Satisfaction and Pleasure. It is extremely sensible of any Alteration in the State of the included Air, and fully determines that controverted Point, Whether there be any Heat in the Electric Fire. By the enclosed Draught, and the following Description, you will readily apprehend the Construction of it.

A B is a Glass Tube about eleven Inches long, and one Inch Diameter in the Bore. It has a brass Feril cemented on each End with a top and bottom Part, C and D to be screwed on, air-tight, and taken off at Pleasure. In the Center of the bottom Part D, is a male Screw, which goes into a brass Nut in the Mehogany Pedestal E. The Wires F and G are for the Electric Fire to pass thro' darting from one to the other. The Wire G extends thro' the Pedestal to H; and may be raised or lowered by Means of a Male Screw on it. The Wire F may be taken out, and the Hook I be screwed into the Place of it. K is a Glass Tube with a small Bore open at both Ends, cemented in the brass Tube L which screws into the top Part C. The lower End of the Tube K is immersed in Water, coloured with Cocheneal, at the Bottom of the Tube AB. (I used at first coloured Spirits of Wine; but, in one of the Experiments I made, it took Fire.) On the Top of the Tube K is cemented, for Ornament, a brass Feril, with a Head screwed on it which has a small Air-hole thro' its Side at a. The Wire b is a small round

PLATE VI.

Page. 389.

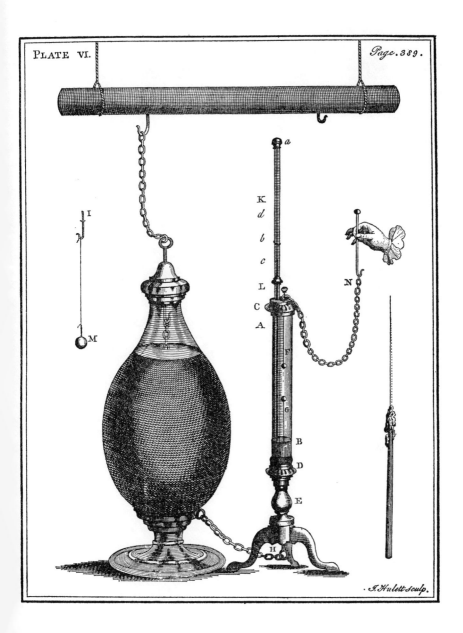

J. Hulett sculp.

Spring that embraces the Tube K so as to stay wherever it is placed. The Weight M is to keep strait whatever may be suspended in the Tube AB on the Hook I. Air must be blown thro' the Tube K into the Tube AB, till enough is intruded to raise, by its elastic Force, a Column of the coloured Water, in the Tube K, up to c, or thereabouts; and then, the Gage-wire b being slipt down to the Top of the Column, the Thermometer is ready for Use.

Exp. 7. I set the Thermometer on an Electric Stand, with the Chain N fixed to the Prime Conductor, and kept it well electrised a considerable Time but this produced no sensible Effect. Which shews that the Electric Fire, when in a State of Rest, has no more Heat than the Air and other Matter wherein it resides.

Exp. 8. When the Wires F and G are in Contact, a large Charge of Electricity sent thro' them, even that of my Case of five and thirty Bottles, containing above thirty square Feet of coated Glass, will produce no Rarifaction of the Air included in the Tube AB. Which shews that the Wires are not heated by the Fire's passing thro' them.

Exp. 9. When the Wires are about two Inches apart, the Charge of a three pint Bottle, darting from one to the other, rarifies the Air very evidently. Which shews, I think, that the Electric Fire must produce Heat in itself, as well as in the Air, by its rapid Action.

The Charge of one of my Glass Jars, which will contain about five Gallons and a Half, Wine Measure, darting from Wire to Wire, will, by the Disturbance it gives the Air in the Explosion, repelling it in all Directions, raise the Column in the Tube K up to d, or thereabouts; and the Charge of the above-mentioned Case of Bottles will raise it to the Top of the Tube. Upon the Air's coalesing, the Column, by its Gravity, instantly subsides till it is in Equilibrio with the rarified Air; it then gradually descends, as the Air cools, and settles where it stood before. By carefully observing at what Height above the Gage-wire b the descending Column first stops, the Degree of Rarifaction is discovered; which, in great Explosions, is very considerable.

Expt. 10. I hung in the Thermometer, upon the Hook I, successively, a Strip of wet Writing Paper, a wet flaxen and woolen Thread, a Blade of green Grass, a Filament of green Wood, a fine silver Thread, a very small brass Wire, and a Strip of gilt Paper; and found that the Charge of the Glass Jar, passing thro' each of these, especially the last, produced Heat enough to rarify the Air very perceptibly. The Charge of the Case of Bottles sent thro' the brass Wire consumed great Part of it into Smoke. The Thermometer appeared quite opaque with it.

Expt. 11. I then suspended, out of the Thermometer, a Piece of brass Wire, not quite so small as the former, about twenty four Inches long, with a Pound Weight at the lower End; and by sending the Charge of the Case of Bottles thro' it, discovered a new Method of Wire-drawing: The Wire was red hot, the whole Length, well anealed, and above an Inch longer than before. A second Charge melted it; it parted near the Middle, and measured, when the Ends were put together, four Inches longer than at first. This Experiment I remember you proposed to me, as worth trying, before you left Philadelphia; in Order to find whether the Electricity, in passing thro' the Wire, would so relax the Cohesion of its constituent Particles, as that the Weight might produce a Separation; but neither of us had the least Suspicion that any Heat would be produced.

Expt. 12. That I might have no Doubt of the Wire's being *hot* as well as red, I repeated the Experiment on another Piece of the same Wire, encompassed with a Goose-quill filled with loose Grains of Gun-powder; which took Fire as readily as if it had been touched with a red-hot Poker. Also Tinder, tied to another Piece of the Wire, kindled by it. I tried a Wire about twice as big but could produce no such Effects with that.

Hence it appears that the Electric Fire, tho' it has no sensible Heat when in a State of Rest, will, by its violent Motion and the Resistance it meets with, produce Heat in other Bodies, when passing thro' them, provided they be small enough. A large Quantity will pass thro' a large Wire without producing any sensible Heat; when the same Quantity passing thro' a very small one, being there confined to a narrower Passage; the Particles crowding closer together and meeting with greater Resistance, will make it red hot, and even melt it.

Hence Lightning does not melt Metal by a cold Fusion, as we formerly supposed. But when it passes thro' the Blade of a Sword, if the Quantity be not very great, it may heat the Point so as to melt it, while the broadest and thickest Part may not be sensibly warmer than before.

And when Trees or Houses are set on Fire by the dreadful Quantity which a Cloud, or the Earth, sometimes discharges, must not the Heat, by which the Wood is first kindled, be generated by the Lightning's violent Motion thro' the resisting combustible Matter?

If Lightning, by its rapid Motion, produces Heat in itself as well as in other Bodies, (and that it does, I think, is evident from some of the foregoing Experiments made with the Thermometer) then its sometimes singeing the Hair of Animals killed by it, may easily be accounted for. And the Reason of its not always doing so, may, perhaps, be this: The Quantity, tho' sufficient to kill a large Animal, may, sometimes, not be great enough or not have met with Resistance enough, to become by its Motion burning hot.

We find that Dwelling Houses, struck with Lightning, are seldom set on Fire by it; but when it passes thro' Barns with Hay or Straw in them, or Store-Houses containing large Quantities of Hemp, or such like Matter, they seldom, if ever, escape a Conflagration. Which may, perhaps, be owing to such Combustibles being apt to kindle with a less Degree of Heat than is necessary to kindle Wood.[9]

We had four Houses in this City, and a Vessel at one of the Wharfs, struck, and damaged, by Lightning last Summer. One of the Houses was struck twice in the same Storm. But I have the Pleasure to inform you, That your Method of preventing such terrible Disasters, has, by a Fact which had like to have escaped our Knowledge, given a very convincing Proof of its great Utility, and is now in higher Repute with us than ever.

Hearing, a few Days ago, that Mr. William West, Merchant in this City,[1] suspected that the Lightning, in one of the Thunder-

9. The Dalibard translation printed in *Gazette . . . de Médecine* begins with the next paragraph and continues through the next to last paragraph of the letter.

1. William West (1724–1782), Irish born, migrated to America about 1750 and engaged profitably in the Indian trade. He was one of those who gave evidence in 1754 on the distance from Pa. settlements to the Forks of the Ohio (above, V, 224). He represented Cumberland Co. in the Assembly, 1756–57. West was a founder, 1771, and president, 1774–76, of the Friendly Sons of St. Patrick. With a nephew of the same name he developed a substantial trade to St. Eustatius during the Revolution. *PMHB,* LXXXVI (1962), 131–8.

Storms last Summer, had passed thro' the iron Conductor which he had provided for the Security of his House; I waited on him to enquire what Ground he might have for such Suspicion. Mr. West informed me that his Family and Neighbours were all stunn'd with a very terrible Explosion, and that the Flash and Crack were seen and heard at the same Instant. Whence he concluded that the Lightning must have been very near; and, as no House in the Neighbourhood had suffered by it, that it must have passed thro' his Conductor. Mr. White, his Clerk, told me that he was sitting at the Time by a Window, about two Feet distant from the Conductor, leaning against the Brick Wall with which it was in Contact; and that he felt a smart Sensation, like an Electric Shock, in that Part of his Body which touched the Wall. Mr. West further informed me, that a Person of undoubted Veracity assured him, that, being in the Door of an opposite House on the other Side of Water-street, (which you know is but narrow) he saw the Lightning diffused over the Pavement, which was then very wet with Rain, to the Distance of two or three Yards from the Foot of the Conductor. And that another Person of very good Credit told him, that he, being a few Doors off, on the other Side of the Street, saw the Lightning above, darting in such Direction that it appeared to him to be directly over that Pointed Rod.

Upon receiving this Information, and being desirous of further Satisfaction, there being no Traces of the Lightning to be discovered in the Conductor, as far as we could examine it below, I proposed to Mr. West our going to the Top of the House to examine the Pointed Rod; assuring him that, if the Lightning had passed thro' it, the Point must have been melted; and, to our great Satisfaction, we found it so. This Iron Rod extended in Height about Nine Feet and a Half above a Stack of Chimnies to which it was fixed; (but, I suppose, three or four Feet would have been sufficient.) it was somewhat more than Half an Inch Diameter, in the thickest Part, and tapering to the upper End. The Conductor from the lower End of it to the Earth, consisted of square iron Nail-rods, not much above a Quarter of an Inch thick, connected together by interlinking Joints. It extended down the Cedar Roof to the Eaves, and from thence down the Wall of the House, four Story and a Half, to the Pavement in Water-street, being fastened to the Wall, in several Places, by small iron Hooks. The lower

End was fixed to a Ring in the Top of an iron Stake that was drove about four or five Feet into the Ground. The above-mentioned Iron Rod had a Hole in the Top of it, about two Inches deep, wherein was inserted a brass Wire, about two Lines thick, and, first put there, about ten Inches long, terminating in a very accute Point; but now its whole Length was no more than [seven] Inches and a Half, and the Top very blunt. Some of the Metal appears to be missing; the slenderest Part of the Wire being, as I suspect, consumed into Smoke. But some of it, where the Wire was a little thicker, being only melted by the Lightning sunk down, while in a fluid State, and formed a rough irregular Cap, lower on one Side than the other, round the upper End of what remained, and became intimately united therewith.

This was all the Damage that Mr. West sustained by a terrible Stroke of Lightning. A most convincing Proof of the great Utility of this Method of preventing its dreadful [effects]. Surely it will now be thought as expedient to provide Conductors for the Lightning as for the Rain.

Mr. West was so good as to make me a Present of the melted Wire; which I keep as a great Curiosity, and long for the Pleasure of shewing it to you. In the mean Time, [I beg] your Acceptance of the best Representation I can give of it, which you will find by the Side of the Thermometer, drawn in its full Dimensions as it now appears.[2] The dotted Lines above, are intended to shew the Form of the Wire before the Lightning melted it.

And now, Sir, I most heartily congratulate you on the Pleasure you must have in finding your great and well-grounded Expectations so far fulfilled. May this Method of Security from the destructive Violence of one of the most [awful] Powers of Nature, meet with such further Success, as to induce every good and grateful Heart to bless God for [the] important Discovery. May the Benefit thereof be diffused over the whole Globe. May it extend to the latest Posterity of Mankind; and make the Name of FRANKLIN like that of NEWTON, *immortal*. I am, Sir, with sincere Respect, your most obedient, and most humble Servant

EBENZR. KINNERSLEY

2. See the lower right corner of the illustration on p. 287. In printing Dalibard's translation, Dubourg placed a footnote here: "Nous n'avons point fait graver ici la figure, qui ne nous a pas paru assez importance."

To Dr. Benjamin Franklin F.R.S. In London.

Endorsed at the top: Read at R.S. Novr 18. 1762. March 24 1763. April 14 1763.

Endorsed on a separate page: XXII For Experiments in Electricity: in a Letter from Mr. Ebenezer Kinnersley to Benjamin Franklin LLD. R.S. Ph. Trans. Vol. 53. p. 84.

From William Heberden[3]   AL: Historical Society of Pennsylvania

[Before March 20, 1761?][4]

Dr. Heberden sends his compliments to Dr. Franklin and desires the favor of his company at dinner on friday the 20th of March at half an hour past three.

From David Hall   Letterbook copy: American Philosophical Society

Sir,   Philada. March 24. 1761.

I received a few Lines from you by Captain Bolitho,[5] owning the Receipt of mine,[6] with the Renewal of the £300 and Damages; and am glad to hear you think of being able to be here soon.

Inclosed I have sent you the third Copy of a Bill of Exchange for Two Hundred Pounds Sterling on Messieurs Trecothick, Apthorp, and Thomlinson, Merchants in London; the first and second Copies of which were sent you (Via New-York,) by the Edward, Captain Davis, and the General Wall Packet Boat, Captain Lutwyche.[7] I am, Sir, Yours, &c.   D. HALL.

To Mr. Franklin By the Indian Trader, Captain Robinson[8]

3. On Dr. Heberden, see above, VIII, 281 n.

4. March 20 fell on a Friday in both 1761 and 1767. According to editorial practice, this document is placed at the earlier of the two dates.

5. *Pa. Gaz.,* March 24, 1761, reported the entry of the *Myrtilla,* Capt. John Bolitho. The letter which she carried has not been found.

6. That of Aug. 26, 1760 (above, p. 187) containing a bill for £360, drawn by Scott and McMichael, Philadelphia merchants, to cover two earlier protested bills.

7. For these bills, see above, pp. 273, 278.

8. *Pa. Gaz.,* March 26, 1761, reported the clearance of the *Indian Trader,* Capt. Anthony Robinson.

From John Balfour and Company[9]

ALS: American Philosophical Society

Sir   Edin[burgh]: March 26th 1761

The occasion of my giving you this trouble is to inform you that in the later end of December or the beginning of January last, I receivd a bill from Mr. David Hall, of which you have an exact double on the other side. This bill when presented at London was refusd to be paid, upon which it was returnd regularly protested.[1] I did not chuse to send it back to Philadelphia, (as the expence will come very high) without first accquainting you, as I imagin'd you might probably take it up, for Mr. Halls honour. You will therefore be so good as [to] inform me in course, whether you incline to do this or not.[2] I thought it my duty in civility to Mr. Hall, to make this tryall before I sent away the bill. My Respectfull Compliments to your Son, and believe me to be with great Esteem Sir Your most Humble Servant

JOHN BALFOUR & CO.

PS The Books I sent to Mr. Hall has answerd his purpose very well, and he has wrote for another parcel. I have sent him out also a good Cargo of Bibles.

Addressed: To / Dr Frankline at his Lodgeings / in Craven Street in the Strand / London

Notations on address page in BF's hand: Black Swan Court [Bark-

---

9. John Balfour (d. 1795) was a bookseller and papermaker in Edinburgh, former apprentice of his brother-in-law Gavin Hamilton, with whom he published the *Edinburgh Chronicle,* 1759–60. BF probably met Balfour, a friend of William Strahan, during his Edinburgh visit of 1759. H. R. Plomer, G. H. Bushnell, E. R. Dix, *A Dictionary of the Printers and Booksellers . . . from 1726 to 1775* (Oxford, 1932), p. 281. Some years later difficulties arose between Balfour and BF over a shipment of books to James Parker of N.Y., instigated perhaps by BF, perhaps by Strahan, which Parker did not want. See also J. Bennett Nolan, *Benjamin Franklin in Scotland and Ireland* (Phila., 1938), pp. 47–9.

1. The bill in question was drawn by Scott & McMichael, Philadelphia merchants, on George and James Portis in London; see below, pp. 298, 302–3. In 1760 the Portises had refused for some time to pay two bills which Hall had bought from Scott & McMichael and sent to BF; see above, p. 34 n.

2. For BF's reply see below, p. 298.

ing?] Lane—behind the Change   Cateaton Street opposite the Church[3]

Endorsed: Balfour Edinbh. Mar 26. 1761

To Mary Stevenson   ALS: Yale University Library

My dear Friend   Cravenstreet, Monday March 30. 1761

As you have been so good as to forgive my long Delay of writing to you and answering your always agreable Letters,[4] I shall not now trouble you with the Apology I had written on that head in one of my Pieces of Letters never finish'd.

Supposing the Fact, that the Water of the Well at Bristol is warmer after some time pumping, I think your manner of accounting for that increas'd Warmth very ingenious and probable.[5] It did not occur to me, and therefore I doubted of the Fact.

You are, I think, quite right in your Opinion, that the Rising of the Tides in Rivers is not owing to the immediate Influence of the Moon on the Rivers.[6] It is rather a subsequent Effect of the Influence of the Moon on the Sea, and does not make its Appearance in some Rivers till the Moon has long pass'd by. I have not express'd myself clearly if you have understood me to mean otherwise. You know I have mention'd it as a Fact, that there are in some Rivers several Tides all existing at the same time; that is, two, three, or more, Highwaters, and as many Low-Waters, in different Parts of the same River, which cannot possibly be all Effects of the Moon's immediate Action on that River; but they may be subsequent Effects of her Action on the Sea.

In the enclos'd Paper you will find my Sentiments on several

---

3. The reason for these notations is not clear. Cateaton Street (more properly Catte), parallel to and north of Cheapside, was later renamed Gresham Street.

4. Apparently BF had not written Polly since November 1760; see above, pp. 247–52.

5. See above, pp. 217–18, for Polly's speculations about the causes of this phenomenon.

6. See above, pp. 195, 213–18, for an exchange of letters between BF and Polly about tides in rivers.

Points relating to the Air and the Evaporation of Water.[7] It is Mr. Collinson's Copy, who took it from one I sent thro' his Hands to a Correspondent in France some Years since; I have, as he desired me, corrected the Mistakes he made in transcribing, and must return it to him; but if you think it worth while, you may take a Copy of it: I would have sav'd you any trouble of that kind, but had not time.

Some day in the next or the following Week, I purpose to have the pleasure of seeing you at Wanstead;[8] I shall accompany your good Mama there, and stay till the next Morning, if it may be done without incommoding your Family too much. We may then discourse any Points in this Paper that do not seem clear to you; and taking a Walk to some of Lord Tilney's Ponds,[9] make a few Experiments there to explain the Nature of the Tides more fully. In the mean time, believe me to be, with the highest Esteem and Regard, my dear good Girl, your sincerely affectionate Friend

B FRANKLIN

My very respectful Compliments to good Mrs. Tickel, and to Mrs. Rooke and Miss Pit.[1] If the above propos'd Visit should not be convenient let me know by a Line when it may be more suitable.

Miss Stevenson

7. In a letter of Jan. 13, 1761, Polly appealed to her "indulgent Preceptor" to explain evaporation; see above, pp. 269–70. The paper BF now sent her cannot be certainly identified, but it may well have been his letter to John Perkins, Feb. 4, 1753, on waterspouts (above, IV, 429–42), or the paper entitled "Physical and Meteorological Observations, Conjectures and Suppositions" (1751?), read to the Royal Society Dec. 23, 1756 (above, IV, 235–43). The letter on waterspouts seems the more likely because Polly discussed it and Perkins' reply in her letter to BF of April 27, 1761, below, p. 308.

8. A village about ten miles from London where Polly spent much of her time attending to two elderly aunts, Mrs. Tickell and Mrs. Rooke.

9. John Tylney, Earl Tylney of Castlemaine (1712–1784), F.R.S., 1746. His grandfather, Sir Josiah Child (1630–1699), writer of a popular treatise on trade and governor of the East India Company, 1681–3, 1686–8, had purchased Wanstead Abbey in 1673 and had spent "prodigious" sums in planting "walnut-trees about his seate, and making fish-ponds, many miles in circuit." *DNB*; G. E. Cockayne, ed., *The Complete Peerage*, III (London, 1913), 92.

1. Miss Pitt was a friend of Polly's; she went to Jamaica in 1763.

To John Balfour

ALS (copy) and draft: American Philosophical Society

Sir, London, April 2. 1761

As Messrs. Portis did the last Summer pay me two Bills of the same Drawers after a Protest,[2] I sent my Son to know if they would do the same with regard to this Bill, in case it should be once more offer'd to them; but they persisted in their Refusal. Had it been a Bill of Mr. Hall's Drawing, I should immediately pay it as you propose, for his Honour. But as it is a Bill drawn by others, which he has paid his Money for in Philadelphia, I think it fittest that the Bill be return'd to him, with the Protest, that he may recover Damages of the Drawers.[3] My Son joins in Compliments, with Sir, Your most obedient Servant B FRANKLIN

Mr Balfour

Copy

To Josiah Quincy[4]

ALS: American Philosophical Society

Dear Sir, London, April 8. 1761

I received your very obliging Letter of Dec. 25.[5] by the hand of your valuable Son,[6] who had before favour'd me now and then

---

2. See above, pp. 177–8.

3. For BF's comments to Hall on this incident, see below, pp. 301–2.

4. Josiah Quincy had come to the Pa. Assembly in 1755 to solicit aid for a projected New England expedition against Crown Point. See above, VI, 3 n.

5. Not found.

6. Edmund Quincy (1733–1768), A.B., Harvard, 1752, merchant, and "zealous Whig" during the controversy with Great Britain, came to London in 1760 to ask the Society of Arts (above, VI, 187 n) to help in establishing a potash industry in Mass. It is not clear whether he meant to persuade the Society to offer premiums for production or merely to ascertain the amount and the conditions under which they were awarded. In discharging his mission he was assisted by Thomas Hollis and, we may presume, by BF himself. In 1766 he wrote Hollis that "the manufacture of potash is now so firmly established, it needs no farther assistance from the society . . . ." [Francis Blackburn], *Memoirs of Thomas Hollis, Esq. F.R.S. and A.S.S.* (2 vols., London, 1780), I, 120, 337–8; William S. Pattee, *A History of Old Braintree and Quincy* (Quincy, 1878), pp. 589–90.

with a kind Visit. I congratulate you on his Account as I am sure you must have a great deal of Satisfaction in him. His ingenuous, manly and generous Behaviour, in a Transaction here with the Society of Arts, gave me great Pleasure as it was much to his Reputation.

I am glad my weak Endeavours for our common Interest,[7] were acceptable to you and my American Friends. I shall be very happy indeed if any Good arises from them. The People in Power here do now seem convinc'd of the Truth of the Principles I have inculcated, and incline to act upon them; but how far they will be able to do so at a Peace, is still uncertain, especially as the War in Germany grows daily less favourable to us.[8]

My Kinsman Williams[9] was but ill inform'd in the Account he gave you of my Situation here. The Assembly voted me £1500 Sterling, when I left Philadelphia, to defray the Expence of my Voyage and Negociations in England, since which they have given nothing more, tho' I have been here near four Years. They will, I make no doubt, on winding up the Affair, do what is just; but they cannot afford to be extravagant as that Report would make them.[1]

I rejoice with you sincerely on the Happiness you enjoy in the Nuptial State, of which you speak so feelingly. I can easily con-

7. BF's Canada Pamphlet; see above, pp. 47–100.

8. In 1760 Frederick II's enemies captured Berlin, occupied Saxony, and took much of Silesia and East Prussia. On his part Frederick routed the Austrians and Imperialists at Torgau, Nov. 3, 1760, but this victory was so costly that he was compelled to spend much of 1761 on the defensive. Stimulated by the expense and indecisiveness of the conflict and by Israel Mauduit's famous pamphlet *Considerations on the present German War* (London, 1760), British public opinion began in 1761 to grow actively hostile to the King of Prussia's cause. Gipson, *British Empire*, VIII, 59–61.

9. Jonathan Williams, Sr. (above, I, lvii), Boston merchant and husband of BF's niece, Grace Harris Williams (C.5.3). What rumor Williams had heard about BF's affairs is not known.

1. On Feb. 19, 1763, some three months after BF's return, the Assembly voted him an annual salary of £500 sterling for his six years' service in England. Norris submitted accounts to the Assembly, Feb. 16, 1763, showing that BF had spent £714 10s. 7d. "in the immediate Service" of the province in England. Thus, of the £1500 which the House had remitted to him £785 9s. 5d. remained in his hands. The Assembly subtracted this sum from the £3000 voted him on Feb. 19, and on March 4, 1763, Norris signed a certificate, payable to BF, for the balance of £2214 10s. 7d. 8 *Pa. Arch.*, VI, 5402, 5405, 5414.

ceive all you express, when I recollect the amiable Person, sprightly, sensible and chearful Conversation, of the Lady that favour'd us with her Company on that agreable Tour.[2] Pray make my best Respects acceptable to her; and do me the Justice to believe that no one more sincerely wishes a Continuance of your Felicity, than, Dear Sir, Your most obedient and most humble Servant   B FRANKLIN

Josa. Quincy Esqr

Endorsed: Dr. Franklin

To John Winthrop[3]   ALS: American Philosophical Society

Sir,   London, April 8, 1761
   I did myself the Honour of writing you a few Lines the 20th of February last[4] inclosing a Piece of Dr. Pringle's on the Subject of Fiery Meteors which he sent you on hearing your ingenious Account of one lately appearing in New England read to the Royal Society.[5] This is chiefly to cover my Friend Mr. Kennicott's Papers relating to the Hebrew Bible, and to request, that if any ancient Manuscripts of that Book are in your College Library (of which indeed I have not much Expectation) you would be so good

2. Quincy married his second wife, Elizabeth Waldron, on Feb. 19, 1756. John Adams, who in 1759 was courting Hannah Quincy, Josiah's daughter by his first wife, observed that Quincy "fondly doats" on his "young" and "very fruitful" wife. Lyman H. Butterfield, et al., eds., *Diary and Autobiography of John Adams* (4 vols., Cambridge, Mass., 1961), I, 87, 102 n, 177 n. It is not clear to what "agreable Tour" BF is here referring.
   3. For John Winthrop, Hollis professor of mathematics and natural philosophy at Harvard, see above, IV, 261 n; V, 267; VI, 404 n.
   4. Not found.
   5. Winthrop's paper about a meteor which appeared in the vicinity of Taunton, Mass., May 10, 1759, "An Account of a Meteor seen in New England, and of a Whirlwind felt in that Country," was read at the Royal Society, Jan. 15, 1761, and published in *Phil. Trans.*, LII, Part I (1761), 6–16. Dr. John Pringle (above, VI, 178 n) could have sent him either his "Several Accounts of the fiery Meteor, which appeared on Sunday the 26th of November, 1758 . . .," read at the Royal Society, Feb. 8, 1759, or his "Some Remarks upon the several Accounts of the fiery Meteor . . . and upon other such Bodies," read on Dec. 20, 1759. These pieces were published in *Phil Trans.*, LI (1759), 218–59, 259–74.

as to send him an Account of them.[6] My respectful Compliments to Mr. President Holyoke,[7] and any enquiring Friends at Cambridge. With great Esteem, I am, Sir, Your most obedient humble Servant   B FRANKLIN

Addressed: To / Mr Winthrop / Professor of Philosophy / of Harvard College / Cambridge / per favour of / Mr Quincy[8]

Endorsed: Dr. Franklin 8 April 1761 Dr Franklin[9]

To David Hall   ALS: Boston Public Library

Dear Friend,   London, April 9. 1761
   I receiv'd yours of Feb. 9. with the Bill for £200 for which I thank you. I shall take care to send the Lower Case Brevier r's, that you write for and acquaint Mr. Strahan with what you mention.[1] The Loss of Faulkner and Lutwydge has baulkt Correspondence between Philadelphia and London a great deal.[2] I lately

6. Benjamin Kennicott (1718–1783), F.R.S., was a Biblical scholar whose consuming interest was the establishment of an accurate text of the Old Testament, finally published as *Vetus Testamentum Hebraicum cum Variis Lectionibus* (2 vols., Oxford, 1776–80). *DNB*. He was probably sending Winthrop a copy of his first annual report of progress (published December 1760); this and its nine successors were later conveniently collected as *The Ten Annual Accounts of the Collation of the Hebrew MSS* (Oxford, 1770). On Nov. 17, 1761, Winthrop wrote BF that Harvard had no ancient Hebrew MSS.
   7. On Edward Holyoke (1689–1769), who presented BF his Harvard A.M. diploma in 1753, see *Sibley's Harvard Graduates,* V, 265–78.
   8. Edmund Quincy; see the preceding document.
   9. On the blank spaces of this four-page sheet Winthrop wrote drafts of his reply to BF and of letters to Dr. Pringle and Gov. Jonathan Belcher, Jr., all dated Nov. 17, 1761.
   1. For Hall's letter of Feb. 9, 1761, in which the foregoing matters are mentioned, see above, pp. 273–4.
   2. The *Friendship,* Capt. Nathaniel Falconer, which cleared Philadelphia in the latter part of December 1760, was taken by a French privateer and carried into Bayonne. *Pa. Gaz.,* Dec. 25, 1760, April 30, 1761. The *General Wall* packet, Capt. Walter Lutwidge, which sailed from New York, March 3, 1761, was attacked on March 20 "150 Leagues to the Westward of the Lizard" by the *Biscayen* privateer, Capt. LaFargue. After a "stout Engagement of three Hours and an Half" during which Lutwidge was mortally wounded, the *General Wall* threw her mail overboard and struck her colors. After paying a ransom of £600, she was allowed to sail for Falmouth, arriving there on

receivd the enclos'd from Edinburgh, and sent the Answer you will find copy'd on the Back.[3] I cannot but blame Messrs. Scot and McMichael, for continuing to draw on such Correspondents, after what pass'd last Year,[4] and think they ought now to suffer a little. As the Goods you order'd from Mr. Balfour were or would be sent,[5] I judg'd your Affairs would not suffer by my not taking it up, for otherwise I should have done it. I hope you will not disapprove my Conduct in this Respect, being, dear Friend, Yours affectionately   B FRANKLIN

Addressed: To | Mr David Hall | Printer | Philadelphia | Via Boston Free B FRANKLIN

Endorsed: Mr. Franklin April 9. 1761.

In another hand: For Perusal.

To Henry Potts[6]   LS: Public Record Office, London[7]

Thomas Boone, governor of New Jersey,[8] wrote John Pownall, secretary of the Board of Trade, Jan. 12, 1761, complaining of the route by

---

March 25, 1761. *N.-Y. Mercury,* March 9, 1761; *Pa. Gaz.,* May 21, 1761; *London Chron.,* March 26–8, 28–31, 1761.

3. John Balfour's letter of March 26, 1761, and BF's reply of April 2, regarding a bill of exchange drawn by Scott & McMichael of Philadelphia on George and James Portis of London which Hall had bought and sent to Balfour and which had been protested. See above, pp. 295, 298.

4. On the Portises' refusal in 1760 to pay two bills of Scott & McMichael which Hall had bought and sent to BF, see above, p. 34 n.

5. In his letter of March 26 Balfour had told BF of receiving a further order for books from Hall and that he had already sent "a good Cargo of Bibles."

6. Potts was secretary of the Post Office, 1760–62, 1765–68; see above, p. 179 n.

7. The letter is in WF's hand. It is located in C.O. 5/978, fos. 49–60, where Potts's covering letter to Pownall, mentioned at the end of the headnote, immediately precedes it.

8. Thomas Boone (1731?–1812), governor of N.J., 1760–61, then of So. Car., 1761–66. In the latter colony, where he had inherited extensive estates, he provoked a long controversy with the Assembly by refusing to administer the oath of office to one of its newly elected members, Christopher Gadsden. Charged with subverting the Assembly's privilege of determining the validity of the election of its own members, he went to England in 1764 to defend

which the postriders traveled through New Jersey between Philadelphia and New York. On April 1, 1761, the Board of Trade ordered an extract of this letter sent to Henry Potts of the Post Office.[9] Boone apparently wrote in similar vein directly to Lord Bessborough, one of the joint postmasters general. Potts, in turn, sent these papers to Franklin for comment and received the reply printed here. On April 23, Potts sent Franklin's report to Pownall with a short covering letter.[1]

Sir   Craven Street. April 23d. 1761

In obedience to the Commands of His Majesty's Postmaster General, signified to me by you, I have considered Governor Boone's Letter to my Lord Bessborough and the Extract of his Letter to John Pownall, Esqr. Secretary to the Board of Trade, containing a Complaint of some Inconveniency to him arising from "the Posts not passing thro' Perth Amboy and Burlington[2] (the Route established by Act of Parliament[3]) in their way between Philadelphia and New York"; and alledging, that "thro' this Omission it has happen'd and may happen again that Dispatches received by him from the Plantation Office could not be answered by the first Pacquet, whence he may sometimes appear tardy to their Lordships with all the Inclinations to be otherwise, &c."

It is true that the Post Route was thro' the Towns of Burlington and Amboy in New Jersey, before and at the Time of making the

himself and never returned to America. Lewis B. Namier, "Charles Garth and His Connexions," *Eng. Hist. Rev.*, LIV (1939), 462–70.

9. *Board of Trade Journal,* 1759–63, p. 185. The pertinent extract from Boone's letter is printed in 1 *N.J. Arch.,* IX, 249.

1. Potts's letter was read at the Board of Trade, May 1, and the matter seems thereupon to have dropped from consideration. *Board of Trade Journal,* 1759–63, p. 185.

2. Governors of N.J. usually lived in either Perth Amboy or Burlington, since the Assembly, which met alternately in these towns, refused to pay their house rent if they lived elsewhere. Edgar J. Fisher, *New Jersey as a Royal Province* (N.Y., 1911), pp. 73–4.

3. 9 Anne, c. 11 (1710), "An Act for establishing a General Post-Office for all Her Majesties Dominions . . . ." Among a multitude of other things, this statute set postal rates between New York, Perth Amboy, and Burlington and from the latter two towns to places sixty and one hundred English miles distant and "thence back again." BF's contention that it did not forbid the establishment of a New York to Philadelphia mail route bypassing Perth Amboy and Burlington, appears to have been well founded. *Statutes of the Realm,* IX (London, 1822), 393–404.

Act of Queen Anne for Establishing the Post Office, and therefore those Towns were mentioned in the Act so far as to settle the Rates of Postage between them and the Cities of New York and Philadelphia; but it has never been understood that the Route was established by such mention of those places, or that the Act bound the Post Office to continue the Posts in any Route then used, if one better and more Convenient could be found. Nor indeed would such Restraints in an Act of Parliament relating to America, be of utility, but the Contrary, For our first settlements there being near the Sea, the first Roads are of course along the Coast where interrupting Waters from Bays and inlets are more frequent, and Rivers wider and more difficult of Passage, but in Process of time, as the People settle farther back and clear the upland Country, more convenient Roads are found, the Bays and Inlets avoided, and the Interruption of Ferries less frequent, as many Rivers are fordable up the Country, that cannot be cross'd near their Mouths but in Boats.

Something like this has been the Case with regard to the Old and New Roads thro' the Province of New Jersey. As soon as the New road in the upper parts of that Province was open'd, Travellers between Philadelphia and New York began gradually to abandon the old Road, which was not so convenient; and after some time, on an Application made to Col. Spotswood,[4] then Deputy Postmaster General, the Post Route was also chang'd from the Old Road to the New.

This Change was made about Thirty Years ago, and some Years before I had any Concern in the Office;[5] but as it was a Matter much talk'd of at the time, I remember well the Reasons that were given for the Change which were these, viz.

That the Ferry over the River Delaware from Bristol to Burlington, to be pass'd in travelling the old Road, was a Mile and half wide, and in Winter often incumbered with Ice, so as greatly

4. Alexander Spotswood, former lieutenant governor of Virginia, was deputy postmaster general for North America and the West Indies, 1730–40. See above, II, 235 n.

5. In his letter to Pownall Boone alleged that BF himself had changed the route "and that too upon some Pique." BF was appointed postmaster at Philadelphia in 1737 (above, II, 178–83) and joint deputy postmaster general for North America in 1753 (above, V, 18).

to delay the Post. That the old Road, from Burlington to Amboy was for 50 Miles chiefly a heavy loose Sand, very fatiguing to the Horses: That being thro' a barren Country, it was not well inhabited, nor the Inns well supply'd with Provisions: That being less travelled than formerly, there was not the same Care taken to provide suitable Accomodations for Travellers; so that no Gentleman passing between New York and Philadelphia tho' desirous of riding Post, could well travel with him; That this gradual disuse of the Road occasion'd less Care to be taken of the Bridges which were often out of Repair, so that in rainy Seasons crossing the Brooks and Branches of Rivers became dangerous and sometimes impracticable to the great delay and Injury of Travellers: That the Ferry over to Amboy necessary to be pass'd on this Road, was near two Miles wide, being at the Mouth of Raritan River, and often so rough from high Winds, or so incumbered with Ice as to be impassable for many Hours, to the great Delay of the Post as well as other Travellers; and after the Post was got to Amboy, he had still three large Ferries to cross between that Place and New York, viz. the Ferry over to Staten Island, the Ferry from Staten Island to long Island 3 Miles wide, and the Ferry from Long Island to New York; in all which Places the Ferrymen were generally very dilatory and backward to carry the Post in bad Weather, availing themselves of every excuse, as they were by Law to receive no Ferriage of him. On the other Hand, the new Road was over better Ground and kept in better Repair; there were every where good Accomodations at the Inns; Delaware River was to be cross'd at Trenton, and Raritan River at Brunswick, where they were both narrow, and the latter fordable at Low Water; and the People at Elizabeth Town Point, undertook voluntarily to have a stout Boat always ready to carry the Post and his Company directly to New York, by which the three last mention'd Ferries were avoided.

The Change being accordingly made, the Post went no more thro' Burlington and Amboy; but those Places on that Account suffered very little Inconveniency; For an Office was still continu'd at each of them; and their Letters sent over to proper Places on the New Post Road, to be carried forward by the Post: and this was easy to do, it being only cross the Ferry from Burlington to Bristol, thro' which the Post goes; and but 4 Miles from Amboy to Woodbridge thro' which he also goes. And the Letters for Burlington were in like manner sent over to that Office from Bristol, and those for Amboy sent to that Office from Woodbridge. Tho' the Letters to and from each Place by Post were always extreamly few, as they are Towns of little or no Foreign Trade, the chief Dealing of Amboy being with New York, and that of Burlington with Philadelphia, to and from which Places Boats are going almost every day, by which they always chose to send their Letters, even when the Post pass'd thro' them. On the other hand, two other large and thriving Towns, who make much more use of the Post, are accomodated by it on the New Road, viz. Trenton and Brunswick; not to mention Prince town where a College is lately erected, Woodbridge and Elizabeth Town, thro' all which Places the new Road passes, and where Offices have been long establish'd.

It is now near 24 Years that I have been concern'd in the Management of the offices between Philadelphia and New York, and in all that time have had no Complaint made to me of Inconvenience from the Posts continuing the Route I found them in. And I must own myself at a Loss to conceive the difficulty Governor Boone mentions of his Corresponding regularly with the Board of Trade, and that "Dispatches receiv'd from their Lordships *could not* be answered by the first Pacquet, tho' [thro'] the Posts Omission of Burlington and Amboy in their Route." His Excellency resides at Amboy, and the Letters for him which arrive at New York in the Pacquet, must be forwarded to him at farthest within three days, as the Post goes from New York twice a Week and passes within 4 Miles of Amboy at Woodbridge, where the Governor's Letters are left, and sent to him immediately by a special Messenger from the Office there. The Post returns twice a Week from Philadelphia to New York, and passing thro' Woodbridge takes up and carries forward any Letters left there. The Pacquet stays at New York at least 20 Days, and during that time the Post passes 6 times thro' Woodbridge to New York, and would carry forward any Letters the Governor should lodge at Woodbridge for that purpose. And if he happens to be at Burlington with his Assembly, the Post passes equally often thro' Bristol (within a Mile and half of him only just cross a Ferry) where it cannot be much Trouble to send his Letters. So that on the whole I am persuaded it must appear, when duly consider'd, that his Excellency's Want of Punctuality in his Correspondence with their Lordships cannot justly be charg'd to the Account of the Post Office.

Mr. Barnard,[6] immediate Predecessor of Governor Boone tho' he also liv'd at Amboy, made no Complaint of this kind that I ever heard of. Nor did the next preceeding Governor Belcher,[7] tho he liv'd great Part of his time at Burlington. The Governors of New Jersey have sometimes liv'd on the New Road, at Trenton and at Elizabeth Town; and as there is no fix'd Place of Residence for Governors in that Province, future Governors may happen to chuse some of the Towns on the New Road; so that if the Post Route were chang'd to Gratify Governor Boone, the next Governor might desire to have it back again.

And I apprehend that the Delays formerly experienced so frequently in the Detention of the Post by the wide Ferries in Winter, would if the Old Route was resum'd, occasion great Dissatisfaction to the Governors of Pensilvania, New York and New England, who as well as the Merchants of their great Trading Towns would probably remonstrate warmly against it.

Nevertheless, if His Majesty's Postmaster General should upon the whole think fit to order the Old Route to be resum'd, and the New One with all the Offices so long established upon it to be drop't it is my Duty to carry their orders into Execution, which I shall do with great Readiness and Fidelity. I am, sir Your most obedient humble servant   B FRANKLIN

To Henry Potts, Esqr.

Endorsed:[8] New Jersey letter from H Potts Esqr. Secry to the Post Master Genl. to Mr Pownall, dated April. 29. 1761. inclosg the Copy of a Letter to him from Mr Frunklyn, joint depy. post Master Genl. in No. America relatin to the Alteration which Mr. Boone desird might be made in the route of the post through New Jersey.

Recd Read May 1 1761

K. 11.

---

6. Francis Bernard, governor of N.J., 1758–60. See above, VIII, 202 n.
7. Jonathan Belcher, governor of N.J., 1747–57. See above, I, 176 n.
8. Apparently in the hand of a clerk at the Board of Trade.

From Mary Stevenson

Draft: American Philosophical Society

Dear Sir   Wanstead, April 27. 1761

Had I never known you I could not have read those Writings you were so obliging to put into my Hands[9] without entertaining the highest Esteem for you, but as I have had the Happiness of experiencing your Condescension and Candour Gratitude and Affection are join'd to my Esteem, and together fill my Heart with Sentiments I am not able to express. You assert your Opinion with so much Modesty, and maintain your Argument with such Clearness, that every sensible Heart must be charm'd, and every unprejudic'd Mind convinc'd. It is indeed Presumptious in me to give my Judgment, yet my Friend I know will lend a partial Attention.

Your Notion of the Water Spout appears to me most probable,[1] for the Facts, which your Correspondent J.P. proves to support his, are not so fully related as those you mention, nor does he remove every Objection so satisfactorily as you do. Most of the Effects he speaks of may, I apprehend, happen in an ascending Spout; beside, tho you are of Opinion the generality ascend you don't say that others may not descend; therefore, supposing those Accounts to be true, your Argument is not confuted.

The Gentleman who asserts that "The increase of the Surface of any Body lessens its Weight in Air Water or any other Fluid, as appears by the Slow descent of Leaf-Gold in the Air,"[2] was rather too hasty; for, I apprehend, tho it is slow in descending, will not rise in the Air without some Force to carry it up. You have answer'd him very fully. The same Gentleman says, "It surprizes him a little that Wind generated by Fermentation is new to you, since it may every day be observed in fermenting Liquor."[3] I should be glad

9. On a visit to Wanstead early in April BF apparently gave Polly several scientific papers in addition to the one he sent her on March 30. For the purpose he may have borrowed from Peter Collinson parts of the "great Philosophical Pacquet" he had sent his friend in June 1755. See above, v, 115, 333; VI, 83–4.

1. This paragraph comments on the correspondence between BF and John Perkins of Boston in 1752–53 on waterspouts and related phenomena. See above, IV, 358–60, 429–42, 489–95.

2. From Cadwallader Colden's essay enclosed with his letter to BF, Nov. 29, 1753 (above, v, 124), to which BF replied, Dec. 6, 1753 (above, v, 146).

3. In the same essay Colden had declared that "A Remarkable intestinal motion like a violent fermentation is very observable in the cloud whence the [water]spout issues" (above, v, 126). In reply BF "would only say, that the

to have your Thoughts upon that Subject when you have Leisure. I don't conceive how the Fermentation of Liquor-producing Wind can be applied to the Clouds, unless they were confin'd in a Cask. Upon looking again at your Answer I find your Opinion the same, and perhaps I ought not to call it mine, but acknowledge it was borrow'd tho I did not know it was. However, I am contented to borrow from you, and care not how far I run in your Debt, for I am already so deep in it that I can never pay, therefore must resign myself to you to be disposed of as you think fit.

The Letters upon other Subjects I have not yet read, when I have I shall let you know whether or not I can understand them. You are to check me when I go to far; I have given you Power, and you have promis'd to exert it. The least Hint from you is sufficient to stop me in any pursuit, and as my chief aim in this was to keep up a Correspondence with you, I shall drop it whenever you bid me, if you will but allow me often to subscribe myself Dear Sir your sincerely affectionate humble Servant   M. STEVENSON

From Mr. Chambers[4]   AL: American Philosophical Society

Thrift Street Thursday Night [c. April 1761][5]
Mr. Chambers's Compliments to Mr. Franklin and being dis-apointed of the pleasure of meeting him at the Philadelphia Coffee House to day desires the favour of him to send to send [sic] his Letters by the Bearer; as being to set out for Portsmouth early tomorrow morning he fears it will be out of his power to wait upon before that time.

Addressed: To / Dr. Franklin / at Mrs. Stephenson's / Craven Street.

Opinion of Winds being generated in Clouds by Fermentation, is new to me, and I am unacquainted with the Facts on which it is founded" (above, v, 147). Colden's response that Polly quotes here is from his letter to BF of April 2, 1754, and the rest of his passage justifies Polly's rebuttal that his analogy relates only to gases produced by liquids fermenting in closed containers. Above, v, 257.

4. Not identified; apparently an English acquaintance, though not a close friend, about to sail to America.

5. So dated because in the following July (below, p. 332) Isaac Norris indicated that BF had recommended "Mr. Chambers" in a letter of April 14, 1761 (not found).

From Isaac Norris

Letterbook copy: Historical Society of Pennsylvania

Dear Friend B Franklin,   Fairhill May 1st 1761

I have been so very Unwell all this last Winter, and the Early part of this Spring that my Attendance on the Assembly has been Very Inconvenient and Troublesome to me, and if my ill state of Health Continues and I have no Reason to Expect much Alteration I must be oblig'd to quit all close Attention or attendance on publick Affairs. This I concieved I had a Right to some Time ago but Necessity will now Oblige me to Insist upon it,[6] and I could wish to see them in Abler hands, whose Strength might be Equal to the Burthen. I have received yours of November 19. 22d and the 16th of December last[7] and approve of your conduct in the purchase of stocks till the Province may have Ocaision to Draw for the sums lodg'd there, tho' we had high Flights in our last Session of Assembly, upon the uncertainty and Jeopardy that Mony was in under its present situation.[8] I cannot presume there will be any necessity of being more particular as you will see from the Governor Message[9] and the minutes which the Commitee will Transmit[1] how very Anxious a few among us are to have that Mony out of your possesion however disadvantageous it might be to the Publick to draw it out at this Time. I own it is my Private Opinion that if the

6. In September 1759 Norris had appealed, publicly though unsuccessfully, to the voters of Philadelphia Co. to elect someone to replace him in the Assembly. In *Pa. Gaz.*, Sept. 24, Oct. 1, 1761, he again requested to be relieved, citing his "advanced Years," his health, and "other Reasons of Importance," but as before his constituents re-elected him. See above, VIII, 441 n.

7. For these letters, in which BF reported receiving Pa.'s share of the parliamentary grant for 1758 and investing part of it, see above, pp. 244–5, 245–6, 253–4.

8. No information has survived from the records of the Assembly sessions of Jan. 5–March 14 and April 2–23, 1761, about the "high Flights" Norris says took place over BF's disposition of the parliamentary grant. The matter became a critical issue in the election campaign of 1764.

9. In a message of April 22, 1761, Governor Hamilton urged the Assembly to use the province's share of the parliamentary grant in BF's hands to support a body of troops General Amherst had asked for. 8 *Pa. Arch.*, VI, 5246–51.

1. No minutes sent to BF by the Assembly's Committee of Correspondence have been found.

second Allotment and the 3d too² were in the same place and under the same Direction it would not give me one Moments uneasiness so different are Mens Thots and fears on the same subject.

As there seems no probability of a Peace this Winter³ I could wish our Governor had passed our Bill for Granting five hund[red] men in Adition to the Three we had Granted out of the Residue of the Hundred Thousand pound Act passed in 1760 for the service of the current Year⁴ but that it seems could not be obtain'd tho the fund for sinking the Bills of Credit to be struck for that purpose was as near as the Circumstance would admit the same with the Act allowed by his Majesty for Receiving the first allotment⁵ and to which the Lords of his Majestys privy Council had Reported "The Board of Trade had made no Objections" Tho' in that particular if I Remember Right They had not strictly considred the Report of the Lords for Trade and Plantations in the conclusion of their observations and Report upon that Act,⁶ As the Clerk has

2. The House of Commons voted £200,000 on March 30, 1760, and the same amount on Jan. 20, 1761, to reimburse colonial military expenses of 1759 and 1760 respectively. *Votes of the House of Commons,* 1759–60, p. 379; 1760–61, p. 154.

3. Abortive peace negotiations began at the end of March 1761 (Gipson, *British Empire,* VIII, 208–25), but nothing was known of them in Philadelphia at the time Norris was writing. Preliminary articles between Great Britain and France were not signed until Nov. 3, 1762.

4. Under considerable pressure from Governor Hamilton and General Amherst, the Pa. Assembly reluctantly voted, March 13, 1761, to raise and support 300 men to garrison the posts between Philadelphia and Pittsburgh to replace British troops transferred to other service. Hamilton approved the act the next day. On April 7, following the reading of a letter from William Pitt asking that Pa. raise two-thirds the number of men provided the year before, the House voted, 15 to 12, against increasing the number of men already authorized. But again pressed by Hamilton and Amherst, the Assembly reversed itself and presented a bill, April 17, for 500 additional men and the issue of £30,000 in bills of credit to pay for them. As had happened so often before, Hamilton strongly objected to the terms of the measure, the members refused to accept his amendments, the bill failed of passage, and the House adjourned, April 23, without complying with Pitt's directive. 8 *Pa. Arch.,* VI, 5209–11, 5217–20, 5222–53 *passim; Pa. Col. Recs.,* VIII, 577–8, 581, 583–4, 588–94, 596–8, 602–12; *Statutes at Large, Pa.,* VI, 91–3.

5. The Agency Act, passed Sept. 29, 1759; see above, VIII, 333, 442 n; this volume, p. 186 n.

6. For the Board of Trade Report, June 24, 1760, and the Order in

notice of this Conveyance I presume the Commitee will send you a copy of that Bill and the Governors proposed Amendments to which the House would not agree.[7] I have now wrote to Joseph Sherwood one of the Executors of Richard Partridge from whom I received a letter some time ago inclosing Richard Partridges Account current with the Province upon which there will be a Ballance due to the Estate,[8] but as by J Sherwoods letter it does not appear who was the other Executor or Executors for I could never learn their Names, nor what Power they have to recieve Mony due to the Estate and as the Account is not Signed by any Body, I have wrote to him and must Request you will be so good to advise them in the proper Vouchers and orders proper to be Transmitted and I will take care to see them paid what Ballance the House may Allow due and Payable to the Estate and I should be pleased that this was done as soon as conveniently may be.

We had strange Accounts of Governor Dennys Reception on his Arrival or Rather his Non Reception, for it was Reported that as soon as he landed he Received such UnWelcome Advices that he imediatly disguised Himself and Run off to Spain or Portugal.[9] As I find you had frequently seen him I should be pleased if you would take the Trouble to bestow a word or two on the little Gentleman, whose Venality when he found he was to be superceded, did him no credit here Even Amongst his friends if he had any Real Friends at the Time of his Taking shipping with his Wife and family. I am your Assured Friend ISAAC NORRIS

Council, Sept. 2, 1760, on the Agency Act and 18 other acts passed by the Pa. Assembly in 1758–59, see above, pp. 164–7, 209.

7. For these amendments, submitted to the House on April 21, 1761, see 8 *Pa. Arch.*, VI, 5245–6, *Pa. Col. Recs.*, VIII, 610–11.

8. Richard Partridge (above, V, 11–12 n), for many years agent for Pa., died on March 6, 1759. Norris laid his accounts, showing a balance due of £184 17s. 5d., before the Assembly in September 1761. They were referred to the Committee for Incidental Charges, which reported, Sept. 19, that the province owed Partridge £152 7s. 5d., which sum Norris eventually paid to his executors, Sherwood and Thomas Corbyn. 8 *Pa. Arch.*, VI, 5262; Norris to Joseph Sherwood and Thomas Corbyn, Oct. 19, 1761, Hist. Soc. Pa.

9. Far from fleeing England upon his arrival, Denny settled in or near London, playing the man about town, until his death in 1765. His lucrative sale of flags of truce while in Pa. almost caused the British ministry to prosecute him. Nicholas B. Wainwright, "Governor William Denny in Pennsylvania," *PMHB*, LXXXI (1957), 194–5.

From John Rice[1]   ALS: Historical Society of Pennsylvania

Sir[2]   4th May 1761

Agreable to your Orders I have bought for to morrow £5000. 3 per Cents Consolidated at 87½ per Cent,[3] which I hope you'l Approve off, the 4 per Cents are at a 100½[4] but in my Opinion they will come down to your price, being oblige to attend Sir Thomas Robinson[5] on particular Business to morrow hope you will accept of my friend Mr. Trigg,[6] if not back in proper time to attend your Acceptance. I am Sir Your Humble Servant

JNO RICE

Addressed: To / Benjamin Franklin Esqr. / in Craven Street / Strand

Endorsed: Letter from J. Rice Broker (1761)

[*Also on cover another notation almost illegible:*] Turtile [?]

---

1. John Rice was a respected broker in New John's Street. In 1762, however, he was nearly ruined by ill-advised speculation and the dishonesty of some of his customers. To recoup his losses he forged powers of attorney and embezzled his clients' stocks until, discovery being imminent, he fled to Cambrai, France, in December 1762. He was arrested, extradited, and hanged at Tyburn, May 4, 1763. *Gent. Mag.,* XXXII (1762), 599; XXXIII (1763), 207–10; *London Chron.,* May 3–5, 1763.

2. The initials I.N. have been added just below the salutation, indicating that either at this time or later BF submitted this letter to Isaac Norris, the speaker.

3. On May 5, 1761, BF recorded payment of £4375 for these annuities plus £25 for Rice's commission "on this and the former Provincial Stock, being in all £20,000 at ⅛ per Cent." "Account of Expences," p. 60; *PMHB,* LV (1931), 130. Rice's signed receipt of the same date, among BF's papers in Hist. Soc. Pa., contains an error in addition, acknowledging a total of only £4399, instead of £4400 as shown in BF's record.

4. The 4 per cent annuities of 1760. *London Chron.,* May 2–5, 1761.

5. There were two Sir Thomas Robinsons prominent in London in 1761. One (1695–1770) had been ambassador to Austria, 1730–48, secretary of state for the Southern Department, 1754–55, and subsequently master of the wardrobe to George II; he was created Baron Grantham April 7, 1761. The other (1700?–1777), called "long Sir Thomas," had been governor of Barbados, 1742–47, and was an amateur architect and bon vivant. See *DNB* for both men. Because of the former diplomat's recent advancement to the peerage when this letter was written and the former governor's frequent financial difficulties, it seems probable that "long Sir Thomas" was Rice's client.

6. Not identified, but probably a business associate of Rice.

From Henry Potts

ALS: American Philosophical Society

Sir   General Post Office May 6. 1761

The Letter which you left with me last Week[7] I read to my Lord Bessborough[8] who Orderd me to Acquaint you he desired Mackrath[9] might be removed Directly and that you would appoint the Person Post Master at Charles Town that was recommended by Governor Littleton some time ago, I shall Acquaint the Governor on Friday next with this Nomination.[1] I am Sir Your most Obedient Servant.   HENY. POTTS. Secy.

To Benjamin Francklin Esqr.

From Henry Wilmot[2]

ALS: American Philosophical Society

Sir,   Greys Inn, 8th May 1761.

I am informed by Mr. Penn, that the £100,000 Act passed by Mr. Hamilton,[3] has been transmitted to you under Seal. This I presume is with an Intention to be presented to the Councill. If You have any thoughts of presenting it, I should be very glad, if before you do it, you wou'd allow me a Quarter of an hours Conversation with you on this head, and I will meet you, when and

---

7. Not found; the letter referred to certainly dealt with a different matter than that of April 23 (above, pp. 302–7).

8. One of the joint postmasters general.

9. Thomas MacKreth had been commissioned postmaster at Charleston, So. Car., by BF and William Hunter, July 11, 1760. See above, v, 452 n.

1. The appointment is puzzling. According to Hennig Cohen (*The South Carolina Gazette*, Columbia, So. Car., 1953, p. 243), Peter Timothy (above, v, 341 n), son of BF's old journeyman Louis Timothée, was postmaster at Charleston from 1756 to 1766 and perhaps longer. Apparently, after BF and Hunter had appointed MacKreth in 1760, Gov. William Henry Lyttelton of So. Car. had either requested the reinstatement of Timothy or the appointment of some new candidate of his own. The editors have found too little information on the Charleston Post Office to permit a resolution of the problem.

2. Ferdinand J. Paris' successor as the Penns' agent and solicitor; see above, p. 16 n. 1. Minis Hays (*Calendar of the Papers of Benjamin Franklin*, I, 22) incorrectly suggests that the writer was "[Sir John Eardley?] Wilmot," a puisne judge of the King's Bench.

3. The Supply Act of April 12, 1760; see above, pp. 43–4 n.

where you please, having something I think, and therefore, I hope, you will think, material to say to you, before that Act is presented.[4] I am with the greatest regard. Sir. Your most Obedient humble Servant.   HENY: WILMOT

Addressed: To | Ben: Franklin Esqr in | Craven Street | Strand.

Endorsed: Mr. Wilmot Sollr

[*Also noted in a list on the cover:*] Hall Hunter Parker Thomson Mrs. F. Sally.[5]

To Edward Penington[6]   ALS: American Philosophical Society

Sir,   London, May 9. 1761
I inclose you a Letter from your Kinsman Mr. Springet Penn, with whom I had no Acquaintance till lately, but have the Pleasure to find him a very sensible discreet young Man, with excellent Dispositions, which makes me the more regret that the Government as well as Property of our Province should pass out of that Line.[7] There has, by his Account, been something very mysterious

4. For BF's reply, setting an appointment at Craven Street on Monday, May 11, see below, p. 318.

5. This list of friends and relatives, in BF's hand, probably served as a reminder of letters received or to be written.

6. Edward Penington (1726–1796) was a successful Philadelphia Quaker merchant, an assemblyman (1761–62), and a judge of the Court of Common Pleas. Elected a delegate to the First Continental Congress, he refused to serve and was subsequently twice arrested on suspicion of being a Tory. *DAB.* His grandfather Edward Penington (1676–1701) was a half-brother of Gulielma Springett (1644–1694), who was William Penn's first wife; she was the great-grandmother of Springett Penn (1739–1766), whose Pa. estates are the subject of this letter. Thus Edward Penington and young Springett Penn were second half-cousins once removed. Since the Proprietor Thomas Penn was the son of William Penn's second wife, he and Penington were not related. But because Penington lived in Pa. and was related, however distantly, to Springett, Thomas Penn chose him to represent the youth in a Pa. land transaction, an action the Proprietor almost immediately regretted. Penn to Richard Peters, Dec. 8, 1759, Penn Papers, Hist. Soc. Pa.; see also above, pp. 260–2.

7. In 1731, after years of litigation, John, Thomas, and Richard Penn, the sons of William Penn by his second wife, bought the claims of their elder half-brother's son, William Penn 3d (father of Springett) to the soil and

in the Conduct of his Uncle Mr. Thomas Penn towards him.[8] He was his Guardian; but instead of endeavouring to educate him at home under his Eye in a manner becoming the eldest Branch of their House, has from his Infancy been endeavouring to get rid of him. He first propos'd sending him to the East Indies: when that was declin'd, he had a Scheme of sending him to Russia; but the young Gentleman's Mother[9] absolutely refusing to let him go out of the Kingdom, unless to Pensilvania to be educated in the College there; he would by no means hear of his going thither, but bound him an Apprentice to a Country Attorney in an obscure Part of Sussex; which after two Years Stay, finding that he was taught nothing valuable, nor could see any Company that might improve him, he left and return'd to his Mother, with whom he has been ever since, much neglected by his Uncle, except lately that he has been a little civil to get him to join in a Power of Attorney to W. Peters and R. Hockley[1] for the Sale of some Philadelphia Lots, of which he is told three undivided fourth Parts belong to him; but he is not shown the Right he has to them; nor has he any Plan of their Situation by which he may be advis'd of their Value; nor was he told 'till lately that he had any such Right, which makes him suspect that he may have other Rights that are conceal'd from him. In some Letters to his Father's elder Brother Springet Penn[2] whose Heir he is, he finds that Sir William Keith survey'd for him the said Springet a Manor of 75,000 Acres on Susquehanah, which he call'd Springets-bury,[3] and would be glad to know what became of that Survey, and whether it was ever convey'd away. By

---

government of Pa. The transaction, so far as it related to government, was not completed until 1744.

8. Thomas Penn was Springett's great-uncle, not uncle.

9. Anne Vaux Penn (d. 1767), William Penn 3d's second wife.

1. William Peters (1702–1789), lawyer, judge, and register of the Admiralty (1744–71), succeeded his younger brother Richard as secretary of the provincial Land Office, serving from 1760 to 1765. DAB under "Richard Peters (1744–1828)." Richard Hockley was the provincial receiver general.

2. Springett Penn the elder (1701–1731).

3. The warrant of survey for Springettsbury (in York Co., Pa.), signed by Governor Keith and dated June 18, 1722, is printed in Pa. Col. Recs., III, 184–5. A re-survey, ordered by Gov. James Hamilton in 1762 but not completed until 1768, showed that the manor contained 64,520 acres. 3 Pa. Arch., IV, no. 63.

searching the Records, you may possibly obtain some Light in this and other Land Affairs that may be for his Interest. The good Inclinations you have shown towards that Interest, in a Letter that has been shown to me, encourage me to recommend this Matter earnestly to your Care and Prudence; and the more private you carry on your Enquiries for the present the better it will be. His Uncle has lately propos'd to buy of him Pensbury Manor House,[4] with 1000 Acres of that Land near the House, pretending that his principal Reason for desiring it, was not the Value of the Land, but an Inclination he had to possess the antient House of the Head of the Family, and a little Land round it just to support it. You know the Situation of that Manor, and can judge whether it would be prudent to sell the Part propos'd from the rest, and will advise him concerning it. He has refus'd to treat about it at present, as well as to sign the Power of Attorney for the Sale of the City Lots; upon which his late Guardian has brought in an Account against him, and demands a Debt of £400 which he urges him to pay, for that as he says he very much wants the Money, which does not seem to look well. Not only the Land Office may be search'd for Warrants and Surveys to the young Gentleman's Ancestors, but also the Record Office for Deeds of Gift from the first Proprietor and other subsequent Grants or Conveyances. I may tell you in confidence, that some Lawyers here are of Opinion, that the Government was not legally convey'd from the eldest Branch to others of the Family; but this is to be farther enquir'd into, and at present it is not to be talk'd of. I am, with much Esteem, Sir, Your most humble Servant   B FRANKLIN

Mr E. Pennington

Endorsed: B Franklin May 9 1765

4. A two-story brick mansion built by William Penn. Pennsbury Manor, on which the house stood, contained 8431 acres and was about twenty-five miles from Philadelphia on the Delaware River near the present Tullytown. *PMHB*, LIX (1935), 91–3.

To Henry Wilmot[5]

ALS: American Philosophical Society

Sir,   Cravenstreet, Saturday May 9. 1761
I have received the Act you mention,[6] and if tis convenient to
you to call at my House on Monday morning any Hour before
One, I shall be glad to see you and converse with you on the Sub-
ject;[7] being with great Esteem, Sir, Your most obedient humble
Servant.   B F

To—Wilmot Esqr

From Mary Stevenson

ALS and draft: American Philosophical Society

Dear Sir   Wanstead May 19th. 1761.
In my last[8] I communicated what occurr'd to me upon first
reading your Letters.[9] I receive so much Pleasure from what you
say or write, and it is with such Facility I comprehend, or fancy I
comprehend, what you mean, that attending to you is my Darling
Amusement. I have not many Opportunities of conversing personally with you, but I make up that Deficiency by a frequent
Perusal of your Writings.

5. As in the case of Wilmot's letter of May 8 (above, p. 314), to which this
is a reply, I. Minis Hays suggests an incorrect identification as "[Sir John
Eardley?] Wilmot." *Calendar of the Papers of Benjamin Franklin*, III, 452.

6. The Supply Act of April 12, 1760; see above, pp. 43–4 n.

7. Thomas Penn reported the meeting between BF and Wilmot on Monday, May 11, to Richard Peters a month later: "Mr. Wilmot has had a conference with Mr. Franklin, who has had exemplified Copies of Bills sent him,
but not any orders to present them, he was charged to let Mr. Franklin know
we had had information that the Assembly was in a better disposition, that
we were very desirous to shew ourselves equally disposed and therefore
would not take any step to widen the breach again, and cautioned him against
it, he said he had yet received no orders, that if he did to present Bills he must
do it, but if any thing was left to his discretion he should exercise it, and that
he thought what Mr. Wilmot said to him was very proper." Penn to Peters,
June 13, 1761, Penn Papers, Hist. Soc. Pa. Apparently this Supply Act was
never presented to the King in Council; see above, pp. 201–2 n.

8. Above, pp. 308–9.

9. The scientific letters, written in 1752–54, which BF gave Polly in April
1761; see *ibid.*

I must beg the Exertion of your wonted Patience while I relate what occurr'd to me upon the Reason you give why there
is no salt Rain.[1] If the Vapours are rais'd from the Sea by Heat
only, and the Salt does not rise with the Water because it is
heavier, I imagine it would be easy to render salt Water fresh
by Distillation; but if, as you say, the Air attracts the Water
and will not take hold of the Salt, then something must be found
to attract the Salt so forcibly as to separate it from the Water.
Doc. Hales,[2] I have heard, has discover'd a Method of making
salt Water fresh, which if I was acquainted with might let me
see my Conception is not entirely false, or convince me of my
Ignorance.

I must not give the Name of Candour to the Manner you regard
whatever I say or do, that being, according to my Acceptation of
the Word, to signify a mild Justice: But you look upon me with a
fond Partiality, and I am as proud that you do so as if I was really
Mistress of the Excellence you ascribe to me. This appears like
begging your Flattery, tho' I only mean to give you my Sentiments
of the fine things you say. I have been insensibly drawn from what
I was going to say further upon that Passage in your Letter which
occasion'd those Conjectures I have had the Assurance to trouble
you with. I was greatly pleas'd with the Piety of your Expression.
If the *Knowledge* I gain from your Instructions is small I am certain
to receive one Advantage, I shall be taught to pay a grateful
Adoration to the Great Creator whose Wisdom and Goodness are
so manifest in the Operations of Nature. I would not have trusted
myself in the Hands of a Philosopher who regards only Second
Causes. There are indeed I believe none who entirely deny a First,
but there are many who do not give him the Honour due as my

---

1. In a letter to John Perkins, Feb. 4, 1753 (above, IV, 440–1), BF argued
that there was no salt rain because it had "pleased the Goodness of God so to
order it" that air, which attracted water and brought rain, would not "attract
the Particles of Salt." For this dispensation "Let us adore him with Praise and
Thanksgiving!"

2. Polly is probably referring either to Stephen Hales's *An Account of a
Useful Discovery to Distill double the usual quantity of Sea-water* (London,
1756), or to his *Philosophical Experiments . . . showing how Sea-water may be
made fresh and wholesome* (London, 1739). BF apparently supplied her with
both works later in the summer; see below, p. 338. For Hales, see above, IV,
315 n.

Friend and Preceptor does. May that Almighty Being shower down Blessing on his Head!

I have read those Letters on Electricity, but I want to be a little better acquainted with that Branch of Philosophy to be able to say anything upon them. Before you leave England I hope to spend some few days with you, and then, if you think proper, I shall be glad to receive some Information. I find your Notion of Light the same as I had before met with in *Spectacle de la Nature*.[3]

My Mother tells me you are soon to be at Mr. Stanley's,[4] so I hope for a short Interview with you.

I am with the highest Esteem and Gratitude Dear Sir your affectionate obedient Servant   M STEVENSON

3. Stan V. Henkels Catalogue, no. 1262 (July 1, 1920), 49–50, prints a document in a hand identified as that of an amanuensis which is called "Philosophical Queries and Answers in all probability written for Miss Mary Stevenson, as dictated by Dr. Franklin." This document which contains quotations from letters of BF and his scientific correspondents begins with a question about respiration in humid air put by Jonathan Todd, March 6, 1753 (above, IV, 451–4). BF's answer, May 3, 1753 (above, IV, 472–4), follows. Then comes a passage about "Damp Winds" from BF to Colden, Dec. 6, 1753 (above, V, 144–7). Next are Cadwallader Colden's speculations about the transmission of heat, April 2, 1754 (above, V, 256–8). The document concludes with an expression of BF's views about the nature of light, April 23, 1752 (above, IV, 299–300), and with a passage from Pluche's *Spectacle de la Nature* on the same topic. While it is not impossible that BF strung these quotations together, Polly seems in fact to have been their compiler. She had been closely reading Pluche since BF gave her the first volumes in the spring of 1760; see above, p. 102 n. Moreover, during April 1761 she had read at least two of the letters quoted in the document here described, they being among the scientific letters which BF gave her earlier that month; see above, p. 308 n. The document appears, then, to have been written by Polly pursuant to BF's advice "to read with a Pen in your Hand" and to record "short Hints of what you find that is curious or may be useful"; see above, p. 117. It was probably written during the spring of 1761—in any case no later than August 1761 when Polly returned the papers to BF.

4. John Stanley (1714–1786), an accomplished blind organist and a composer of some of "the best English instrumental compositions of the eighteenth century." In 1758 he advised BF about buying a harpsichord (above, VII, 383–4) and in 1770 he took Josiah Williams (C.5.3.1), BF's blind grand-nephew, as a pupil. *DNB*. He was a member of the circle of friends which included Dr. John Hawkesworth (above p. 265 n) and Polly Stevenson.

From David Hall

Letterbook copy: American Philosophical Society

Sir   Philada. June 1. 1761.

Your Favour, by Captain Hammit, came safe to hand last Week, for which I am obliged to you.[5]

Inclosed you have the first Copy of a Bill of Exchange for One Hundred Pounds Sterling, drawn by Lieutenant Thomas Vaughan on John Calcroft Esq; Westminster,[6] for which, as usual, please give me Credit, and Advise of its coming to Hand. Should be mighty glad to see you here again, in order, among other Things, that we might get our long standing Account settled. You talk often of coming, but it seems to be a difficult Matter for you to get away. I am, Sir, Yours. &c.   DAVID HALL.

Exchange of above Bill 73 and a Third

To Benjamin Franklin Esq.,
Sent by the Willy, Captain McConnell, to Cork.[7]

Second Copy of the above Bill sent by the Knuttsford, Captain Williams, to Liverpool.[8]

The Society of Arts: Notice of Committee Meeting

Printed form with MS insertions in blanks: American Philosophical Society

In the Franklin Papers there are a number of printed notices of committee meetings at the Society of Arts (above, VI, 187 n), an organiza-

5. The *Dragon,* Capt. Francis Hammett, sailed from Portsmouth, March 31, 1761, and arrived in Philadelphia, May 24, 1761. *Pa. Gaz.,* May 28, 1761. BF's letter has not been found.

6. Thomas Vaughan was commissioned a captain in the 45th Regiment, April 7, 1761. Worthington C. Ford, ed., *British Officers Serving in America. 1754–1774.* (Boston, 1894), p. 101. John Calcraft (1726–1772), M. P., 1766–72, made a fortune as a regimental agent during the Seven Years War, was a follower of Pitt and Shelburne, and served as an intermediary in delicate political negotiations between various factions. Namier and Brooke, *House of Commons,* II, 170–4.

7. *Pa. Gaz.,* May 28, 1761, recorded the clearance of the *Willey,* Capt. J. M'Connell.

8. *Pa. Gaz.,* June 4, 1761, recorded the clearance of the *Knuttsford,* Capt. R. Williams.

tion to which BF was devoted as his attendance record—some fifty-odd appearances at meetings between 1759 and 1762—attests. At various times he sat on the Committees of Agriculture, Mechanics, Polite Arts, and Chemistry and on Dec. 3, 1760, he was elected co-chairman (with John Pownall) of the Committee of Colonies and Trade, a position to which he was re-elected in the following December.[9] The document printed below is the earliest surviving example of the Society's notices. The others will not be separately printed.

SOCIETY'S OFFICE
For the Encouragement of Arts, &c. in the Strand.

June 10 17 *61*

SIR,

YOUR Attendance is desired at a COMMITTEE appointed to meet at this Office, on *Friday next* the *12.* Day of *June Inst* at *7* o'Clock in the *After* noon, to *consider Articles in Agriculture*
[*Committee*] *of Mechanics meet on Saturd: next at 11. to determine the Comparative Merit of the Tide Mills.*[1]

By Order of the Society,
PETER TEMPLEMAN, Secretary.[2]

Addressed: To | Dr. Franklin | Craven Street | Strand

9. E. N. da C. Andrade, "Benjamin Franklin in London," *Journal of the Royal Society of Arts*, CIV (1956), 227–8.

1. In 1759 the Society offered a premium of £50 for a model of a tide mill (a mill whose shaft was driven by the motions of the tide). Although two prizes of £20 were awarded in 1760, one of £60 and another of 10 guineas in 1761, and one of 20 guineas in 1762, none of the models was really successful, for the contestants could not wholly solve the problems created by variation in the velocity, and periodic reversal in the direction, of the flow of water. Robert Dossie, *Memoirs of Agriculture and other Œconomical Arts,* I (London, 1768), 112–13; Derek Hudson and Kenneth W. Luckhurst, *The Royal Society of Arts* (London, 1954), p. 112.

2. Peter Templeman (1711–1769), B.A., Cambridge, 1731, M.D., Leyden, 1737, author and editor of several medical works and translator of Norden's *Travels in Egypt and Nubia,* was elected secretary of the Society of Arts in 1760, after having served for two years as Keeper of the Reading-Room at the British Museum. *DNB.*

From [John Peter Miller]³ Extract: Princeton University Library

[Ephrata, June 16, 1761]
Extract of a Letter from one of the People called Dunkards,
dated Ephrata June 16th. 1761, to Benjamin Franklin Philadelphia.

The respect you was so kind as to send to the father⁴ and to the
Societies, was received very well,⁵ as it came from an old Friend
who was acquainted with the society from its Infancy.⁶ The father

3. So identified because John Peter Miller (1709–1796) appears to have
been the only member of the Ephrata community who corresponded with
BF and because the reference to the passage of "26 years since we first eat
together the bread of tribulation" is evidently an allusion to Miller's conver-
sion in 1735 by the founder of the Ephrata community, Johann Conrad
Beissel (1690–1768). Miller emigrated to Pa. in 1730, was ordained by the
Presbytery of Philadelphia in 1731, and began preaching to German Re-
formed congregations on the frontier. Reputed to be one of the most learned
ministers in Pa., he shocked the province when he renounced his charge and
became a disciple of Beissel, a journeyman baker turned evangelist, who advo-
cated triple immersion, Sabbatarianism, and celibacy. Miller lived for a while
as a hermit but in 1735 joined Beissel and his followers at Ephrata whence
they had retired to lead a monastic life. Upon Beissel's death, Miller became
the leader of the Ephrata group. For a thorough study of the Ephrata community and its leaders, see Julius F. Sachse, *The German Sectarians of Pennsylvania*, II (Phila., 1899).
4. Johann Conrad Beissel.
5. On Feb. 20, 1761, BF recorded the purchase of "2 glasses for the Brethren
at Ephrata." He sent these glasses, "with cut Shanks and feet" costing 7s. 6d.
to Isaac Norris, who received them on May 27, 1761, and apparently forwarded them to Ephrata shortly afterwards. "Account of Expences," p. 58;
PMHB, LV (1931), 130; Norris' MS account book, 1735–65, Lib. Co. Phila.
6. According to Sachse, BF attended some of the open-air evangelistic
meetings that Beissel and two of his associates conducted in 1729 from the
Court House steps in Philadelphia, near the recently established New Printing Office of Franklin & Meredith. The pietistic German and the printer
became acquainted and in 1730 BF was commissioned to bring out three of
Beissel's works: *Mystische und sehr geheyme Sprueche, welche in der Himlischen
schule des heiligen geistes erlernet; Göttliche Liebes und Lobesgethöne;* and *Die
Ehe das Zuchthaus fleischlicher Menschen.* Others of Beissel's works issued
from BF's press in 1732 and 1736. Sachse, *German Sectarians*, II, 154, 159–68;
Evans, 3251–53, 3503, 3986. Beissel's beliefs were strongly influenced by
theosophy and Rosicrucianism. In spite of diligent efforts, the present editors
have found no evidence that BF, though an acquaintance of Beissel and his
early printer, ever personally adopted any Rosicrucian beliefs, as has sometimes been publicly asserted.

has now reached 70 years; according to his constitution he is semper idem, but by a task of 46 years, (for so long he has been employed in the Vineyard of God,) he is reduced to such a Condition, that he is, as I may say justly, a very quick and lively skeleton. When he arrived in these parts of the world he cast his eyes upon a certain solitary place, in order to spend the residue of his Days in an Hermetical life, but he had not long tasted the sweetness of that Paradisacal life in a retired solitude now called Ephrata, before he was commanded by Divine Providence, who dictates all his resolutions, and to whom he stipulated an inviolable obedience to appear publickly. Thus pretty early the Hermetical life was Metamorphised into a Monasterial one, and Ephrata designed at first for an Hermitage, has become now without any mans premeditation, the Camp of a Solitary Congregation, in which character it was hitherto maintained by mere accidental events, and as self will was deemed an unpardonable error, every individual was careful to yield himself to the winkings of Providence.

It is now more than 26 years since we first eat together the bread of tribulation, and have been in that space alternately visitted by heavenly comfort and many Tryals, as they commonly succeed each other. Never was a people of such different sexes, manners, professions, dispositions and inclinations, and that in the prime of their age, assembled into a body as we then was, and in a way so far removed from all advantages with which we were invested by our natural birth-right. Thanks be unto God who has removed the obstacles. I never could discover by what means this body was cemented so strongly together, neither did the father who was before so well acquainted with this way, think that so many would hold out, as he wished to live so long as to see some of his followers grey-headed, which has happened to his satisfaction. He was, ever since I knew him, an enemy to self interest, even in the most innocent things, and has adopted that generous principle of disinterested love by which he was guided hitherto. And as God is justly call'd a fathomless ocean of love, he judged that his Ambassadors should by all means strive to bring his Philanthrophy to the light, and to paint him in such a shape as to intimidate good people, is doing wrong, since we are naturally so shy of him, that we always keep at a Distance from him.

Two things he observed strictly in his course; not to run before

Providence, neither by a Laziness too common in our Days, to sit still when God wants hands. Being thus submissive to Divine Instruction, he had the good fortune to find the middle road, whilst he has seen many that fell upon either of those two extremes to suffer Shipwreck, and he used to say that to suffer the operations of God was more than our own Operations. Concerning his conversation he was always upright, but not elated in his mind; and altho' he suffered in his Sphere of Activity the Vicisitudes of Day and night, yet never did appear the least marks of Dispair in his countenance, by which any one could be dejected. He often said, that he would rather die than discourage any one upon the way of Self Denial. In the cause of God, a bolder Person has never been seen—he was never surprised by any flattery—but as for his own Abilities, his concomitant Attributes are Trembling and Bashfulness.

And as I have the honour to try your Patience by this long Detail, I cannot but give my Pen some further relaxation; I think in exalting the Mediatorship of our blessed Saviour no man ever went too far, neither can go too far, as it is an inexhaustable Treasure to all that want Comfort, but surely our own Nobility [?], and especially our free will is suppressed too much. Are we not destin'd to bear fruits in the house of God? The excellency of our Soil will not be discovered while it remains uncultivated; but by bearing fruits its faculties will be so exhausted, that it now and then must be watered by the heavenly riviluts [rivulets], and it is known by experience that whosoever will bear good fruits must navigate against both wind and tide, and will find the current against him all his life time.

But to return, I hope you will allow the Sisters a Paragraph in this Letter.[7] They have received your compliments very decently, and wish all prosperity to you and your worthy family. They have so far transcended the limits of their Sex, that they joined among

7. Toward the end of 1735, Beissell organized the women at Ephrata, some of whom had left home and family to follow him, into what he called the Order of Spiritual Virgins. The Sisters lived in the Kedar, a three-story building originally intended as a house of worship, cooked communal meals, and wore habits resembling those of the Capuchins. In 1771 their number was 26, although as many as 75 had lived at Ephrata. Sachse, *German Sectarians*, II, 254–8, 298, 309–11. John Peter Miller to BF, June 12, 1771. APS. It is not known what compliments BF paid the Sisters.

themselves in a visible Body, independant of any mans Government upon earth, except that they are under a fathers Tutorship. And altho' enclosed into their Appartment, yet their odoriferous fragrancy broke out every where. If I say that they are upon a Level with the Brethren, I do no Justice to their Character, I could say more, if I did not abhor all flattery. Let this be as it will, they have either more zeal for the life to come, or are naturally more inclined than we to a retired life, whilst on the contrary, in our Male-Breasts the revolting faculties of the Lapse are so abundantly collocated, that from thence hardly proceedeth anything else but rebellion and disobedience.

Concerning the Brethren, it is true that the body of our Society consisteth chiefly of Veterans, who by a long experience are inured to a life exposed to so many hardships; but the Addition we have received since, have not reached that Zeal which burned in our breasts when we listed first, and was consequently not so successful in their Spiritual Warfare. Such a nice Scheme adopted in the foundation of this Society has hitherto found more admirers than followers.

Endorsed: Copy of a letter from the Dunkards to Benjamin Franklin.

To [Springett Penn?][8]   Draft: Detroit Public Library

Sir   Friday June 30. 61
I have not yet obtained the Opinion of my Lawyer on the Title &c.[9] and am to be out of town tomorrow and next Day, but on Friday purpose to be in the City and to call on you. I am Sir, Your humble Servant   B FRANKLIN

8. The reference to the opinion of BF's lawyer "on the Title" provides a clue to the possible identity of the addressee. As the result of a recent interview with Springett Penn (above, p. 315), BF appears to have initiated an inquiry, in the strictest secrecy, into the validity of the title of Thomas and Richard Penn to the proprietorship of Pa. This note appears to be a response to Springett's queries about the progress of the investigation.
9. Crossed out: "but expect it in a Day or two. I shall be out of"

To Mary Stevenson   ALS: American Philosophical Society

Cravenstreet July 7. 1761

This is just to acquaint my dear Polly, that her good Mama, Mr. and Mrs. Strahan, and her Friend Franklin, purpose to be at Bromley on Tuesday Morning next, to have the Pleasure of seeing Dr. and Mrs. Hawkesworth and the agreable Miss Blunt's, dining there and returning in the Evening.[1] They carry down with them Miss Peggy Strahan,[2] and leave her there instead of Miss Stevenson who is to come to Town with them. This is the Scheme; but all this in case it will be agreable to our Friends at Bromley, of which you are to let us know. Mr. Strahan is here with us, and we all join in drinking your Health with that of our Bromley Friends. 'Tis 11 a Clock at Night, and the Post rings his Bell, which obliges me to conclude, dear good Girl, Your affectionate Friend

B Franklin

Mama says God bless you. Peter[3] could find me no better Paper.

Endorsed: July 7—61

1. For Dr. John Hawkesworth, a successful writer and editor who helped his wife run a school at Bromley, Kent, see above, p. 265 n. The "agreable Miss Blunt's," Catherine (1727–1775) and Dorothea (1733–1809), close friends and cousins of Polly, were granddaughters of Sir John Blunt (1665–1733), the able, though unscrupulous, financier who directed the spectacular operations of the South Sea Company in 1719–20 and lost a fortune when the Bubble collapsed. With Dorothea (Dolly) Blunt BF formed one of those playful, affectionate relationships which he enjoyed so much and for which he had so great a capacity. When Polly Stevenson married William Hewson in 1770 he and Dolly "agreed to love each other better than we ever did, to make up as much as we can our suppos'd Loss," but although they corresponded frequently and saw each other at intervals, Dolly never enjoyed the abiding love and concern with which BF favored Polly. Whitfield J. Bell, Jr., "All Clear Sunshine," APS *Proc.*, c (1956), 528, 529; John Carswell, *The South Sea Bubble* (Stanford, 1960). BF and his party arrived at Bromley on Wednesday, July 15, 1761. William Strahan to David Hall, July 15, 1761, APS.

2. Strahan's younger daughter Margaret, whom BF affectionately referred to as "little Peggy" or "my little Wife," apparently because she had "made choise" of him for a husband when she should grow up. Strahan to BF, May 27, 1782.

3. BF's Negro servant; see above, VI, 425 n.

327

From Mary Stevenson

ALS: American Philosophical Society

Bromley July 8. 1761.

Soon after my Eyes were open this Morning they were blest with a Letter from my dear and honour'd Friend.[4]

Mrs. Hawkesworth (for I have not seen the Doctor, but they seem to have both one Soul) bids me tell you they approve all your Scheme except that part of it which relates to me; and they shall expect to see all their Friends, who design them that Pleasure, next Tuesday. It is uncertain where I shall be then, but if I am not gone from hence I need not tell you I shall receive additional Happiness, tho what I enjoy is so great that I can scarce wish for more. Except those Hours I have spent with you, I never had my Time so fill'd up as it is now. Chearfulness, Benevolence and Goodsense reigne here. When my Dolly and I are by ourselves our Conversation generally turns upon two Gentlemen, whose Praises we repeat with Delight, and whose Virtues we resolve to imitate. I won't tell you who they are.[5]

Give my Duty to my dear Mother; and believe me to be with all imaginable Gratitude and Esteem Dear Sir Your most affectionate Servant and (as you permit to say so) Your faithful Friend
M STEVENSON.

Addressed: To / Dr. Franklin / Craven street / in the / Strand

From James and Ann Overall: Assignment

Copy: Commissioner of Records, City of Philadelphia

July 11, 1761

ABSTRACT: Ann Overall, wife of James Overall of Wellingborough [England], clockmaker, is niece and heir-at-law of Thomas Hine [here spelled "Hind"] late of Philadelphia, shoemaker, deceased, she being the only child and heir-at-law of Janes [*illegible*], her late mother, deceased, who was only surviving sister and heir-at-law of the said Thomas Hine. Whereas, by indenture dated July 30, 1760, between James and Ann Overall and John Overall of Wellingborough and by fine agreed to and since levied,[6] "All the Messuages Cottages Land Tenements

4. See immediately above.
5. Obviously BF and Dr. Hawkesworth.
6. A fine was a process of conveyancing which, among other advantages,

328

Plantations and Hereditaments" of James and Ann Overall in Phila-delphia or elsewhere in Pennsylvania formerly belonging to Hine and by his death descended to Ann, were conveyed to the use of such person or persons as James and Ann Overall might, during their joint lives, grant them to by deed or other properly executed writing; and whereas Benjamin Franklin "of Philadelphia aforesaid now residing in Craven Street in the City of Westminister Esqr." has contracted with the Over-alls for the purchase of the fee and inheritance of the house and lot here-inafter mentioned for £350, this indenture witnesses that James Overall and Ann his wife, acknowledging receipt of the said £350, do, and each of them does, grant and sell to Franklin all that messuage and lot on the north side of High Street, Philadelphia, bounded east by the lot of William Biles, west by the lot late of Sarah Read, widow, north by other land of Sarah Read, and south by High Street, which said house and lot were lately in the occupation of Mary Jacobs,[7] with the appur-tenances and all other lots and houses of James and Ann Overall, or either of them, in Philadelphia. The Overalls declare that the fine or fines shall inure "to the only Use and absolute Behoof" of Franklin, his heirs and assigns forever. Each of the Overalls covenants that one or both of them has the right to convey this property and that they or others claiming under them will upon request perform all reasonable acts for the further perfecting this grant, provided the person or persons making such further assurance be not required to travel more than ten miles from his or her place of abode.[8] Signed, sealed, and delivered by James Overall and Ann Overall (first being duly stamped) in the pres-ence of A. Winterbottom, Old Broad Street, London, and Thos. Coulthard, Clk. to Mr. Winterbottom. A receipt follows for £350 from

enabled a married woman effectually to convey her property. W.S. Holds-worth, *An Historical Introduction to the Land Law* (Oxford, 1927), pp. 116–18.

7. This property was in the block between Front and Second Streets, 20 ft. to the east of the house of Robert Grace, in which the Franklins had lived earlier and where the printing-office of Franklin and Hall still operated. According to a survey of about 1812, this lot measured 17 ft. 5 in. wide by 102 ft. deep (see next note). BF continued to receive rent from Mary Jacobs until 1789. Penrose R. Hoopes, "'Cash Dr To Benjamin Franklin,'" *PMHB*, LXXX (1956), 46–73.

8. To BF's annoyance, he discovered a few months later that, in spite of the Overalls' assurances to the contrary, the property had been mortgaged to a man named Spofford and the house was in great need of repairs. In the distribu-tion of BF's real estate among the heirs of his daughter Sarah Bache, January 14, 1812, this property passed to her daughter Elizabeth Harwood (D.3.4). Department of Records, Recorder of Deeds, City of Philadelphia, Book 1 C, 19, pp. 7–8, 15.

Franklin dated the same day. Acknowledged, also the same day, by James Overall and (separately and privately) by Ann Overall before Sir Thomas Blakiston, Lord Mayor of London, who also certifies that Abraham Winterbottom appeared before him the same day and made oath (which follows) that the Overalls signed in the presence of the two witnesses and that his and Thos. Coulthard's signatures are in their own handwritings. Recorded Dec. 12, 1761.

From David Hall   Letterbook copy: American Philosophical Society

Sir,   Philada. July 20. 1761.

Your Favour I received relating to Scott and McMichael's protested Bill,[9] for which am obliged to you, and much approve of your Conduct in that Affair.

Bills, at present, are so very high, that I do not know what to do about remitting you; they ask now Seventy-seven and a Half; however, if I don't hear quickly of your embarking for this Place, shall soon remit you more.

I think you should immediately order Caslon to cast the same Quantity of Brevier you sent over lately, and to do it with all Expedition.[1] My Reason for it is, That our Advertisements, for a considerable Time past, have been very bulky, and often continued for a great While,[2] which obliges us, many times, to distribute the standing Ones, in order to set up the new, which is a Loss; or else set many of them on Bourjois, which is also a very great Disadvantage.[3] I am, Sir, Yours, &c.   DAVID HALL

To Mr. Franklin.

Sent by the Philada. Packet, Capt. Budden.[4]

9. See above, pp. 301–2.

1. On Feb. 22, 1760, BF had paid William Caslon for a font of brevier type. It was shipped to Hall in the *Beulah*, Capt. James Gibbon, and arrived in Philadelphia about the first of June 1760. Hall acknowledged its receipt on July 2, 1760. See above, pp. 34 n, 179.

2. Issues of *Pa. Gaz.* for the first half of 1761 contain numerous long ("bulky") advertisements for lotteries, book sales, the Pa. Land Co., and imported goods.

3. Bourgeois (9 point) type, being larger than brevier (8 point), was less economical of space.

4. *Pa. Gaz.*, July 23, 1761, recorded the clearance of the *Philadelphia Packet*, Capt. Richard Budden.

From Isaac Norris

Letterbook copy: Historical Society of Pennsylvania

Dear Friend B F   Fairhill July 21st. 1761.

I am to acknowledge the receipt of your favours of the 27th of febry, and 14th of April, with my Account Current, the Articles of which Agree with my Remittences, and I return my Acknowledgments for Your Care in transacting them,[5] the Sence of the House Could not be Depended Upon in Relation to the Province Mony in your hands, Till their last Adjournment on the 23d of April, without giving any orders to the Trustees for drawing Bills,[6] and tho' by Law perhaps the Trustee's have the power, I know they will Not Venture to Draw for that Mony Without an order of the Assembly, so That As they Stand Adjourned to the begining of Sept. it will Continue in its present Situation, At least Till that Time,[7] Under These Circumstances it Would have been of Advantage to the Province had You Venturd to Deposite the remainder of That Mony on the Same Terms with the £15,000 but the Reasons Advanced for Not doing it have Great weight;[8] and we must be satisfyd with what has been done. On the 1st of May last I wrote my Sentiments Upon it, and gave hints of the Motion of one of our Members[9] on That occasion, but as he was not Seconded, it drop'd, he was very earnest for having the Mony drawn for Imeditatly, but as Nothing further was done in it, That Mony

5. Neither letter has been found. Norris' account book, 1735–65 (Lib. Co. Phila.), shows that on May 27, 1761, he received a detailed account from BF listing receipts and expenditures of £4775 6s. 4d. between Jan. 3, 1759, and Feb. 20, 1761. For a description of this account, see above, VIII, 147–8.

6. For Norris' mention, May 1, 1761, of "high Flights" in the Assembly over BF's investment of the parliamentary grant for expenditures of 1758, see above, p. 310.

7. For the Assembly's action on the parliamentary grant for expenditures of 1760, see below, pp. 358–9.

8. In December 1760 BF had bought £15,000 of the 4 percent annuities of 1760 for £13,781 17s. 6d. Since stocks were "still falling," he had decided against investing the remainder of the parliamentary grant in his hands until he could do so more profitably. See above, p. 254.

9. Probably William Allen, who later boasted of having been instrumental in depriving BF of the management of the next parliamentary grant. Lewis B. Walker, ed., *The Burd Papers. Extracts from Chief Justice Allen's Letter Book* ([Pottsville, Pa.], 1897), p. 49.

will in all liklihood be Continued in the Stocks till their rise may Encourage the House to give orders for drawing for it, Whether that may happen at their Next Seting, or be left to the Suceeding Assembly, is Uncertain, What Can I say to your Seperate Paper,[1] I am sorry for it, and have somtime since wrote to my old Acquaintance on that head, I have not yet mentiond Any Thing of his former Letter, to me, but shall Take Care to do what is Necessary on my part on the first Sutible Opportunity. I have not yet heard where Mr. Chambers,[2] recommen[d]ed under the 14th of April is, but learn upon enquiry That he has Not yet reached this Place, Whenever he does, I shall be pleas'd to do him all the Good Offices in my Power. I am obligd to Close My Brother Just Now Sending me up the Two Bills, of Exchange[3] and Informing me That Capt. Budden has left Town[4] and I must Depend Upon Some Persons following him, I am, Your affectionate Friend I N

I have inclosed two Bills of Exchange for £100 sterling each
No. 37 John Hunter on Messrs. Thomlinson Colebrooke

Nesbitt & Hanbury	£100. 0. 0.
38 Ditto On Ditto	100. 0. –
	£200 0. 0

1. Not found, but probably relating to Robert Charles's decision to resign his position as Pa. agent. Charles had informed Norris of it in a letter of Oct. 16, 1760, which the speaker received "at the end of January" and to which he replied May 31, 1761 (letterbook copy, Hist. Soc. Pa.) asking for the agent's accounts with the province "as soon as possible." Norris informed the Assembly of this resignation in September 1761. 8 *Pa. Arch.*, VI, 5262. The date of Charles's letter invalidates Richard Jackson's assumption (in a letter to BF, April 4, 1763) that the Assembly's refusal to honor the two agents' signed undertaking before the Privy Council Committee, Aug. 28, 1760, on the taxation of proprietary estates, had caused Charles's resignation, for news of the Committee hearing and the agents' action had not even reached Philadelphia when Charles wrote. His reasons for giving up the agency are obscure; they may have involved dissatisfaction over his salary and BF's greater prominence in the negotiations with governmental officials.

2. See above, p. 309.

3. BF recorded the receipt of these bills on Sept. 23, 1761. "Account of Expences," p. 61; *PMHB*, LV (1931), 131.

4. *Pa. Gaz.*, July 23, 1761, reported the clearance of the *Philadelphia Packet*, Capt. Richard Budden. She arrived at Gravesend, Sept. 3, 1761, *London Chron.*, Sept. 3–5, 1761.

Which please to receive for my Account, Bills are become so scarce and the Exchange so high that it is difficult now to procure them. I detain my Brother's Man in hopes to reach Captain Budden. I N

NB This Letter was designed to go by Captain Budden but it got to Town too late for him and CN informs me that he put it on board Captain Marshall in a Schooner Via Corke which saild the 30th July.[5]

BF rec this Letter ackd 8br. 9th. 1761

First Bills of Excha £200. o.

To Samuel Preston Moore ALS: Haverford College Library

Dear Sir, London, July 24. 1761
I have the Pleasure of sending you enclos'd the Royal Approbation of your Act.[6] What the Expence of the Solicitation will be, I cannot yet tell you, not having yet receiv'd the Bills. But I shall discharge it, and acquaint you per next Opportunity.[7] With great Esteem, I am, Dear Sir, Your most obedient humble Servant

B FRANKLIN

S.P. Moore Esqr

From Mary Stevenson ALS: American Philosophical Society

Dear Sir Wanstead July 30th. 1761.
I cannot return your Book[8] without making some little Acknow[le]dgment of my Obligation. You did me great Honour by

---

5. *Pa. Ga*., July 23, 1761, reported that the schooner *Creighton*, Capt. W. Marshall, was outward bound for Cork; but the issue of August 6 reported the clearance of the schooner *Triton*, Capt. W. Marshall, for Cork.

6. The Pa. act of Sept. 27, 1757, empowering Moore, his wife, and his father-in-law to grant land titles on behalf of their beneficiaries received the royal approbation on June 25, 1761; see above, pp. 271–2 n, and below, p. 340.

7. The expenses for soliciting the confirmation of Moore's act were £36 15*s.*; see below, p. 340.

8. Evidently a rather loose use of the word, because in another place Polly

333

entrusting me with it, and I receiv'd a high Pleasure in the Perusal. Give me leave to say the Pleasure I receiv'd proceeded not wholly from the Merit of the Writings, but from my Esteem and Affection for the Author; yet I will so far compliment my Understanding to think I should have been instructed and convinc'd by the same Words deliver'd by another, tho' I should not have been equally delighted. I told Dr. Hawkesworth, the other day, he was a dangerous Man: I thought you so, long ago. For you have such a Power of Perswasion you can make me think what you please. How happy is it a good Heart is join'd to that Power!

I cannot longer indulge myself in this pleasing Employment, for I have appointed to spend the day, with Mr. and Mrs. Lehook,[9] at the Devil's House, a Place by the Water side, where we hope to see the West-India Fleet pass,[1] and we are to go soon. I therefore took some of your morning (not Dr. Hawkesworth's) for a last look at the Book, and to assure you I am Dear Sir Your gratefully affectionate Servant   M STEVENSON.

My Duty to my Mother.

Addressed: To | Dr. Franklin.

---

writes of returning BF's "Manuscript" (below, p. 354) and because in replying to this letter on Aug. 10, 1761 (below, pp. 338–9), BF acknowledged receiving his "Papers," by which he almost certainly meant the scientific letters, written in 1752–54, which he sent Polly in April; see above, p. 308 n. The papers may, of course, have been bound up to protect them, giving them the appearance of a book. Polly left the papers with John Stanley (above, p. 320 n) from whom BF received them in a little more than a week.

9. Probably Ronjat Lehook and his wife. *London Chron.,* May 29–June 1, 1762, reported that Lehook, "an eminent merchant of this city," died at Wanstead on May 29, 1762.

1. A report from Deal, July 26, stated that ninety ships from the Leeward Islands had arrived under convoy and had sailed for the river, and a report of the next day recorded the arrival at Deal of "about thirty merchant ships from Jamaica." Both in *London Chron.,* July 25–28, 1761.

Record of Stock Purchases

Copy:[2] Historical Society of Pennsylvania

I. N.

1761 July 5th. paid for £10,000 Scrip of 1761[3]
the preceeding Payments being

made	£4,800: —: —
28 paid for this Monthly Payment	1,000: —: —
Augst. 14 paid the Remaining Payments	3,000: —: —
	£8,800: —: —

£10,000 Stock at 88 P Ct. per
London Chron. No. 707
from July to July 7: 1761[4]

Commission £4,800. for	
Brokers	12: 10: —
	£8,812: 10: —
do. Cash recd for advanced Payments made this day on the Scrip[5]	16: 7: 10
Nt Cost of £10,000 Stock	£8,796: 2: 2

Endorsed: July. 1761 Ten thousand Pound Scrip at 88 per Cent. the Net Cost £8,796. 2. 2 No. 4

2. In a clerk's hand. The endorsement, I.N., in the left-hand corner shows that BF submitted this document, as he did every other paper relating to his stock purchases for the province, to Speaker Norris.

3. This was BF's final purchase on the province's behalf. Between December 1760 and August 1761 he had paid £26,977 19s. 8d. (including broker's commissions and deductions for pre-payments) for stock whose face value was £30,000. See above, pp. 254, 313. BF recorded the present series of payments in his "Account of Expences," p. 60; *PMHB,* LV (1931), 131.

4. *London Chron.,* number 707 (July 4–7, 1761), lists the price of "Scrip. 1761" at "88 a 87⅜."

5. BF recorded receiving this sum in "Account of Expences," p. 61; *PMHB,* LV (1931), 131.

From Isaac Norris

Letterbook copy: Historical Society of Pennsylvania

B F   Augt 5th 1761

I wrote the Above[6] in much haste, and yet it got To Town too late, but my Brother informs me he forwarded it a few days after by Capt. Marshall in a Schooner bound to Corke, which may Possably reach London Sooner Than if it had been sent by Capt. Budden; There is an Account in Town That the Ship Indian Trader is Taken off our Capes, and a Rumour That Budden is also taken; But the Last I hope is not True.[7] I have set my self A very great Task in order to settle Effectualy the Account of the Books I had of Osborn's Parcel,[8] which is To Transcribe My Catalogue of Them, and which would have been needless, had your Son had Time, as he intended to have Calld on Me, and Counted the Numbers from my lists Of Them, with Their Titles. There are some in the Assembly Library which I will Endeavor to get the House to Take if they Incline to it, and Then Settle with Them, I have many remaining after taking all the Several Editions of the Same Book, and Several of the Same Edition which I have given away, Chas. Thomson[9] had a few of Them, what shall be done with the remainder many are Rotten, having been laid in some Celler as I suppose, and not a few have Their leaves entirely

6. See above, pp. 331–3.

7. *Pa. Ga₮.*, Aug. 6, 1761, reported that the *Indian Trader*, Capt. Anthony Robinson, was taken and carried into Bayonne. On October 15, however, it reported that the ship was retaken by the *Admiral Durrell*, privateer, and sent to Guernsey. *London Chron.*, Aug. 27–29, 1761, reported that Captain Budden in the *Philadelphia Packet* had reached Spithead; and in the issue of Sept. 3–5 that he had passed Gravesend on September 3.

8. Probably the "parcell of Old Books" which Thomas Osborne (above, VII, 176 n) originally sent James Read and which, through means not altogether clear, had come into Norris' possession. Norris had hoped to settle his account with Osborne in April 1758, but, having been prevented by "frequent Interruptions," he directed BF, Jan. 17, 1759, to pay the bookseller £40. BF complied on June 7, 1759, but apparently the sum was insufficient. See above, VIII, 57–8, 169–70, 228–9. "Account of Expences," p. 41; *PMHB*, LV (1931), 120. The "intricate Account" seems to have been still unsettled in 1764. Osborne to BF, November 1764, APS.

9. For Charles Thomson, author of *An Enquiry into the Causes of the Alienation of the Delaware and Shawanese Indians*, see above, VII, 266 n.

Stuck Together with Printer's Ink. They are not, at best, for Common reading, and perhaps would not be of any Advantage To an Auction of Books Suited to the Present Taste of Readers; I imagine this has fallen under your Notice in former Sales; however I will endeavour to finish my part as Soon as I Can. I have not mentiond in any of my Letters, since the 22d of October last[1] That Thomas Lloyd After I had Clos'd That letter, calld upon me for it, pretty late at Night, and Just at parting proposed That he might be Taken or Some Unforeseen Accident might happen on his Voyage, by which he might be Necessitated To make use of the Credit of his Friends whilst abroad, and desird I would give him one, to the Value of about A hundred pounds, this I did in a Separate letter which he did not Expect To make Use of, but if he presents the Letter be so kind as to pay it.[2] I am, &c.   I N

I have enclosed second Bills of Exchange for £200 Sterling.

[*In the margin:*] BF recd this ackd 8br. 9. 1761[3]
2d. Bills.

To Deborah Franklin   ALS: American Philosophical Society

My dear Child   London, Aug. 7. 1761

I wrote to you June 13. July 11. July 22. and July 24.[4] I have now little to add, except to acquaint you that we continue pretty well, tho' I begin to feel the want of my usual yearly Journeys.[5] We shall therefore, having little to do at present, set out in a few Days for Harwich and possibly may take a Trip over to Holland,[6] but purpose to be again in London, God willing, before the Coronation. My Love to my dear Sally, whom with you I long to see, and to all Friends. I am, my dearest Debby Your ever loving husband   B FRANKLIN

1. See above, p. 239.
2. BF recorded paying Thomas Lloyd (above, VI, 380 n) £50 on June 10, 1761, and again on July 5, 1761. "Account of Expences," p. 60; *PMHB*, LV (1931), 131.
3. Not found.
4. None of these letters have been found.
5. For these earlier journeys, see above, VIII, 114–15, 133–46, 430–1, and this volume, p. 231 n.
6. For BF and WF's trip to the Netherlands, see below, pp. 364–8.

To Mary Stevenson

ALS: Yale University Library[7]

Dear Polley, Cravenstreet, Aug. 10. 61

I received yesterday my Papers.[8] I had sent for them before to Mr. Stanley's, but Peter found no one at home. It has however been of no Damage to me, except being so long without the Pleasure of reading your agreable little Letter that accompanied them.

We are to set out this Week for Holland, where we may possibly spend a Month, but purpose to be at home again before the Coronation.[9] I could not go without taking Leave of you by a Line at least, when I am so many Letters in your Debt.

In yours of May 19.[1] which I have before me, you speak of the Ease with which Salt Water may be made fresh by Distillation, supposing it to be, as I had said, that in Evaporation the Air would take up Water but not the Salt that was mix'd with it. It is true that distill'd Sea Water will not be salt, but there are other disagreable Qualities that rise with the Water in Distillation; which indeed Several besides Dr. Hales[2] have endeavoured by sundry Means to prevent; but as yet their Methods have not been brought much into Use. I have his Pieces on the Subject, which I will leave with your Mother for your Perusal, as you may possibly make her happy a Day or two with your Company before our Return.

I have a singular Opinion on this Subject, which I will venture to communicate to you, tho' I doubt you will rank it among my Whims. It is certain that the Skin has *imbibing* as well as *discharging* Pores;[3] witness the Effects of a Blister Plaister, etc. I have read that a Man hired by a Physician to stand by way of Experi-

7. Printed as Letter LII in *Exper. and Obser.*, 1769 edit., pp. 458–60, but with the omission of the first paragraph and the postscript. Sparks, Bigelow, and Smyth all reprinted the text with these omissions.

8. For these papers and Polly's covering letter, see above, pp. 333–4.

9. On BF and WF's trip to the Netherlands, see below, pp. 364–8.

1. Above, pp. 318–20.

2. For Dr. Steven Hales's treatises on the distillation of sea water, see footnote to the letter cited immediately above.

3. In his treatise on "The Animal Oeconomy," written in 1733 and 1734 and sent to BF in 1745, Cadwallader Colden proposed that the skin "may perspire and absorb at the same time" through "*absorbent Vessels* intermix'd with the perspiratory Ducts on the external and internal Superficies of the Body." BF found this theory an improvement on Hales's hypothesis, advanced in his *Vegetable Staticks* (1727), that the body was alternately in

ment in the open Air naked during a moist Night, weighed near 3 Pounds heavier in the Morning. I have often observ'd myself, that however thirsty I may have been before going into the Water to swim, I am never long so in the Water. These imbibing Pores, however, are very fine, perhaps fine enough in filtring to separate Salt from Water; for tho' I have been soak'd by swimming, when a Boy, several Hours in the Day for several Days successively in Saltwater, I never found my Blood and Juices salted by that means, so as to make me thirsty or feel a salt Taste in my Mouth: And it is remarkable that the Flesh of Sea Fish, tho' bred in Salt Water, is not salt. Hence I imagine, that if People at Sea, distress'd by Thirst when their fresh Water is unfortunately spent, would make Bathing-Tubs of their empty Water Casks, and filling them with Sea Water, sit in them an Hour or two each Day, they might be greatly reliev'd. Perhaps keeping their Clothes constantly wet might have an almost equal Effect; and this without Danger of catching Cold. Men do not catch Cold by wet Clothes at Sea. Damp but not wet Linnen may possibly give Colds; but no one catches Cold by Bathing, and no Clothes can be wetter than Water itself. Why damp Clothes should then occasion Colds, is a curious Question, the Discussion of which I reserve for a future Letter, or some future Conversation.[4]

Adieu, my dear little Philosopher. Present my respectful Compliments to the good Ladies your Aunts, and to Miss Pitt; and believe me ever Your affectionate Friend and humble Servant

B FRANKLIN

P.S. I begin to see a Rival in Dr. Hawkesworth.[5] But, what is uncommon with Rivals, the more he likes you, and you him, the more, if possible, I shall esteem you both.

"imbibing" and "perspirable" states and made "a little Machine to try an Experiment" to test it. See above, III, 33–5, 47. Thus BF's opinion on the actions of the pores was by no means as "singular" as he implied.

4. By 1773 BF had concluded that neither dampness nor wetness caused colds, that their causes were "totally independent of wet and even of cold." BF to Barbeu Dubourg, March 10, 1773, Dubourg, ed., *Oeuvres de M. Franklin* (2 vols., Paris, 1773), II, 311.

5. In her letter of July 30, 1761, Polly had commented that Hawkesworth was a "dangerous Man" because of his persuasiveness. Writing to BF, Nov. 8, 1769, Hawkesworth reported: "I have just received a Line from the Virgin Mary, and I dine with her at Kensington on Fryday; I hope there will be no Jealousy in Heaven for my wife will be of the Party." Haverford Coll. Lib.

From Francis Eyre: Bill and Receipt

DS: Library Company of Philadelphia

BENJAMIN FRANKLYN ESQR

For Samuel Preston Moore's Private Act of Assembly,
past in Pensilvania and confirmed by His Majesty in Council.[6]

1761.

16. Janry.	Fees at the Council Office		
	Order referring said Act to a Committee	3: 2: 6	
	Copy of the Act annexed	1: –: –	
20.	Committee Order referring it to the Board of Trade	2: 2: 6	
	Copy of the Act annexed	1: –: –	
5 June	Committee Report thereon	1: 10: –	
25 Do.	Order confirming the Act	4: 2: 6	
	Record Keepers Fee	2: 2: –	14: 19: 6

NB. This Act was referr'd among Others
by Mr. Penn, who payd for it in the
Gross, yet the Fees are thus charged
to Mr. Eyre.

NB. also, The Board of Trade referr'd it
with Others to their Counsel, And
have hitherto made no Demand; If
they do their Fees will be inserted.

Paid Sir Mathew Lamb Counsel to the Board of Trade, his Fee, on this Act being referr'd to him	5: 5: –
Do. to his Clerk	–: 5: –
Do. for a Copy of his Report	–: 10: 6
For all my own Trouble Attendances at the Publick Offices getting this Act passed through, Copys thereof and the Orders &c.	10: 10: –
Paid Porters Petty Expences and Gratuitys	5: 5: –
	£36: 15: –

RECED the 10th. of August 1761, of Benjamin Franklyn Esqr. thirty six Pounds fifteen Shillings, in full by me   FRAS. EYRE[7]

Recd. Jany. 18 1762 of S.P.Moore the above sum in Current money at 75 percent per C[urren]t Exchange amounting to £64. 6. 3.   D FRANKLIN

To Samuel Preston Moore ALS: Library Company of Philadelphia

Dear Sir,   London, Augt. 13. 1761.

Inclosed I send the Account of Charges in Solliciting your Act, amounting to £36 15s. 0d.[8] The Act itself with the Royal Approbation engross'd on Parchment, I sent you per Mr. Wells,[9] and hope it will get safe to hand. I am, with great Esteem, Dear Sir, Your most obedient humble Servant   B FRANKLIN

S. Preston Moore Esqr

Addressed: To / Samuel Preston Moore Esqr / Philadelphia / Per favour of / Mr Hilborne[1]

Notation on address page:[2]

```
36. 15. 0
18.  7. 6
 9.  3. 9
64.  6. 3
     18. 3
63.  8. 0
      9. -
```

6. This bill well illustrates what it cost a colonial, whose affairs necessitated a private act, to get that act confirmed in Great Britain. For the circumstances in this case and the procedures involved, see above, pp. 271–2 n, 278, 279, 333, and the letter immediately below.

7. BF recorded this payment in "Account of Expences," p. 61; *PMHB*, LV (1931), 131.

8. For Moore's Act, see the document immediately above and the references cited in its first footnote.

9. Not identified.

1. Not identified.

2. Down through the first addition these figures indicate Moore's method of determining in Pa. currency the amount he was to pay DF for this bill of £36 15s.: the amount in sterling plus 50 per cent and 25 per cent, equalling 75 per cent exchange. See the end of the document immediately above. The significance of the remaining figures escapes the editors.

Of the Meanes of Disposing the Enemie to Peace

Printed in *The London Chronicle*, August 11–13, 1761; also rough notes and draft: American Philosophical Society

This paper was part of Franklin's campaign to prevent a premature and disadvantageous peace. As such, it is closely linked in argument as well as in purpose with "A Description of those, who, at any rate, would have a Peace with France," published in *The London Chronicle*, Nov. 22–24, 1759 (above, VIII, 446–7). In this instance he employed one of his characteristic devices: a composition of his own which he gravely attributed to another source. The supposititious author was Tommaso Campanella (1568–1639), a Dominican (not a Jesuit as Franklin and others thought him to have been), who wrote in 1601 a treatise called *De Monarchia Hispanica Discursus*, recommending a suitable foreign policy to the Spanish government. First published in a German translation, 1620, later in several Latin editions, it appeared in an English translation by Edmund Chilmead in 1654. William Prynne gave it further circulation in England about 1660, when he reissued the Chilmead text under the title *Thomas Campanella an Italian Friar and Second Machiavel*. This title and Prynne's comments gave the author an almost wholly undeserved reputation for nefarious intrigue, which he still retained a century later when Franklin concocted his spurious chapter and cited it as coming from a non-existent English translation.

Among Franklin's surviving papers is a two-page set of rough notes enumerating the classes of Englishmen whom he was about to describe as eager for a premature peace and listing some of their supposed unpatriotic motives. He checked most of them off his list as he wrote. There also survives a draft of the paper as a whole, with the introductory and concluding paragraphs by "A Briton" added at the end and a notation as to where they were to go in the fair copy. There are numerous revisions in the draft; a few will be indicated in footnotes to illustrate Franklin's methods of composing and polishing such writings.

To the Printer of the London Chronicle. [August 13, 1761]
SIR,

I send you for your excellent Paper, an extract from the famous Jesuit Campanella's discourses address'd to the King of Spain, intituled, *Of the Meanes of extending the Greatnesse of the Spanish Monarchie.*[3] The language is a little antiquated, being the old

3. The introductory paragraph of the draft differs almost completely from the printed version. Campanella is not named, but the *Chronicle's* corres-

translation in the edition of 1629; but the matter contain'd is so *apropos* to our present situation (only changing *Spain* for *France*) that I think it well worth the attention of the Publick at this critical conjuncture, as it discovers the arts of our enemies, and may therefore help in some degree to put us on our guard against them. After discoursing largely on the wars to be made, particularly against England and Holland, the conquests to be attempted, and the various means of securing them when gained, he comes to his

CHAP. XIV.

Of the Meanes of disposing the Enemie to Peace.[4]

"Warres, with whatsoever prudence undertaken and conducted, do not always succeed; many thinges out of mans power to governe, such as dearthe of provisions, tempests, pestilence, and the like, oftentimes interfering, and totally overthrowing the best designes; so that these enemies* of our Monarchie, though apparentlie at first the weaker, may, by disastrous events of warre on our part, become the stronger; and though not in such degree as to endanger the bodie of this great kingdome, yet,[5] by their greater power of shipping and aptness in sea-affaires, to be able to cut off, if I may so speak, some of its smaller limbes and members, that, being remote therefrom, are not easilie defended; to wit, our islands and colonies in the Indies; thereby however depriving the

*England and Holland.

———

pondent says he had lately met with "an old Quarto Book on a Stall, the Title Page and the Author's name wanting, but containing Discourses address'd to some King of Spain." The last leaf of the translation, he says, recorded that the book had been "printed at London by Bonham Norton and John Bill, Printers to the King's most excellent Majesty, M,DC,XXIX." From references in the text the letter writer concludes that the author must have been a Jesuit.

4. In the draft BF first wrote conventionally "Means" and "Enemy," and started the text with his usual spelling. Before he had finished the first sentence, however, the idea of using archaic spellings apparently occurred to him. He went back and overwrote some words in the forms which appear here and continued in his draft, whenever he remembered to do so, to write "Warre" instead of "War," "Meanes" instead of "Means," "hardie" instead of "hardy," and the like. Archaisms he had overlooked at the time he apparently inserted in the fair copy to be sent to the newspaper.

5. After "stronger" BF first wrote "so far at least as," then substituted "and tho' . . . kingdom, yet" in the draft.

bodie of its wonted nourishment, so that it must thenceforthe languish and grow weake, if those parts be not recovered, which possibly may, by continuance of warre, be found unlikely to be done. And the enemie, puffed up with their successes, and hoping still for more, may not be disposed to peace on such termes as would be suitable to the honour of your Majestie, and to the welfare of your State and Subjectes. In such case, the following meanes may have good effect.

"It is well known, that these northerne people, though hardie of bodie, and bold in fight, be neverthelesse, through overmuch eating and other intemperance, slowe of wit and dull in understanding, so that they be oftimes more easilie to be governed and turned by skille than by force. There is therefore always hope, that by wise counsel and dextrous managemente, those advantages which through cross accidents in warre have been lost, may again with honour be recovered. In this place I shall say little of the power of money secretly distributed amongst grandees or their friends or mistresses,[6] that method being in all ages known and practised. If the *minds* of enemies can be *changed*, they may, be brought to grant willingly and for nothing, what much golde would scarcelie have otherwise prevailed to obtaine. Yet as the procuring this change is to be by fitte instruments, some few doublones will not unprofitablie be disbursed by your Majestie; the manner whereof I shall now brieflie recite.

"In those countries, and particularly in England, there are not wanting men of learning, ingenious speakers and writers, who are neverthelesse in lowe estate and pinched by fortune; these being privatelie gained by proper meanes, must be instructed in their sermons, discourses, writings, poems and songs, to handle and specially inculcate points like these which followe. Let them magnify the blessings of peace and enlarge mightily thereon, which is not unbecoming grave Divines and other Christian men;[7] let them expatiate on the miseries of warre, the waste of Christian bloode, the growing scarcitie of labourers and workmen, the dearness of

6. BF first added above the line "or Mistresses," then struck out these words and substituted "or Paramours," then apparently returned to his first addition in the fair copy.

7. BF first wrote "Prelates and Christian Men," then substituted "Divines" and politely added "other."

all foreign wares and merchandises, the interruption of commerce by the captures or delay of ships,[8] the increase and great burthen of taxes, and the impossibilitie of supplying much longer the expence of the contest; let them represent the warre as an un-measurable advantage to particulars, and to particulars only (thereby to excite envie against those that manage and provide for the same) while so prejudicial to the Commonweale and people in general: let them represent the advantages gained against us as trivial and of little import; the places taken from us as of small trade or produce, inconvenient for situation, unwholesome for ayre and climate, useless to their nations, and greatly chargeable to keepe, draining the home Countries both of men and money: let them urge, that if a peace be forced on us, and those places withheld, it will nourishe secret griefe and malice in the King and Grandees of Spain, which will ere long breake forthe in new warres, wherein those places may again be retaken, and lost with-out the merit and grace of restoring them willingly for peace-sake: let them represent the making and continuance of warres from view of gaine, to be base and unworthie a brave people; as those made from view of ambition are mad and wicked; and let them insinuate that the continuance of the present warre on their parte, when peace is offered,[9] hath these ingredients strongly in its nature. Then let them magnifie the great power of your Majestie, and the strength of your kingdome, the inexhaustible wealthe of your mines, the greatness of your incomes, and thence your abili-tie of continuing the warre; hinting withal, the new alliances you may possibly make; at the same time setting forth the sincere dis-position you have for peace, and that it is only a concerne for your honour and the honour of your realme, that induceth you to insist on the restitution of the places taken. If with all this they shrewdly intimate and cause it to be understood by artfull words, and beleeved, that their own Prince is himself in heart for peace on your Majesties termes, and grieved at the obstinacie and perverse-ness of those among his people that be for continuing the warre, a marvellous effect shall by these discourses and writings be pro-duced; and a wonderful strong party shall your Majestie raise

8. "The interruption . . . of ships" was a marginal insertion in the draft, further amplified in the printed version.

9. "When peace is offered" does not appear in the draft.

among your enemies in favour of the peace you desire; insomuch that their own Princes and wisest Councellours will in a sort be constrained to yeeld thereto. For in this warre of words, the avarice and ambition, the hopes and fears, and all the croud of human passions, will, in the minds of your enemies, be raised, armed, and put in array, to fight for your interests, against the reall and substantiall interest of their own countries. The simple and undiscerning many, shall be carried away by the plausibilitie and well seeming of these discourses; and the opinions becoming popular,[1] all the rich men, who have great possessions, and fear the continuance of taxes, and hope peace will end them, shall be imboldened thereby to cry aloud for peace; their dependents who are many, must do the same: all marchants, fearing loss of ships and greater burthens on trade by farther duties and subsidies, and hoping greater profittes by the ending of the warre, shall join in the cry for peace: All the usurers and lenders of monies to the state, who on a peace hope great profit from their bargaines, and fear if the warre be continued, the State shall become bankeroute,[2] and unable to pay them: these who have no small weight, shall joine the cry for peace: All the gowne and booke statesmen, who maligne the bold conductors of the warre, and envie the glorie they may have thereby obtained; these shall cry aloud for peace; hoping, that when the Warre shall cease, such men becoming less necessarie shall be more lightelie esteemed, and themselves more sought after:[3] All the officers of the enemies armies and fleets, who wish for repose, and to enjoy their spoiles, salaries, or rewards, in quietness, and without peril, these, and their friends and families, who desire their safetie, and the solace of their societie, shall all cry for peace: All those who be timorous by nature, amongst whom be reckoned men of learning that lead sedentarie lives, using little exercise of bodie, and thence obtaining but few and weake spirits; great Statesmen, whose natural spirits be exhausted by

1. The first part of this sentence, through "popular," was a marginal insertion in the draft.
2. Thus in the draft. This form of "bankrupt," derived from the French, was commonly used in the sixteenth and early seventeenth centuries, but had become obsolete by BF's time. *OED*.
3. "All the gowne and booke statesmen . . . more sought after" is a marginal insertion in the draft.

much thinking, or depress'd by over-much feasting; together with all women, whose power, weake as they are, is not a little among such men; these shall incessantly speake for peace: And finallie, all Courtiers, who suppose they conforme thereby to the inclinations of the Prince;* all who are *in* places of profit, and fear to lose them, or hope for better; all who are *out* of places, and hope to obtain them; all the worldly-minded clergie, who seeke preferment; these, with all the weight of their character and influence, shall joine the cry for peace, till it becomes one universal clamour, and no sound but that of *Peace, Peace, Peace,* shall be heard from every quarter. Then shall your Majesties termes of peace be listened to with much readiness, the places taken from you be willingly restored, and your kingdome, recovering its strength, shall only need to waite, a few years for more favourable occasions, when the advantages to your power proposed by beginning the warre, but lost by its bad successe, shall, with better fortune, be finallie obtained."

What effect the artifices here recommended might have had in the times when this Jesuit[4] wrote, I cannot pretend to say; but I believe, the present age being more enlightened, and our people better acquainted than formerly with our true national interests, such arts can now hardly prove so generally successful. For we may with pleasure observe, and to the honour of the British people, that though writings and discourses like these have lately not been wanting, yet few in any of the classes he particularises seem to be affected by them; but all ranks and degrees among us persist hitherto in declaring for a vigorous prosecution of the war, in preference to an unsafe, disadvantageous peace.[5]

Yet, as a little change of fortune may make such writings more attended to, and give them greater weight, I think the publication of this piece, as it shows the spring from whence these scribblers draw their poisoned waters, may be of publick utility. I am, Sir, yours, &c.   A BRITON.

*Ad Exemplum Regis, &c.

4. The draft reads "our Author" instead of "this Jesuit."
5. The draft concludes this sentence: "to an unsafe, disadvantageous, or dishonourable Peace."

From Isaac Norris

ALS: American Philosophical Society; letterbook copy: Historical Society of Pennsylvania

Dear Friend B Franklin   Fairhill, Augt. 19th. 1761

Your Wife has very kindly sent me Notice that if I write by this Post it will reach the Packet from N. York[6] and that She will take care of the conveyance. I write therefore to acknowledge the receipt of yours 9th May and the 13th of June last[7] which came to my Hands the 12th. Instant. I am well pleased with the Additional purchase of Stock on Account of the Province[8] and hope the whole may be invested in them as I believe no part of that Mony will be drawn out 'till they Rise as must certainly be the Case upon a Peace.

As the Lords of the Treasury have apportioned the Parliamentary Grant for 1759 I presume the House at their next Meeting will by a Law impower some Persons to receive it,[9] and take care that it shall be appropriated to the lessning our Taxes and Sinking the Bills of Credit already issued in due time.[1] It is unfortunate for the Province that a suitable provision had not been made in the Law passed by Govr. Denny[2] which might have been done by a few Words, but that cannot now be amended.

The Assembly immediatly on hearing the accession of his present Majesty to the Throne of G. Britain addressed, and I know the Address and a Copy have been transmitted by different Conveyances but I do not know by what Vessels they were sent.[3] I hope,

6. DF erred. The *Earl of Halifax* packet, Capt. Bolderson, sailed from N.Y. the day this letter was written and arrived in Falmouth Sept. 14. *London Chron.*, Sept. 17–19, 1761.

7. Neither of these letters has been found.

8. A reference to BF's purchase, May 5, 1761, of £5000 of the "3 per Cent Consolidated at 87½ per Cent." See above, p. 313.

9. See above, p. 223 n.

1. For the arrangements made by the Assembly in its September session for the management of the parliamentary grant for 1759, see below, p. 359 n.

2. The Agency Act of Sept. 29, 1759; see above, VIII, 442 n.

3. George III succeeded to the throne on Oct. 25, 1760. The Pa. Assembly adopted an "Address of Condolence to his present Majesty, on the late Death of his Royal Grandfather, and of Congratulation, on his own happy Accession to the Crown of Great Britain" on Feb. 3, 1761, and ordered that copies be sent to its agents for presentation to the King. 8 *Pa. Arch.*, VI, 5176, 5185–6.

however they may have escaped the Enemy. I have already mentioned my Letter of Credit to Colo. Lloyd which he asked of me and I gave him after my Letter by him was sealed up. I now approve of that payment to him and shall Credit it in your Account with me.[4] I have already sent Two Bills of Exchange the first and Second by way of Cork. I now inclose the third Bills John Hunter on Messrs. Thomlinson &c. No 37 and No 38 for a Hundred Pounds Sterling each.[5] Captain Hammet will sail in a few Days[6] as I am informed and by him I propose to add Duplicates of what I have written by way of Corke. I am your Assured Friend

ISAAC NORRIS

Please to purchase for me to make my Stock an even Sum in Hundred Pounds.[7]

From David Hall   Letterbook copy: American Philosophical Society

Sir,   Philada. Aug. 24. 1761.

In my last to you, of the 20th ult.[8] by the Philadelphia Packet, Capt. Budden, I owned the Receipt of yours relating to the protested Bill of Scott and McMichael, and signified my Approbation of your Conduct in that affair. In it I told you, that Exchange was at Seventy-seven and a Half, which was the Reason you had no Remittance from me by that Opportunity; and as they are now at Eighty, you have none by Hammit,[9] not caring to give so high an

4. For BF's payments to Col. Thomas Lloyd, see above, p. 337 n.

5. For these bills, see above, p. 332.

6. *Pa. Gaz.*, Aug. 27, 1761, reported the clearance of the *Dragon*, Capt. Francis Hammett.

7. The letterbook copy bears the notation: "B Franklin received this Letter and the Bills which were paid See his Letter Novr 25, 1761." BF's reply (not found) probably also reported that two days earlier he had complied with Norris' request about investments. BF's account with Norris (above, VIII, 147–8) shows that up to this time he had purchased for the speaker £4525 par value of stock and that on Nov. 23, 1761, he assigned to Norris "£375 of my Stock at 71⅛," making himself thereby creditor in the amount of £266 14s. 4½d. sterling. He recorded this transfer in "Account of Expences," p. 62; *PMHB*, LV (1931), 131.

8. See above, p. 330 n, for notes on matters mentioned here.

9. *Pa. Gaz.*, Aug. 27, 1761, recorded the clearance of the *Dragon*, Capt. Francis Hammett.

Exchange, but should be very glad to know your Mind on that Head. I likewise told you, that I thought it would be best for you immediately to order Caslon to cast the same Quantity of Brevier you sent over some time ago, and to have it ready to come as soon as possible, as our Advertisements of late have been very bulky and often continued long, which occasions us either to distribute them before they are done with, in order to set up the new Ones, which is a great Loss; or to compose many of them on Bourjois, which is also a considerable Disadvantage. I am Sir, Yours, &c.

DAVID HALL.

To Mr. Franklin

Sent by the Dragon Capt. Hammit, to London

From Thomas Ronayne[1] with Notes for a Reply

ALS: American Philosophical Society

Sir   Corke August the 26th. 1761.

I beg Leave to Communicate to you a few Experiments and observations on Electricity, both common and atmostpherical, and to have your opinion of them.

It seems to me that Electricks per Se or Non Conductors do not contain more of the Elctrick Fluid than Non Electricks.[2] For An Insulated Wire being heated at one end, and having Light threads hanging from any Part of it did not shew the Least sign of being Electrified when a Stick of wax was applied to the heated part of the wire; tho' wax becomes non Electrick by melting: Neither did an In[s]ulated Wire shew any Sign of Electricity after a Piece of

1. Thomas Ronayne (d. c. 1800), scion of an old Irish family, probably acquired his interest in science from his father Philip Ronayne (c. 1683–1755), a friend and correspondent of Newton. Interested in "atmospheric Electricity," the son began "experiments on the Air" in 1761 and "those on the Clouds" in 1762. *Journal* of the Cork Hist. and Archaeol. Soc., second series, XXIII (1917), 99–104. While BF's full reply to this letter has not been found, they corresponded further in 1766 and 1772.

2. To understand Ronayne's experiments it should be remembered that at this time the term "electrick per se" was commonly used for a substance (such as glass or wax) which in its normal state could store an electric charge but not transmit it, and "non electrick" for one (such as copper) which transmitted it but seemingly could not store it.

Melted Glass coold on it; tho' (According to Mr. Willson[3]) melted Glass is non electrick.

The Expansion, or contracktion of a body Seems not to Electrifie it for a Wire put in an open thermometer of Spirit of Wine, non electrick; or oil of Turpentine an electrick per se; Shew'd no Sign of electricity either when the Liquor contracted or expanded. The Air in a Room may be electrified either positively or negatively by applying either the hook or coating of a charg'd Phial to one end of an insulated Wire sharp Pointed at the other end.

The Electricity of the Air shews itself only by causing cork balls hung in contact, or threads, to repell each other. In a frost, in a fog, and sometimes in a Mist with small Rain I have found the Air without Doors to be electrified, and even in a frosty Night tho there was no Aurora Borealis; in all these Cases the Electricity was positive. When the Summer came I never could find the Air to be electrified except from Thunder or Showers and then the Electricity was sometimes negative, and sometimes positive. And was much Stronger than that in the winter. We had two Thunder Storms this Summer. In the 1st. I try'd Mr. Cantons curious Electrometer Described Phil: Transac. Vol 48 Part 2d. No 93[4] which I allways carry in my Pocket along with a stick of sealing wax and another of Glass but the wind agitated the Cork Balls in such a manner that I could not satisfie my self; *which is an inconvenience I know not how to remedy.*[5]

The Next day I satisfied mySelf both by the Electrometer and by holding a Pole round which a Wire was twisted while I Stood on wax. There were changes from negative to positive and from that to negative and lastly to positive.

3. For Benjamin Wilson, electrician and portrait painter, see above, IV, 391 n; VIII, 239–63.

4. Canton's "Electrometer" was a "small narrow box with a sliding cover" inside of which was a pair of pea-sized cork or elder balls attached to a wire "by linen threads of six inches long." The cover being pulled back and the balls being permitted to dangle in the air, they could by their attraction or repulsion determine the nature of the charge in the atmosphere. John Canton, "A Letter to the Right Honourable the Earl of Macclesfield . . . concerning some new electrical Experiments," *Phil. Trans.*, XLVIII (1754), 780–5.

5. The italicized words, here and in the queries below, are lightly underlined in the MS. Perhaps BF, not Ronayne, did this in preparation for drafting the notes of a reply which are here printed at the end of Ronayne's letter.

Queries concerning Thunder

How do the Clouds or Air become electrified? Why is the Electricity of the Clouds so Strong; when that of the Air is so weak. Why does not the Electrick Fire in or about a Cloud dissipate it; or at Least hinder it from Raining? *Was Rain Water caught in an electrick per se ever found to be electrified? Is a Cloud electrized more in Proportion than any other body? Were Light bodies ever observ'd to be attracted towards an Electrified Cloud?*

What is the Cause of the continued length of a Clap of Thunder? Can Fire balls and other Phoenomena seen with or without Lightning be accounted for by electrical Principles? In haste I am with Sincere respect, Your Most obliged humble Servant

THOS. RONAYNE

Addressed: To / Benjamin Franklin Esqr. / of / Philadelphia

[*On another page in Franklin's hand in red ink:*]

The Balls may be kept from the Wind by hanging them from the Cork within a thin Glass Phial; where they will nevertheless be affected by the State of Electricity in the Air.

Rain water, caught during a Thundershower, has been found to be electrified.

Small Fragments of Cloud are often seen to be attracted to the large Body of Cloud of a Thunder Gust. The Leaves on the Tops of Trees are observ'd to be drawn up wards when the Great Cloud first comes over them, and the Dust is also drawn up.

A number of Strokes from Cloud to Cloud, though all at the same Instant, will give Sounds that arrive at the Ear in Succession according to the different Distances.

From Mary Stevenson

ALS: American Philosophical Society

Dear Sir   Cravenstreet, Augt. 29. 1761.

I arriv'd here, very opportunely for my Mother and myself, on the day a Letter was to be sent to you, which saves her the Trouble and affords me the Pleasure of writing.[6] I am first to present her

6. BF and WF were traveling in the Netherlands with Richard Jackson; see below, pp. 364–8.

Thanks for your two kind Letters,[7] and then I must acknowledge my Obligation for your Remembrance of me in them.

No Person has call'd here except Mr. Johnston[8] for the Glasses, and the packet has not been sent for. My Mother receiv'd your Letter for Mrs. Franklin which she will take care of.[9] This is all she orders me to tell you, only she bids me add all the civil Things I can say to you for her; but as I judge of her Breast by my own, I think it will not be in my power to say all she means, for I never can express myself fully, and therefore I shall decline saying anything.

I have your Letter now before me in which you applaud the Zeal of the Romanists, and censure us (too justly I fear) with Indifference. I wish all the Members of the Reform'd Church had your Piety, and I wish that we could boast of you for one of the Pillars of it. Forgive me my dear Friend! I have a little Zeal for Religion, and I know nothing that would promote the Cause of it so much as Dr. Franklin's adding the Performance of it's Rituals to that inward Devotion of his Heart and his truely Virtuous Conduct.

A necessary Train of Thought brings to my Mind that your Rival (as you are pleas'd to call him[1]) with his amiable Partner, and my two Friends make us happy with their Company to day:[2] Indeed, Sir, I love him much, I love you *very* much, you may judge then what Pleasure it gives me to find you love each other. God bless my two amiable Friends! and may they continue to love her whose grateful Heart is highly sensible of the Obligation, and will most faithfully return it.

I thank you, my dear Preceptor, for your kind Letter which I receiv'd a few days before you left England.[3] To let you see I don't lose the Instructions you give, I remember'd you had related to me all which you then wrote, and that it might not slip my Memory I had pen'd it down. This did not lessen the Pleasure of

7. Not found.
8. Not identified.
9. Probably the letter BF wrote DF from Antwerp; see below, pp. 356–7.
1. Dr. John Hawkesworth; see above, p. 339.
2. Catherine and Dolly Blunt; see above, p. 327 n. Her other close friend, "Miss Pitt," had come to Craven Street with her, as the postscript mentions.
3. That of Aug. 10, 1761; see above, pp. 338–9, on the distillation of sea water and citing Stephen Hales's treatises on that subject.

your Letter, but rather added to it by confirming what I had written to be right. I have not yet seen the Book you left for me. Mr. Stanley apologiz'd to me about your not receiving your Manuscript sooner;[4] but I told him the delay was not attended with any bad Consequences.

I left my Aunts[5] this morning at Wanstead, both now pretty well, but my Aunt Rooke is just recovering from a fit of the Gout. All the rest of your Friends that I know are well. My Mother joins in every good and fervent Wish for you Welfare with Dear Sir your most sincere and affectionate humble Friend

M STEVENSON

Pitt, who came with me, desires her best Respects. God send you safe to us!

Dolly comes to me while I am writing and says, "Do you think it worth while to say anything for me?" She loves and honours you much.

Dr. Hawkesworth says I know his Heart, and I know he loves and honours you. I would have him write this himself, but he says he will not take anything from me.

My Mother I know would chuse something to be said from her to your Son, but as she don't tell me what I leave it to you; and if it may be done without impropriety you may say he has my good Wishes with hers.

Addressed: To / Dr. Benj. Franklin / to be left at the Post Office at / Amsterdam

From Mary Stevenson Draft: American Philosophical Society

Dear Sir Wanstead Septr 10. 1761.

I don't know whether to say I fear or I hope this won't reach you before you leave Holland, for I don't care how soon we have you in our Island again, and I wish you had no Attachment ever to draw you from it again, that is I wish your Attachments were all here.

4. For this "Manuscript" and John Stanley's connection with it, see above, pp. 333–4 n.
5. Mrs. Tickell and Mrs. Rooke.

My Mother wanted me to write another Letter to you while I was with her,[6] but my Time was so taken up with seeking for Places at the Coronation[7] that I had not Leisure during my stay which was very short, being oblig'd to attend my Friends the Miss Blunts,[8] who favour us with their Company at Wanstead. I just found Time to look into the Books you left for me of Dr. Hales,[9] which gave me a high Opinion of his Benevolence. The Methods for distilling Sea Water as you observe cannot be brought much into Use. The Expedient you propose for relieving the Distress People at Sea suffer from Thirst would be easy and you have prov'd it by Experiment to be efficacious. I don't doubt that you have made it publick, and I hope it will prove successful. You take notice that Men do not catch Cold by wet Clothes at Sea: I somewhere met with a Proposal for preventing the bad Effects of the exessive Dews in hot Countries by wetting the Clothes with Salt Water. I should ill deserve your good Opinion if I conceal'd my Errors from you who so candidly look over them, therefore I must confess that I did not express myself as I meant, for you understood that I thought Salt Water could with Ease be made fresh by Distillation, supposing it to be, as you had said, that in Evaporation the Air would take up Water but not the Salt that was mix'd with it. Now I conceiv'd that the Air had no Action in the Distillation and therefore the Particles of Salt which would be forc'd up by the Heat with the Water, not meeting the Air to repel them, would remain with it.[1] I find, however, I was not wrong in supposing part of the Salt must be detain'd by somewhat to which it will adhere.[2] I shall not trouble you any further at present with my

6. For the letter Polly wrote BF while visiting her mother, see immediately above.

7. The coronation of George III and Queen Charlotte took place on Sept. 22, 1761. Polly may have been seeking seats in the galleries in Westminister Hall and Westminister Abbey or in one of the houses or booths erected along the procession route, more likely the latter. For a detailed account of the coronation ceremonies, see *The Annual Register*, IV (1761), 215–42.

8. Catherine and Dolly Blunt.

9. See above, p. 338, for BF's promise to put Stephen Hales's treatises on the distillation of salt water at Polly's disposal and for his proposals on which Polly comments later in this letter.

1. For Polly's sentiments on the distillation of salt water, see above, p. 319.

2. Above the line at this point Polly inserted "to prevent it rising with," but it is not clear where she intended these words to go. Probably the sentence

Philosophy, because I must leave room for my Mother to write to you about Business, as I am not with her to do it. I was resolv'd nothing should prevent my writing to day as I promis'd I would send her a Letter for you, but I am afraid she will think it almost too late. The Stanleys and Hawkesworths dine with us to day.³ I shall tell the Doctor I have written to you to day and he will say, *If the Letter is not seal'd say something for me.* I believe I may venture to say he esteems you highly, and, what he thinks is more, loves you heartily. I should have a very indifferent Opinion of him if he did not, and could neither esteem or love him, for with the greatest Esteem and warmest Affection I am my honour'd Friend most sincerely yours   M STEVENSON.

To Deborah Franklin   ALS: American Philosophical Society

My dear Child,   Utrecht in Holland, Sept. 14. 1761
    I wrote to you just before we left London, that we were about to make a short Tour to Holland.⁴ I wrote to you since from Antwerp in Flanders,⁵ and am now to acquaint you, that having seen almost all the principal Places and Things worthy Notice in those two Countries, we are now on our Return to London, where we hope to be next Saturday or Sunday, that we may not miss the Coronation. At Amsterdam I met with Mr. Crellius, and his Daughter that was formerly Mrs. Neigh; her Husband Dr. Neigh died in Carolina, and she is married again and lives very well in that City.⁶ They treated us with great Civility and Kindness; and will be so obliging as to forward this Letter to you, a Ship being bound to New York from Amsterdam. We are in good Health, and have

should have concluded "to which it will adhere to prevent it rising with [the Water]."
    3. The Hawkesworths and Stanleys are mentioned in practically every letter which BF and Polly exchanged in the summer of this year.
    4. For the fullest surviving account of this tour, see below, pp. 364–8.
    5. This letter, apparently forwarded by Mrs. Margaret Stevenson, has not been found; see above, p. 353.
    6. For Joseph Crell, formerly the printer of a German newspaper in Philadelphia and partner of John Franklin in the Braintree glass factory, his daughter Anna, and her two husbands, the second of whom, Francis Farquhar, kept a tavern in Amsterdam, see above, IV, 65 n, 77–8 n.

had a great deal of Pleasure, and receiv'd a good deal of Information in this Tour that may be useful when we return to America. My Love to my dear Sally, and affectionate Regards to—all Pennsylvania. Billy presents his Duty. I am, my dear Debby, Your ever loving Husband   B FRANKLIN

Addressed: To | Mrs. Franklin | at the Post-Office | Philadelphia

Added on back: Forwarded by Yr Most Obt | JNO: GREENWOOD[7] | Amstr:

From Isaac Norris

Duplicate: American Philosophical Society; letterbook copy: Historical Society of Pennsylvania[8]

Duplicate.

Dear Friend B Franklin   Fairhill, Septr. 30th 1761
    A few Days before the last Assembly rose[9] I received your Letter of the 10th of July by the Packet, It came to Hand very seasonably and was read in the House on the 23d of September.[1] The Mem-

7. Probably John Greenwood (1727–1792), a painter and art dealer, who was born in Boston, spent several years in Surinam, moved to Amsterdam in 1758, and settled in London in 1764. *DNB*. A portrait of BF's sister-in-law Elizabeth, Mrs. John Franklin (C. 8), has been attributed to Greenwood, and the art historian, Alan Burroughs, has suggested that Greenwood may also have done the first known painting of BF (above, II, frontispiece), although in recent years he and others have attributed it to Robert Feke. Charles Coleman Sellers, *Benjamin Franklin in Portraiture* (New Haven and London, 1962), pp. 24–25.
    8. Norris sent BF both an original (not found) and a duplicate, unsigned but in his own hand. In the duplicate he deleted two paragraphs and part of the postscript, but the missing passages have fortunately survived in his letterbook copy. At the appropriate places the deletions are noted and the omissions supplied from the letterbook copy.
    9. The Pa. Assembly adjourned on Sept. 26, 1761, having been in session since September 7. 8 *Pa. Arch.*, VI, 5271.
    1. BF's letter has not been found. According to *Votes and Proceedings* it was read before the House on Sept. 19, 1761, not the 23d as Norris says. If by the letter's arrival "by the Packet" Norris meant the *Pitt* packet, which reached N.Y. on the evening of September 18 (*N.-Y. Mercury*, Sept. 21, 1761), his date for the reading is more probable since mail from N.Y. could not reach Philadelphia overnight. There is a possibility, however, that he meant

357

bers were all well Satisfied with the Succinct Account therein given of the Situation of the Publick Mony under your Care,[2] but the pressing Necessities of the Merchants and the strong Reports of a Peace, which gained Credit generally among the People[3] induced the House to order the Trustees "forthwith" to draw Bills of Exchange upon you for the net Proceeds of the first Parliamentary Grant and Allotment to this Province,[4] And I apprehend the Merchants will hurry the printing and drawing these Bills as soon as possible for which Reason I shall endeavour to get as speedy Conveyances as I can for this Intelligence and take due Care in transmitting Copies for fear of Miscarriage. The House at their last Sitting sent up to the Governor a Bill for receiving the remaining Proportions of the year 1759 and all Such future Parliamentary Grants as may be allotted to this Province[5] which the Governor enacted into a Law without any Amendments. By this Law Jno Sergant and Geo Aufrere of your Recommendation and

---

the brig *Yarmouth-Packet*, which had arrived in Philadelphia from Yarmouth by the beginning of September (*Pa. Ga{.*, Sept. 3, 1761). In that case the Assembly minutes were probably correct and would be consistent with the vote of the same day (mentioned below) to order bills of exchange drawn on BF as soon as possible.

2. For BF's investments for the province, see above, pp. 253, 313, 335.

3. On July 9, 1761, *Pa. Ga{.* published the declaration of France, Austria, Russia, and their allies, delivered at London, March 31, 1761, proposing a peace conference at Augsburg and the counter-declaration of Britain and Prussia, April 3, 1761, accepting the proposal. For the next two months the paper teemed with the accounts of the preparations for the conference (which never met) and with reports of preliminary negotiations conducted simultaneously in Paris by the British plenipotentiary, Hans Stanley, and in London by the secretary of the French Foreign Office, M. de Bussy. A dispatch from London, printed in the *Ga{ette*, Sept. 24, 1761, giving assurances with the "utmost confidence, and from the best authority, that we are at the very eve of a peace" was typical of the optimism which colored the news during this period. Beginning in October, however, more sober assessments of the European situation began to reach Pa., although it was not until December that the *Ga{ette* carried news of the failure of the Anglo-French negotiations, of the fall of Pitt, and of the imminence of a Spanish war. For the abortive negotiations in 1761, see Gipson, *British Empire*, VIII, 204–22.

4. The Assembly adopted this order to the Trustees of the provincial Loan Office on Sept. 19, 1761. 8 *Pa. Arch.*, VI, 5262–3.

5. For the parliamentary grant for 1759, see above, p. 223 n. Later grants will be discussed in succeeding volumes.

David Barclay junior and Jno Barclay formerly proposed by the Governor are empower'd to apply for and receive all such Monies as are or may be apportioned to this Province and when the Mony is received and Notified to the Trustees they, the Trustees, are to draw Bills of Exchange for the Amount in the Manner directed by the Act.[6] But as it was foreseen that the Application for, and receipt of the Grant of the Year 1759 and such future Allotments as might be made with other Circumstances which must attend before the Act could be effectually complied with, your Friends in the House, first moved and procured the present Nomination, as they judged it would not be agreeable or sute your Circumstances to be detained from your Family merely to attend that particular Business. But as I had no Intelligence in this Affair I had no part in the Debates or the Resolutions of the House on this Clause of the Act.[7]

The Committee have Reported and the House agreed to a ballance of £152. 7s. 5d. due to the Estate of R. Patridge[8] which I desire you would be pleased to pay to his Executors they giving an Acquittance on the payment thereof, and charge it to my Account. I have never heard from Sherwood but once and could never get any information of the other Executor nor have I received

6. For the "Act for appointing Certain Persons ... to apply for and receive the Distributive Shares and Proportions ... allotted to the Province out of the Sum or Sums of Money granted, or to be granted, by Parliament to his Majesty's Colonies in America," passed by the Assembly on Sept. 19, 1761, and signed by Governor Hamilton on September 26, see *Statutes at Large, Pa.*, VI (1759–65), 114–18. John Sargent (above, VII, 322 n) and George Aufrere (1715–1801), a wealthy merchant of Huguenot descent, M. P. for Stamford, 1765–74, had been authorized—along with BF, Robert Charles, and two other men—by the Assembly order of Oct. 18, 1760 (above, p. 237 n), to receive Pa.'s share of the parliamentary grant for 1758. On Sept. 25, 1760, and April 22, 1761, Hamilton had unsuccessfully recommended that the Assembly join the Barclays (above, p. 190 n) to its own appointees to receive the parliamentary grants. *Pa. Col. Recs.*, VIII, 501, 610.

7. At this point Norris inserted the following bracketed sentence: "Here was a Clause to pay the Executors of R. Partridge which I omit." The omitted clause, actually a paragraph, is preserved in Norris' letterbook copy and is supplied at this point by the editors.

8. For Richard Partridge, formerly the agent of Pa., see above, p. 312 n. The Assembly's Committee on Incidental Charges brought in a report on his accounts on Sept. 19, 1761, which the House apparently adopted the same day. 8 *Pa. Arch.*, VI, 5262.

any answer from J. Sherwood as, in respect to time, I might have expected before now but as the Business can be effectually accomplished there pray be so kind, to take the trouble of finishing it with the Executors of Richard Partridge whoever they may be.[9]

I have already sent Three Bills of Exchange, that is to Say, the First Second and third Bills for £200. sterling drawn by Colonel Hunter on Messrs. Thomlinson &c.[1] so that as I have only the Fourth Bill by me I do not think it necessary to transmit it till I hear of the Others which I hope will get safe to your Hand. But I now inclose a First Bill drawn by J. Logan and Jno. Smith on Giles Bailey and Archibald Drummond Physicians in Bristol which I purchased of my Daughter for £97. 10s. 8d. Sterling which please to receive for my Account.[2]

I shall have some Mony to receive for my Friend R. Charles in Bills when the Trustees shall draw in Virtue of our late Act but as that may not happen till 6 or 8 Months hence and I am willing and desirous he should have it sooner be pleased to pay him £200 Sterling and charge the said Sum to my Account.[3] I would have sent the inclosed Bill to himself if it had been an even Sum but,

9. Partridge's executors were Joseph Sherwood and Thomas Corbyn. In the margin Norris wrote, "I retract this Order," the reason being, as he explained to BF on Oct. 19, 1761, that the executors had written him directing the "Settlement of their Accounts here."

1. For these bills, see above, pp. 332, 349.

2. For James Logan, Jr., see above, III, 390 n, and for John Smith, above, III, 240 n; V, 423 n. Both Norris and Smith were married to sisters of James Logan, Jr. The daughter here mentioned was either Mary Norris (1740–1803), who married John Dickinson in 1770, or Sarah Norris (1744–1769). BF recorded the receipt of this bill on Dec. 28, 1761. "Account of Expences," p. 62; *PMHB*, LV (1931), 131. At this point in the duplicate letter Norris inserted the following bracketed statement: "a Clause to pay R. Charles omitted here." The omitted "clause" (actually a paragraph) is supplied from the letterbook copy.

3. For Robert Charles's resignation as Pa. agent, see above, p. 332 n. His accounts were to be paid from the province's share of the parliamentary grant for 1759, but Norris believed that this money would not be available for many months, since the Pa. act of Sept. 26, 1761, appointing persons to receive it, could not be presented in England and confirmed in a shorter time. Hence the order to BF. Norris to Charles, Oct. 19, 1761, Hist. Soc. Pa. In the margin of the letterbook copy Norris wrote, "I contravene this Order," the reason being, as he wrote BF, also on October 19, that he had in the meantime purchased bills for £200 and intended to send them directly to Charles.

'bating Ceremony, I presume he will receive it more expeditiously in the present Mode.

I find One Thos. Burgh Esqr.[4] presented to the Parliament a Method for determining the Area's of all Right-lined Figures for which he received a Parliamentary Reward and on his Principles both Gibson and Wilson in their several Treatises of practical Surveying[5] have essay'd Some Improvement on Burgh's Invention and of late Our blundering John Gordon has upon the Same Foundation essayed a new Traverse Table[6] which pleases me much better than either Gibsons or Wilsons. I have never seen Burgh's Method, nor do I know when he presented it to Parliament but if it is published, I should be pleased to have it, and also Gibsons Treatise of practical Surveying which I have seen tho' I am sensible there is a pretty deal of triffling Stuff in it, particularly his Proposals of first protracting and then weighing an Irregular Figure to find its Area by proportioning the Weight of it to an Irregular-Figure given. I am &c   I. N.

ps October 19. 1761

The above Letter having misst the Packet,[7] I have since received Letters and am now so differently Situated that I do retract my

4. Thomas Burgh was the author of *A Method to Determine the Areas of Right-Lined Figures Universally* (London, 1724).

5. Robert Gibson's *A Treatise on Practical Surveying* and Henry Wilson's *Surveying Improved* went through numerous editions in the eighteenth century.

6. For BF's non-committal endorsement of *John Gordon's Mathematical Traverse Table, &c.*, on March 11, 1757, see above, VII, 144–5. On April 4, 1761, Gordon presented a copy of his book to the Pa. Assembly, which judged that it contained "some Things which may be useful, and deserve Encouragement" and voted him £10 on April 10, 1761. 8 *Pa. Arch.*, VI, 5232, 5235–6.

7. The *General Wall* packet, Capt. Thomas Robinson, sailed from N.Y. for Falmouth on Oct. 7, 1761. *Pa. Gaz.*, Oct. 15, 1761. In Norris' letterbook this letter with its postscript is followed directly by that of October 19 (see below, pp. 370–1). In the margin at the beginning of the entry of the present letter Norris noted: "One of these Two Letters to BF sent by Brig Sally Capt. Hervey to Hollyhead and Duplicate I gave to Wm. Fisher via Bristol by each of them went Sept. 30 and October 19. B F. received this Letter Ackd. Janry 7, 1762." *Pa. Gaz.*, Sept. 10, 1761, had reported the clearance of the brig *Sarah*, Capt. W. Harvey, for Holyhead (Wales), but it must have been held up in the lower bay waiting for a convoy and so was able to receive additional mail.

Orders[8] for payment of £152. 7s. 5d. to the Executors of R. Partridge and also for the payment of £200 Sterling to Robert Charles. And refer to My Letter of this Date.   I NORRIS

From [Charles Norris and Thomas Leech][9]

Draft: Historical Society of Pennsylvania

I. N.[1]   Octr. 1. 1761

We have now to Acquaint You that by a Resolve of the House of Assembly of this Province the last week We were Ordered Imediately to draw on You for the Parliamentary Grant Allotted for this Province by the Lords of the Treasury for the 1758. And We are now preparing the Bills of Exchange and Geting all things in readiness for that purpose.[2]

We are in Behalf of the Trustees Your assured Friends

To Benja: Franklin Esqr

Sent 2 to New York—1 of which Suppose went per Pacquet.[3]
1 to Hollyhead per Brig Sally Capt. Hervey Oct. 17. 1761
Sent I:Ns. Letters to B.F and R.C per ditto.

Pa. Gaz., October 22 reported the clearance for Bristol of the ship *Sarah and Katherine,* Capt. W. Condy. Apparently Fisher, a Philadelphia merchant, was a passenger on this ship.

8. At this point Norris inserted in the duplicate the following bracketed statement which concluded the postscript: "to pay R. P. Executors and R C omitted." The editors have supplied the remainder of the postscript from the letterbook copy.

9. So identified because on Nov. 17, 1761, BF acknowledged receiving from these two trustees of the General Loan Office "a Notification (dated Octob. 1. 1761)" that the trustees had been ordered to draw upon him for Pa.'s share of the parliamentary grant for 1758; see below, p. 383. For the Assembly's order to the Trustees to draw on BF, Sept. 19, 1761, see 8 *Pa. Arch.*, VI, 5262–3.

1. The initials "I.N." in the upper left hand corner indicate that this paper, like many others relating to Assembly business, was turned over to Speaker Isaac Norris and filed by him.

2. An undated draft memorandum (also initialed "I.N.") explains that because of the heavy subscription for these bills of exchange by merchants, no one person was to be allowed to subscribe to more than £500 worth. The memorandum then gives the "Form of the Bills" to be printed. Hist. Soc. Pa.

3. For the departure of the packet *General Wall* and the brig *Sally* (or *Sarah*) see the next to last footnote to the document immediately above.

To John Hunter[4]

ALS: Library of Congress

Dear Sir, London, Octobr 9. 1761

I am extreamly concern'd at the News of the Death of my dear Friend Mr. Hunter, with whom I had so long liv'd and transacted Business with the most perfect Harmony.[5] It was the more surprizing to me, as his last Letters mention'd an entire Freedom from his old Complaints, and a perfect Establishment of his Health.[6] His Death is not only a Loss to his Friends; I think it a great one also to his Country. For he had Abilities for Publick as well as private Business, an excellent Understanding with the best Dispositions in the World. I would write to poor Polly[7] on the melancholly Occasion, but at present—I cannot; tho' I condole with her most sincerely. I purpose to be in America early in the Spring, when a Settlement may be made more easily between his Executors, (one of which I imagine you are) and myself.[8] But in

4. See above, VI, 223 n, for Col. John Hunter, Va. merchant, agent for Thomlinson & Hanbury of London, who were contractors for transferring funds to the British forces in America. This and previous volumes contain many references to bills of exchange he had drawn on his principals which Norris or Hall bought and sent to BF.

5. William Hunter, BF's colleague as deputy postmaster general, and a printer of Williamsburg, died at his house Aug. 12, 1761. The notice from Williamsburg printed in *Pa. Gaz.*, Sept. 10, 1761, described him as "a Gentleman endowed with many amiable Qualifications, which render his Death much regretted by all who had the Pleasure of his Acquaintance." His exact relationship to John Hunter has not been determined.

6. After a long sojourn in England for his health he had returned to Va. in the spring of 1759. Above, VIII, 324, 340. No letters from him to BF thereafter survive, but in one to DF, July 22, 1759, among BF's papers (APS), Hunter reported that "I have at length happily succeeded in the Recovery of my Health, having been perfectly well for a Twelve Month past."

7. Hunter's unmarried sister Mary, who had been his traveling companion in England.

8. BF settled Hunter's post office accounts with the executors in the spring of 1763; he then collected and remitted to England the balance due amounting to "more than £400 Sterling." BF to Anthony Todd, June 1, and BF and John Foxcroft to Todd, June 10, 1763, both in Yale Univ. Lib. The settlement of Hunter's personal and printing accounts with BF, which took much longer, is discussed in a series of letters from James Parker to BF printed in 2 Mass. Hist. Soc. *Proc.*, XVI (1902), 193–220. BF also took charge of the education of Hunter's natural son William, Jr., boarded him at the Franklin home, and

363

the mean time, as I may possibly be detained longer than I expect, it will be a Satisfaction to have a Line here from you on the State of our Accounts which I think you can easily obtain, as I know he was always very exact and regular in them. My best Respects to good Mrs. Hunter, and believe me, with the sincerest Esteem, Dear Sir, Your most obedient and most humble Servant

B FRANKLIN

Col. Hunter

Addressed: To / Col. John Hunter / Mercht / Hampton / Virginia / Free / B FRANKLIN

Endorsed: London Benja: Franklin 9 Octor: 1761

William Franklin to Sarah Franklin

Copy (incomplete):[9] American Philosophical Society

In the summer of 1761 Franklin took his customary annual trip for health and pleasure. This time, instead of traveling in Great Britain, he made his first visit to the Continent, journeying through the Austrian Netherlands and the Dutch Republic (now Belgium and the Netherlands). This letter gives the only extensive surviving account of the expedition. From it may be deduced the probable itinerary of the travelers, Franklin, his son William, and his friend Richard Jackson. They left London about August 15[1] and, apparently landing at Antwerp, toured the Austrian Netherlands, visiting Brussels, Ghent, and Bruges. They seem then to have traveled up the west coast of Holland, passing through Delft, the Hague, Leyden, and Haarlem, and arriving at Am-

---

enrolled him in the Academy in Philadelphia. In DF's and BF's Memorandum Book, 1757–1776 (described above, VII, 167–8), are several entries regarding payments by Hunter's executors in settlement of postoffice business and others concerning Billy Hunter's expenses.

9. In what appears to be DF's hand, an attribution supported by the spelling, which is characteristically phonetic and unorthodox. Possibly Sally dictated from the original while her mother made a copy for circulation among relatives.

1. BF recorded the receipt of an interest payment from the Bank of England "just before we left London Viz. Augt. 14." "Account of Expences," p. 61; *PMHB*, LV (1931), 131.

sterdam. From here the party turned southward, journeying through the interior of the country, stopping at Utrecht, and sailing for England from either Rotterdam or Antwerp. They were away from London a little over five weeks.

London, Octr 10, 17[61]
I wrote to my Dear Sister a long Leter in April last, via N. York, which I fear has Miscarried, as she makes no Mention of it in those Leters I have had the Happyness of Reciveing from her,[2] it was mear Chit Chat and I keep't no Copy of it or I should send it by this Oppertunity. There was Inclosed one of Lady Northumberland's Cards which you rote for,[3] but as that is Lost I have sent you another. I acknowledg'd the Reciept of and thank you for your acceptable Present of two Pair work'd Ruffles, and Inform'd you that as there was no Bosom or Chitterlins[4] to either (without which they Could not be worn here) I would endeavour to have one Pair maid out of the Two, which I thought Could have been eaisily done, as the work'd part of one was narrower [torn] than the other, but the Lady's tell me that that Scheme won't answer, by reason of the Scollop being so very different; so I have Concluded to git the Woman who taught you that kind of work (as she Stays in London this winter)[5] to Compleat them for me. If she won't undertake it, I must keep them as they are till I have the Pleasure of seeing you in Philadelphia. The Poor Woman is bin Extreemly ill treated by her Father-in-law who sent for her over, he haveing taken her Child from her, and turn'd her out of Doors without so much as haveing paid one farthing of her Expences. It gave me Great Pleasure that you were so lucky as to find a Bottle of Rhenish in my Room on the Occasion you Mentioned, as

2. WF's and Sally's letters have not been found.
3. Elizabeth Seymour Percy (1716–1776), Countess and later Duchess of Northumberland, was one of the famous hostesses of her day. For a description of a party at Northumberland House, London, in 1762 attended by over three hundred people, see Frederick A. Pottle, ed., *Boswell's London Journal 1762–1763* (London, 1950), pp. 70–1. How and when WF had met her is not clear. Her husband, Hugh Percy (formerly Smithson), Earl of Northumberland and in 1766 first Duke of Northumberland of the third creation (1715–1786), had been F.R.S. since 1736 and BF may have come to know him at the Society. *DNB*.
4. Chitterlings: ruffles.
5. Not identified, but possibly Mrs. Henry Flower (above, VIII, 424).

Nobody could be more welcome than Mr. Hughes[6] to any thing Belonging to Wm. Franklin.

Before this Comes to hand you will probably have heard that my Father and I have lately maid a small Tour through Flanders and Holland, we were accompany'd by Mr. Jackson of the Temple, and upon the whole spent our time with much Pleasure, and I hope some profit. I kept a Sort of Journal,[7] and took Memorandums of whatever I thought remarkable, it is too long to Transcribe, or I would have sent you a Copy; but when I have the Happiness of seeing you we will Read it over together. In genaral we saw all the principal Cities and Towns in the Dutch and Austrian Netherlands, and at the most Considarable staid 3 or 4 Days. Att Brussels we were at Prince Charles of Lorrains,[8] in whose Cabinet, which is full of Art and Nature, we saw an Apperatus for trying my Father's Experiments in Electricity. The Magnificence and Riches of The Roman Catholic Churches here and at Ghent, and Bruges and Antwerp, particular the latter, surpass'd any thing I had ever seen before or Conceived. In all these town's there are English Nunneries, to one of which (a very elegant Building for English Lady's of great Families only) we went and saw the Nuns, but they Being at there Devotions we could have no Conversation with them, Indead they did no look very inviting but on the contaray appeard like Cross Old Maids who had forsakin The World becaus the World had first forsaken them—at Leyden we visited Professor Muschenbrook who first dy[scovered?] the Electrical Bottle, he was extreemly Glad to see my Father, and told him he was about Publishing a Work in which he should make Considerable Use of a Leter he had Received from him [from]

6. John Hughes, one of BF's most faithful correspondents; see above, VI, 284–5 n; VIII, 90–1.

7. Not found.

8. Charles-Alexandre, Duke of Lorraine and Bar (1712–1780), a double brother-in-law of Empress Maria Theresa, was supreme commander of the Imperial armies during the War of the Austrian Succession and at the beginning of the Seven Years' War. He was relieved of his command after his defeat by Frederick II at Leuthen (Dec. 5, 1757). He was a popular governor-general of the Austrian Netherlands, 1755–80, and was an avid though indiscriminate collector of medals, miniatures, rare books, plate, elaborate mechanical contrivances, minerals, exotic grains, and stuffed birds. J. Schouteden-Wery, *Charles de Lorraine et son Temps* (Brussels, 1943).

America,[9] But poor Gentleman though he appeared in witts and Health he died a Forginight after.[1] At the Hague we Received great Civilities from Sir Joseph Yorke, our Ambassador there,[2] with whom we din'd in Company with most of the Forign Ministers. We din'd also at Count Bentinck's who is at the Head of the Nobility in Holland[3]—at Amsterdam we were Recommended to thee Hopes,[4] who are Rank'd amounge the greatest Merchants in Europe, one of them sent us his Coach to carry us to se every thing curious in the City, here we meat with Mr. Crelius, and his Dogter that was Marry'd to Dr. Nye, he dying in Carolina she Came over to Holland and is Marry'd to a Scotsman who keeps a Tavarn.[5] In North Holland the People are in Many Respects different from those of the South, and even excell them in the Cleanliness of their Homes and Streets, which one would think allmost Imposiabel. We were at Harlem Delft and Utrecth, and twice [*torn:* at Leyden?].

The Most disagreable Circumstance I met with in Holland, was

9. Pieter van Musschenbroek, inventor of the Leyden jar (above, VIII, 329 n), was engaged in preparing his *Introductio ad Philosophiam Naturalem* (2 vols., Leyden, 1762), a revision and extension of his *Epitome Elementorum physica-mathematicorum, conscripta in usus academicas* (Leyden, 1726). BF's letter to him has not been found.

1. Musschenbroek died on Sept. 19, 1761. P. C. Molhuysen and F. K. H. Kossman, eds., *Niew Nederlandsch Biografisch Woordenboek*, X (Leyden, 1937), 659. If WF's statement is accurate, BF and his party were in Leyden on Sept. 5, 1761.

2. Sir Joseph Yorke (1724–1792), British minister at the Hague since 1751, had been raised to the rank of ambassador in the spring of 1761. He remained in the Netherlands until 1780 and will appear frequently in these volumes during the period of the American Revolution.

3. William Bentinck, Lord of Rhoon and Pendrecht, Count of the Holy Roman Empire (1704–1774), president of the College of Deputies of the States General, was the younger son of William III's devoted servant, William Bentinck, first Earl of Portland (1649–1709). *Niew Nederlandsch Biografisch Woordenboek*, I (Leyden, 1911), 302–3.

4 . Thomas and Adrian Hope. Their nephew Henry Hope (1736–1811), said to have been born in Boston, joined his uncles in Amsterdam in 1760 after London experience and took over the business in 1780, managing it with such acumen that at his death he was called the "most eminent merchant of his time." Retiring to England in 1794, he turned the business over to his grand-nephew, John Williams Hope. *Gent. Mag.*, LXXXI (1811), 292–3.

5. For Joseph Crell, his daughter Anna, and her second husband, Francis Farquhar, see above, IV, 65 n, 77–8 n.

their Continual Smoaking of Tobaco. I don't Recolect that I saw more than one Dutch Man without a Pipe in his Mouth, and that was a fellow who had hung in Chains so long that his Head had drop'd off. There Very Children are taught Smoakin from the Moment they leave Sucking, and the Method they take to teach them is, to give them when they are Cutting their Teath, an Old Tobaco pipe which is Smoak'd Black and smooth to rub their Gums with insted of Coral. But what Suppriz'd me most of all was the seeing at one of the [*illegible*] Houses a Man of ninety Dragd out his Partner and dance a Minuet smoaking most solemnly a long Pipe during The whole time. Our Passage over to Holland was Plesant enough, we haveing fine Weather and the whole Cabbin to ourselves: But our return was as disagreeable as possiable: haveing hard Blowing contrary winds, and upwards of 50 Passengers of different Nations, in a Small sloop, who not being able to Stand the Dek on Account of the weather all Crowded below. Here we soon become most Sea sick, and however it might be with the Lading of other Vessel's, I can assure you that on Board ours there was no such thing as *Inside Contents unknown* for my part what ever I Might have been formerly I think I must now be one of the best natur'd Men living, as old Neptune and Eolus took that oppertunity of depriveing me of Every bit of Gaul I had in my Body. I risisted as much as I Could, and would feign have sav'd a littel for my Enimies, but there was no making those old Gentlemen hear Reason nothing less than all would satisfy them. We luckily however Sprung a Leek so as to keep the Pumps almost Continuelly a going, which Obliged the Captain to bear away for the first Port the wind would let him make, or else we Should probably have been beating another Day or two in that blessed Situation before we Could reach the Port we were distined to. Though we landed 60 Miles farther from London than we Expected, yet we made shift to get there time enough for the Coronation,[6] for which we had engag'd Places so as to see the Procession before our departure, I however did not make use of mine haveing a Tiket giveing me by which I was enable to see the whole Ceremony in the Hall, and to walk in the Procession quite into the Abbey. By this means [*remainder missing*].

6. For a detailed account of the coronation of George III and Queen Charlotte, Sept. 22, 1761, see *The Annual Register*, IV (1761), 215–42.

To William Coleman[7]

LAS: Yale University Library

Dear Sir,   London, Oct. 12. 1761

I have received your obliging Favours of July 16. and Augt. 15. for which I thank you.[8] The Transit I think would not have appear'd at Philadelphia, if any body had been ready there to observe.[9] It is so far West, that Venus was off the Sun's Disk before he rose there. I send you Ferguson's Book on the Subject to which I was a Subscriber, and also a large Scheme of the Transit he has since presented to me.[1] At the next Meeting of the Society, which is in November, we shall have all the Observations laid before us, except the most remote, and I will immediately send you a Copy.[2] I have not yet heard that the Books sent the Library Company by Becket,[3] are got to Hand. Mr. Collinson sends a few, he tells me per this Ship. With the greatest Esteem, I am, Dear Friend Yours affectionately   B FRANKLIN.

Addressed: To | William Coleman Esqr | Philadelphia

Endorsed: London October 12th. 1761 from B. Franklin

7. For Coleman, one of BF's earliest Philadelphia friends, see above, II, 406 n.

8. Not found, but probably containing comments on Lord Kames's *Principles of Equity;* see below, p. 376.

9. The transit of Venus, June 6, 1761, was not visible in the continental American colonies, and in any case, the one useful telescope in Philadelphia was out of commission at the time. Harry Woolf, *The Transits of Venus: A Study of Eighteenth-century Science* (Princeton, 1959); Brooke Hindle, *The Pursuit of Science in Revolutionary America 1735–1789* (Chapel Hill, 1956), pp. 98–100. See above, IV, 415–22, for the efforts in America to observe the transit of Mercury in 1753 to provide information and experience useful for the transits of Venus in 1761 and 1769.

1. James Ferguson (above, VIII, 216 n) had published *Astronomy Explained on Sir Isaac Newton's Principles* in 1756 with a second edition in 1757. It contained a method for using the transit of 1761 to determine the distances of the planets. His pamphlet *A Plain Method of Determining the Parallax of Venus by her Transit over the Sun* (London, 1761) was probably the "large Scheme" BF sent to Coleman.

2. Brief reports on the observations in London were read at the Royal Society, June 11, 1761, and others from England and continental centers on Nov. 5, 12, 19, and 26, 1761, and Jan. 6, 1762, and were printed in *Phil. Trans.*, LII (1761–62), Part I.

3. The books BF had ordered through Thomas Becket in January; they

From Isaac Norris

Letterbook copy: Historical Society of Pennsylvania

Dear Friend BF   Fairhill, Octobr 19th. 1761

I find my Last of the 30th of September[4] mist the Packet by which it was intended so that having since that Date received yours of 7th August[5] and a Letter from the Executors of R. Partridge by which they Order and direct the Settlement of their Accounts here I retract my former Order to pay them the Ballance of R P. Account as it will suit me better to settle and discharge that Account here in pursuance of their said Order. I have now procured Bills of Exchange which I shall remit directly to my old Friend R. Charles for which Reason I contravene my Order to pay him the £200 mentioned in mine of the 30th of September last.[6]

The distresses of the Merchants for want of Bills of Exchange at a reasonable Price and the Strong Rumours of a Peace which gained Credit at the same Time induced the last Assembly to order the Trustees "forthwith" to draw Bills of Exchange for the first Parliamentary Grant which they are now drawing to make up about £26.000 sterling the greatest Part of which is already drawn and Subscriptions for the whole some Time since compleated.

As the Merchants are limited in the Sums and obliged to pay for the Bills in our Paper Currency only[7] the Bills perhaps may not be sent by the Vessels now ready to sail for London and other

---

were shipped on the *Dragon*, Capt. Hammett, which arrived in Philadelphia, May 24, 1761; see above, pp. 274–7.

4. See above, pp. 357–62, for that letter and many of the matters mentioned in this one.

5. Not found.

6. Immediately following this document in the letterbook is a letter to Robert Charles of the same date explaining that because it would take several months to get the money due Pa. from the second parliamentary grant, "I have advanced my own Mony on the Credit of our Act and have now inclosed Two Bills of Exchange for £100 sterl. each No. 48 and No. 49 drawn by the Trustees on Benjamin Franklin who received the first Allotment."

7. Because of the heavy demand for bills, the trustees of the Loan Office decided to limit each purchaser to £500 sterling. Undated memorandum, Hist. Soc. Pa. On Sept. 25, 1761, the Assembly recommended that the trustees sell "none of the said Provincial Draughts for less than Seventy per Cent. Exchange, Pennsylvania Currency." 8 *Pa. Arch.*, VI, 5267.

Ports in England to more than ½ or ⅔ds of the Whole Sum. But their Necessities are so great that I believe the Remainder will soon follow. I was of Opinion that the House had better defer their Order for drawing Bills till we had had a Confirmation of a Peace, but as every Body did or affected to, believe the Reports Current at that Time the Province must take the Chance of the Stocks to answer their Bills now drawn.

I have given your Account Current Credit for the Mony paid Col. Lloyd, both Payments amounting to the Sum of One Hundred Pounds Sterling.[8] I have mentioned Som'thing on this Head in some of my former Letters.

I found at the End of last Year that several of the Members were well acquainted with R. Charles's declining the Agency of this Province,[9] tho' not from me, however, as I proposed to inform the House of it when the Year expired, I acted accordingly, and the present Assembly have complied with his Request so that it now only remains to settle and discharge his Accounts In Order to which I shall remit Bills of Exchange to himself as I apprehend this Method will be more acceptable to him than the Manner before proposed. If the price of Stocks should encourage at the Time of receiving this Advice or during your stay in England, be pleasd to invest what Mony I may have in your Hands in the consolidated Annuities in Addition to what I have already there or in any other of the publick Funds,[1] thô I suppose the prizes [prices] of all are very soon brought to an equal value by the Stockjobbers according to their several Purchases.

I would chuse mine to lye together as I think the Sum will be too inconsiderable to be seperated—but in this use your own Judgment. I am your Affectionate Friend   I NORRIS

Whilst I am writing I am informed that Captains Gibbons, Friend, and Bradford are arrived[2] but as they bring me no Letters I have nothing futher to add.

8. See above, p. 337 n.
9. On Charles's resignation of the agency, see above, p. 332 n.
1. BF appears to have fulfilled this commission by assigning Norris £200 of his own stock on Jan. 30, £100 on Feb. 12, and £150 on Feb. 16, 1762. The current market value of the stock was £289 5s. "Account of Expences," pp. 62–3; PMHB, LV (1931), 131–2.
2. The James and Mary, Capt. John Bradford, and the Beulah, Capt. James

The Trustees inform me they have taken Care to advise Their drawing.[3]

[*In the margin:*] Added—I have enclosed a Second Bill of Exchange ut Supra for £97. 10s. 8d. Sterling.

Endorsed: See page 125 Sent by Captn Hervey and W. Fisher B F recd it. ackd. Janry 7. 1762[4]

From the Trustees of the General Loan Office: Bill of Exchange[5]

Printed form with blanks filled in: The Franklin Inn, Philadelphia

Exchange for *£300 Sterling*   [No. *96*]

Philadelphia, *October 20th* 1761.
At Thirty Days Sight of this our Fourth per Exchange (our First, Second and Third, of the same Tenor and Date, unpaid) pay unto *John Reynell*[6] or Order, *Three hundred* Pounds Sterling, for Value received, and charge it to the Province of Pennsylvania; but if it is not paid at said Thirty Days Sight, then pay INTEREST on that Sum, from the Expiration of the said Thirty Days, until paid, at the Rate of Six Pounds per Centum per Annum; and if this Bill and Interest is not paid in one Year from

---

Gibbon, left Spithead, Aug. 14, 1761, convoyed by H. M. S. *Intrepid,* Capt. John Hale, and arrived in Philadelphia, Oct. 17, 1761. The *Carolina,* Capt. James Friend, arrived the same day. *Pa. Journal,* Oct. 22, 1761.

3. See above, p. 362. This sentence was added in the letterbook at a later time.

4. No letter from BF to Norris of this date has been found.

5. An example of the printed bills of exchange the trustees of the General Loan Office had prepared for use in drawing funds from the parliamentary grant of 1758. The text follows precisely the form of their undated draft memorandum now among the Isaac Norris Papers, Hist. Soc. Pa. See above, p. 362 n. No attempt has been made to locate and reproduce other surviving bills of this series.

6. John Reynell (1708–1784), Quaker shipping and commission merchant of Philadelphia, treasurer of the Pa. Hospital, 1751–52; president of its Board of Managers, 1757–80. *PMHB,* LVI (1932), 158–86. Frederick B. Tolles, *Meeting House and Counting House: The Quaker Merchants of Colonial Philadelphia 1682–1763* (Chapel Hill, 1948), contains much information on Reynell's business activities and reproduces a silhouette now in Hist. Soc. Pa.

the Date hereof, we do hereby oblige ourselves, our Heirs, Executors, and Administrators, to pay the said Bill with Interest from the Date thereof, at the above Rate, until paid, when it shall be returned with a Protest to us, but no other Damages; on this Condition, nevertheless, that if Payment be not demanded within Six Months after the Date of the said Protest, the Interest from that Time shall determine and cease.   CHAS. NORRIS
THOS LEECH
MAHLON KIRKBRIDE

To   *Benjamin Franklin Esqr.*
in London

Endorsed: Pay the Contents to Hillary & Scott[7] on Order
JOHN REYNELL

To William Cullen[8]

MS not found; reprinted from John Thomson, *An Account of the Life, Lectures, and Writings of William Cullen, M.D.* (Edinburgh and London, 1859), I, 140.

Dear Sir,   London, 21st, October 1761
I hear, that since I had the pleasure of seeing and conversing with you on the subject, you have wrote some of your sentiments of Fire, and communicated them to the Philosophical Society.[9] If so, as it may be some time before their publication, I should think myself extremely obliged to you if I could be favoured with a copy, as there is no subject I am more impatient to be acquainted with. It should go no further than my own closet without your permission.

I thank you for the civilities you were so good as to shew my friend Mr. Shippen, whom I took the liberty of recommending to your notice the last year.[1] Give me leave to recommend one friend

7. Probably a Liverpool mercantile firm; see above, p. 41.
8. Professor of chemistry at Edinburgh; see above, VII, 184 n.
9. No such paper appears in the third volume of *Essays and Observations, Physical and Literary* (1771) of the Philosophical Society of Edinburgh. It may never have been published; John Thomson mentions that various essays on heat survive among Cullen's papers. *An Account of the Life, Lectures, and Writings of William Cullen, M.D.* (Edinburgh and London, 1859), I, 54.
1. See above, pp. 219–20.

more to your advice and countenance. The bearer, Mr. Morgan,[2] who purposes to reside some time in Edinburgh for the completion of his studies in Physic, is a young gentleman of Philadelphia, whom I have long known and greatly esteem; and as I interest myself in what relates to him, I cannot but wish him the advantage of your conversation and instructions. I wish it also for the sake of my country, where he is to reside, and where I am persuaded he will be not a little useful. I am, with the greatest esteem and respect, Dear Sir, your most obedient and most humble servant,

B. FRANKLIN

To Lord Kames

LS:[3] Scottish Record Office

My dear Lord,   London, Octr. 21, 1761[4]

It is long since I have afforded myself the Pleasure of writing to you. As I grow in Years I find I grow more indolent, and more apt to procrastinate. I am indeed a bad Correspondent; but what avails Confession without Amendment!

When I come so late with my Thanks for your truly valuable

2. John Morgan (1735–1789) was the son of Evan Morgan (1709–1763), BF's friend and associate in the Library Co., the Association, the Hospital, and the Pa. Assembly, and with BF one of the provincial commissioners in 1755. The father's name has appeared often in earlier volumes; see esp., VI, 285 n. John graduated in the first class of the College of Philadelphia, was apprenticed to Dr. John Redman, served as surgeon with the provincial troops, and went to England in 1760. He spent a year studying in London with Dr. John Fothergill and others, then went to Edinburgh, where he received the M.D. degree in 1763. After further study in Paris and Italy, he returned to America in 1765 and won adoption of his proposal for the establishment of a medical school in connection with the College of Philadelphia. He was thereupon appointed professor of the theory and practise of physic. Early in the American Revolution Congress appointed him director general of hospitals and physician-in-chief of the army. Increasing complaints against him—inspired as he believed by the jealousies of his subordinates—led to his removal from these posts early in 1777, and he thereafter confined himself to his work at the Hospital and Medical School and to his private practice. *DAB;* Whitfield J. Bell, *John Morgan Continental Doctor* (Phila., 1965).

3. The body of the letter is in WF's hand; the signature and address in BF's.

4. For some reason not now clear, Sparks (*Works,* VII, 231–4), gave the date as November 1761. Bigelow and Smyth, reprinting from Sparks, did the same.

Introduction to the Art of Thinking, can I have any Right to enquire after your Elements of Criticism?[5] I promise myself no small Satisfaction in perusing that Work also, when it shall appear. By the first you sow thick in the young Mind, the Seeds of Good Sense concerning moral Conduct, which as they grow and are transplanted into Life must greatly adorn the Character, and promote the Happiness of the Person. Permit me to say, that I think I never saw more solid useful Matter contain'd in so small a Compass, and yet the Method and Expression so clear, that the Brevity occasions no Obscurity. In the other, you will by alluring Youth to the Practice of reasoning, strengthen their Judgment, improve and enlarge their Understanding, and increase their Abilities of being useful. To produce the Number of valuable Men necessary in a Nation for its Prosperity, there is much more Hope from Schemes of *early Institution* than from those of *Reformation*. And as the Power of a single Man to do National Service, in particular Situations of Influence, is often immensely great; a Writer can hardly conceive the Good he may be doing when engag'd in Works of this kind. I cannot therefore but wish you would publish it as soon as your other important Employments will permit you to give it the finishing Hand.

With these Sentiments you will not doubt my being serious in the Intention of finishing my Art of Virtue.[6] 'Tis not a mere ideal Work. I plann'd it first in 1732. I have from time to time made and caus'd to be made Experiments of the Method, with Success. The Materials have been growing ever since; the Form only is now to be given; in which I purpose employing my first Leisure after my Return to my *other* Country.

Your Invitation to make another Jaunt to Scotland, and Offer to meet us halfway *en famille,* was extreamly obliging. Certainly I never spent my Time any where more agreeably, nor have I been in any Place, where the Inhabitants and their Conversation left

5. Lord Kames published his *Introduction to the Art of Thinking* in January 1761. It included BF's "Parable against Persecution" without attribution or permission (see above, VI, 116–17), but BF does not allude to that fact here. *The Elements of Criticism* appeared in 3 vols., in March 1762 (*Gent. Mag.,* XXXII, 147) and BF told Kames, Aug. 17, 1762, that he planned to read it on the voyage home.

6. On BF's cherished project, never finished but partly incorporated in his autobiography, see above, p. 104 n.

such lastingly pleasing Impressions on my Mind, accompanied with the strongest Inclination once more to visit that hospitable friendly and sensible People. The Friendship your Lordship in particular honours me with, would not, you may be assured, be among the least of my Inducements. My Son is in the same Sentiments with me. But we doubt we cannot have that Happiness, as we are to return to America early in the next Spring.

I am asham'd that I have been so useless a Member to your Philosophical Society since they did me the Honour of admitting me. But I think it will not be long before they hear from me.[7] I should be very glad to see Dr. Cullen's Paper on *Fire*.[8] When may we expect the Publication? I have, as you have heard, been dealing in *Smoke:* and I think it not difficult to manage, when one is once acquainted thoroughly with the Principles. But as the Causes are various so must be the Remedies; and one cannot prescribe to a Patient at such a Distance without first having a clear State of its Case. If you should ever take the Trouble of sending me a Description of the Circumstances of your smoaky Chimnies, perhaps I might offer something useful towards their Cure.[9] But doubtless you have Doctors equally skilful nearer home.

I sent one of your Principles of Equity a Present to a particular Friend of mine, one of the Judges of the Supream Court in Pensylvania,[1] where, as there is no Court of Chancery, Equity is often mix'd with the Common Law in their Judgments. I since receiv'd two Letters from him. In the first when he had read but Part of the Work he seem'd to think something wanting in it. In the latter he calls his first Sentiments in question. I think I will send you the Letters though of no great Importance, lest since I have mention'd them you should think his Remarks might be of more Consequence: You can return them when any Friend is coming this Way.

7. BF sent a letter to David Hume with an account of lightning rods, Jan. 21, 1762. It was read to the Philosophical Society of Edinburgh and printed (though with an incorrect date) in its *Essays and Observations, Physical and Literary*, III (Edinburgh, 1771), 129–40.
8. See the letter immediately above.
9. Kames responded in a letter of November 22 (not found), which BF answered, Jan. 27, 1762, asking for further particulars, as "it is so difficult at this Distance to employ any Skill I may have in those Matters for your Relief." Scottish Record Office.
1. Presumably William Coleman; see above, pp. 104, 369 n.

May I take the Freedom of recommending the Bearer, Mr. Morgan,[2] to your Lordship's Protection. He purposes residing some time in Edinburgh to improve himself in the Study of Physick, and I think will one day make a good Figure in the Profession, and be of some Credit to the School he studies in, if great Industry and Application join'd with natural Genius and Sagacity[?], afford any Foundation for the Presage. He is the Son of a Friend and near Neighbour of mine in Philadelphia, so that I have known him from a Child, and am confident the same excellent Dispositions, good Morals, and prudent Behaviour, that have procur'd him the Esteem and Affection of all that know him in his own Country, will render him not unworthy the Regard, Advice and Countenance your Lordship may be so good as to afford him.

My Son (with whom I have lately made the Tour of Holland and Flanders) joins with me in the best Wishes for you and Lady Kames, and your amiable Children. We hope, however far we may be remov'd from you, to hear frequently of your Welfare, and of the Fortunes of your Family: being with the sincerest Esteem and Regard, My dear Friend, Yours most affectionately

B FRANKLIN

Lord Kames

Addressed: To | The Rt. Honble Lord Kames | Edinburgh

Endorsed: 21 October 1761

To Mary Stevenson   ALS: American Philosophical Society

Cravenstreet, Oct. 29. 61.

My dear Polly's good Mama bids me write two or three Lines by way of Apology for her so long omitting to write. She acknowledges the Receiving two agreable Letters lately from her beloved Daughter, enclosing one for Sally Franklin which was much approv'd (excepting one Word only) and sent as directed. The Reasons of her not Writing are; That her Time all Day is fully taken up during the Day-Light, with the Care of her Family and —laying abed in the Morning. And her Eyes are so bad, that she cannot see to write in the Evening—for Playing at Cards. So she

2. See above, p. 374 n.

377

hopes, that one who is all Goodness, will certainly forgive her, when her Excuses are so substantial. As for the Secretary, he has not a Word to say in his own Behalf, tho' full as great an Offender, but throws himself upon Mercy; pleading only that he is with the greatest Esteem and sincerest Regard his dear Polly's ever affectionate Friend   B FRANKLIN

Compliments to the good Family, and to Mrs. Byrd[3] if still with you. We shall be glad to see Mr. White[4] as often as agreable to him.

Endorsed: Oct 29—61

To the Earl of Bessborough ALS: American Philosophical Society

Craven Street
My Lord,   Friday Evening. [October 1761][5]
Calling at the Board this Morning, I was informed that Application had been made by Governour Fauquier[6] for a Commission to his Secretary as my Colleague in the American Office.[7] It is my Duty to acquiesce in your Lordship's Pleasure if after reading

3. Not identified.
4. In one of the letters to her mother mentioned above, Polly seems to have said that this young man was soon coming to London. Writing to an unnamed young cousin, apparently in the army overseas, Dec. 17, 1761, Polly reported that "Your old Companion Tom White is come to England, and his brother Hugh is settled in Jamaica." APS. "Mr. White" is not otherwise identified.
5. William Hunter, joint deputy postmaster general of North America, died Aug. 12, 1761, and BF had learned of his death by early October; see above, p. 363. If Governor Fauquier of Va. had recommended a successor promptly, as he probably did, his letter would also have reached London in October, thereby occasioning BF's letter.
6. Francis Fauquier (1704?–1768), lieutenant governor of Va., 1758–68, and acting governor during the entire period.
7. John Foxcroft (d. 1790), Fauquier's secretary, served as joint deputy postmaster general of North America until the disruption of the British postal service in the colonies following the outbreak of the Revolution. A Loyalist, he was vigorously abused as formerly a "needy Domestic" and now a "Mushroom Gentleman" in 1775 by William Goddard, then a Baltimore printer. *PMHB,* XXVII (1903), 501–2. After the Revolution Foxcroft was appointed British agent for the packet service in New York City.

this you should think proper to gratify the Governor by such an Appointment. But I conceive that the Application to your Lordship was founded on a Supposition of a Vacancy to be supply'd, which I apprehend not to be really the Case. The Commission I have had the Honour so recently to receive from the Goodness of your Lordship and Mr. Hampden,[8] grants the whole Office, Powers and Salary, to *the Survivor* of the two Persons therein appointed; and therefore, notwithstanding the Decease of Mr. Hunter, there is properly no Vacancy; unless you should think fit to make one by revoking that Commission; which, when my long and faithful Service of 24 Years in the Post Office,[9] is considered, I hope will not be done. During the greatest Part of that time, I had the Burthen of conducting the whole American Office under others, with a very slender Salary; and it has been allow'd, that the bringing the Office to what it is, from its former low insignificant State, was greatly owing to my Care and Management. And now that in the Course of Things some additional Advantage seems to be thrown in my Way, I cannot but hope it will not be taken from me in favour of a Stranger to the Office; especially as Governor Fauquier has in his Disposition many Places of Profit in his Government as they fall, and therefore cannot long want an Opportunity of gratifying the Services of his Secretary.[1]

I beg your Lordship to excuse the Freedom I have taken in this Representation; and believe me to be, with the most perfect Respect and Attachment, My Lord, Your Lordship's most obedient and most humble Servant   B FRANKLIN

I was at your Lordship's Door to day, but did not find you at home.

8. Bessborough and Robert Hampden (formerly Trevor) were joint postmasters general of Great Britain and so had the right to name their American deputies. On Aug. 12, 1761—the very day Hunter died—they reappointed BF and Hunter to the American office following the accession of George III, an event requiring new commissions for all public officials. Ruth L. Butler, *Doctor Franklin Postmaster General* (N.Y., 1928), p. 71.

9. BF had been postmaster of Philadelphia, 1737–53, and deputy postmaster general since 1753.

1. Despite BF's request, announcement was made in November of Foxcroft's appointment to succeed Hunter as deputy postmaster general for America with BF. *Gent. Mag.*, XXXI (1761), 539.

From David Hall

Letterbook copy: American Philosophical Society

Sir,   Philada. Nov. 4. 1761.

I received yours, (Via New-York) relating to the order of Forty Pounds Sterling, in Favour of Mr. Palomba,[2] which is paid, at the Rate of Seventy per Cent. Exchange, that being the Exchange the Trustees of the Loan-office drew for.

Remember me kindly to your Son, and tell him, I received his by Palomba, but never heard any thing of the Letter he mentions to be sent by Mr. Quincy Via Boston.[3]

I wrote you by two or three other Vessels, desiring you to order Caslon to cast, and send by the first Ship, the same Quantity of Brevier you last sent, which I hope is at Sea before this reaches.[4] If the War is not at an End before you leave England, hope you will order it so, that the News Papers will come regularly by the Packets, as they now do. I am, Sir, Yours very sincerely

DAVID HALL

To Mr. Franklin

Sent by the James and Mary Captain Bradford.[5]

From Isaac Norris

Letterbook copy: Historical Society of Pennsylvania

Dear Friend BF   Fairhill, Novr. 4th. 1761

I sent by Captain Hervey bound to Hollyhead and by Wm. Fisher to Bristol Originals and Duplicates of Mine of the 30th Septr. and of the 19th of Octobr Last[6] which inclosed First and Second Bills of Exchange for £97 10s. 8d. Sterling. I now remit the Third Bill drawn by JL and JS. on G. Bailey and A. Drummond Physicians in Bristol for the aforesaid Sum of £97 10s. 8d. Sterling. I have now likewise inclosd a First Bill of Exchange

---

2. BF's letter has not been found nor has Mr. Palomba been identified.

3. Edmund Quincy, son of Josiah Quincy of Boston; see above, p. 298 n.

4. See above, pp. 330, 350.

5. *Pa. Gaz.*, Nov. 5, 1761, reported the clearance of the *James and Mary*, Capt. J. M. Bradford; *London Chron.*, Dec. 24–26, 1761, reported that it had passed Gravesend December 25.

6. See above, pp. 357–62, 370–2.

drawn by the Trustees of the L. Office on your self No. 121 for £100. Sterling which please to carry to the Credit of My Account[7] it needs no indsorsing but to prevent Accidents I have Transcribed the Above Order on the Bill. Pray take the Trouble of investing this with the Ballance of my Mony in your Hands in the Stocks in addition to what I have already there.[8] I leave it to your own Judgment, but refer to mine of the 19th. of Octobr last if that Letter has come to Hand, In which I prefer the Lodging all my Mony in the Same Fund, unless you See Cause to seperate it. There are Several Vessels going nearly at the Same Time so that I shall close this with Design to let it lay with My Brother for the First Opportunity. I am your Affectionate Friend   I N

BF arrived at Philada. Novr. 1 : 1762.[9]

Endorsed: By Captn Bradford[1] This did not go by Bradford who left his Bag—but soon after

First Bill £100.0—BF received This Acknowledged in his of Feb. 13. 1762[2]

From Mary Stevenson   ALS: American Philosophical Society

Dear Sir   Wanstead, Novr. 9th. 1761.
    I had rather you should find me deficient in any Point than that of Gratitude; therefore I will not delay acknowledging your Favour of the 29th.[3] tho I am not prepar'd to write to you, having made very little Improvement lately in any kind of Study.
    I cannot recollect what word in my Letter to Miss Franklin was so unfortunate to meet your Disapprobation.[4] I am oblig'd to you

7. BF recorded the receipt of this bill on Jan. 27, 1762. "Account of Expences," p. 62; *PMHB*, LV (1931), 131.
8. For BF's compliance with this request, see above, p. 371 n.
9. Carefully hand-printed at the end of the letterbook copy.
1. *Pa. Gaz.*, Oct. 29, 1761, reported that the *James and Mary*, Capt. John Bradford, was outward bound. Her clearance was reported in the next issue, Nov. 5, 1761.
2. Not found.
3. Above, pp. 377–8.
4. In his letter of October 29 BF had said that her letter to Sally "was much approv'd (excepting one Word only) and sent as directed."

for telling me when I do wrong, but you should say in what, otherwise I remain in Ignorance and cannot mend. I am sensible I often fail in my Attempt to write correctly, tho I confess I have taken some pains to do it.

I know my Mother don't love writing, so I don't often expect a Letter from her; and I know your Time is too much, and too well, employ'd to desire you should write often to me. If I have a Place in your Heart and, sometimes, in your Thoughts I am satisfied; and when you have Leisure to send me a few Lines I receive a very high Pleasure.

I am extreamly oblig'd to you for your kind Invitation to my young Friend,[5] who I hope will have Sensibility enough to accept it with Pleasure when he is acquainted with it. He set out for Mr. Mure's, at Saxham,[6] the day after I wrote to my Mother in his Behalf, and I have not yet heard of his Return. I know your Partiality to your Polly makes you overlook her Impertinence, and you are ever ready to grant all her Requests. Believe me to be with the utmost Gratitude for your unmerited Favours, and the highest Esteem of your Worth Dear Sir your faithful and affectionate   M STEVENSON

From Isaac Norris

Letterbook copy: Historical Society of Pennsylvania

Benja. Franklin   } Infra
By Captn. Bradford }   Nover 16 [1761]
Above is the Substance of my Last.[7] I now send the Second Bill of Exchange No. 121 for £100. Sterling drawn by the Trustees on your Self. Please to Credit my Account Current with That Sum. I am afraid our last Assembly have been too precipitate in drawing These Bills but it is now too late to recall it. I am your assured Friend   I N.

To Benja Franklin

5. Presumably the "Mr. White" mentioned in BF's letter of October 29.
6. Mr. Mure is not identified. Great Saxham and Little Saxham are in Suffolk, near Bury St. Edmunds.
7. His letter to BF of Nov. 4, 1761, above, pp. 380–1. It should be consulted for matters mentioned in this letter.

NB. I. Johnston[8] Sent a Third Bill. B F recd the Bill See his Letter of the 13. Febry. 1762[9]

Endorsed: Second Bill Excha for £100. o. o BF recd this Bill Benja. Franklin arrived at Philad November 1st. 1762.[1]

To Charles Norris and Thomas Leech

ALS: Historical Society of Pennsylvania; LS duplicate, New Jersey Historical Society[2]

I. N.[3]

Gentlemen;   London, Nov. 17. 1761

I have this Day received from each of you, a Notification, (dated Octob. 1. 1761) that by a Resolve of the Assembly, you are ordered immediately to draw on me for the Whole of the Parliamentary Grant to our Province for the Year 1758.[4] As I had acquainted the House from time to time, thro' the Speaker, with the Purchases of Stock I had made with that Money for the Account of the Province,[5] which would have reap'd the whole Benefit of the expected Rise on a Peace, I suppose the House have been induc'd *now* to order the Drafts on the Apprehension that Peace might probably be concluded about the Time of their Arrival in England. Unfortunately the Negociations have been broken off,[6] and the Stocks have thereupon fallen considerably, so that if our £30,000, which cost us £26,994. 7s. 6d.[7] be sold at

8. Not identified.

9. Not found.

1. Neatly hand-printed at the bottom of the page.

2. The duplicate, in WF's hand, lacks Isaac Norris' initials and the address page.

3. Added later, indicating that the speaker received this ALS copy for filing from his brother and Leech.

4. See above, p. 362.

5. For BF's investments on behalf of the province, see above, pp. 253, 313, 335. Most of his letters to Norris about these investments, including his "Succinct Account . . . of the Situation of the Publick Mony," July 10, 1761, have not been found.

6. Negotiations had come completely to an end by September 26; see above, pp. 358 n.

7. BF arrived at this sum by adding £13781 17s. 6d., invested Dec. 18–23,

the present Rates, it will not Net more than £23,837. 10s. 0d. whence, instead of a Gain of 5 or £6000 that we should probably have had by Delaying to draw till a Peace, we shall now incur a Loss *here* of £3156. 17s. 6d. However, the Delay, so far as it has gone, may, by the intermediate extreme Rise in the Price of Bills at Philadelphia far overballance this Loss, so that on the whole, with the Interest received here, the Province may be Gainer, which I sincerely wish. But I send you this early Notice of the present State of Things, by different Conveyances, that if not too late, you may judge whether it will not be proper to avoid Drawing for more than will probably be in my Hands; since if you should go far beyond what the Stocks when sold will produce, it will be impossible for me duly to honour all your Drafts. I am, with the utmost Respect for yourselves and the Assembly, Gentlemen, Your most obedient and most humble Servant

B Franklin

p.s. Stocks by this Day's Paper[8]
3 per Cent. Consol[idated]
          (of which we have £5,000)—at 72½ to 71¼
4 per Cent. 1760   (of which we have £15,000)—at 86½ to 86
3 per Cent. 1761   (of which we have £10,000)—at 73¾ to 73⅛
What they were when I bought may be seen in my former Letters to the Speaker.[9]

I shall state and send the whole Account per next Pacquet.[1]

Cha. Norris and Thos. Leech Esqrs.

Addressed: To / Cha. Norris and Thos. Leech, Esquires / Philadelphia / To be sent from Portsmouth / by a New York Ship: / but if the Fleet is sail'd to / be return'd to B. Franklin, Craven street London

Endorsed: Benja Franklin to the Trustees L. O Novr. 17 1761

1760, £4400 (including broker's commission), paid May 5, 1761, and £8812 10s. (again including broker's commission) paid July-August, 1761. BF did not deduct a rebate of £16 7s. 10d. for advanced payments for the stock bought in July and August.

8. *London Chron.,* Nov. 14–17, 1761.

9. BF bought the 3 per cent Consolidateds at 87½, the 4 per cents at 92 to 91¾, and the 3 per cents, 1761, at 88.

1. See below, p. 392, for an account of the sale of the 4 per cents, 1760.

From John Winthrop
Draft:[2] American Philosophical Society

Dr. Franklin, Sir   Cambridge 17 9br 1761

I received your favor of 20 Feb. and 8 April last, the former inclosing Dr. Pringles paper on an extraordinary meteor, and the later Mr. Kennicotts papers relating to the Hebrew Bible.[3] I am infinitely[?] obliged to you for introducing me to so valuable acquaintance as Dr. Pringle, several of whose curious papers I perused in the Phil. Trans. and whose correspondence I shall highly esteem; and agreeable to a hint you have given me, have enclosed a letter directed to him, which I beg you'd be so good as to send him.

I'm sorry we are not able to contribute towards Mr. Kennicott's design of revising the edition of the Hebrew Bible; but as you readily judge, new Countries are not the most likely places to look for ancient MSS in. I have, however, thoroughly searched our College Library with this view; and find several editions which I am sensible can be of no service in the affair; but not so much as 1 MS. I couldn't tell what better to do in the next place than to consult our old Rabbi Mr. Monis.[4] All the information I can get from him is, that MSS of the whole Old Testament are very rare; MSS of the Pentateuch are common in every Synagogue; tho he couldn't certainly inform me of any in America. Most of those

2. Winthrop wrote this and drafts of letters to Jonathan Belcher and John Pringle on the empty pages of BF's letter of April 8, 1761. Parts of the draft are interlined or overwritten to the point of virtual illegibility, and he used abbreviations and contractions which are almost unrecognizable to the reader (e.g., "pr" for "paper," and "svl" for "several"). The editors have used their best efforts to decipher his words and to place them in the correct order, but confess that they cannot guarantee the results in every instance.

3. The letter of February 20 not found; for that of April 8 and footnotes on the papers by Pringle and Kennicott, see above, pp. 300–1.

4. Judah Monis (1683–1764), Hebrew scholar, educator, was born either in Italy or Algiers and educated in Jewish schools at Leghorn and Amsterdam. Migrating to Jamaica, Long Island, and then to New York City, he was described as a merchant but probably also served as rabbi in both places. He moved to Boston in 1720 and presented the draft of a Hebrew grammar to the Harvard Corporation. He was publicly baptized in 1722 and was a professing Christian during the rest of his life. Harvard appointed him instructor in Hebrew in 1722 and gave him the M.A. degree the next year, and he continued to teach there until his retirement in 1760. His Hebrew grammar, the first in America, was published in 1735. *DAB; Sibley's Harvard Graduates*, VII, 639–46.

copies I presume must be modern, and so of little Authority. [*illegible*] moreover the book of Esther.[5]

Give me leave now sir to congratulate you on the honorary distinctions conferred on you at home;[6] which if I may be allowed to express my sentiments and those of my acquaintance are but just acknowledgements of your merit. I hope, you are pursuing your philosophical inquiries with the same happy success as formerly: and shall look upon your correspondence as a great obligation, when you can find leisure to favor me with it. And if it shall be in my power to render you or any of your learned Friends the least service in this part of the world, I shall do it with the utmost pleasure, being with great esteem Sir, etc.

To Thomas Ringgold[7]

Draft (incomplete):[8] American Philosophical Society

This note serves to introduce both the present document and the one immediately below.

Lord Baltimore, the Proprietor of Maryland, and his governors and supporters in the province continuously and successfully thwarted the desire of the House of Delegates to appoint an agent to represent its interests and point of view in England independently of the Proprietor. Several times, therefore, the leaders of the House were forced to rely on the good offices of an agent of another assembly. Such a situation occurred in 1761–62 and Franklin was the man to whom they turned for help.[9]

5. Because of cancellations and interlineations in the MS it is impossible to determine Winthrop's intended placing of these words.

6. Probably a reference to BF's honorary doctorate at the University of St. Andrews and his admission to freemanship in Edinburgh, Glasgow, and St. Andrews; see above, VIII, 277–80, 434–5, 436, 439. The words "at home" were often used by colonials, even as late as this, with reference to Great Britain.

7. Thomas Ringgold (1715–1772), planter and merchant of Chestertown, Md., had acted as agent for Franklin & Hall, 1754, to collect debts due the *Pennsylvania Gazette* on the Eastern Shore. See above, IV, 471 n; V, 202–3. He was elected a member of the Md. House of Delegates from Kent Co. in 1761 to fill a vacancy and took his seat April 13. *Md. Arch.*, LVI, 437.

8. Only the first page survives and that has a piece torn out near the bottom.

9. The account which follows is based on the journals of both houses of the Md. Assembly during the session of April 13—May 6, 1761. *Md. Arch.*, LVI, 406–7, 411–12, 420–5, 456–8, 466–8, 474–5, 480, 487.

The death of King George II and the accession of his grandson George III led Governor Sharpe[1] to propose, April 15, 1761, that the two houses of the Assembly join him in an address of condolence and congratulation to their new King. The House of Delegates and the Council agreed and each appointed members of a joint committee to prepare the address. As originally drafted, probably by two councilors, it was a wholly innocuous document, couched in the usual language of adulation of the deceased monarch and of loyalty and devotion to the "Sacred Person" of his successor. On April 22, however, the Lower House instructed its representatives, by a vote of 24 to 17, to propose the addition of a paragraph complaining of the lack of "proper Means of obtaining Access to the Throne," and asking for a full inquiry into the reasons why Maryland had during the present war "in so small a Degree exerted it's Force for the Service" of the late King. The proposed addition urged that the Delegates be allowed to "raise a Support for an Agent, who may lay all their Grievances which they suffer under the Government of the Lord Proprietary" before the new King, and it expressed a wish that in the meantime he would continue "that favourable Opinion which, we hope, you have hitherto maintained of your Protestant Commons of the Province of Maryland," whose members were unexceled in loyalty by subjects in any of the King's dominions.

When this paragraph was offered at the committee meeting the next day, the councilors present walked out "without saying one Word," returned to the Upper House (as the Council was called in its legislative capacity), and reported the proposed addition, "so extremely improper and foreign to the subject of the Address," and so "apparently intended to cast an injurious Blemish upon his Lordships Government." As a result of the impasse which followed, the governor and Upper House alone adopted the address as originally prepared and sent it to Lord Baltimore on April 29 for presentation. The Lower House adopted its own longer version and asked Sharpe, May 1, to affix the provincial great seal, a request with which he quite understandably refused to comply. Five days later he prorogued the Assembly to August.

Apparently a group of members of the Lower House decided almost at once to ask Franklin to present their address to William Pitt for submission to the King. While neither their letter of May 9 nor Franklin's reply of August 7 to Thomas Ringgold, one of their number, has been found, his efforts on their behalf and his gentle hint for their future action on the matter of an address are both apparent from the incomplete letter printed here and the longer one immediately following.

1. Horatio Sharpe (1718–1790), was governor of Md., 1753–69.

Mr. Ringold

Dear Sir, London, Nov. 26. 1761

The above is a Copy of my last. On my Return from a little Tour I made thro' Flanders and Holland, I found a Duplicate of the Papers you sent me, and among them the Address which had before been omitted. Inclos'd is my Letter to the Gentlemen who did me the Honour of recommending that Matter to my Care; by which you will see its present Situation. As your House may probably at their meeting this Winter, think proper to address his Majesty on his happy Nuptials,[2] the Congratulation on his Accession may be blended with it; and the other Matter couch'd in a Memorial or Petition by it self, agreable [to] Mr. Wood's[3] Advice, which if done, I am persuaded will be attended with good Effects; for at present the Proprietor and Governors Friends have possess'd the Ministry with an Opinion that the Failure of Supplies in your Province was totally owing to the Obstinacy of the Assembly, and their Disinclination to his Majesty's Service.

I thank you for the Pains you have taken in applying to Mr. Green concerning my old Account.[4] I think he uses me extreamly ill, and makes me very bad Returns for so long Forbearance and Kindness: I shall find myself obliged to sue him at last.

The Retaining of Canada is now become so popular a Point here, that I imagine nothing but some fatal Change in our [Affa]irs can make any Ministry think themselves [justi]fiable or safe in giving it up. I flatter m[yself] that the Pamphlet you are pleas'd to spe[ak of fa]vourably[5] may have had some Share in [producing] this Effect which [*remainder missing*].

2. On Sept. 8, 1761, George III married Princess Charlotte Sophia (1744–1818), younger sister of Adolphus Frederick IV, reigning Duke of Mecklenburg-Strelitz. They saw each other for the first time only on their wedding day.

3. Robert Wood (1717–1771), under secretary of state under Pitt and Egremont.

4. Jonas Green (1712–1767), printer and postmaster at Annapolis; see above, III, 153 n. BF's account with Green, covering the years 1740–49, is in Ledger D; it remained unsettled by Green or his heirs as late as 1786. George Simpson Eddy, *Account Books Kept by Benjamin Franklin "Ledger D" 1739–1747* (N.Y., 1929), p. 66. Writing to DF in 1757, BF had declared that Green "has not an honest Principle, I fear"; above, VII, 277.

5. BF's Canada Pamphlet.

To Edward Tilghman, William Murdock, Matthew Tilghman, Charles Carroll, Thomas Ringgold, and John Hammond[6]

ALS not found; reprinted from *National Intelligencer*, July 7, 1824; draft (last part only): American Philosophical Society

Gentlemen: London, Nov. 26, 1761

In mine of the 7th of August to Mr. Ringold, I acknowledg'd the Receipt of yours of May 9th, which had then just come to hand,[7] but without the mentioned Address. Soon after, taking the Opportunity of the Vacation of Business in the Public Offices here, I went abroad and was absent making the Tour of Holland and Flanders with my Son, till towards the End of September. At my Return I received a Duplicate of your first Dispatches, with the Address. Having carefully read your Votes, and acquainted myself with every thing proper to be said in defence of your House, I endeavoured to see Mr. Pitt, in order to deliver him your Letter, and at the same time make him acquainted with the Particulars for which you had referr'd him to me. He was always extreamly difficult of

6. For the background of this letter see the headnote to the document immediately above. The men addressed were all members of the anti-proprietary or "country" party in the Md. House of Delegates:

Edward Tilghman (1713–1786) of Queen Anne Co., was high sheriff, 1739–42; assemblyman, 1746–50, 1754–71; speaker, 1770–71; member of the Stamp Act Congress, 1765.

William Murdock, a very active assemblyman representing Prince George Co., was a member of the Stamp Act Congress, 1765.

Matthew Tilghman (1718–1790), brother of Edward, represented Talbot Co., 1751–58, 1768–74, and Queen Anne Co., 1760–61; speaker, 1773–74; delegate to the Continental Congress, 1774–76; president of the Md. Constitutional Convention, 1776; and member of the Md. Senate, 1776–83. *DAB.*

Charles Carroll ("the Barrister," 1723–1783), a distant cousin of the more famous Charles Carroll of Carrollton, was educated at Eton and at Clare Coll., Cambridge; called to the bar from the Middle Temple; returned to Md. in 1746. He represented Anne Arundel Co. for many years and was president of the Md. Convention of 1775.

On Thomas Ringgold see the first footnote to the preceding document.

John Hammond matriculated at Oriel Coll., Oxford, 1758; Middle Temple, 1760. He succeeded his recently deceased father Philip as delegate from Anne Arundel Co. in the session beginning April 13, 1761.

7. Neither letter found.

Access, and more so about the Time of his intended Resignation, which follow'd before I could have an Opportunity of Speaking with him.[8] I then sent your Letter to him with the Address inclos'd, by my Son, who assists me here, supposing Mr. Pitt would deliver the Address to his Successor Lord Egremont, as he accordingly did. As soon as the Bustle occasion'd by the Resignation was a little over, we made Enquiry after the Address at the Secretary's Office, in order to urge the Presenting it. After several Attendances together and separately to no Purpose, my Son at length met with Mr. Wood, who was under Secretary to Mr. Pitt, and continues in the same Office under Lord Egremont. He enter'd into a free Discourse on the Conduct of your Province, and express'd a great deal of the Resentment entertain'd against your Assembly by the Ministry here, with whom you at present stand in a very bad Light. My Son, who knows your Affair as well as I do, took occasion to justify you, and to satisfy him that you had been much misrepresented, by informing him of many Particulars in your favour that were quite unknown to the Ministers, owing to your not being allow'd an Agent here, which he seem'd greatly surpriz'd at.[9] As to the Address he said, it had not been presented, nor would be, the foreign Matter mix'd in it, making it quite improper; for that if it was presented, it must of course be printed in the Gazette; and then there would appear a heavy Charge against an Officer or Servant of the Crown, publish'd by Authority, without his having had any Opportunity of being heard in his own Defence, which was not thought equitable. That the Assembly themselves would be very sensible of the Irregularity, and probably complain of it as an Injury, if a Charge of their[1] Governor against them, should be inserted here in the Gazette, without Enquiry or Hearing. He was glad however for their sakes to learn that they desir'd an Enquiry

8. William Pitt resigned as secretary of state, Oct. 5, 1761, when the Cabinet would not support his demand for an immediate declaration of war against Spain. Sir Charles Wyndham, 2d Earl of Egremont (1710–1763), took his place.

9. Controversies between the House of Delegates and the governor and Council, very similar to those in Pa., including the issue of taxation of proprietary estates, had produced a virtual stalemate in Md. and had prevented the passage of adequate appropriations for carrying on the province's share of the war effort.

1. The surviving page of BF's draft begins at this point.

from a Consciousness that they could justify themselves; and concluded with Advising that they should make their Address of Congratulation distinct from their Complaint, and send them separately, and they might be assur'd that the Address would be favourably receiv'd, and an Enquiry order'd immediately to be made as they should desire.

I am extremely sensible, Gentlemen, of the Honour done me by the Confidence you have plac'd in me; and it would be no small Pleasure to me to be able to render any Service to the Assembly of Maryland. If such an Enquiry should be order'd while I reside here, you may depend no Pains or Care shall be wanting on my Part to place your Conduct in a just Light, and to remove the Imputations it at present labours under. In the mean time, I shall take every Opportunity in Conversation or otherwise of vindicating you, where it may be proper and seasonable.[2]

With great Respect, I am, Gentlemen, your most obedient humble Servant,   B. FRANKLIN.

To E. Tilghman,
    Wm. Murdock,
    Mat. Tilghman,
    Cha. Carroll,   } Esqrs.—Maryland.
    Thos. Ringold,
    Jno. Hammond,

2. On April 15, 1762, the House of Delegates voted that an address of condolence and congratulation be prepared and sent to George III. As drafted and adopted, April 24, the address was in general confined to condolences on the death of George II and congratulations on the new King's accession and marriage; but the House could not resist including a passage begging his Majesty "to suspend every unfavorable Sentiment of the People of Maryland or their Representatives 'till the real Causes of it are laid open to your royal Consideration." The House voted that the address should be sent to BF for presentation by a committee, four of whose six members were among the men to whom BF had addressed the present letter. *Md. Arch.,* LVIII, 132, 146, 148, 172–4. Writing to Cecilius Calvert, May 11, 1762, Governor Sharpe indicated that the House of Delegates had prepared the new address in consequence of BF's advice. *Ibid.,* XIV, 53.

Account of Sales of Stock Copy: Historical Society of Pennsylvania

I.N.[3]

Sold for Benj: Franklin Esqr[4]

1761

Novbr. 26 £700 4 per cents	to Wm: Morris	at 83½	£584.	10	–
£1000	to J. Ruddell	at 83⅜	833.	15	–
£1200	to S: Cazalet	at 83⅜	1000.	10	–
£800	to T. Brooksbank	at 83¼	666.	–	–
£1000	to T. Roberts	at 83¼	832.	10	–
£600	to Huntridge & Co.	at 83¼	449.	10	–
£500	to T. Brooksbank	at 83¼	416.	5	
Nov. 27. £500	to J. Tench	at 83	415	–	–
£600	to T. Bretland	at 82¾	496.	10	
£200	to W Chapman	at 82¾	165.	10	
£550	to Ja Cappes	at 82½	453.	15	
£350	to Maddison & Co.	at 82½	288.	15	
Nov. 28. £1400	to J. Linde	at 82⅝	1156.	15	
Nov. 30. £600	to Sr. W Hart	at 82¾	496.	10	
£1000	to Jo Hilton	at 82⅝	826.	5	
Dec. 1. £1000	to Jno Wood	at 82¾	827.	10	
£500	to R Roberts	at 82¾	413.	15	
Dec. 2. £1200	to Ja Scott	at 83¼	999	–	–
£700	to P How	at 83¼	582.	15	
£600	to Sr. W Hart	at 83⅜	500.	5	–
£15000[5]			12455.	5	–
		Brokerage	18.	15	
		Per E SHERVELL	£12436.	10	

Endorsed: Acct Sales of the £15000 4 per Cents. No. 6.

From James Brown[6] Copy: Historical Society of Pennsylvania

I.N.[7]

Benj. Franklin. Esqr.　　　　Lombardstreet 27th Novr. 1761

I have sent herewith a letter of Attorney to be Executed by you before two Witnesses to empower me to transfer the Fifteen

3. Isaac Norris' notation of receipt of this document.

4. James Brown of Henton Brown & Son (see the document immediately below) and his broker, E. Shervell, managed the sale of the £30,000 of stock which BF had bought with the parliamentary grant for 1758.

Thousand Pounds 4 per Cents.[8] as I could not do it without, you'll please to return it per Bearer as it must be lodg'd at the Bank this afternoon—£8000 being sold for to morrow morning and must be done then as the Persons who bought it will stay no longer—it being sold to be transferr'd this morning and it was with difficulty they were prevail'd on to take it to morrow. I am for Father and Self most Respectfully Yours   JAS. BROWN

I have sent back your Bank Book apprehending it was sent per Mistake.

Addressed: To | Benj. Franklin Esqr. | from J. Brown | Banker in Lombard Street | respecting the Sale of Stocks.

From Henton Brown   Copy: Historical Society of Pennsylvania

I.N.

B. Franklin Esqr.   London the 28th. Novr 1761.

Esteemed Friend

I did not fully speak to the Proposition respecting the £3000.[9] as I had not any discourse with my Son[1] respecting it in which affairs we always consult and act in concert. We have now considered the proposition maturely and think it of that nature that when thou comes to reconsider it in all its parts must appear a Thing not eligible for us. First because it may put us on any emergencies into the same condition thou art with respect to the sale of Stocks. Secondly the locking up so large a Sum for so long a time will manifestly be a great loss to us as by the lowness of

---

5. Between Dec. 18 and Dec. 23, 1760, BF bought £15,000 of the 4 per cents, at 92 to 91¾; see above, p. 253.

6. James and his father Henton Brown were BF's bankers; see above, p. 218 n.

7. Indicating the ultimate submission of this document to Isaac Norris.

8. For the sale of this block of stock, see the document immediately above.

9. It is not clear what this proposition was, but it seems likely that BF had asked his bankers to lend £3000 on the security of some of the Pa. stocks, so that BF could honor the bills of exchange he was receiving from the province without selling stocks at the current low price. When the price of stocks rose sufficiently the Browns would sell the security and repay their loan from the proceeds.

1. James Brown; see the document immediately above.

Stocks and the purchase of Navy bills gives so great an advantage over common Interest. 3dly. in case of any prospect of a peace the money would be out of our power and we should lose the advantage of the rise of Stocks. 4thly. the nature of this business subjects us to unforeseen fluctuations and by which we are liable to sudden and peremptory calls arising from contingent circumstances together with our engagement and the great demands there will be for the new Loan renders such a dependance on our part not suitable, but that no disappointment may happen when the bills shall become due we will advance the £3000—to give opportunity to provide the money from private hands on condition that we shall be at full liberty to dispose of the Stock transferred to us when we shall think proper.[2] I am for self and Son thy Obliged Friend   HENTON BROWN

The Broker has sold £1400 more since writing the above 82⅝[3]

Endorsed: Novr 28th 1761 Copy of Henton Brown (Banker) Letter, relating to the Bills[4]——recd Febry 13th. 1762. under Cover from Benja. Franklin

To Deborah Franklin

ALS (fragments only):[5] American Philosophical Society

[November? 1761][6]

[*First part missing*] Billy is now down at Bath. Inclos'd is a Letter I have just receiv'd from him inviting me there.[7] But I must not at

2. While declining BF's original proposition, the Browns were apparently willing to lend him £3000 temporarily until he could make other arrangements.
3. See above, p. 392.
4. Up to this point the endorsement is in BF's hand; the remainder is in that of Isaac Norris.
5. Only the lower half of a single sheet survives, with writing on both sides. What remains of the first page appears to be in Polly Stevenson's hand (as though she were acting as BF's amanuensis); the second page is unmistakably in BF's hand.
6. So dated because of the reference to BF's daily expectation of bills drawn on him by the trustees of the General Loan Office (see above, p. 383) and the mention of a mortgage on the Overall property.
7. Not found.

present leave London, as I daily expect Bills drawn on me by the Trustees.

I shall be glad to receive from you, and hope it is on the Way, an Account of what is due on Mr. Spoffords Mortgage, as I have Hopes of recovering it of the Sellers, who never acquainted me that such Mortgage subsisted, tho they must have known it.[8] Also I hope soon to receive a Copy of the Will you mention.

I inform'd you in a former Letter that I had sent the Harpsichord with our Friend Amos in Capt. Fingloss.[9] Mr. Stanley has now given me a List of the best Music for that Instrument and the Voice, which I shall soon procure and send [*one half page missing*].

[Mrs.] Stevenson and Miss desire their Compli[ments] to you and Sally. I am, my dear Debby, Your ever loving Husband

B FRANKLIN

I do not enclose Billy's Letter, as there is nothing material in it, and my Pacquet is like to be full large.

8. BF had apparently discovered that the property on Market St. which James and Ann Overall had sold to him July 11, 1761 (above, pp. 328–9) had previously been mortgaged to one Spofford. The will mentioned in the next sentence was probably that of Ann Overall's mother by which she had inherited the property.

9. BF had written DF, Feb. 19, 1758, that Dr. John Stanley, the blind organist, had advised him against buying a particular harpsichord he was then considering getting for 40 guineas as a gift for Sally; above, VII, 383. On June 22, 1759, he recorded having "Paid Bailey for Harpsichord £42 0s." "Account of Expences," p. 42; *PMHB*, LV (1931), 121. Apparently he waited for more than two years before sending it to America—for what reason is not clear—but he failed to record at any time the charges for its transportation. *London Chron.*, Oct. 15–17, 1761, reported from Deal, October 16, that the *Prince George*, Captain Finglass, had come down from London bound for Philadelphia. It reached that city during the second week of January 1762, bringing English news as late as November 9. *Pa. Gaz.*, Jan. 14, 1762. "Our Friend Amos" has not been identified.

To Thomas-François Dalibard[1]

MS not found; translation of extract reprinted from *Gazette d'Epidaure, ou Recueil de Nouvelles de Médecine*, III, no. XI (Feb. 6, 1762), 81.[2] (Bibliothèque Nationale)

Monsieur,   [December 9, 1761]
Il y a quelques années que la guerre a interrompu notre correspondance. Mon ami le Docteur Shippen[3] partant pour voir Paris, j'ai profité de cette occasion pour vous communiquer l'extrait ci-joint d'une Lettre que j'ai reçûe de M. Kinnersley que j'imagine qui vous fera plaisir.[4] Je suis, etc.   BENJAMIN FRANKLIN

To Joshua Babcock[5]   ALS: Yale University Library

Dear Sir   London, Decr. 10. 1761
I have been favour'd with yours by your valuable Sons, on whose promising Worth I congratulate you and good Mrs. Bab-

1. The French scientist who translated BF's *Exper. and Obser.* and the first to carry out his proposed experiment to prove the identity of lightning and electricity; see above, IV, 302 n.
2. The title page of the bound volume bears the title of the journal as given here with the added words: "Avec des Réflexions, Pour simplifier la théorie et éclairer la practique. Par. M. Barbeu Dubourg" and a list of the editor's titles and society memberships. Individual issues, however, are more simply headed *Gazette de Médecine*, and the journal is usually so catalogued.
3. William Shippen, Jr., who had recently received his M.D. degree at Edinburgh; see above, p. 219 n.
4. Kinnersley's letter of March 12, 1761; see above, pp. 282–91. In *Gazette de Médecine*, III, no. VII (Jan. 23, 1762), 49–53, Dubourg had printed a paraphrase of that part of Kinnersley's letter describing how a lightning rod had saved William West's house from injury and had mentioned Dalibard's intention of printing an exact translation. In no. X (February 3) Dubourg informed his readers that the translation would shortly appear in this journal and expressed astonishment that the Royal Society of Science in Paris had never printed Dalibard's account of his great experiment at Marly-la-Ville, May 10, 1753. Immediately following the printing of the present extract of BF's letter appears (pp. 82–6) Dalibard's translation of Kinnersley's report on the West incident. In no. XXXII (April 21), 256, Dubourg printed a translated extract of a letter from BF, March 20, 1762, thanking Dalibard for the translation and publication of the Kinnersley account.
5. On Joshua Babcock, physician and storekeeper of Westerly, R.I., Ezra Stiles's "stay-at-home Protestant," see above, VI, 174 n.

cock.[6] I should be glad to see them oftner than I do. But young Men find in England, Amusements more agreeable than the Company of old ones. The Colonel is gone down with my Son to Bath, where I last Night had the Pleasure of hearing they were both well.[7]

It gives me Pleasure to learn that my Endeavours here for the Good of our Northern Colonies, have met with the Approbation you mention, among my Countrymen.[8] The Negotiations for a Peace, in which Canada was to be for ever ceded to England, are unfortunately broken off, but there is nevertheless great Reason to believe it will not be given up, unless some fatal Change should happen in our Affairs.[9] The Nation is now so fully convinc'd of the Importance of retaining it; that a Minister without evident Necessity, will hardly venture to relinquish it.

My best Respects attend you and yours. Remember me to your Neighbours the good Samaritans: to Mr. and Mrs. Ward, Mr. Eeles, &c.[1] With the greatest Esteem, I am, Dear Sir, Your most obedient humble Servant   B FRANKLIN

6. Babcock's letter not found. The Babcocks had four sons: Henry (1736–1800), Luke (1738–1777), Adam (1740–1817), and Paul (b. 1748). The one referred to here as the "Colonel" was Henry, B.A., Yale, 1752; an officer in the R.I. militia who had served at Crown Point and Ticonderoga. He was a member of the R.I. Assembly, 1766–69, and served briefly in the militia again early in the Revolution. If only one of his younger brothers accompanied him to England in 1761 it was probably Luke, B.A., Yale, 1755, who kept shop in New Haven and became postmaster there in 1767. Two years later he went to England for Episcopal ordination and was a missionary of the Society for the Propagation of the Gospel in Yonkers, N.Y., 1771–77. Like many Episcopal clergymen in the northern colonies, he was a Loyalist at the outbreak of the Revolution. Dexter, *Biog. Sketches*, II, 277–80, 362–4; Wilkins Updike, *A History of the Episcopal Church in Narragansett*, D. B. Updike, ed. (Boston, 1907), II, 47–58.

7. See above, p. 394, for WF's visit to Bath.

8. Probably a reference to the Canada Pamphlet.

9. Negotiations between Great Britain and France, conducted simultaneously in London and Paris during the late spring and the summer of 1761, were broken off in September. A proposed general congress of all the warring powers at Augsburg never met. Gipson, *British Empire*, VIII, 204–22.

1. Samuel and Anna Ward of Westerly (the latter the sister of Catherine Ray), and probably the Rev. Nathaniel Eeles (1711–1786), A.B., Harvard, 1728, minister at nearby Stonington, Conn. *Sibley's Harvard Graduates*, VIII, 407–16.

P. S. I enclose you some Seeds of the true Tartarian Rhubarb.[2] It is distributed by Order of the Society of Arts. There is no doubt but it will grow with you.

Dr. Babcock

Addressed: To / Dr Babcock / at Westerly / Rhodeisland Governmt / Free / B FRANKLIN

Endorsed: Ben Franklin Esq. of 10 Decr. 1762 from London with seed of Tartarn Rhubarp Recd 21 Aprl. 1762

Another note in an almost illegible hand: Tower Hills April 21. 1762 By My Master and forwardd by Ser [?] Hurd Ser John Cass[?]

To David Hall Duplicate ALS: Glassboro (N.J.) State Teachers College

Copy

Dear Mr. Hall   London Decr. 10, 1761

Enclos'd are some Letters for you, left with me by Mr. Strahan. I have some Time since bespoke the Brevier you last desired, and hope it will now soon be ready.[3]

In your last you desire to know my Mind about Remitting, the Price of Bills being so high with you. What Money I have here is chiefly in the Funds, from whence I cannot withdraw it for present Use without great Loss, compar'd with the Price it will bear at a Peace. I am therefore very willing to allow the Price Bills may be at with you, for any Sums you may find convenient to remit to me. And they will be of particular Service about the Time of my leaving England, which I purpose the Beginning of the Summer, as I shall want to bring many Things with me. I now hope soon for

2. The Tartarian rhubarb (*Rheum officinale*) was introduced to Europe from China through Russia and promoted in Great Britain by BF's friend Sir Alexander Dick (above, VIII, 440 n). It was highly prized for its medicinal uses. In 1774 the Society of Arts awarded its gold medal to Dick for his contribution. Robert Dossie, *Memoirs of Agriculture and other Œconomical Arts* (London, 1768–82), II, 258–91; III, 208–25.

3. For matters mentioned here, see Hall's letter of Aug. 24, 1761, above, pp. 349–50. That of November 4 had not yet reached England when BF wrote the body of this letter.

the Pleasure of seeing you; being with great Esteem, Dear Friend, Yours affectionately B FRANKLIN
Pray send me the printed Votes of 1759, 60 and 61.
Jan. 9. 1761 [*sic*]. I have now receiv'd the above-mention'd Votes.[4] BF.
Addressed: To / Mr David Hall / Printer / Philadelphia / Free / B FRANKLIN
Endorsed: Franklin Decr. 10. 1761.[5]

To Edmund Quincy[6]   LS: Massachusetts Historical Society

Sir, London Decr. 10, 1761
I should sooner have answer'd your obliging Letter of Jany. 9.[7] but that I hoped from time to time I might be able to obtain some satisfactory Answers to your Queries. As yet I have done little, that kind of Information being look'd upon as a Part of the Mysteries of Trade, which the Possessors are very shy of communicating. But I think I am now in a Train of obtaining more, of which I hope soon to give you a good Account. In the mean time I may inform you that great Quantities of Wine are made both here and at Bristol from Raisins, not by private Families only for their particular Use, but in the great Way by large Dealers, for the Country

4. Possibly received a few days after Christmas with Hall's letter of November 4; see above, p. 380 n.
5. Hall acknowledged receiving this letter, April 15, 1762. It probably arrived during the first week of April on the *Pennsylvania Packet,* Capt. W. Gardner. *Pa. Gaz.,* April 8, 1762.
6. Edmund Quincy (1703–1788), A.B., Harvard, 1722; brother of Colonel Josiah (above, VI, 3 n) and uncle of the Edmund Quincy who had visited BF the previous winter and spring (above, p. 298 n). A business partnership in Boston with his brother Josiah continued until 1750 when it was dissolved and Edmund's sons then joined him in a new firm. He removed to the ancestral home in Braintree in 1753, leaving the business for the most part to the somewhat incapable younger men, and went bankrupt four years later. Although he tried farming, merchandizing, and the retail liquor business, he gained most of his income during the rest of his life from fees earned as justice of the peace and of the quorum. *Sibley's Harvard Graduates,* VII, 106–16.
7. Not found.

399

Consumption. As New England trades to Spain with their Fish, it would I imagine, be easy for you to furnish yourself at the best hand with Plenty of Raisins, and from them produce a genuine Wine of real Worth, that might be sold with you for good Profit. Being lately at a Friend's House where I drank some old Raisin Wine that I found to be very good, I requested the [*torn*[8]] sound and good.[9] It is thought here, that by far the greatest Part of the Wine drank in England is made in England. Fine Cyder or Perry is said to be the Basis, Sloes afford Roughness. Elder Berries Colour. And Brandy a little more Strength. But of this I have no certain Account. The Porter now so universally drank here, is, I am assured, fined down with Isinglass or Fish Glue, for which £60,000 per Annum is paid to Russia. Of late it has been discovered, that this Fish glue is nothing more than the Souns[1] of Cod or other Fish extended and dry'd in the Sun, without any other Preparation: So you may make what Quantity you please of it, and cheap, Fish being with you so plenty. I heartily wish you Success in your Attempts to make Wine from American Grapes.[2] None has yet been imported here for the Premium.[3] With great Esteem, I am, Sir, Your most obedient humble Servant   B FRANKLIN

8. Enough of the bottom of the sheet has been torn off to account for the loss of one or possibly two lines of text here and at the end of the postscript. Part of the frank on the address page is lost for the same reason.

9. The friend has not been certainly identified. In the Franklin Papers, XLIX, 72c, APS, is an undated recipe for making raisin wine, endorsed in BF's hand "From Mr. Viney whose Wine was remarkably good." This was Thomas Viny, a London coachmaker, whose friendship with BF seems to date only from about 1770. For this reason the editors have tentatively dated the recipe as of that year, but it is remotely possible that BF and Viny had known each other much longer and that BF was here referring to Viny's product. In that case the missing part of the sentence may have said that BF had asked for the recipe and was sending a copy to Quincy with his commendation.

1. Sounds: the organs of fish, primarily air bladders.

2. Some years earlier BF had met Quincy during a trip to Boston, and learning of his interest in growing wine grapes, had gone to great pains to send him parcels of slips from Rhenish grape vines grown in Pa. L.H. Butterfield et al., *Diary and Autobiography of John Adams* (Cambridge, Mass., 1961), I, 125–6.

3. Beginning in 1758 the Society of Arts had been offering premiums for wines produced in the colonies. Robert Dossie, *Memoirs of Agriculture, and other Œconomical Arts*, 1 (London, 1768), 239–41.

P.S. The Negotiations for a Peace, in which Canada was to be forever ceded to England, are at present broken off.[4] But whenever they are resum'd, I am persuaded that will be [torn].

N.B.[5] One Ezl. [Ezekiel] hatch, near Greenwoods Mastyard, tells me that, the Cod Souns or other may be Sav'd by stringing up and drying, that under this Circumstance they will not dissolve in any liquor hot or Cold; but that taken and wrapp'd up in Clean linnen Cloath or other Cloath, and covered up in embers so as to wast them, they will then dissolve—and that they will answer the End of Glue; but not so well of Cod as the Souns of hake, which is catch'd in or near the fall; those many Joyners at distant places use as Glew for their Cabinet work: roasted first in order to dissolve as Glew.

Addressed: To / Mr Edmund Quincy / at Braintree or / Boston / [Fr]ee / [B Fr]ANKLIN

From Ezra Stiles
Draft: Yale University Library

Sir   Newport, Decr. 30. 1761
I once more attempt to reach you with a Letter, which the Fate of war has I suppose hitherto intirely prevented. We are extremly sorry to know that Mr. Pitt has resigned the Seals: and have scarcely yet learned enough about the Earl of Bute (except from Scotsmen) to form an Idea of him.[6] The only obnoxious Thing in

4. See above, p. 358 n.
5. This note, written lengthwise in the margin, is in an unknown hand. It probably represents a memorandum added by Quincy or by some friend to whom he had shown BF's letter. Ezekiel Hatch has not been identified; a Nathaniel Greenwood had started a shipyard in Boston about 1665 near the foot of Salutation Alley where the Union Wharf later stood. The shipyard was carried on by Greenwood's descendants until 1741, when it was sold. Another Nathaniel Greenwood, "Mast Maker," is listed in Boston in 1774. *New-Eng. Hist. and Gen. Reg.*, XXVII (1873), 30; *Sibley's Harvard Graduates*, V, 483; VI, 471; I Mass. Hist. Soc. *Proc.*, XI (1869–70), 393.
6. John Stuart, 3d Earl of Bute (1713–1792), succeeded to his father's title in 1723. An accidental meeting in 1747 with Frederick, Prince of Wales, led to his becoming a favorite in the household of the prince and princess, a relationship which continued and even grew stronger with the princess and her young son Prince George after the death of Frederick, 1751. Though

Mr. Pitts Character that any in this Country (except the Jacob-
ites) are toutched with, is his being an Advocate for Exercising
the Militia on Sunday[7]—for the Sanctity of the Day apart: this
washing up and resting once in a while is healthy—but Training
days in New England are the hardest Days work in the year. That
Men and Cattle lie by one day in a week or thereabouts I believe
beneficial: in a well constituted community for Industry and social
Life, I believe 100,000 industrious Farmers or other Laborers
would accomplish more work in a year, desisting and resting every
seventh day than by incessant and unremitted Labor. And the
same holds good of Oxen, Horses. Whether we consider Health,
or fruits of Labor, these weekly recruits are necessary for Man
and beast—so wise was the mosaic Institution! To me who am a

---

holding no political office, Bute was the new heir's constant companion and
confidant and Princess Augusta's political adviser. Upon the accession of
George III, Oct. 25, 1760, Bute began at once to exercise great influence in
the government as the King's spokesman and virtual prime minister. He became secretary of state for the Northern Department in March 1761 and two
months later was elected one of the Scottish representative peers in the House
of Lords. A political opponent of William Pitt and an advocate of immediate
peace with France instead of extension of the war to Spain as the other wanted,
he engineered Pitt's resignation, Oct. 5, 1761, and took over complete control of the administration. Although events forced him to declare war on
Spain, Jan. 4, 1762, his earlier unpopularity with the English public, as a
favorite and a Scotsman, continued unabated. He took office as first lord of
the Treasury in May 1762, put through the preliminary treaty of peace, Nov.
3, 1762, and the definitive treaty, Feb. 10, 1763, and with the aid of Henry
Fox drove Newcastle, Grafton, Rockingham, and their Whig followers from
public posts. Partly because he had now obtained the peace he had long sought,
but also because of the public dislike of his person and policies, he resigned
in April 1763 and was succeeded by George Grenville. His close personal
relationship with George III had come virtually to an end by 1765. *DNB.*

7. After one failure in 1756, Pitt proposed and drove through Parliament
in 1757 An Act for the better ordering of the Militia in the several Counties
of that Part of Great Britain called England, 30 Geo. II, c. 25. As originally
presented, the bill provided that the smallest local units of the militia were to
assemble and drill three Sundays out of every month in the year, immediately
after divine service, and the next larger units on the fourth Sunday of every
month. *A Bill For the better ordering of the Militia Forces In the Several
Counties* . . . (London, [1757]), pp. 16–17 (Yale Univ. Lib.). Apparently because of public criticism (e.g., *Gent. Mag.,* XXVII, Jan., Feb. 1757, 29–30,
58), the bill was amended before passage to substitute Monday drills for these
units and to exclude Sunday exercises entirely.

Believer of Revelation, there is another Argument for desisting from Secular Labors on the Lords Day, which doubtless has no Weight with Mr. Pitt.

But excepting this and some few Reflexions on the dissenters which I hope they do not disserve, Mr. Pitt is deservedly in the highest Reputation among us[8]—I believe never was a Minister of State tread [treated?] with so much honor and Affection by us in New England—we almost idolize him: his being in the privy Council and in the House of Commons, has given us the greatest *Confidence* as well as Spirit and Alacrity. In short (I hope without Reason, but so it is) we know not how to confide in any one personge below the Crown. We have such an Idea of the universal Corruption, and of the national Jockying, that we fail of feeling assured, with respect to any of the illustrious Personages in public Administration, that they will subordinate their own to the Interest of the public, that they will not sacrifice the great public Interest when it interferes with their own Interest or that of their Friends and Connexions or prospect of Honor Preferment whether at his own high price most may not be bo't to abandon the National Interest &c. But we believe in Mr. Pitt we have a Confidence in him, in his Integrity and patriot faithfulness to the national Interest, more than his Capacities tho' extraordinary—I say we have a *Confidence* in Mr. Pitt, which I do think that I may do him the Honor to resemble to that Confidence which with infinitely greater Justice ought to be and is exercised by the Body of the intelletual World in him who consults for all, with whom is the Guidance and Administration and Guardianship of the universe. I have the honour to be Dear Sir Your most obedient servant   EZRA STILES

Dr Franklin London

8. Stiles also expressed his enthusiasm for Pitt's character and leadership elsewhere in his writings and sermons, though never more forcefully than in this letter. Edmund S. Morgan, *The Gentle Puritan A Life of Ezra Stiles, 1727–1795* (New Haven and London, 1962), pp. 212–15, 228.

From Miss Ralph[9]

AL: University of Pennsylvania Library

Decr. 31. 1761.

Miss Ralphs best respects wait upon Dr. Franklin, she with Pleasure, informs him that her Pappa, as the Doctor Said, yesterday, was out of Danger; but, he remains very Low, and weak, She is very Sorry, that she had not the Pleasure of seeing Dr. Franklin, a Tuesday;[1] but, she having set up all Night, was oblig'd, to go to Bed, in the Morning. She desires her Compliments to Mrs. Stephenson.

Addressed:[2] To / Dr [?] / Franklin / in / Craven Street / in the Strand / *London*

Notes on the cover:[3] Mr Lo
Mrs
Mr AC
Dr R
Mrs R
Mr R

9. The English-born daughter (first name unknown) of BF's old friend James Ralph; see above, I, 58 n. Leaving an American family behind, Ralph had gone to England with BF in 1724 and had remained there, as a professional writer. In 1757 BF told DF that he had seen Ralph, who had married again and had one child; above, VII, 274. His home was in Chiswick, in the western outskirts of London, about three miles from Craven St. In spite of the optimistic tone of his daughter's note, he was now in his last illness. He died Jan. 24, 1762, and his daughter also died on the following March 1, in her eighteenth year. *London Chron.*, Jan. 23–26, March 2–4, 1762; Thomas Faulkner, *The History and Antiquities of Brentford, Ealing, and Chiswick* (London, 1845), pp. 354–5.

1. BF had apparently gone to Chiswick to see Ralph on Tuesday, December 29.

2. The letter sheet was oddly folded; only "Franklin" being in the normal place and the other words appearing at different angles on the flaps.

3. Scrawled in what appears to be BF's hand; the significance of the notes is not clear, although two may stand for Dr. William Rose of Chiswick and his wife. Rose became one of Ralph's executors. "James Ralph," *DNB.*

404

Index

Abercomby, James, reports on troops, 241, 246

Absenteeism, in Ireland and colonies, 86–7

Academy of Philadelphia: lotteries help to support, 158; patronized by Proprietors, 158–9

Account of the New Invented Pennsylvania-Fire-Places, An, sent to Kames, 5

Addison, *The Tatler*, satire on knowledge without morality, 122 n

Admiral Durrell (ship), retakes *Indian Trader*, 336 n

Advertising, Baskerville uses BF letter for, 258–9

Aesop, Baskerville edition of, 258

Africa, supplies manpower for colonies, 51

Agency, Md., Assembly desires, 386–7

Agency, Pa.: accounts of, 12; Eyre's bill for representing Pa. Assembly, 22–4; difficulty over funds for, 44–6; financial arrangements for, 299; R. Charles resigns from, 332 n, 371

Agency Act (1759): Penn opposes, 16; Eyre presents separately to Privy Council, 26 n, 126; loses priority at hearings, 128; Board of Trade reports favorably on, 164–7; defect in, 165; terms and history summarized, 186 n; confirmed by lapse of time, 209; BF to invest Pa. share of parliamentary grant, 223. *See also* Parliamentary grant

Agency Bill (1760): Assembly passes, 225; legislative history of, 225 n; terms of, 225–6; fails of passage, 232–3, 234

Agents, colonial, often receive parliamentary grants, 236

Agriculture, Society of Acts to consider, 322

Air: effect on barometer, 119–20; properties of, 269–70; electricity in, 284–5; electrical thermometer for, 286–9; and evaporation, 296–7, 355; may be electrified, 351

Albany (sloop): brings Pitt letter, 28; sails from Charleston, 28 n

Albany Plan of Union, mentioned, 90 n

Alexandria, center of trade, 82

Algiers, potential enemy, 74

Alien decedents, act for the relief of heirs of: Board of Trade reports adversely on, 163–4; committee recommends disallowance, 205; disallowed, 210

Alison, Francis, caustic reference to, 115 n

Allen, William: executes deed of trust, 36–7; caustic reference to, 115 n; inquires about captured letters, 222; praises Canada Pamphlet, 227; not to be in Assembly, 234; plans trip to London, 234 n; opposes BF's management of parliamentary grant, 331 n

Allen & Marder, bill drawn on, 188

Allen, Fort, garrisoned, 10–11

Almanacs, numerous in Philadelphia, 39–40

Alva, Duke of, and Dutch revolt, 91

Amazon River, water fresh as far as the sea, 248

Amboy, N.J. *See* Perth Amboy

America: peculiar problems of security, 61–3; as frontier of British Empire, 74; self-interest vis-à-vis Canada, 75–6; potential inland commerce, 81; potential products of inland regions, 81; rivers, aid communication, 92

America (ship), carries mail, 33 n, 37 n, 235

American Almanack, The, published, 40

Americanisms, BF replies to Hume's criticisms of, 229–30

Amherst, Jeffery: urges Assembly support, 28, 310 n; sends forces to subdue Cherokee, 30 n; takes Montreal, 226 n; mentioned, 182

Amsterdam: trade route to, 82; BF and WF visit, 356, 367

Amu Dar'ya (Oxus) River, on trade route, 82

Anglo-Dutch War, end of, 66 n

Annapolis, Md., salt water in Bay at, 250

Annuities. *See* Stocks

Antigua, B. Mecom printer in, 19 n

Antwerp: gains and loses Flemish industry, 84; BF and WF visit, 356, 366; fine churches in, 366

Apples, DF sends to BF, 25, 27

Apthorp, Charles (1698–1758), identified, 273 n

Apthorp, Charles Ward (d. 1797): identified, 273 n; draws bill of exchange, 273

405